MW00755405

ADVISORY EDITOR: BETTY RADICE

TITUS LIVIUS was born in 59 B.C. at Patavium (Padua) but later moved to Rome. He lived in an eventful age but little is known about his life, which seems to have been occupied exclusively in literary work. When he was aged about thirty he began to write his *History of Rome*, consisting of 142 books, of which thirty-five survive. He continued working on it for over forty years until his death in A.D. 17.

BETTY RADICE read Classics at Oxford, then married and, in the intervals of bringing up a family, tutored in classics, philosophy and English. She became joint editor of the Penguin Classics in 1964. As well as editing the translation of Livy's *The War with Hannibal* she has translated the Latin comedies of Terence, Pliny's letters, *The Letters of Abelard and Heloise* and Erasmus's *Praise of Folly* for the Penguin Classics. She has edited and annotated her translation of the younger Pliny's works for the Loeb Library of Classics, and translated from Italian, Renaissance Latin and Greek for the Officina Bodoni of Verona. She is collaborating as a translator in the Collected Works of Erasmus in preparation by the University of Toronto, and is the author of the Penguin reference book *Who's Who in the Ancient World*. She is an honorary fellow of St Hilda's College, Oxford.

ROBERT MAXWELL OGILVIE was educated at Rugby and Balliol College, Oxford. He was a fellow of Clare College, Cambridge, from 1955 to 1957 and of Balliol from 1951 to 1970. He was headmaster of Tonbridge School from 1970 to 1975, and Professor of Humanity at the University of St Andrews from 1975 until his death in November 1981. He was the author of a standard commentary on Livy, Books I–V, and, with the late Sir Ian Richmond, of a standard commentary on Tacitus's *Agricola*; in addition he wrote books on Roman religion and on the influence of the classics on English life. His main interests were early Roman history and archaeology, and Roman Scotland.

LIVY

ROME AND ITALY

Books VI–X of
*The History of Rome from its
Foundation*

Translated and annotated by
BETTY RADICE

with an introduction by
R. M. OGILVIE

PENGUIN BOOKS

Penguin Books Ltd, Harmondsworth, Middlesex, England
Viking Penguin Inc., 40 West 23rd Street, New York, New York 10010, U.S.A.
Penguin Books Australia Ltd, Ringwood, Victoria, Australia
Penguin Books Canada Limited, 2801 John Street, Markham, Ontario, Canada L3R 1B4
Penguin Books (N.Z.) Ltd, 182–190 Wairau Road, Auckland 10, New Zealand

This translation first published 1982
Reprinted 1986

Copyright © Betty Radice, 1982
Introduction copyright © the Estate of R. M. Ogilvie, 1982
All rights reserved

Printed and bound in Great Britain by
Cox & Wyman Ltd, Reading
Filmset in Monophoto Bembo by
Northumberland Press Ltd, Gateshead, Tyne and Wear

Except in the United States of America,
this book is sold subject to the condition
that it shall not, by way of trade or otherwise,
be lent, re-sold, hired out, or otherwise circulated
without the publisher's prior consent in any form of
binding or cover other than that in which it is
published and without a similar condition
including this condition being imposed
on the subsequent purchaser

CONTENTS

TRANSLATOR'S PREFACE

This translation of Livy, Books VI–X, with its introduction by R. M. Ogilvie, is the second of the four volumes of Livy's *History of Rome from its Foundation* in the Penguin Classics. The other three are *The Early History of Rome* (Books I–V) by Aubrey de Sélincourt and R. M. Ogilvie; *The War with Hannibal* (Books XXI–XXX) by Aubrey de Sélincourt and Betty Radice; *Rome and the Mediterranean* (Books XXXI–XLV) by Henry Bettenson and A. H. McDonald.

The text translated is that of the Oxford Classical Text, with very few exceptions; in places where the text is defective I have supplied a few words and indicated these by brackets or a note. Like the first volume, and unlike the third and fourth, this one has no chronological index, as the early dates are not always precise (those at page heads are often only approximate). Instead, the five books are analysed in the Introduction, pp. 17–20. The Select Bibliography covers available editions of the text as well as books and articles on Livy and the historical background to the period about which he is writing.

Many have judged that Livy's literary virtuosity outshines his historical acumen. For the Emperor Caligula he was a 'wordy and inaccurate historian' (*verbosum in historia neglegentemque*[1]) whose works should be suppressed along with those of Homer and Virgil – hardly a pronouncement to deserve much attention. But even Quintilian, who properly appreciates Livy as a stylist, thinks that the 'rich creaminess' of his writing – the much-quoted *lactea ubertas*[2] – does not inspire confidence in his reliability. Perhaps no one has been so blunt as Macaulay, who declared roundly that 'No historian, with whom we are acquainted, has shown so complete an indifference to truth. He seems to have cared only about the

---

1. Suetonius, *Gaius* 34.2.
2. *Institutio oratoria* X.1.32.

picturesque effects of his book, and the honour of his country.'[3] But Macaulay continues immediately 'On the other hand, we do not know, in the whole range of literature, an instance of a bad thing so well done. The painting of the narrative is beyond description vivid and graceful. The abundance of interesting sentiments and splendid imagery in the speeches is almost miraculous. His mind is a soil which is never over-teemed, a fountain which never seems to trickle. It pours forth profusely; yet it gives no sign of exhaustion.' Today perhaps we can better appreciate what Livy achieved by his use of the tradition and his predecessors to produce a mainly 'solid and dependable account'.

Livy's Latin is never anything but a challenge. As the Introduction remarks (p. 13), a translation cannot hope to recapture the sound and subtle variety of the great dramatic speeches; and it may not do much better with the crisp sentences of narrative or the moving simplicity which presents the bewildered emotions of the Roman army trapped at the Caudine Forks (IX.2.10–11). There are also humorous touches, which must be lightly conveyed: the pipe-players plied with strong drink (IX.30.7–9); the women's quarrel over the cult of Chastity (X.23.3–10); and the Fabia sisters' embarrassment over their socially different marriages (VI.34.6–10). The range of Livy's vocabulary is a perpetual delight – the poetic words, often Virgilian in flavour, the metaphor in a single verb: *fluctuare*, for instance (VI.13.3), is much more than our 'fluctuate'; *saginare* (VI.17.3) 'to fatten up'; *occinĕre* (VI.41.8; X.40.14) of a bird which squawks or croaks – a rare and raucous-sounding word which, incidentally, Erasmus was pleased to use of the pulpit oratory of his day. I can only hope that some of my enjoyment in trying to serve Livy well in translation reaches his English readers, whether Latinists or not.

My special thanks are to R. M. Ogilvie for his introduction and generous help with details of interpretation, to Elizabeth

3. *The Works of Lord Macaulay: Essays and Biographies* (London, 1945), i, pp. 192–3; quoted in K. R. Prowse, 'Livy and Macaulay' in T. A. Dorey (ed.), *Livy*, p. 161.

Radice for her expert typing, to Judith Wardman for her meticulous copy-editing, and to my friends and members of my family for continuing to bear with my preoccupations, sometimes to their neglect.

Highgate, 1981   BETTY RADICE

Robert Ogilvie died sadly young in November 1981, before he could read the proofs of his introduction to this book or give a final informed opinion on its notes and index. The loss to what was planned as a collaboration is great; far greater is the loss to classical scholarship of his work in wider fields. Livy's *Rome and Italy* therefore offers gratitude for his personal interest and for his services to the Penguin Classics, and may serve as a reminder to its readers of all that we owe him.

                                                              B.R.

INTRODUCTION

Livy (Titus Livius) was born at Padua in northern Italy in 59 or possibly 64 B.C. We know little about his family background, except that Padua, a city famous for its moral rectitude, had suffered severely in the Civil Wars. Livy himself may have been prevented from going to the university in Greece, as most educated young Romans went, but he made a study of philosophy (according to the elder Seneca, he wrote philosophical dialogues) and other traditional subjects. Nor does he seem to have aimed at a public career either at the bar or in politics; we have no record of his holding any office or engaging in public activity. Instead he devoted the course of a long life to writing his *History of Rome,* which comprised 142 books (thirty-five are still extant; 150 were probably planned) from the foundation of Rome down to 9 B.C. Most of his life was passed at Rome. His reputation brought him into contact with Augustus, but there is little evidence of intimacy between the two men, except that about A.D. 8 Livy helped the young Claudius (the future emperor) with his literary efforts.[1] Augustus, indeed, disapproved of Livy's outspoken treatment of the recent past (Tacitus says that he called him a Pompeian[2]) and a note in the summary of Book 121 states that this book (and presumably the remaining books, which dealt with Augustus's principate) were not published until after the emperor's death in A.D. 14, for fear, we may assume, that they might give offence. Thus, although in touch with the seat of power, Livy retained an uninvolved independence. He was criticized by a contemporary, Pollio, for his 'Paduanness' (*Patavinitas*) – a provincial manner of speech.[3] His local patriotism is clearly displayed in X.2 where he writes about a nautical festival at Padua. It is notable that he is not referred

1. Suetonius, *Claudius* 41.1.
2. Tacitus, *Annals* IV.34.
3. Quintilian VIII.1.3, I.5.56.

to by any contemporary writer. He died at Padua, not Rome, in A.D. 17.[4]

Livy differed from the great majority of his predecessors in that he was not a public man: he did not turn to history as a recreation. For him it was life. We would not expect to find in him the crude political interpretations of history, discussed in the following section, which characterized the approach of earlier writers. Yet it would be a mistake to think of Livy's history as unconcerned with the problems of his generation. The difference between Livy and the others is that his philosophical detachment enabled him to see history in terms of human characters and representative individuals rather than of partisan politics. Livy accepted a tradition going back to Aristotle (especially in the *Rhetoric*) and to Thucydides, which explained historical events by the characters of the persons involved. As Aristotle said, 'actions are signs of character'. Because people are the sort of people that they are, they do the sort of things they do, and the job of the historian is to relate what happens to the appropriate character. Equally, however, it follows that if similar characters occur in 300 B.C. and 20 B.C. their possessors will tend to act in a similar way, so that one can infer from what a man of a certain character did in 20 B.C. what a similar character must have done in 300 B.C. Human nature, Thucydides argued, is constant and hence predictable. This philosophy helps to account for the readiness with which historians transferred events from the recent to the remote past (see below, p. 22) but Livy used it as the framework of his history. Instead of a barren list of unconnected events Livy constructs a series of moral episodes which are designed to bring out the character of the leading figures.

This technique, which is particularly to be appreciated in the first half of Book VII, had a further advantage besides giving unity and shape to the narrative. It helped Livy to bring the tale alive. The climax of almost every moral episode is a short speech or dialogue uttered by the principal characters. It was

4. See P. G. Walsh, *Livy: His Historical Aims and Methods*; R. M. Ogilvie, *A Commentary on Livy 1–5*, Introduction; T. A. Dorey (ed.), *Livy*.

a device used, for example, by Horace in his *Odes*, to highlight the key moment of the story. But ancient literary criticism insisted that where an author composed a speech either in history or in oratory it should fit the character of the speaker. Thucydides was often criticized for the sameness of his speeches. To achieve the right effect Livy deployed the whole range of the Latin language, but the subtlety of his tones is inevitably lost in any translation, however good. Sometimes he sets out to re-create the great rhetorical effects of the orators of his youth, such as Cicero or Hortensius. When we read the speeches of Appius Claudius (VI.40–41) or M. Valerius Corvus (VII.40) we can hear the thundering periods, the political clichés, the emotive vocabulary of the late Republic. For these men were statesmen, and that is how statesmen speak. On other occasions Livy captures the special tone of his speakers. Marcus Manlius is the boastful demagogue and the story of his downfall is built round his character. In the same way Livy shapes his material to bring out the aristocratic arrogance of Ap. Claudius, the heroic strain of self-sacrifice in the Decii, or the calm skill of M. Fabius. It is important to remember, while reading a translation, that to a Roman's ears each of Livy's characters would have sounded real because he was made to speak in a distinctive and fitting manner.

Livy made history comprehensible by reducing it to familiar and recognizable characters, but the process was one which could not be divorced from his attitude to his own times and his vision of the future. In the Preface he asserts that the present state of Rome was the direct consequence of the failure in moral character of the Romans. 'I would have the reader trace the process of our moral decline, to watch, first, the sinking of the foundations of morality as the old teaching was allowed to lapse, then the rapidly increasing disintegration, then the final collapse of the whole edifice, and the dark dawning of our modern day when we can neither endure our vices nor face the remedies needed to cure them.' It was a commonplace among Roman historians that things had got worse and worse; Sallust, for instance, blamed the destruction of Carthage and the capture of Greece for the start of the deterioration, because the one removed an enemy that had kept Rome on her toes, the other familiarized Rome with the enervating vices and luxuries of the Greek world. For Livy the cause of the decline is an infection contracted by contact with foreigners, especially Easterners; compare XXXIX.6.7: 'the origin of foreign luxury was brought into the City by the army that served in Asia.' No particular date could be put on the outbreak of the disease; it was a slow process which went back to the Carthaginian wars and beyond. Nor should it be ascribed to divine agency. Livy's attitude to the gods is ambivalent. On the one hand he is reluctant to accept divine intervention in human affairs and almost always offers a rationalistic explanation as an alternative (as in VIII.6 when Annius Setinus falls to his death). On the other hand he is fascinated by religious phenomena such as prodigies, or the *devotio* of P. Decius Mus, and, like Horace and many other Romans, he regards the performance of traditional religious rites as essential for the wellbeing of the State.

But the disease is not incurable. Although Livy's pessimism is pervasive (cf. X.9.5–6, where he says that the Lex Valeria forbade the scourging or beheading of anyone who appealed, 'but if the law was disregarded on either point it did no more than term it "a wicked deed". Such was the sense of shame amongst men at that time that this, I suppose, was thought to impose a legal sanction which would be sufficiently binding. Today hardly anyone would seriously utter such a threat'), yet he did believe that strong, authoritative measures could correct and improve behaviour. His attitude is seen most clearly in his favourable treatment of the elder Cato, the Censor; see especially XXXIV.4.8: 'Diseases must be known before their cures are found; by the same token, appetites come into being before the laws to limit their exercise.' There is no doubt that at least in the early years he saw Augustus as a man who could heal the sickness of Rome, Augustus who had 'brought peace to the world by land and sea' (I.19.3) and who was the 'founder and restorer of all our temples' (IV.20.7). Livy had probably started to write in 29 B.C. when settled conditions began to be reinstituted after the decisive battle of Actium (31 B.C.), and published Books I–V about 27 B.C. Books VI–X therefore will have been written in the following years but they afford no internal evidence for dating, unless, perhaps, there are contemporary overtones in the digression on Alexander the Great.

Livy's own contribution was to write, on a scale never before attempted, a detailed and living history which would not only be a memorial to the greatness of Rome but would also identify the ills of Rome and their causes. 'The study of history', he says (Preface 10), 'is the best medicine for a sick mind; for in history you have a record of the infinite variety of human experience plainly set out for all to see; and in that record you can find for yourself and your country both examples and warnings: fine things to take as models, base things, rotten through and through, to avoid.'

There is, therefore, a real sense in which Livy's *History* was deeply rooted in the Augustan revival. Despite stories that Livy's recitations from it in Rome were poorly attended, its fame was immediate. There is a tale of a man who came all the way from Cadiz just to look at Livy (Pliny, *Letters* II.3.8). And it quickly established itself as a classic, being accepted as such by Tacitus (*Agricola* X.3) and by the critic and rhetorician Quintilian. It superseded previous histories so completely that only scattered fragments of them have survived. Its very size, however, deterred people from reading it all, so that at an early date abridgements were made. A senator, Mettius Pompusianus, had an anthology of speeches from Livy which earned him death at the hands of the emperor Domitian, and Martial refers to a 'pocket' Livy (*Epigrams* XIV.190). These abridgements, of which three survive in part or whole, meant that by later antiquity only the most readable and exciting books of the original were still in circulation. The Christian apologist Lactantius knew only the first book.[5] The great pagan senator, Q. Aurelius Symmachus, was responsible about A.D. 396 for a new edition of the first ten books, presumably because they evoked for him the finest spirit of classical Rome, and it is to this edition that we owe the survival of these books through the Dark Ages.

5. R. M. Ogilvie, *The Library of Lactantius* (Oxford, 1979), p. 42.

THE SCOPE OF BOOKS VI–X

The plan of Livy's *History* is still a matter of dispute, but it is generally agreed that, at least for the early part, he composed in units of five books (e.g. from the Foundation of the City to the Gallic Sack) and that these units themselves are grouped in larger units of fifteen books (e.g. I–XV the Conquest of Italy, XVI–XXX the Carthaginian Wars, XXXI–XLV the Conquest of the East). It is reasonable to believe that Livy had mapped out the rough outline of the whole *History* before he began to write it and that he planned 120 books (i.e. eight groups of fifteen), but that when he finished them he was induced to continue with a further thirty books dealing with contemporary events, which he did not live to complete.[6] Books VI–X then form the central portion of the first main section, and cover the dramatic century from the apparent collapse of Rome after her defeat by the Gauls in 386 B.C. to her emergence as the premier power in Italy in 293. This fact helps to explain one of the more unexpected features of the Pentad, namely the highly rhetorical digression on Alexander the Great (IX.17–19), in which Livy compares the rival claims of Alexander and the Romans to be the greatest power in history.

It has been thought that this digression was an early literary exercise which Livy chose to insert into his history at this point, but on closer inspection it becomes clear that it has a special relevance to the period when Livy was composing these books. Contemporary Greek historians (Timagenes, Metrodorus and others) were at this time comparing the Romans unfavourably with the Parthians, just when Augustus was successfully negotiating for the return of the standards lost by Crassus at the disastrous battle of Carrhae (53 B.C.) against the Parthians. The pivotal position of the digression on Alexander within the framework of the first fifteen books establishes the superiority of the Romans in the face of all comers – Etruscan, Greek,

6. See T. J. Luce, *Livy: The Composition of his History.*

Carthaginian or Parthian. Alexander was no match for the rugged determination of the Romans. The digression falls nearly in the centre of Books II–XV (Book I is concerned with the kings, and the history of the Roman Republic begins with Book II), and it serves to highlight the theme of the first section of the *History* – how from humble beginnings Rome became a world power.

Within this overall design each of the individual books has its own architecture.

Book VI has a clear structure. After a preface and preliminary chapters on the alarms of war, it divides into two principal sections. The first contrasts the virtues of the loyal and constitutional Camillus, winning victories for Rome abroad, with the evils of Manlius, who stirred up class warfare at home (VI.6–20). Manlius is executed, a man who 'would have been memorable had he not been born in a free State'. A short interlude follows, as Rome deals with the Volscians, Tusculum and Praeneste (VI.21–30). The second section, of comparable length, relates the conflict between the patricians and the plebeians over their constitutional rights, particularly exacerbated by the hardship caused by the laws of debt (VI.31–42). The book ends with the passing of the Sextio-Licinian rogations (see pp. 83 and 96), which resolve, at least temporarily, the conflict. The book is framed by the great speeches which bring the central issues out into the open (VI.6, Camillus; VI.18, Manlius; VI.36–7, Sextius and Licinius; (VI.40–41, Appius Claudius).

Book VII is more complex. There are two well-marked breaks in it. At VII.18.1 Livy writes: '(The consuls) entered office that same day, in the four-hundredth year from the founding of Rome, the thirty-fifth from the recovery of the City from the Gauls'. Again, at VII.29.1, the start of the long Samnite wars, he says that 'From now on the wars described will be of greater importance. Our enemies were more powerful, and campaigns lasted longer and were mounted in remote areas.' The book opens with a retrospect – the election of the first plebeian consul (362 B.C.) and the obituary of Camillus. The first section of the main narrative, which deals chiefly with wars against the Gauls, is distinguished by a series of heroic and romantic stories much more reminiscent of Horatius Cocles and Scaevola in Book II than of the sober and factual history which Livy promised at the start of Book VI. These include the episodes of young T. Manlius (VII.4–5, VII.9–10), M. Curtius (VII.6), the centurion Sextus Tullius (VII.13), as well as the feat of M. Valerius Corvus (VII.26). In his usual way Livy makes these stories instructive and vivid, but it seems as if he is deliberately writing them up as legends to point an effective contrast with the historical realities which characterize the Samnite war. The second section is very much of an interlude made up of political and military events covering the years 352–340 B.C. The third section, however, is once again given a deliberate ring-structure: it opens with the speech by the Campanian envoys, made all the more impressive by its echoes of Thucydides (VII.30), followed by the reply of the Roman Senate (VII.31), and closes with the divided Roman army being reunited by T. Quinctius and M. Valerius Corvus (VII.40–41). These speeches serve not just to round off the narrative but also to bring out the important moral themes (obligations of friendship, loyalty to the State and to one's officers and comrades) which Livy saw as being a powerful and creative force in the history of Rome.

Book VIII has the clearest plan of all. The early part is taken up with the revolt of the Latins (338 B.C.) and its consequences, the latter part with Roman expansion into south Italy. It is divided in the middle by a brief digression on the death of Alexander of Epirus (VIII.24), but it is held together by a common theme – the principle of obedience to superior authority. At the beginning of the book (VIII.7) T. Manlius executes his son for disobeying his orders, although he displayed great initiative and gallantry and was a notable success. At the end Q. Fabius is spared the same fate when he disobeys the orders of his dictator, L. Papirius. Livy brings out the parallel by describing the enraged Papirius as 'praising with nearly every other word the deed of Titus Manlius' (VIII.30; cf. VIII.34, 'the precedent of Manlius'). The moral is clearly stated by Papirius (VIII.35) when he bids Fabius show 'that you have learned the lesson which this day has taught you – that in war and in peace you are able to bow to lawful authority.' As is his practice in other books, Livy opens the narrative with a fine speech (VIII.4: L. Annius, the Latin) and rounds it off with a pair of matched speeches (VIII.31 and VIII.32: Q. Fabius and L. Papirius).

Book IX is remarkable in being divided into two not quite equal halves by the strange excursus on Alexander the Great (IX.17–19: see pp. 16–17). The first part of the book is cleverly constructed to balance the Roman defeat at the Caudine Forks with their avenging victory at Luceria. It is ushered in by a speech of sombre menace by C. Pontius, while the turning-point in Roman fortunes, which stems from Roman insistence on moral rectitude at all costs, is marked by the speeches of the defeated consul Spurius Postumius (IX.9) and of C. Pontius (IX.11). The second part, which involved Livy in trying to put some kind of shape on a great deal of miscellaneous and disconnected material, is held together by the common theme of Roman expansion in Italy against a variety of peoples (Umbrians, Paelignians, Samnites etc.). The disaster of the Caudine Forks, which at the start of the book looked like a fatal blow to Rome's ambitions, is seen to be the prelude to an almost irresistible advance, but such an advance depended on the solidarity of the Roman political scene dominated by the sinister figure of Appius Claudius (IX.33–4, IX.46).

Book X ends on the high note of the battle of Aquilonia (X.38–43), which, although not in fact the end of the Third Samnite War, was the last major engagement, after which it was only a matter of time before the Samnites had to concede defeat. Livy signalizes both the importance of the battle and its position as the climax to these five books by stressing the total commitment of the Samnites (X.38), and his account of it is a brilliantly romantic piece of writing. But the rest of the material for the book did not lend itself easily to an ordered structure, because the Third Samnite War was spasmodic. Livy alternates military activities in Samnium itself with the operations in Etruria and details of Roman politics. One thread which runs through the book is the continuing tradition of certain families, especially the Fabii, Decii and Papirii, but the central focus is the dramatic narrative of the battle of Sentinum and the *devotio* of Publius Decius Mus (X.27–9), one of the legendary moments of Roman history.

Livy opens Book VI with these words:

> The history of the Romans from the foundation of the City to its capture, first under kings, then under consuls and dictators, decemviri and consular tribunes, wars abroad and dissensions at home, I have set out in five books, covering matters which were obscure both through their great antiquity, like objects dimly perceived in the far distance, and because in those days there were few written records, the only reliable means of preserving a memory of past events. A further reason was the loss of most of such accounts as were preserved in the commentaries of the pontiffs and other public and private records when the City was destroyed by fire.

In fact there is no archaeological evidence for a conflagration of Rome. So what in practice was the evidence that Livy used in the compilation of his history? Basically he had three categories at his disposal: the writings of earlier historians, the researches of antiquarian scholars such as Cornelius Nepos and M. Terentius Varro (*d.* 27 B.C.), and original records (e.g. inscriptions, sculpture, paintings, documents, records of the various priesthoods, lists of consuls and triumphs and so on[7]).

There is very little to suggest that Livy searched out and inspected the records for himself. He certainly did not consult the Annals of the Pontifex Maximus, which apparently were the accumulated contents of a list of notices which the Pontifex Maximus published annually on a whitened board. It is uncertain how far genuine notices go back, perhaps to 390 (386) B.C., perhaps only to 304 with the activities of Cn. Flavius (Livy IX.46.1–5). He takes Augustus's word for an important

7. See B. W. Frier, *Libri Annales Pontificum Maximorum: The Origins of the Annalistic Tradition* (American Academy in Rome, 1979).

inscription which was still visible in Rome in his day (IV.20) and relies on hearsay for the bowls which Camillus dedicated in the temple of Jupiter (VI.4). Furthermore, chance has preserved some epigraphic material which gives versions of events that differ from the received account told by Livy. There are fragments of a painting on the Palatine Hill depicting the activities in the Samnite wars of a Fabius otherwise unknown to history[8]; and a fresco in an Etruscan tomb portrays a hero, Mastarna, whose rôle in Roman politics would have been obliterated but for a stray reference in a speech of the emperor Claudius. Nor does Livy seem to have made extensive use of the researches of others. He does refer once to the antiquarian L. Cincius for details about the ceremony of driving nails into the walls of the temple of the goddess Nortia (VII.3.7), and it is likely that he derived his account of the origins of Roman comedy (VII.2.4–12) from Varro. But such use of scholarly sources is exceedingly unusual, perhaps not because Livy was uninterested in historical oddities but because scholars like Varro did not offer him the framework of an extensive account which was essential for the flow of his narrative.

In the main, then, he relies on the histories of his predecessors. At X.17.11 he clearly implies that he has consulted at least four different accounts, and at X.18.7, three. He names a number of writers. One is C. Licinius Macer, who was tribune of the plebs in 73 B.C. (VII.9.4, IX.38.16, IX.46.3, X.9.10). Another is L. Calpurnius Piso, consul in 133 B.C. (IX.44.3, X.9.12), who was probably the first Roman historian to make use of the annual records kept by the pontiffs. He also cites two contemporaries of Macer's, Valerius Antias (IV.23.1 *et passim*) and Q. Claudius Quadrigarius (VI.42.5, VII.19.13 *et passim*), who seems to have begun his history from the Gallic Sack. A more recent writer was Q. Aelius Tubero (X.9.10), the son of a friend of Cicero's. One famous name that Livy mentions is Q. Fabius Pictor (VIII.30.9, X.37.14), the first Roman historian who wrote (about 200 B.C.) an account of Rome in Greek, with special emphasis on the early centuries,

8. *Affreschi romani dalle raccolte dell'Antiquarium communale* (Rome, 1976).

with a view to impressing on the Greek world that Rome was as civilized and cultured as any Hellenic city; but it is doubtful whether Livy actually made first-hand use of Pictor.

All these historians, even Pictor, have certain features in common. They were, for the most part, politicians who turned to the writing of history as a leisure pastime; they were not interested in historical research as such but were concerned to use history as a means of reflecting the issues and controversies of their own times. Licinius Macer, who was a partisan of Marius, rewrote history to foreshadow the policies and events of the Marian regime; Valerius Antias seems to have espoused the cause of Sulla and to have reflected Sulla's political settlement in his narrative of early Roman history. It is, therefore, to be expected that the story of M. Manlius, which Livy inherits from them and rewrites in his own colours, should be redolent of the ideals and slogans of the Gracchi and later democratic reformers.

Secondly, they had great pride in their own families. Sometimes this pride may have been based on family records or family memories, but, even so, such evidence has to be treated with caution.

> Speeches in praise of the dead are indeed extant; for families kept them as a sort of honour and a record, in order to preserve the memory of the achievements of the family and document its nobility. Of course the history of Rome has been falsified by these speeches; for there is much in them which never happened – invented triumphs, additional consulships, false claims to patrician status, and so on.
>
> (Cicero, *Brutus* 62)

Livy laments that family pride had made it impossible to discover who actually was dictator in 322 B.C. (VIII.40.4), and in VII.9.3–6 he says that Licinius Macer was always promoting the claims and prestige of the Licinii. Something of this process can be seen in the prominent position given in these books to the Fabii and the Valerii.

But the problem faced by Pictor or Piso or Tubero was essentially no different from that faced by Livy himself. They too had to construct a narrative from whatever material they could lay hands on, and that amounted to family traditions and the annual records of the Chief Pontiff eked out by inscriptions, customs and monuments. Licinius Macer was unusual in the extent of his antiquarian curiosity; he even discovered a linen book with a list of magistrates, probably covering the years 445–367 B.C. Fabius Pictor may have been more inventive than most, particularly when dealing with the legends of early Rome. Since, however, the work of all these earlier historians only survives in fragments, it is futile to try to reconstruct their tone and contents. What should not surprise us is that they frequently disagree over names (e.g. VIII.23.17) or numbers or facts. Indeed, it seems quite likely that the whole chronological framework which Livy inherited for this period is out of true by some four years, as a result of critical gaps in the evidence (see below, p. 32). It is instead a matter for surprise and thankfulness that the tradition is as full and as reliable as it is. In so far as we can understand what did happen in the years 386–293 B.C., Livy seems to have given us a solid and dependable account.

THE HISTORY[9]

The century was dominated by two inter-related developments – the political evolution of the Roman constitution and the expansion of Roman power in Italy. Both of these are fully and fairly treated by Livy, even if his view is coloured by later political thinking and by honest patriotism. (It is disconcerting to find how little interest Livy, a Paduan, shows in non-Roman peoples.)

The capture of the city by the Gauls, immigrants from the Celtic lands north of the Alps, had left the Romans in a very weak position. It took them a full twelve years before they could build a wall to defend Rome (VI.32.1), and the very fact that a wall was thought necessary at all is proof of their shattered morale. The disaster must also have affected their

9. The best short account is by M. H. Crawford, *The Roman Republic*.

relations with their neighbours, above all with the towns of Latium. For the past century Rome and the Latins had been united by a formal treaty negotiated by Spurius Cassius (c. 493), which provided for joint military action and reciprocal political benefits in mutual trade (*commercium*), intermarriage (*conubium*) and mobility (*migratio*). In practice Rome had acquired the position of senior partner in this alliance and had tended to act, as against Veii, unilaterally. The Latins took advantage of the Gallic Sack to assert their independence once more, but such a move was inevitably short-lived. Rome was too large, too prosperous and too strategically situated to be constricted in that way. A series of minor provocations culminated in a decisive war in 338 B.C. (VIII.9–10), which broke the Latins for ever and established the unchallenged supremacy of Rome in central Italy. The war, however, had other, perhaps more important consequences, because it forced the Romans to devise new constitutional arrangements to deal with defeated enemies. Some of the Latins were allowed to continue the old reciprocal rights; others were directly incorporated into the Roman citizen-body, thereby losing their independent identity; for others a new status was invented – citizenship without the vote (*civitas sine suffragio*), which imposed certain burdens (taxation and military service) but granted considerable privileges. The voting disqualification was not controversial because it was grounded on the simple fact that the communities concerned were too far distant from Rome to be able to exercise any voting rights regularly.

The settlement of 338 was to have profound consequences for the Roman world. It not only reasserted Rome's hegemony but created a new social organization which was ultimately to enable people on the banks of the Euphrates or under the shadow of Hadrian's Wall to identify themselves as Romans, as is vividly brought out by Plutarch's dialogue *On the Failure of the Oracles*, where travellers gather at Delphi from the ends of the world and exchange stories within the context of a single civilized world.

As Rome began to reassert her power over her neighbours it was inevitable that she should be drawn to the rich lands of the south, especially Campania. Three very different peoples had a stake in the area. The first were the Etruscans, who, recognizing both the fertility of the region and its enormous mineral deposits, as well as the advantages of its communications with the Greek mainland, established a substantial presence there in the sixth century, but that presence was short-lived. The increasing pressure of hill-people on their lines of communication and a disastrous defeat in the naval battle of Cumae in 474 B.C. effectively forced the Etruscans to give up their aspirations. The Greeks, however, had been there much earlier; the colony of Pithecusa (Ischia) probably dates back as far as 775 B.C. Like the Etruscans they were attracted by the resources of the area and subsequently did very good business with the Etruscans themselves, as the wealth of imported pottery indicates. But once again it was the native hill-peoples who exercised the strongest pressure. Capua, one of the biggest Etruscan-Greek cities fell in 423 B.C., and Cumae, perhaps the most prestigious of all the Greek colonies in the west, was taken over in 421.

Who were these hill-peoples, known to us as Samnites?[10] Basically of the same ethnic, cultural and linguistic stock as the Romans themselves, they occupied the great mountain massif in the centre of Italy south of Rome, stretching from Aufidena in the north to Venusia in the south. Their home-lands offered good but limited grazing and the water supply was chancy, so that the rich fields of the Campanian region always beckoned, and when over-population intensified their problems, they, like the Volscians to the north, began to infiltrate the coast-land. Although they were a peasant society with few urban centres (Bovianum and Maleventum are exceptional, but even they were not large), they were highly organized and disciplined. Livy gives an account of the solemn oath taken by their picked troops when a campaign was started (IX.39.5, X.38.12). Even more interesting is the ceremony described by the geographer Strabo called the 'Sacred Spring' (*Ver sacrum*: Strabo V.4.12; cf. Livy XXII.9.10, XXII.10.2). In a crisis the

10. For the Samnite wars see E. T. Salmon, *Samnium and the Samnites*.

Samnites would promise to dedicate to their chief god Mamers (Mars) everything that was born in the following spring. The ceremony was institutionalized so that the children born on such an occasion were required when they grew up to leave their tribe and, following the lead of some sacred animal, settle elsewhere. This enforced emigration was a natural solution of the problem of over-population.

By the middle of the fourth century the Samnites had penetrated as far as the River Liris, the natural frontier between Latium and the south. There is good agricultural land here and rich minerals in the Monte della Meta. At the same time the Romans were feeling their way down south, and in 354 B.C. they subscribed a treaty with the Samnites which seems to have recognized their respective spheres of influence (VII.19.4), as well as making provision for mutual help against marauding armies of Celts who had spilled over from Gaul into Italy. The treaty is in line with the one which the Romans concluded with Carthage six years later, in 348, and indicated how they were concerned to define their international position. Both treaties presuppose that Rome was the major power in Latium and so anticipate the state of affairs that prevailed formally after the defeat of the Latin revolt in 338 B.C. Indeed, the Samnites actually gave Rome support in that revolt, presumably as part of their treaty obligations. But the alliance was bound to be unstable because each nation was competing for the same prizes. In VII.29 ff. Livy records that between 343 and 341 the Romans and Samnites actually engaged in open warfare, probably over rival claims to parts of Campania. This First Samnite War has often been disputed because many of the details given by Livy are clearly fictitious and no other historian refers to it, but some sporadic fighting would be entirely in character with the uneasy peace of the times.[11]

By now, however, there was a confident political situation at Rome, and a number of able men, both patrician and plebeian (see below, p. 33), such as L. Papirius Cursor, Q. Fabius Rullianus, Q. Publilius Philo and P. Decius Mus, were

11. E. T. Salmon, op. cit., pp. 181 ff.

united on a common policy of securing Rome's control over Campania and the adjacent territory, especially to the north-east. Their motives are clear. They knew what valuable commercial and maritime outlets they would gain with the Greek world; they prized the fertile, partly volcanic land; they needed the mineral resources. So the start of the Second Samnite War (326–304) was a result of planned provocation. The first stage was to take over northern Campania with such important industrial towns as Cumae, Suessula and Acerrae, and this they achieved by 332 (VIII.17.12). The second was to secure as far as possible a ring of friendly allies which was to include Alexander of Epirus (VIII.17.9), the Lucanians and the Apulians (VIII.25.3, VIII.27.2), although these alliances did not always endure. The third, in 328 B.C., was to plant a Latin colony, in territory which the Romano–Samnite treaty recognized to be Samnite, at Fregellae on the left bank of the River Liris – a strategic site which commanded the line of the Via Latina and a route leading from the Trerus valley over the mountains to the sea near Tarracina (Anxur) and which also guarded a vital river-crossing (VIII.22.2).

These moves were designed to precipitate action, and the Samnites retaliated by capturing control of the old city of Naples (Palaepolis) in 327 B.C., thereby threatening the Roman settlements in Campania. War was declared (VIII.23.10), and it proved to be a long-drawn-out and bitter war, because the Samnites could match the Romans in toughness and resources. They also had the advantage of a mountainous and difficult country to which they could retreat to recoup and from which they could launch lightning raids against Roman detachments. The war, therefore, despite Livy's frequent mention of enormous Samnite losses and proud Roman triumphs, turned out to be signally inconclusive. The Romans suffered at least one major reverse at the Caudine Forks in 321 (IX.2–12) when they tried to force a decisive success, but the battle has been invested with such romantic pathos that it is difficult to know either how serious the defeat really was or how grave the consequences. It is certainly true that Rome was never able to press home the advantage. They did indeed capture a number of key places, including Saticula, Luceria, Teanum and, for a while, the provincial capital Bovianum, but in a series of engagements, such as those at Lautulae in 315 (IX.22–3) or at Anagnia in 306 (IX.42–5), the Samnites managed to elude them, and there seemed no prospect of achieving a final victory.

Nevertheless the Romans had the ascendancy. They were gradually restricting the Samnites to the hills and taking over more of the strategic sites. They were even able to complete the Via Appia in 312 B.C. It had involved an enormous expenditure of money and the deployment of thousands of peasants as soldiers, with all the disruption that that entailed for the cultivation of the land. It was the start of a long military process which was to mean that, during the last two centuries B.C., 'the median size of the army amounted to 13% of adult male citizens.'[12] The Samnites, on the other hand, had suffered heavily, even if not on the scale reported by Livy, and were on the defensive. So it is understandable that when the Samnites made peace overtures in 304 the Romans should have been willing to agree to a treaty (IX.45.1–4) which effectively gave Rome control of the whole of the Liris valley.

But the treaty was only a breathing-space. The Samnites knew that the Romans were intent on their complete subjugation – they were already beginning to mark out plots of land for Roman settlers near Bovianum. To survive the Samnites needed allies who would divert and distract the Roman advance. At the beginning of the third century the Celts were on the move again and another marauding army of Gauls was at large in Italy. At the same time the great Etruscan cities north of Rome were impatient with the treatment they were receiving from the Romans, who had paraded their force throughout Etruria in 302 B.C. (X.3–4), and the Umbrians, one of the biggest hill-peoples in central Italy, had been provoked by the Roman annexation of the town of Nequinum (Narnia) in 299 (X.9–10). Rome's actions in both cases had almost certainly been designed to forestall trouble

12. K. Hopkins, *Conquerors and Slaves* (Cambridge, 1978), p. 31.

from those quarters so that she could concentrate on Samnium, but the effect was the opposite of what was intended. It offered the opportunity to an adventurous and determined Samnite leader, Gellius Egnatius, to forge a quadruple alliance against Rome. Rome for her part had not been idle. She pressed ahead with the foundation of strategic colonies, constructed the vital military highway, the Via Valeria, across Central Italy, and renewed alliances with peoples to the south, such as the Lucanians and the Apulians.

The Third Samnite War probably began in 298 B.C., but the fighting was desultory and inconclusive until 296, when Gellius Egnatius, in a quite unexpected and untypical move, burst out of Samnium with a very large force and joined the Gauls, Etruscans and Umbrians in Etruria (X.18–19). This at once changed the nature of the whole war, and offered the Romans the chance of the decisive battle that had escaped them for so long. That chance came in 295 at Sentinum (Sassoferato), when the Romans engaged the Gauls and Samnites in the absence of the Etruscans and Umbrians, who were engaged on other operations (X.27–9). The battle was closely fought and the casualties high (9000 Romans; 25,000 Samnites and Gauls), but the Romans carried the day and Samnite manpower was decimated. Thereafter the power of Samnium was broken, and it only remained for Rome slowly to mop up the survivors. A further victory in 293 at Aquilonia, on the borders of Samnium (X.38–43), opened the way to the heartlands of the Samnites.

It is appropriate that these five books of Livy should end with his stirring account of the battle of Aquilonia; for, although the war was to drag on for a further three years, this was the real finale. Rome's southern frontier moved from the River Liris to the River Volturnus and her territory now stretched eastwards as far as the Adriatic. She acquired huge quantities of loot, which radically transformed her economy: Livy says that at Papirius Cursor's triumph 2,533,000 pounds of bronze were displayed (X.46.5; cf. X.46.14). And with the Samnites and the Umbrians becoming her 'allies' she now had undisputed mastery over the whole of central Italy. She was ready for the next challenge and the next advance.

This brief sketch of the Samnite wars reveals one significant fact. Towards the end of the fourth century the Romans adopted a more aggressive and planned policy than can be discerned before. The Second Samnite War was a calculated and deliberate act. How had this new political confidence come about?

To understand this we have to go back to the beginning of the Republic. The class of society that was eligible to hold power was known as the patricians, and they were the descendants of 'fathers' (*patres*) who had been members of the Senate under the kings. Even down to the last days of the Roman world, senators were known as 'conscript fathers'. The reasons for this were partly sociological (in a primitive society power is bound to be concentrated in the hands of a few large families) and partly the effect of the Roman sense of continuity (the *mos maiorum* or custom of one's forefathers), but the chief reason was religious. Religion and politics were never divorced at Rome: there was no separate class of 'religious' people; every leading politician was himself a member of one of the main colleges of priests (*pontifices*, augurs, *quindecimviri sacris faciundis, epulones*) and would be called upon in the course of his political duties to preside at sacrifices and other religious events. In particular he would have to seek the will of the gods by taking the auspices, which involved the study of the flight of birds observed under special circumstances. It was this religious prerogative that singled out the patricians; it was only they who had the right to take the auspices and so to hold the consulship, and who enjoyed various other religious privileges, such as that of celebrating triumphs.

The patricians were, however, a closed group. Technically, once the kings, the source of religious ennoblement, had been expelled, no new patricians could be created, though there is one version of the family history of the Claudii which asserts that they migrated to Rome some years after the expulsion of Tarquinius Superbus and were given patrician status (Livy II.16.3–5). Nevertheless, as the fifth century progressed there is no doubt that the monopoly of political and religious power by a small class began to give rise to difficulties. In the first place, as one would expect, new families appeared on the scene and acquired wealth and importance but were denied the highest political office. Secondly, the patrician families themselves seem to have declined. Many of them were Etruscan by origin, and with the collapse of Etruria in the middle of the fifth century some of them simply disappear: perhaps they died out, perhaps they withdrew to their native homelands. But the Larcii, Menenii and others who are so prominent in the early years of Republican history are heard of no more. Thirdly, the complexity of government increased. By the end of the century Rome was often fighting on at least four fronts – against Etruscans, Gauls, Volscians and Aequi. This put great pressure on Roman resources, not only on manpower but on leadership. In their characteristically flexible way the Romans seem at first to have resolved the difficulty by creating a new chief magistracy – tribunes of the soldiers with consular authority. This solution enabled them both to elect non-patricians to positions of supreme command and to vary their number according to the number and seriousness of the threats with which they were faced. Consular tribunes, although not necessarily elected every year, seem to have lasted from 444 to 367 B.C. But the decline of the patricians and the rise of the new, rich plebeian families meant that the latter could not be denied for ever the religious and political power associated with the consulship. The situation was aggravated by the disaster of the Gallic Sack, which left Rome poor and weak.

Something of the tension comes through in the story of Marcus Manlius, although it must be remembered that Livy's account of these events has been so heavily coloured by subsequent political crises, in particular the affair of Catiline in 63 B.C., that very little trust can be put in any of the details that he gives. The issue was not the rights of the proletariat and

poor people – that was to come later. It was about the rights
of a few rich and ambitious families who felt that, since they
contributed so much to the welfare of Roman society, they
were unjustly deprived of their due rewards. There is no doubt
that this led to massive civil disturbance in the 370s, even
though Livy's statement that there were no magistrates in
Rome from 375 to 371 (VI.35.10) is almost certainly mistaken.
He is attempting to find an explanation for a serious chronological shortcoming in his sources, which have extended the
history of the Republic by four or five years. Roman annalists
placed the expulsion of the Tarquins in 510 B.C. and the Gallic
Sack in 390; the true dates were 507 and 386 respectively, and
Livy had to fill the gap as he came closer to more accurately
documented times.

The remedy which the Romans adopted was a bold one. In
367 B.C. a law was finally passed, after years of argument,
which laid down that one of the consuls in any year should be
a plebeian. Subsequent legislation opened the other magistracies to plebeians in the same way. Whether the Sextio–
Licinian law was really framed in the exact terms which Livy
gives (VI.42.9–14) is perhaps doubtful. Although we have
reliable lists of magistrates throughout most of the fourth
century, it is not always easy to tell whether they come from
patrician or plebeian families. C. Marcius Rutulus, for instance,
who is always claimed as the first plebeian dictator and censor
(VII.17.6), was probably neither plebeian nor a dictator: his
claims have been invented by later plebeian Marcii after the
family went through a period of total obscurity for 200 years.
What does, however, emerge is that from 367 to 342 B.C. the
patricians seem to have retained a virtual monopoly of the
consulship. It is, therefore, more likely that the Sextio–Licinian
law in fact prescribed that one consul might, rather than
should, be a plebeian.

As the 340s drew on, Rome's commitments also grew. First
came the Latin war, and then the prolonged involvement with
Samnium. As in the fifth century, this entailed both large-scale
mobilization of troops and the services of every rich and able
leader that Rome possessed. In 342 a tribune of the plebs,

Lucius Genucius, secured the passing of three plebiscites. The first prohibited anyone from holding the same office more than once in ten years (VII.42.2), thereby effectively breaking the patrician monopoly. The second, the true purpose of which is not fully understood, prohibited a person from holding two offices simultaneously. The third opened both consulships to the plebeians.

The effect of these measures is reflected in the lists of magistrates, which now show a substantial number of plebeians coming to the fore. Essentially, however, it was an alliance of patrician and plebeian aristocrats effected by a change of technical status, and not an opening of power to the lower classes. Nevertheless, Roman society was changing. The Samnite wars required the conscription of huge numbers of Roman citizens who were thereby absent from their farms for years on end. When they were demobilized they tended to drift to Rome. At the same time the Samnite wars (and later the wars in Greece, Asia Minor and Africa) brought rich rewards to the generals which they could only either spend on luxuries or invest in land. But land worked on a peasant basis is notoriously uneconomical, and the only solution was to replace the peasant small-holdings by large estates worked by slaves. This process again had the effect of increasing the proletariat in the city of Rome itself.[13]

It was this plebeian body which began to become a force in Roman politics at the end of the fourth century. The failure of the coalition of patrician and plebeian nobles to bring the Samnite war to a decisive conclusion created both discontent and economic suffering. Ap. Claudius, although himself a descendant of one of the most intransigent patrician families, took up the cause of the poor. We cannot be sure about his motives, but as censor in 312 he not only inaugurated a major scheme of public works in order to provide employment but also managed to force through three major changes. The first was to distribute the poor (*humillimi*), who had previously been confined to the four urban tribes, among all the tribes.

13. See J. Heurgon, *The Rise of Rome to 264 B. C.* (London, 1973), pp. 195–8.

This secured for the urban proletariat a majority say in the tribal assembly (IX.46.10–11). The second was to make sons of freedmen eligible for office and for membership of the Senate – apparently a short-lived measure. The third was the military reform of manipular tactics, which gave to ordinary soldiers far greater importance and responsibility in the collective unit. At the same time steps were taken to improve the plight of debtors.

When Livy's narrative resumes with Book XXI (after the loss of Books XI–XX), we have moved into the full light of history. At the beginning of the third century Rome might have turned, like Athens, towards a participating democracy, which seems to have been Ap. Claudius's ultimate ideal. In the event she took the second course and developed that nexus of dynastic families, both patrician and plebeian, whose unity under statesmen such as the Scipios and Cato was to bring the great triumphs of the second century, and whose rivalry and disunity were to culminate on the field of Pharsalus in 48 B.C.

Errachd, 1981   R. M. OGILVIE

SELECT BIBLIOGRAPHY

TEXTS, EDITIONS AND TRANSLATIONS

TITI LIVI, *Ab urbe condita* libri VI–X, ed. C. F. Walters and R. S. Conway; Vol. II of Oxford Classical Text (OCT; Oxford, 1919).

LIVY, *Books V–VII, VIII–X*, ed. and tr. B. O. Foster; Vols. III and IV of the Loeb Classical Library (Loeb; London and Cambridge, Mass., 1924, 1926).

TITE-LIVE, *Livres VI–VII*, texte établi et traduit par Jean Bayet; Budé edition (Paris, 1966).

LIVY, *Book VI*, ed. F. H. Marshall (Cambridge, 1903; 3rd edition 1934).

LIVY, *Book IX*, ed. W. B. Anderson (Cambridge, 1909; 3rd edition 1953).

LIVY, *The Early History of Rome* (Books I–V), tr. Aubrey de Sélincourt, with an Introduction by R. M. Ogilvie (Harmondsworth, 1960; revised 1971).

LIVY, *The War with Hannibal* (Books XXI–XXX), tr. Aubrey de Sélincourt, ed. with an Introduction by Betty Radice (Harmondsworth, 1965).

LIVY, *Rome and the Mediterranean* (Books XXXI–XLV), tr. Henry Bettenson, with an Introduction by A. H. McDonald (Harmondsworth, 1976).

BOOKS AND ARTICLES ON LIVY AND THE HISTORICAL BACKGROUND TO BOOKS VI–X

F. E. ADCOCK, 'The Conquest of Central Italy', Chapter XVIII in Vol. VII of the *Cambridge Ancient History* (*CAH*; Cambridge, 1928).

M. H. CRAWFORD, *The Roman Republic* (London, 1978).

T. A. DOREY (ed.), *The Latin Historians* (London, 1966).

T. A. DOREY (ed.), *Livy* (London, 1971).

M. GRANT, Chapters 3 and 4, *History of Rome* (London, 1978).

M. GRANT, *Roman Myths* (London, 1971, 1973).

L. HOMO, 'The Gallic Wars of Rome', Chapter XVII in Vol. VII of the *Cambridge Ancient History*.

M. L. W. LAISTNER, *The Greater Roman Historians* (California, 1947).

T. J. LUCE, *Livy: The Composition of his History* (Princeton, 1977).

A. H. MCDONALD, 'The Style of Livy', *Journal of Roman Studies* (*JRS*) 47 (1957), pp. 155 ff.

A. H. MCDONALD, *Republican Rome* (London, 1967).

R. M. OGILVIE, *A Commentary on Livy 1–5* (Oxford, 1965; revised 1970).

R. M. OGILVIE, *The Romans and Their Gods* (London, 1969).

R. M. OGILVIE, 'Notes on Livy Book IX', *Yale Classical Studies* 23 (1973), pp. 159 ff.

E. T. SALMON, *Samnium and the Samnites* (Cambridge, 1967).

H. H. SCULLARD, *A History of the Roman World* (London, 1935; 3rd edition 1961).

H. STUART JONES and H. LAST, 'The Making of a United State', Chapter XVI in Vol. VII of the *Cambridge Ancient History*.

P. G. WALSH, *Livy: His Historical Aims and Methods* (Cambridge, 1961).

P. G. WALSH, *Livy* (with full bibliography), Greece & Rome New Surveys in the Classics (Oxford, 1974).

G. WEBSTER, *The Roman Imperial Army* (London, 1969).

BOOK VI

1. The history of the Romans from the foundation of the City to its capture,[1] first under kings, then under consuls and dictators, decemviri and consular tribunes,[2] wars abroad and dissensions at home, I have set out in five books, covering matters which were obscure both through their great antiquity, like objects dimly perceived in the far distance, and because in those days there were few written records, the only reliable means of preserving a memory of past events. A further reason was the loss of most of such accounts as were preserved in the commentaries of the pontiffs and other public and private records when the City was destroyed by fire. From now on a clearer and more reliable account can be given of the City's civil and military history, after it made a second start, reborn as it were from its old roots with increased vigour and productivity.

Now it stood at first by leaning on the same support which had raised it up, that is, on its leading citizen Marcus Furius (Camillus), who was only allowed to resign his dictatorship when the official year was ended.[3] It was decided that the tribunes who had been in office when the City was captured should not hold the elections for the coming year, and the State reverted to an interregnum.[4] The citizens were occupied with

1. By the Gauls in 386 B.C. (390 by Roman reckoning).
2. The decemvirate lasted only from 451 to 449 and drew up the law-code of the Twelve Tables. The consular tribunate was created in 444 to increase the number of available military commanders and lasted till 401; cf. ch. 37.5.
3. 30 June.
4. An interregnum was declared on the death or resignation of both consuls before completion of their term of office. The senators chose an interrex as their representative for five days; he renewed the auspices and submitted two names to the assembly. If these were rejected by the people he or his successors continued to nominate candidates until agreement was reached. A list of eight interreges is given in VII.17, and a period of eleven mentioned in VII.21.

unremitting toil and labour to restore the City; meanwhile
Quintus Fabius had no sooner resigned office than he was
indicted by the people's tribune Gnaeus Marcius, on the
charge of having contravened the law of nations by fighting
against the Gauls, to whom he had been sent as an envoy. He
escaped trial by a death so timely that the majority believed
it was self-inflicted. The interregnum began, with Publius
Cornelius Scipio as interrex, followed by Marcus Furius
Camillus, who held the election for military tribunes with
consular authority of Lucius Valerius Publicola (for the second
time), Lucius Verginius, Publius Cornelius, Aulus Manlius,
Lucius Aemilius and Lucius Postumius.

Immediately on entering office after the interregnum, these
men consulted the Senate before anything else on matters of
religious observance. One of their first decrees was for a search
to be made for all that could be found of the treaties and laws:
that is, the Twelve Tables and certain laws of the kings. To
some of these even the common people were given access, but
those which applied to sacred rites the pontiffs suppressed,
largely so that they could keep the minds of the populace under
control through religious awe. They then went on to deliberate
about days of ill omen. The 18th July, which was notorious
for a double disaster, the slaughter of the Fabii at the Cremera
and the shocking defeat at the Allia which led to the destruction
of the City,[5] they named the Day of the Allia after the latter
disaster, and decreed that it should be marked by a cessation
of all business, whether public or private. Because the military
tribune Sulpicius had apparently not obtained favourable
omens before offering sacrifice on 16 July and two days later
had exposed the Roman army to the enemy without gaining
the gods' favour, some think that it was also decreed that
religious rites should not be held on the days following the
Ides, and that subsequently it became the tradition for the same
scruple to extend to the days following the Kalends and Nones
as well.

2. But the Romans were not left in peace for long to discuss

5. II.50–51; V.37–9; cf. Tacitus, *Histories* II.91.

amongst themselves their plans for restoring their State after its disastrous downfall. On the one hand their old enemies the Volscians had taken up arms with the intention of wiping out the name of Rome; on the other, according to traders' reports, the leading men from all the peoples of Etruria had met at the temple of Voltumna[6] and sworn to combine forces in war. There was also fresh alarm at the revolt of the Latini and Hernici, who ever since the battle of Lake Regillus[7] had remained on friendly terms with the Roman people with no suspicion of disloyalty for nearly a hundred years. And so with such serious causes for alarm on all sides, as it was obvious to all that the name of Rome was not only suffering from the hatred of her enemies but was even held in contempt amongst her allies, it was determined that the republic should be defended under the auspices of the man who had brought about her recovery, and that Marcus Furius Camillus should be named dictator. Once appointed he named Gaius Servilius Ahala as master of Horse, and after proclaiming a suspension of public business,[8] he held a levy of the younger men, and even included many of their elders who were still sufficiently strong and active; he administered the oath of allegiance and enrolled them into centuries.

When the army was enlisted and armed he divided it into three. One division he posted in the Veientine region to confront Etruria, and a second he ordered to encamp in front of the City, under the command of the military tribune Aulus Manlius; the division sent against the Etruscans was commanded by the tribune Lucius Aemilius. The third division he led himself against the Volscians, and set out to attack their camp not far from Lanuvium, at a place called 'near the Mecius'.[9] The Volscians had gone to war out of contempt for the Romans, believing that nearly all their young men had

6. The federal sanctuary of the Etruscans at Volsinii (IV.23.5; V.17.6).

7. Where the exiled Tarquins were defeated in 496 according to Roman tradition (II.19–20).

8. The temporary suspension of all legal business in an emergency, known as *iustitium*; cf. VII.6.12, X.21.3.

9. Probably a hill; cf. Plutarch, *Camillus* 34.

been wiped out by the Gauls, but the mere news that Camillus was in command threw them into such a panic that they blockaded themselves behind a rampart, and protected the rampart with piled-up logs, so that the Romans should nowhere be able to penetrate to their defences. On seeing this, Camillus gave orders to throw fire on the barrier that blocked his way. It so happened that there was a high wind blowing against the Volscians, so that he not only blazed a way through but so terrified the enemy with the flames spreading into the camp, the heat and smoke and crackling of the burning green wood, that the Roman soldiers had less difficulty in scaling the rampart and entering the Volscian camp than they had faced when going through the burnt barricade. The enemy were routed and killed, the dictator stormed and captured the camp, and then gave the plunder to the army, an act all the more gratifying to the soldiers as coming unexpectedly from a commander not given to generosity.[10] He then pursued the fugitives, laid waste all the Volscian territory, and forced the Volscians to surrender at last, after seventy years of warfare. After his victory Camillus moved on from the Volscians to the Aequi, who were also making preparations for war, and surprised their army near Bolae, capturing not only their camp but their city too at the first attack.

3. While things went well in the region where Camillus was commander for Rome, elsewhere great danger threatened. Nearly the whole of Etruria was in arms and allies of the Roman people in Sutrium were under siege. Envoys from the town had appeared before the Senate begging for help in their plight, and had obtained a decree that the dictator should bring the Sutrines aid as soon as possible. But the state of the besieged could not wait for the realization of this hope: the citizens were few in number and exhausted by labour, guard duty and wounds, which always bore hard on the same people, so that they had made terms and handed over their town to the enemy. They were actually leaving their homes in a wretched procession, unarmed, each with a single garment, when

10. cf. V.22.1–2 and V.25.11–13.

Camillus arrived with a Roman army. The miserable people
flung themselves at his feet; the leading men addressed him in
words wrung from them by the cruellest necessity, accompanied by the sobs of the women and children whom they
were dragging along to share their exile. Camillus told the
Sutrines to spare their lamentations, for it was to the Etruscans
he was bringing sorrow and tears. He then gave orders for
army packs to be set down, the Sutrines to wait there with the
small guard he left them, and the soldiers to arm and follow
him. With his army thus unencumbered he set out for Sutrium
and found everything there as he expected, with the usual lax
discipline following a success: no pickets outside the walls,
gates open, the victors dispersed and busy taking plunder from
their enemies' homes. For the second time then on the same
day, Sutrium was captured; the Etruscans in their hour of
victory were cut down everywhere by a new foe, with no time
to collect and join their forces or to arm. They made for the
gates, to see if they could escape into the fields, but found them
shut, for that had been the first order of the dictator. Then
some seized their arms, others whom the sudden attack had
found already armed called on their fellows to begin a battle,
and this would have been hotly fought in their desperation if
heralds had not been sent through the town to order arms to
be laid down, the unarmed to be given quarter, and none but
those still carrying weapons to suffer injury. At this, even those
who had been desperately determined to fight to the death,
now that they were offered hope of life, threw down their
swords everywhere and gave themselves up unarmed, as
fortune had made this the safer course. The great crowd was
divided up under guard-parties, and before nightfall the town
was handed back to the Sutrines, undamaged and free from
any ill effect of war, since it had been surrendered under terms.

4. Camillus returned to the City in triumph for his victories
in three concurrent wars.[11] By far the largest number of
captives led before his chariot were Etruscans, and their sale by
auction realized so large a sum that after the married women

11. Victories over the Volscians, the Aequi, and now the Etruscans.

had been repaid for the gold they had contributed,[12] there was sufficient surplus to make three golden bowls: these are known to have been inscribed with the name of Camillus, and up to the burning of the Capitol[13] to have stood in the chapel of Jupiter at the feet of Juno.

That year those of the Veientes, Capenates and Falisci who had gone over to Rome in the course of the wars were admitted to citizenship, and land was allotted to these new citizens. A decree of the Senate was also passed to recall from Veii people who had been too idle to build at Rome and had gone off to Veii and occupied vacant houses there. At first there was grumbling, and the order was flouted, but when a date was fixed and loss of civic rights was threatened for those who had not returned to Rome, their united defiance changed to individual obedience, everyone having fears for himself. The population of Rome increased and everywhere at once buildings sprang up; the State helped with the cost, and the aediles put on pressure as if the work were a public concern, while the individual citizens hurried on to finish their building, fired by their wish to be making use of it. Within the year the new City was standing.

At the end of the year an election was held of military tribunes with consular powers, in which Titus Quinctius Cincinnatus, Quintus Servilius Fidenas (for the fifth time), Lucius Julius Julus, Lucius Aquilius Corvus, Lucius Lucretius Tricipitinus and Servius Sulpicius Rufus were elected. They led one army against the Aequi, not to make war (for the Aequi admitted they were defeated) but out of hatred, intending to destroy their lands completely and leave them no strength for further designs; with the other they invaded Tarquinian territory, where they stormed and captured the Etruscan towns of Cortuosa and Contenebra. At Cortuosa there was no resistance; the town was taken in a surprise attack at the first shout and assault, then sacked and burnt. The people of Contenebra withstood the attack for a few days until the continuous effort, without respite day or night, defeated them:

12. cf. V.50.6–7.   13. In 83 B.C.

for the Roman army had been divided into six sections, each of which took its turn in the battle for six hours, while the townsmen were few in number and therefore compelled to face fresh combatants continuously in spite of their exhaustion. At last they gave in and allowed the Romans to enter the town. The tribunes would have liked the plunder to go to the State, but they took longer to issue the order than to make up their minds; while they delayed the soldiers were already in possession and it could not have been taken from them without causing ill feeling.

In the same year, so that the City's growth should not be limited to private building, the foundations of the Capitol were also laid in squared blocks of stone, a work which commands attention even in the magnificence of the City today.

5. While the citizens were occupied with their building, the people's tribunes were already trying to attract crowds to their meetings by proposing agrarian laws, and held out hope of the Pomptine district,[14] of which for the first time the Romans had undisputed possession as a result of the blow dealt by Camillus to Volscian power. The tribunes brought the charge that the land was in far worse plight by reason of the nobility than it had been because of the Volscians, who had only made forays into it so long as their resources and arms permitted; whereas the nobles were grabbing possession of public land, and there would be no room left there for the common people unless it was shared out before they seized it all. They made no great impression on the people, who were too taken up with their building to be often present in the Forum, and for the same reason were crippled with the expenses they had incurred and had little thought of land when they had no means of stocking it.

There were widespread religious anxieties in Rome, and at that time even the leaders were prone to superstitious fears as a result of the recent disaster; so in order to renew the auspices, there was a return to an interregnum. The office of interrex

14. The region in Latium between Antium and Circeii.

was held in turn by Marcus Manlius Capitolinus, Servius Sulpicius Camerinus and Lucius Valerius Potitus. The last-named held elections for military tribunes with consular power. Lucius Papirius, Gnaeus Sergius, Lucius Aemilius (for the second time), Licinius Menenius and Lucius Valerius Publicola (for the third time), were elected and took office at the end of the interregnum. That year the temple of Mars vowed during the Gallic war was dedicated by Titus Quinctius, one of the two commissioners for performing sacrifices. Four tribes (the Stellatine, Tromentine, Sabatine and Arniensis) were made up of new citizens and added to those existing to bring the number of tribes up to twenty-five.

6. The subject of the Pomptine land was brought up by the people's tribune Lucius Sicinius, before a better-attended meeting of men more ready to change their opinions and be interested in owning land than they had been before. There was also talk in the Senate of war with the Latins and Hernici, but this was postponed through fear of a greater war, since Etruria was under arms. Responsibility again fell on Camillus, as military tribune with consular power. He was given five colleagues: Servius Cornelius Maluginensis, Quintus Servilius Fidenas, Lucius Quinctius Cincinnatus (for a sixth term of office), Lucius Horatius Pulvillus and Publius Valerius. At the start of the year public attention shifted from a war with Etruria, when a party of fugitives from the Pomptine district suddenly arrived in Rome with the news that the people of Antium were under arms and the Latins had dispatched their own younger men to give help, though they insisted that they were only allowing volunteers to serve where they wished and that this was not their official policy.

By now the Romans had ceased to think lightly of any war; and so the Senate gave thanks to the gods that Camillus was in office, for he would have had to be made dictator had he held no official position. His colleagues declared that direction of all affairs should be in one man's hands at a time of serious threat of war, and they intended to subordinate their own power to that of Camillus; nor did they believe their own dignity was in any way diminished by what they had done for his. The tribunes were warmly praised by the Senate, and Camillus, much moved, added his thanks. A heavy responsibility, he said, had been laid on him by the people of Rome in electing him now for the fourth time, and a serious one by the Senate in their high opinions of him, but the most serious of all arose out of the deference of such honoured colleagues. And so if he could add anything to his efforts and his vigilance he would be his own rival, to ensure that the high opinion of him unanimously held by his fellow-citizens should be a lasting one. As for the war with the people of Antium, he believed it was more of a threat than a danger, but he advised them not to make light of the situation even if they need have no fears. The City of Rome was beset by the envy and hatred of her neighbours and therefore needed more than one leader and army to administer its affairs. 'I want you, Publius Valerius,' he said, 'to share my authority and deliberations, and to join me in leading the legions against our enemies at Antium. You, Quintus Servilius, are to mobilize and equip a second army and keep it encamped in the City, ready for action, if in the meantime there is a rising in Etruria like the recent one, or one amongst the Latins and Hernici, this new problem of ours. I am sure you will deal with this in a manner worthy of your father, your grandfather[15] and the six tribunates you have held. A third army must be recruited by Lucius Quinctius out of men invalided out of the army or above military age, and this shall defend the City and its walls. Lucius Horatius is to provide arms, missiles, corn and everything else to meet the demands of the situation. Servius Cornelius, we your colleagues appoint you president of this state council, guardian of religious ceremonies, of elections, the laws, and of all the City's interests.'

All promised loyally to do their best in the duties assigned them, and Valerius, who had been chosen to share the command, added that he would regard Marcus Furius as dictator and himself as his master of Horse; their hopes for the outcome of the war should therefore reflect their confidence in their matchless commander. The senators in their enthusiasm at this

15. cf. IV.21.10 (father); III.6.1 (grandfather).

45

cried out that they had high hopes of the war, and of peace and the City's welfare in general; Rome would never have need of a dictator if she had such men in office, men so united in heart, as ready to obey as to command, and contributing glory to the common stock rather than drawing from it in their personal interests.

7. After declaring a suspension of legal business and holding a levy of troops Furius and Valerius set out for Satricum, where the Antiates had concentrated not only the fighting forces of the Volscians recruited from the younger generation, but also vast numbers from the Latins and Hernici, drawn from peoples who were in excellent shape after a long period of peace. This combination of a new enemy with their old one had a disturbing effect on the army's morale. The centurions reported to Camillus, as he was already drawing up his line of battle, that the soldiers were dispirited and reluctant to arm, were loitering and hanging back as they left the camp, and had even been heard to say that they would be fighting against odds of a hundred to one and an army of such a size as could hardly be withstood even if it were unarmed, still less when armed. He jumped on his horse, and riding between the ranks in front of the standards he faced his troops. 'Soldiers,' he cried, 'what is this gloom, this reluctance, which is so unlike you? Is it the enemy whom you don't know – or me – or yourselves? What else is an enemy but a perpetual opportunity for you to show your mettle and win glory? As for yourselves, under my leadership (to say nothing of your capture of Falerii and Veii and massacre of the Gallic legions when they had occupied your own city) you have recently celebrated a triple triumph for a threefold victory over those very Volscians and Aequi and over Etruria. Or can it be that because I gave you the signal as tribune, not as dictator, you do not recognize me as your commander? I have no wish for absolute authority over you, and you should see in me nothing but myself; my resolution has never gained anything from dictatorship, any more than it lost anything through exile. Nothing in any of us has changed, and we bring the same qualities to this war as we brought to earlier ones. Let us then expect the same outcome. At the first

clash everyone will act in accordance with his training and habit: you will win, they will run away.'

8. He then gave the signal for action, jumped down from his horse, and, seizing the nearest standard-bearer by the hand, hurried him towards the enemy, shouting 'Attack, soldiers!' At the sight of Camillus charging the enemy in person, though his age made him unfit for physical feats, the men all cheered and rushed forward together, everyone taking up the cry 'Follow the general!' It is even said that at Camillus's order the standard was thrown into the ranks of the enemy and the front line of troops was urged on to recover it. That was the first time the Antiates had been forced to give way. Panic spread right through their front lines and back to the supporting troops. It was not so much the drive of the Roman soldiery, inspired by the presence of their leader, which pushed back the enemy, as the fact that nothing alarmed the Volscians so much as the sight of Camillus in person when they encountered him; thus wherever he went he brought certain victory with him. That was especially apparent on the left wing, which had almost been forced back when he quickly seized a horse, galloped up armed with an infantry shield, and restored the battle by his presence and assurance that the rest of the army was winning the day.

The issue was already determined, but the sheer weight of the enemy was a hindrance to their flight, and large numbers were left to be cut down by the exhausted soldiers in a pro- tracted massacre, until violent gusts of wind and a sudden downpour broke up what was more a certain victory than a battle. Then the signal for recall was sounded, and the night which followed ended the campaign without any further action of the Romans; for the Latins and Hernici deserted the Volscians and went off to their homes, having fared no better than their evil intentions deserved. Once the Volscians found themselves abandoned by those on whom they had relied for their rebellion they left their camp and shut themselves inside the walls of Satricum. Camillus at first set about surrounding them with a mound and palisade for an attack by siege, but when he saw that there were no sorties to hinder these operations he concluded that the enemy had too little spirit to make it necessary to wait so long for victory, and urged his men not to exhaust themselves with protracted labour, as in the siege of Vëii, now that victory was in their grasp. The soldiers responded magnificently; he then attacked the walls on all sides, and took the town with scaling ladders. The Volscians threw down their arms and surrendered.

9. However, the general's thoughts were intent on the more serious menace of Antium, the capital of the Volscians, which he believed to have been responsible for the recent war. A city so strong could not be captured except by considerable equipment of engines and artillery; he therefore left his colleague in command of the army and set out for Rome, in order to exhort the Senate to destroy Antium. While he was speaking (I suppose it was the gods' will that Antium should continue in existence a while) envoys from Nepete and Sutrium arrived asking for help against the Etruscans and pointing out that the time in which to give it was short. Thus Fortune diverted Camillus's energies away from Antium to this new area. The two places commanded Etruria, providing both a barrier and a gateway, so that the Etruscans were anxious to occupy them whenever they had any new plan in mind, and the Romans were equally concerned to recover or protect them. The Senate accordingly decided to suggest to Camillus that he should leave Antium in order to undertake a campaign against the Etruscans, and assigned him the city legions commanded by Quinctius (Cincinnatus). He raised no objection, though he would have preferred the trained army accustomed to his command which was in Volscian territory; all he stipulated was that Valerius should share his command. Quinctius and Horatius were sent to replace Valerius against the Volscians.

Furius and Valerius left Rome for Sutrium, where they found that half of the town was already taken by the Etruscans, and the townsfolk in the other half were having difficulty in repelling the enemy attack by means of street barricades. The arrival of Roman support and, still more, the great fame of Camillus's name amongst both enemies and allies for the time being kept the situation from deteriorating further and allowed time for bringing help. Camillus accordingly divided his army and told his colleague to take his forces round to the part of the town held by the enemy and attack the walls – not so much in the hope of taking the city by scaling them as of drawing off the enemy in that direction so as to relieve the strain on the citizens, who were already exhausted with fighting. It would also give himself a chance of breaching the walls without meeting resistance. Both operations were put into effect at the same moment, so that the Etruscans found themselves trapped between two hazards; they saw the walls violently attacked and the enemy already inside the city, and rushed out in a single panic-stricken crowd through the only gate which happened not to be under attack. The massacre of fugitives both in the city and in the countryside was great; the majority were cut down by Furius's soldiers inside the walls, while Valerius's men were more lightly equipped for pursuit, and carried on the slaughter until nightfall made it impossible to see.

Once Sutrium was recaptured and restored to the allies, the army was taken on to Nepete; there the Etruscans were in complete occupation after the town's surrender. 10. It looked as though it would be more difficult to recover, not only because it was entirely in enemy hands but also because the surrender was due to the betrayal of their city by a section of the populace. However, it was decided to send a request to their leaders to sever relations with the Etruscans and themselves to provide the loyal aid which they had begged from the Romans. When the reply came back that they were quite powerless, that the Etruscans held the walls and were on guard at the gates, an attempt was first made to terrorize the townsfolk by devastating the surrounding fields; then when loyalty to their surrender rather than to their alliance proved more binding on them, bundles of brushwood were collected in the fields and the Roman army brought up to the walls. The moat was filled in, scaling ladders set up, and the town taken at the first shout and charge. The people of Nepete were then told to lay down their arms and the order was given to spare the unarmed. The Etruscans were killed, whether armed or not;

the ringleaders of the town's surrender were also executed, but the innocent people were given back their possessions and the town was left with a garrison. Two allied cities were thus won back from the enemy, and the tribunes brought the victorious army back to Rome, covered with glory.

In the same year satisfaction was demanded from the Latins and Hernici, who were asked why in recent years they had provided no military contingent as they had agreed to do. The reply came from a well-attended assembly of both peoples that it was not official policy, which could not therefore be held to blame, if a few of their young men had served with the Volscians; the men had paid the penalty for their misguided decision, and none of them had come back. The reason why they had sent no soldiers was the constant danger from the Volscians – that thorn in their side which so many wars, one after another, had never been able to extract. When this was put to the Senate it was decided that though there might be grounds for war, this was not the time for it.

11. The following year, when the tribunes with consular powers were Aulus Manlius, Publius Cornelius, Titus and Lucius Quinctius Capitolinus, Lucius Papirius Cursor and Gaius Sergius (both for the second time), saw the outbreak of a serious foreign war and an even more serious internal insurrection. The war was started by the Volscians in conjunction with a revolt of the Latins and Hernici; the insurrection originated where such a thing could least have been expected, with a man of patrician family and distinguished reputation, Marcus Manlius Capitolinus. He was an excessively proud man, who despised the other nobles. Marcus Furius alone he envied, for the way he outshone everyone in honours and merits, resenting his unrivalled eminence in both civil and military positions of authority, where, so he said, Furius now stood so high that he treated men elected under the same auspices as servants, not colleagues – in spite of the fact that (if one judged fairly) Marcus Furius could not have rescued the fatherland from its besiegers if Manlius himself had not first saved the Capitol and Citadel. Furius had attacked the Gauls when the gold was being handed out and they were less intent

on fighting in hope of peace, while he had forced them back when they were fully armed and in the act of capturing the Citadel[16]; a good part of Furius's glory rightly belonged to all the soldiers who had been victorious with him, whereas no mortal man had a share in his own triumph. His pride went on swelling as he voiced these opinions, and he had moreover a defect of character which made him impetuous and head-strong, so that when he saw that his abilities did not count as high in the Senate as he thought they should, he became the very first patrician to take up the popular cause and to throw in his lot with the plebeian magistrates.[17] By abusing the patricians and courting the people he was wafted along on a breeze of popular favour rather than of good sense, preferring his fame to be widespread rather than well founded. Moreover, not content with agrarian legislation, which had always pro-vided the people's tribunes with material for civic disturbances, he started to make an attack on credit, believing that debt was a sharper spur to action, since it not only threatened penury and disgrace but terrified the free man with the prospect of fetters and imprisonment. There was in fact a great accumu-lation of debts, contracted through what is highly ruinous even to the wealthy – that is, building. The Volscian war, serious in itself and aggravated by the revolt of the Latins and Hernici, was put forward as a pretext for seeking a more absolute authority, but it was the revolutionary schemes of Manlius which put greater pressure on the Senate to name a dictator. Aulus Cornelius Cossus was elected, and chose Titus Quinctius Capitolinus as his master of Horse.

12. The dictator realized that a greater conflict lay ahead of him at home than abroad, but even so, whether because the war demanded prompt action or because he thought he could add power even to the dictatorship by a victory and triumph, he recruited men and made for Pomptine territory, where he had heard an army had been assembled by the Volscians.

I do not doubt that people who read in all these books about endless wars with the Volscians will feel surfeited by them, but

16. V.47.4 ff.
17. The *tribuni plebis* were not in fact magistrates, i.e. state-officials.

they will also feel as astonished as I did myself when I examined the historians who were more nearly contemporary with these events, and will ask where the Volscians and Aequi got a sufficient supply of soldiers after so many defeats. But since the ancients have passed over this point in silence, what can I adduce except a suggestion such as anyone by conjecture can make for himself? It is probable that either in the intervals between the wars, as happens now when we hold levies, successive generations of younger men were used for these frequent renewals of war; or that the armies were not always conscripted from the same tribes, although it was always the same nation which made war; or that countless numbers of free men were living in districts which today can scarcely provide a meagre recruiting ground for soldiers and would become a desert but for Roman slave-gangs. In any case, the authorities are all agreed that the Volscians had an enormous army, although they had lately been dealt such a severe blow under the leadership and auspices of Camillus. There were also additional forces from the Latins and Hernici, a certain number of troops from Circeii, and even Roman settlers from Velitrae.

The dictator set up camp that day, and next morning, after taking the auspices, came out to offer a victim and sought the favour of the gods. He was in good spirits as he showed himself to the soldiers, who were already arming at sunrise, as they had been told to do, in expectation of a signal for battle. 'The victory is ours, my men,' he said, 'if the gods and their soothsayers can see at all into the future. Therefore, as befits an army full of confidence and hope which is about to engage with an inferior enemy, let us lay our javelins at our feet and arm our right hands with swords only. I wish no one to run forward from the line: you are to stay firm, stand your ground, and receive the enemy's attack. When they have discharged their missiles to no effect and have come rushing up on you where you stand, then let your swords flash out, and let each man remember that there are gods who help the Roman, the gods who have sent him into battle with good omens on his side. You, Titus Quinctius, must hold back your cavalry and watch for the first sign of the battle beginning. When you see the lines are already locked in combat at close quarters, that is the moment to bring in the horse and terrify the enemy when they are already taken up with another fear; charge then and break up their ranks as they fight.' Cavalry and infantry fought as they were bidden; the general did not fail his legions and fortune did not fail the general.

13. The large enemy forces, relying only on their numbers as they scanned both the opposing lines, rashly started the fight and equally rashly broke off. They were bold only in battle cry, throwing of missiles and the first onrush of the battle; sword-fighting, holding ground, an enemy's face flashing its fury they could not stand up to. Their front lines were driven in and panic spread to the supporting troops, while the cavalry added their own terror; then ranks were broken in many places, there was general confusion and the line surged to and fro like the sea. After that, as the first lines collapsed and everyone saw his own turn to be killed was coming to him, they turned and ran. The Romans followed hard on their heels, and so long as they kept their weapons and fled in a packed crowd, it was the infantry's task to keep up the pursuit. But when the enemy were seen to be throwing away their weapons and scattering widely over the land, then came the moment for the cavalry squadrons to be let loose, with orders not to stop to kill individuals and give meanwhile the main body the opportunity to escape – it was enough to throw missiles to frighten them and check their speed, and by riding across their path hold the column until the infantry could catch up and finish the enemy off with a regular massacre. Flight and pursuit did not end till nightfall. The Volscian camp was also taken and plundered the same day, and all the booty handed over to the soldiers, except for men of free status.[18] Most of the captives were from the Latins and Hernici; not all of them were plebeians, who could be expected to have fought as mercenaries, but some young men of high rank were found, clear proof that the Volscian hostilities had been given official support. Some were also recognized as coming from Circeii,

18. These would be sold as slaves and the money paid into the treasury.

53

and from the colonists at Velitrae. They were all sent to Rome, and under questioning by the leading senators gave the same replies as they had done to the dictator, making no attempt to conceal their people's defection.

14. The dictator kept his army in camp, quite confident that the Senate would order war on the rebel peoples, when a more serious outbreak of trouble at home brought him a summons to Rome, where sedition was spreading from day to day and proving more alarming than usual because of the man responsible for it, Marcus Manlius. It was now not only his public speeches but his actions too which were revolutionary under a show of being democratic, and these had to be judged in the light of his intentions. A centurion who had won fame for his military exploits had been condemned for debt. As he was led off to prison Manlius saw him, hurried up in mid-Forum with a party of his supporters, laid hold of him, and held forth about the arrogance of the Senate, the cruelty of moneylenders, the miseries of the people, the merits and misfortune of the man. 'Then it was all for nothing,' he cried, 'that this right hand of mine saved the Capitol and Citadel, if I am to see a citizen and fellow-soldier led off as a captive to slavery and chains, as though the Gauls had been our conquerors!' Thereupon he paid off the debt in full view of the people, set free the centurion by ceremony of scales and bronze,[19] and released him, calling on gods and men to show their gratitude to Marcus Manlius his liberator, the father of the Roman people. The man was surrounded at once by a turbulent crowd and increased the uproar by displaying the scars he had received in the Veientine and Gallic and other successive wars. While he had fought and tried to restore his ruined home, he cried, he had been destroyed by his borrowings, for though he had paid off the capital of his debt many times over, the accumulated interest always swamped the sum on loan to him. That he could see the light of day, the Forum, the faces of his fellow-citizens, was all due to Marcus Manlius; from him he had received all the support which parents give; to him he vowed

19. A symbolic sale from servitude to freedom, in which the debtor struck the scales with a piece of bronze before witnesses.

all his remaining strength, existence and lifeblood; all the ties which had bound him to his country, to the gods of his country and family, now bound him to one man alone. Carried away by these words, the people were already all for a single man, when Manlius did another thing deliberately calculated to be more generally subversive: he put up for sale by auction the farm he held in Veientine territory, in fact the main part of his estates, 'so that I shall not suffer any one of you, fellow-Romans, to be judged, condemned and led off to slavery, so long as anything I possess remains.' This so fired their enthusiasm that they were clearly prepared to follow their champion of liberty in any cause, right or wrong.

As well as this, in his home Manlius made speeches which were more like public harangues, full of accusations against the patricians. Regardless of whether he spoke true or false, he declared amongst other things that the patricians were concealing treasure-hoards of Gallic gold, and were no longer content with possessing State lands unless they could also appropriate State money; if the facts were made public, the people could be freed from debt. Once this hope was held out to them, the commons found their treatment quite monstrous, arguing that when gold had to be raised to buy off the City from the Gauls it had been collected by tax on all, but now the same gold had been recovered from the enemy it had become the loot of a few. They therefore pressed their demands to know where such a sum of stolen money was hidden, and when Manlius put them off with the assurance that he would tell them in his own good time, they dropped everything and could think of nothing else, so that it was clear that their gratitude, if his words were true, or their disgust, if they proved false, would be unbounded.

15. In such a crisis the dictator was recalled from his army and came to Rome. Next day he held a meeting of the Senate, and when he had made sure of the people's support, he ordered the senators not to leave him, came out into the Comitium accompanied by large numbers of them, set up his curule chair, and sent an official to fetch Marcus Manlius. Summoned by the dictator's order, Manlius passed the word to his supporters

that the fight was on, and came to the tribunal with a huge crowd behind him. Senate and people were ranged on opposite sides, looking to their respective leaders as if drawn up for battle. The dictator obtained silence and began to speak. 'I wish the Roman Senate and I could agree with the plebeians on all problems as readily as I am sure we shall do on what regards you, Manlius, and the request I am going to make of you. I am aware that you have raised the citizens' hopes that money lent them can be repaid, without injury to credit, out of the Gallic treasure which you say leading patricians are concealing. I am far from wanting to hinder such a proposal: on the contrary, Marcus Manlius, I am urging you to release the people of Rome from usury, and to force those people who are jealously hoarding public treasure to disgorge their secret spoils. If you fail to do this, either in order to share the booty yourself or because your information is groundless, I shall give orders for you to be taken into custody, and shall not allow you to excite the populace with false hopes a moment longer.'

To this Manlius replied that he was well aware that the appointment of a dictator was not aimed at the Volscians, who were enemies only when it suited the patricians, nor at the Latins and Hernici, who were being driven to take up arms by trumped-up accusations, but against himself and the common people of Rome. The pretence of war had already been dropped and the attack directed against him: now the dictator was coming out as the champion of the moneylenders against the plebs; now in the popular support he personally enjoyed a pretext was sought to bring about his destruction. 'Does it annoy you, Aulus Cornelius,' he cried, 'and you, Conscript Fathers, to see this crowd gathered round me? Why don't you win it from me? Any one of you could do so, by acts of kindness, by standing surety, by striking the fetters off fellow-citizens, by preventing the enslavement of those condemned and assigned to it, by ministering to the needs of others from your own superfluity of wealth. But why do I ask you to spend your own money? Take what is left of the capital sum, subtract from the original loan what has been paid you in interest; then the crowd round me will be no more conspicuous than that round any of you. Why, you may ask, am I the only man to feel concern for my fellow-citizens? I can no more answer that than if you asked why I was the only man to save, as I did, the Capitol and Citadel. Then I gave all the help I could to the community; now I would offer it to individuals. As for the Gallic treasure – it is simple enough, but your questioning makes it difficult. Why do you ask what you know? Why do you order your own purses to be emptied instead of handing them over yourselves – unless there is some fraud involved? The more you order us to expose your tricks, the more I fear you have blown smoke in our eyes as we watched you. And so it is not a case of putting pressure on me to denounce your loot, but of compelling you to give it up.'

16. The dictator told him to come to the point, and insisted that he either substantiate his charge or admit to the crime of bringing a false accusation against the Senate and exposing it to the odium of a theft which did not exist. When Manlius refused to speak at the bidding of his enemies, he ordered him to be taken off to prison. As he was arrested by the officer, Manlius called out 'Jupiter Best and Greatest, Queen Juno and Minerva, and all you other gods and goddesses who dwell on the Capitol and Citadel, do you permit your champion and protector to be harassed by his enemies in this way? Shall this right arm which drove the Gauls headlong from your shrines now be fettered and chained?' No one could bear to see or hear of his shameful plight, yet there were certain actions which the citizens, wholly submissive as they were to established authority, had made inviolable for themselves, and against a dictator's power neither the tribunes of the people nor the people itself dare lift their eyes or open their mouths. But it is generally known that after Manlius was thrown into prison a large proportion of the people put on mourning, men let their hair and beards grow, and a sorrowing crowd gathered round the entrance to the prison.

The dictator held his triumph over the Volscians, but it was one which brought him more unpopularity than glory; there were murmurings that he had won it at home, not on the battlefield, over a Roman citizen, not an enemy, and that the only feature missing from his display of arrogance was the sight of Marcus Manlius led before his chariot. By this time the situation came very near to open strife, and to calm it down, the Senate quickly turned of its own accord to making an offer which no one demanded, and ordered two thousand Roman citizens to be dispatched to set up a colony at Satricum. Two *iugera* and a half[20] of land were assigned each man, but as this was judged a meagre gift to an inadequate number and looked like payment for the betrayal of Manlius, the remedy proposed only aggravated the unrest. Now the Manlian party was even more conspicuous, with its dismal garb and appearance of men under accusation, and the abdication of the dictator after his triumph had removed men's fears and set free their tongues and spirits.

17. And so reproaches were openly expressed against the people, blaming them for always raising their champions to dangerous heights by their support and then abandoning them at times of crisis. This had happened in the case of Spurius Cassius,[21] who had been destroyed when he offered the plebeians a share in the land, and of Spurius Maelius[22] for trying to save his fellow-citizens from starvation at his own expense; it was the same with Marcus Manlius, betrayed to his enemies for extricating the section of the populace he saw sunk deep in debt and bringing them to light and liberty; the plebeians fattened its favourites only for slaughter. Was this what an ex-consul must suffer if he did not respond to a dictator's bidding? Suppose he had lied before, and for that reason found himself unable to reply: what slave had ever been imprisoned for a lie? Had they no recollection of that night which had so nearly been eternal, the last night for the name of Rome? Could they not picture the file of Gauls climbing the Tarpeian Rock, and Marcus Manlius himself, as they had seen him then, armed and covered with sweat and blood, after he had snatched Jupiter himself – one might say – from the hands of the enemy? Was their gratitude to their country's

20. About 1⅔ acres. The *iugerum* measured about ⅔ of an acre.
21. II.41.
22. IV.13 ff.

saviour measured in half-pounds of flour?[23] Would they permit one whom they had made almost a god, and the equal, at any rate in surname, of Capitoline Jupiter, to lie chained in prison and to draw breath in darkness, at the mercy of an executioner's whim? Could it really be true that when one man had been able to save them all, there was no help among so many men for one? By this time it was growing dark, and the crowd still would not disperse from where they stood and were threatening to break into the prison, when they were granted what they intended to take by force, and Manlius was set free by decree of the Senate. Even this did not end the rioting but gave it a leader.

About this time the Latins and Hernici, along with colonists from Circeii and Velitrae, who were seeking to clear themselves of the charge of taking part in the Volscian war and to recover their captives for punishment under their own laws, received a harsh reply – especially harsh in the case of the colonists, because though they were Roman citizens they had formed the heinous plan of attacking their own country. They were accordingly not only refused the captives but received a reprimand which the allies were spared; they were commanded by decree of the Senate to make all haste to leave the City, out of sight and presence of the Roman people, for they would not be covered by the rights of envoys, which were designed for foreigners, not citizens.

18. The insurrection started by Manlius broke out again towards the end of the year, when elections were held at which the following were elected military tribunes with consular powers: Servius Cornelius Maluginensis and Publius Valerius Potitus, both for the second time, Marcus Furius Camillus for the fifth time, Servius Sulpicius Rufus for the second time, Gaius Papirius Crassus and Titus Quinctius Cincinnatus also for the second time. At the beginning of this year there was peace abroad, which was very welcome to patricians and plebeians alike: to the people because they had hopes that while they were not being called up for service by levy and had so

23. V.47.7–8: the donation by each soldier to Manlius for saving the Capitol.

powerful a leader they would be able to break the power of usury; to the patricians because they did not want to be distracted by any external threat from finding a remedy for the city's domestic troubles. Both sides had accordingly taken up their positions with much more vigour, and now the hour of battle was at hand. Manlius was indeed inviting members of the plebeians to his house and discussing plans for revolution with their leaders night and day, for he was much bolder and angrier than before. His fury was roused by the recent humiliations suffered by a spirit unused to insult; and his courage increased with the thought that the dictator had not dared to treat him as Quinctius Cincinnatus had treated Spurius Maelius,[24] and had escaped the bitter resentment aroused by imprisoning him only by resigning his own dictatorship, while even the Senate had found it impossible to endure it. Elated and at the same time exasperated by these thoughts, he began to work on the emotions of the people, which were already roused on his behalf. 'How long,' he asked, 'will you remain unaware of your own strength, which nature has decreed even brute beasts shall know? At least count up your numbers and those of your adversaries. As many as you were as clients around your individual patrons, so many shall you now be against a single foe. If you were going to confront them man for man, I should still believe that you would fight more keenly for liberty than they for domination. Only make a show of war and you will have peace. Let them only see you prepared for violent action and they will give you your due rights of their own accord. We must all unite for one act of daring, or else – divided – suffer every evil. How long will you go on looking for me? I am here, and will fail none of you, but you must see to it that fortune does not fail me. I, your champion, was suddenly brought down when it pleased your enemies, and you all saw led off to prison the man who had held off imprisonment from each one of you. What am I to expect if my enemies dare more against me? To end like Cassius and Maelius? You do well to show your horror. The

24. IV.14.

gods will prevent this, but they will never come down from heaven on my account: they must give *you* the understanding to prevent it, as they granted me as soldier and citizen the understanding to defend you from the barbarity of your enemies and the arrogance of your fellow-citizens. Is there so little spirit in so great a people that the help of the tribunes against your enemies is enough for you? Is your struggle with the senators only to limit the extent you will permit them to lord it over you? This is no natural trait in you: you are slaves of habit. Your sense of superiority towards foreigners makes you think it proper to rule them. Why is that? Because you are used to contending with them for power to rule, whereas, when it comes to the Senate, you make attempts at gaining your liberty, but you are not used to defending it. Even so, with such leaders as you have had, and being the men you are, up to now you have gained as much as you sought, whether by force or good luck. The time has come to try for bigger things. Only test your own good fortune – and me, whom, I hope, you have already successfully proved; you will find it easier to set a ruler over the patricians than it was to establish resistance to their rule.[25] Dictatorships and consulships must be levelled with the ground so that the Roman people can raise its head. Stand by me, then, and stop legal proceedings on debts. For my part I declare myself patron of the plebeians, a title won by my integrity and concern for your interests. If you wish to address your leader by a more striking title of authority and honour, you will find him the better able to win you what you want.'

This was the start, it is said, of Manlius's bid for royal power; but there is no clear record to say with whom he shared his plans or how far they went.

19. On the other side the Senate was discussing the with-drawal of the plebs into a private house – one too which happened to be situated on the Citadel – and the dangerous threat to liberty. The majority clamoured that a Servilius

25. i.e. by the creation of the people's tribunes in 494 after the first Secession of the plebs (II.33.1).

Ahala[26] was needed, one who would not merely exasperate a public enemy by ordering him to be imprisoned but would jettison a single citizen in order to put an end to domestic strife. They settled for a proposal which was milder in its terms but had the same severity, namely that the magistrates should see to it that the State took no harm[27] from the subversive schemes of Marcus Manlius. Thereupon the consular tribunes and the tribunes of the people – for they too had bowed to senatorial authority, realizing that, with general liberty for all, their own power would come to an end – all these men, then, debated what should be done. No one could see a solution except through violence and bloodshed, which would certainly involve a fearful struggle, when the people's tribunes Marcus Menenius and Quintus Publilius spoke up: 'Why are we turning into a conflict between Senate and people what should be no more than the action of the State against a single obnoxious citizen? Why involve the people in our attack on him, when it is safer to attack by means of the people, so that he will collapse under the weight of his own strength? We intend to bring him to trial. Nothing is so unpopular as kingship. As soon as that mob sees that the conflict is not with them, and changes from being his supporters to become his judges, considers that the accused is a patrician while his prosecutors are plebeian, and that the charge of aiming at kingship is before them, they will favour no man in preference to their own liberty.'

20. All present approved, and Manlius was committed for trial. The first effect of this on the plebeians was most disturbing, especially when they saw the accused dressed as a mourner unattended by any of the senators or indeed by his kinsmen or relatives, not even by his brothers Aulus and Titus Manlius, for never before that day had the custom failed to be observed that a man's closest friends should go into mourning at a time of such peril to him. They recalled how when Appius Claudius

26. The master of Horse who cut down Spurius Maelius when he was resisting arrest in 439 (IV.14.6).

27. The formula of the *senatus consultus ultimum* giving the magistrates absolute powers in an emergency.

was taken to prison his enemy Gaius Claudius and the entire Claudian family had gone into mourning,[28] and they supposed that there was a plot to put down the people's friend because he had been the first to forsake the patricians for the common people.

The day of the trial came, but I cannot find in any authority what allegations were brought against the defendant by his accusers which have specific bearing on the charge of his wanting regal power, apart from meetings of the populace, seditious words, his gifts of money and false accusations. I have no doubt these were convincing, since the people's reluctance to condemn him was due not to the issue but the place of the trial.[29] But so that men may know how great were the achievements which were made not only unpopular but even hateful by that infamous hankering after royal power, this point should be made: it is said that Manlius produced nearly four hundred men to whom he had lent money free of interest, thus preventing their goods from being sold up and themselves from being made over to their creditors. Besides this were his military distinctions, which he not only enumerated but produced for all to see; these included the spoils of up to thirty enemies he had killed, and about forty decorations granted him by his generals, outstanding amongst which were two mural and eight civic crowns. Then came the citizens he had saved from the enemy, amongst whom was named in absence Gaius Servilius, the master of Horse. Finally, by way of climax, he is said to have made a speech recounting his military exploits in language as brilliant as his deeds, to have bared his breast, marked with the scars of battle, looked up to the Capitol, and repeatedly called on Jupiter and the other gods to aid his destiny. He besought them to inspire the Roman people, in his hour of peril, with the spirit they had granted him when he defended the Capitoline Hill for the Roman people's safety, and implored his hearers, one and all, to fix their eyes on the

28. cf. III.58; Gaius Claudius was either the uncle or the brother of Appius.
29. The Campus Martius, from which the Capitol could be seen.

Capitol and Citadel and turn to the immortal gods when they passed judgement on him.

As the people were being called by centuries in the Campus Martius and the accused by stretching out his hands to the Capitol had directed his prayers from men to the gods, it became clear to the tribunes that unless men could have their eyes diverted from that reminder of so glorious a deed, they would remain preoccupied with the service done them and never open their minds to the reality of the charge. They therefore adjourned the day of trial and summoned an assembly of the people in the Peteline Wood, outside the River Gate,[30] from where the Capitol could not be seen. There the charge was proved, and the people steeled their hearts to pass sentence of such severity that it was painful even to those who pronounced it. Some authorities say that Manlius was condemned by special officers known as duumvirs,[31] appointed to inquire into cases of high treason. The tribunes threw him from the Tarpeian Rock: so the same place commemorated one man's greatest hour of glory and the supreme penalty he paid.

Marks of ignominy were attached to his name after death: one of an official nature, when because his house had stood on the present site of the temple and mint of Juno Moneta[32] the people were asked to vote that no patrician should live on the Citadel or Capitol; the other which came from his own people, when the Manlian clan issued a decree forbidding anyone in future to bear the name of Marcus Manlius. Such was the end of a man who would have been memorable had he not been born in a free State. Before long the people remembered only his good qualities, now that there was no danger from him, and regretted their loss. Moreover, when plague broke out

30. The Porta Flumentana led directly to the Tiber from between the Capitol and the Aventine Hill.

31. These official prosecutors in the name of the king first appear in the trial for *perduellio* (high treason) of Publius Horatius under Tullus Hostilius; cf. I.26.5–7.

32. The temple housed the linen rolls containing the lists of magistrates; it was vowed by Furius Camillus in 345 and dedicated in 344. cf. VII.28.4–5.

soon afterwards, with no obvious reasons for so serious a calamity, it was attributed by most people to the execution of Manlius: the Capitol (they said) had been polluted by the blood of its saviour, and the gods had been displeased when the man who had snatched their temples from the hands of their enemies had met his punishment practically before their very eyes.

21. Shortage of grain followed the plague, and in the following year, when the news of these two disasters had got abroad, there was fighting on several fronts. The military tribunes with consular authority were Lucius Valerius (for the fourth time), Aulus Manlius, Servius Sulpicius, Lucius Lucretius and Lucius Aemilius (all for the third time) and Marcus Trebonius. With the Volscians, who seemed destined to provide nearly continuous training for Roman soldiery, the colonies of Circeii and Velitrae, which had long been plotting revolt, and the Latins, already under suspicion, a new enemy suddenly sprang to arms: the people of Lanuvium, hitherto a city of complete loyalty. The Senate believed they were prompted by contempt, because the revolt of the Veliterni, who were citizens like themselves, had gone so long unpunished, and decreed that a proposal should be put to the people at the earliest possible moment to declare war on them; and to ensure the readiness of the commons for this campaign, they appointed a commission of five to divide up the Pomptine land[33] and one of three to conduct a colony to Nepete. Then the people were asked to declare war, and despite the efforts of the people's tribunes to dissuade them, all the tribes[34] voted for it. That year was spent on preparations for the campaign, but the army did not take the field because of the plague. This delay could have given the colonists time to beg the Senate's forgiveness (and in fact the majority were in favour of sending envoys to Rome to offer submission) had not the general danger become bound up with the risk to individuals, as can happen; so that the leaders of the revolt from Rome turned the colonies from thoughts of peace in their fear of being the only ones to be

33. cf. ch. 5.1, note 14.
34. Livy means the centuries; the *comitia centuriata* declared war.

charged with the crime, and thereby falling victims to Roman wrath. These men did not stop at opposing the embassy in their own senate; they incited large numbers of the common people to go out pillaging Roman territory, and this fresh outrage put a stop to all hope of peace. That year the Praenestines too were first reported to be in revolt, but to the accusations against them by the Tusculans, Gabini and Labicani, whose borders they had invaded, the Senate gave so mild a reply that it was obvious that they were reluctant to believe in the charges because they did not want them to be true.

22. The following year Spurius and Lucius Papirius, the new consular tribunes, led off the legions to Velitrae, while their four colleagues, Servius Cornelius Maluginensis (elected for the third time), Quintus Servilius, Gaius Sulpicius and Lucius Aemilius (for the fourth time), stayed behind to protect the City and guard against any fresh movements which might be reported from Etruria – for everything in that quarter gave rise to suspicion. Near Velitrae a battle was fought successfully against supporting troops from Praeneste, who almost out-numbered the entire army of colonists: but the town was so near that the enemy soon fled in retreat and found in it their sole refuge. The tribunes refrained from attacking it, for they were not sure of succeeding, and thought they ought not to pursue the fighting to the total ruin of a colony.

The letter they sent to the Senate in Rome with news of victory was more sharply critical of their enemies from Praeneste than of those of Velitrae. As a result, by resolution of the Senate and bidding of the people, war was declared on the Praenestines; they joined up with the Volscians, and the following year attacked the Roman colony of Satricum and took it by storm, in spite of the colonists' stubborn defence, with shocking abuse of their victory in their treatment of captives. This infuriated the Romans, and prompted them to elect Marcus Furius Camillus military tribune for the sixth time. As colleagues he was assigned Aulus and Lucius Postumius Regillensis and Lucius Furius, along with Lucius Lucretius and Marcus Fabius Ambustus. The conduct of the Volscian war was given by special appointment to Camillus, and from the other tribunes he was given by lot Lucius Furius as his assistant. This proved to be less in the public interest than a source of increased reputation for Camillus, both in his official capacity for having restored a situation which had declined through the other's rashness, and personally when he sought to gain from Lucius's error his gratitude and not glory for himself.

Camillus was now far advanced in years, and at the election he was prepared to take the usual oath to plead ill health had he not been prevented by the unanimous wish of the people. But his wits were very much alive thanks to a vigorous constitution, his senses keen and unimpaired, and though he took little part in politics, he was stimulated by war. Four legions were enrolled, each of 4000 men, and the army ordered to assemble at the Esquiline Gate next day. He then set out for Satricum, where the captors of the colony were awaiting him, quite undaunted, as they were relying on their considerable superiority in numbers. They formed up for battle as soon as they saw the Romans approaching, with every intention of risking a decisive engagement, for in this way, they argued, the Romans' numerical weakness would gain nothing from the skill of their pre-eminent commander, on which alone they pinned their hopes.

23. The Roman army was just as impatient, and so was one of its commanders. Nothing delayed the hazard of an immediate engagement but the prudence and authority of one man, who by prolonging the campaign sought an opportunity to improve his resources by strategy. That made the enemy press on still more; they were no longer satisfied with deploying their forces before their camp but advanced into the middle of the open field and, marching practically up to the Roman rampart, paraded their proud confidence in their strength. The Roman soldiers were indignant at this, and much more so was the second of the two tribunes, Lucius Furius, the natural impetuosity of whose youth and temperament was further increased by the hopes of the rank and file, though there was no firm ground at all for their enthusiasm. The men were already excited, but he spurred them on still further by dis-

paraging his colleague's authority in the only way he could –
on the score of age. He kept insisting that war was for young
men, and that the spirit like the body was subject to growth
and decay; the most active of warriors had become a procras-
tinator, the man who used to seize camps and cities at the first
assault the moment he arrived was now sitting still and wasting
time behind his entrenchments. What did he hope would
increase his own strength or weaken the enemy's? What
occasion, what moment, what ground was he preparing for an
ambush? There was no heart or vigour in the old man's tactics.
Camillus had had enough of life and glory; but why should
the State, which ought to be immortal, age and decline in
strength along with the mortal body of a single man?

These speeches won over the entire camp, and when on all
sides there was a demand for battle he addressed his colleague:
'Marcus Furius, we cannot resist the soldiers' enthusiasm, while
the enemy, whose confidence we have increased by our pro-
crastination, insults us with an arrogance no longer to be
endured. You are alone; give way to us all, and accept defeat
in counsel so that you may inflict defeat the sooner in war.'
To this Camillus replied that in the wars which up to that day
had been carried on under his sole auspices neither he nor the
Roman people had regretted either his strategy or its outcome.
But he knew now that he had a colleague who was his equal
in legal power and authority, and his superior in youth and
vigour. And so, though as regards the army he had been
accustomed to rule, not be ruled, he could not prevent his
colleague from exerting his authority. Let him do what he
thought was best for the State, with the gods' blessing. For
himself, he asked the favour not to be put in the front line at
his age: he would not fail to carry out the duties in war proper
to an old man. One thing only he begged of the immortal
gods: that no misfortune should make his own plan of action
prove the better one.

But the men paid no heed to those salutary words; nor did
the gods hear his devout prayers. The man responsible for the
engagement drew up his battle-line, while Camillus strengthened the reserves and put a strong guard in front of the camp.

He then took his stand on rising ground to keep a close watch
on the outcome of the other's tactics. 24. At the first onset and
clash of arms the enemy gave ground, not out of fear but as
a ruse. The ground sloped gently up behind them from the
battle-line to their camp, and as they were well supplied with
men, they had left in the camp several strong cohorts armed
and ready to make a sortie once the battle had begun and their
enemy had approached the rampart. The Romans broke ranks
to pursue them as they retreated and were drawn into an
unfavourable position where they were exposed to attack
from the camp; thus the victors were under threat in their turn,
and because of the new enemy and the slope downhill the
Roman line gave way. They were hard pressed by fresh forces
of Volscians who had attacked from the camp, while the
troops who had given way in pretended flight also renewed
the battle. By then the Roman soldiers were not simply
retreating but, with no thought of their recent impetuosity and
their former glory, had turned tail and everywhere were
running full tilt to recover their camp. At that moment
Camillus was lifted into his saddle by those around him, and
quickly threw in his reserves. 'Soldiers,' he cried, 'is this the
battle you demanded? What man, what god is there whom
you can blame? That rashness then was your own, and so is
this cowardice now. You have followed another leader: now
follow Camillus – to victory as you always did when I led you.
Why look to the rampart and the camp? Not one of you will
enter there unless victory is won.'

It was shame which first checked their headlong rout; then,
when they saw the standards wheeled about and the line
re-formed to face the enemy, while their general, distinguished as he was for his many triumphs and venerable in
years, showed himself amongst the standards in the front
line where there was the heaviest fighting and greatest danger,
one and all they rebuked themselves and each other, and
then their cries of mutual encouragement ran through the
whole army in a resounding clamour. Nor did the other
tribune fail to meet the emergency; sent to rally the cavalry
by his colleague, who was re-forming the line of infantry,

BOOK VI   [24.8]

he spoke no word of reproof (for his share in the blame had
made him less effective) but turned wholly from commands
to entreaties, begging each and every man to save him from
the charge of responsibility for the day's disaster. 'In the face
of my colleague's opposition and refusal,' he cried, 'I chose to
share the general folly instead of the foresight of one man.
Camillus can see glory for himself whether you win or lose:
but my plight will be truly wretched if the battle is not
restored. Misfortune I shall share with everyone, but the disgrace will be mine alone.'

As the battle-line was wavering, it seemed best for the
cavalry to hand over their horses and set upon the enemy on
foot; they were conspicuous for their arms and courage and
went wherever they saw the infantry were hardest pressed.
Neither commanders nor men were lacking in courage for a
supreme effort, and their strenuous exertions and bravery told
in the result. The Volscians scattered in a genuine rout over the
same ground where they had recently withdrawn in feigned
panic; large numbers were cut down both in the actual battle
and in the flight which followed, while others were killed in
the camp, which was captured in the same charge; but more
were taken prisoner than killed.

25. At the count of prisoners several were recognized as
Tusculans. They were separated from the others and taken to
the tribunes, where they admitted under questioning that they
had served under official orders. Camillus was disturbed by the
danger of a war so close at hand, and said he would conduct
the prisoners to Rome immediately, so that the Senate should
not be left in ignorance that the Tusculans had broken their
alliance; his colleague, if willing, should be in charge of the
camp and army meanwhile. A single day had taught Lucius
Furius not to prefer his own counsels to wiser ones, but neither
he nor anyone in the army supposed that Camillus would
calmly overlook his blunder, which had brought the republic
to the brink of sheer disaster. Both in the army and in Rome
everyone said the same: Lucius Furius must take the blame for
lost battles and routs in the changing fortunes of the Volscian
campaigns, while all the glory for victory belonged to

Camillus. The prisoners were brought before the Senate and the Fathers voted for a campaign against Tusculum with Camillus to conduct it, but when he asked for a single assistant to help him and leave was given to him to choose any of his colleagues he wanted, to everyone's surprise he chose Lucius Furius. This leniency mitigated his colleague's disgrace and greatly enhanced his own high reputation.

In fact there was no war against the Tusculans; by maintaining a continuously peaceful attitude they gained a freedom from violation by the Romans such as they could not have won by taking up arms. When the Romans entered their territory, they did not move away from the places near the route of march, nor break off their work in the fields; the gates of the city stood open, and the citizens came flocking out to meet the generals, wearing their togas. Provisions for the army were obligingly brought to the camp from the city and fields. Camillus set up camp opposite the gates, as he wanted to find out whether the same spirit of peace existed inside the walls as was shown in the countryside. He entered the city and saw house doors standing open, shops unshuttered with goods openly displayed, craftsmen all busy at their respective trades, schools humming with voices of pupils, streets busy with women and children going their ways freely among the crowds, wherever the calls of their occupations took them, with no sign of fear or even of surprise. He looked everywhere, trying to see some indication that there had been a war on, but there was no trace anywhere of anything having been removed or brought out for the occasion. All seemed so undisturbed and wholly peaceful that it was hardly believable that so much as a rumour of war had come this way.

26. He was therefore deeply impressed by the enemy's pacific behaviour and ordered their senate to be summoned. 'Men of Tusculum,' he said, 'up to now you alone have found the right arms and true strength to protect your possessions from Roman wrath. Go to Rome, to the Senate; the Fathers will judge whether you deserve punishment for past conduct or pardon now. I will not anticipate your gratitude for what must be an official concession. From me you shall have an

opportunity to ask for mercy; the outcome of your petition is for the Senate to decide as it thinks fit.'

When the Tusculans arrived in Rome, and the dejection of a people who only recently were counted as faithful allies was seen in the faces of their senators as they waited in the vestibule of the Senate-house, the Fathers were moved at once, and bade them be admitted immediately, in a manner more hospitable than hostile. The Tusculan chief magistrate then spoke as follows: 'You declared war on us, Conscript Fathers, and invaded our land, yet we came out to meet your generals and legions no more armed and equipped than you see us now standing at the entrance of your Senate-house. This has always been our way, and that of our commons, and always will be, unless at any time we receive arms from your hands to use on your behalf. We thank your commanders and your armies, for having trusted their own eyes more than their ears, and for committing no act of hostility where they were shown none. The peace which we maintained towards you we now ask of you; divert your war, we beg you, to any place where war exists. If we have to suffer to test the power of your arms against us, we will do so unarmed. Such is our intention, and may the gods grant it a happy outcome to match its loyal sentiments. As for the charges which moved you to declare war on us, though it is pointless to use words to refute what facts have disproved, still, even if they were true, we believe we could safely confess our guilt when our repentance is so clear to see. What matter if men wrong you, provided that you prove worthy to accept such amends.' Such was the speech of the Tusculans. They were granted peace for the time being, and soon afterwards also won full citizenship.[35] The legions were brought back from Tusculum.

27. Camillus was acclaimed for his strategy and courage in the Volscian campaign and his success in the expedition against Tusculum, as well as for his remarkable forbearance and moderation towards his colleagues on both occasions. He resigned his office after the election of military tribunes for the

35. Dionysius of Halicarnassus (XIV.6) quotes this as an example of Rome's good policy of generosity to defeated enemies.

coming year. These were Lucius and Publius Valerius (for the fifth and third time respectively), Gaius Sergius (for the third time), Licinius Menenius (for the second time), Publius Papirius and Servius Cornelius Maluginensis. This year there was also need of censors, especially because of the vague rumours circulating about debts. The people's tribunes even exaggerated the extent of the resentment these caused, whereas it was played down by those in whose interest it was that loans should appear to be endangered more through the bad faith of the debtors than their lack of means. The censors elected were Gaius Sulpicius Camerinus and Spurius Postumius Regillensis. They had already begun their work when it was interrupted by the death of Postumius, for there were religious scruples against replacing the colleague of a censor. Sulpicius accordingly laid down his office and other censors were elected; but there was a flaw in their election and they did not serve. There was strong feeling against electing a third pair, as it looked as if the gods were not going to accept a censorship that year. The tribunes insisted that this was an intolerable mockery of the common people: the Senate, they said, were ignoring the evidence of the public records of each man's personal property because they did not want the total sum of debt to be known, as this would prove that one half of the State had been destroyed by the other half, and all the while the debt-ridden plebeians were exposed to one enemy after another. Wars were now being pursued in any quarter, in-discriminately; the legions had been marched from Antium to Satricum, from Satricum to Velitrae, and thence to Tusculum; now it was the Latins, then the Hernici and Praenestines who were under threat of attack more out of hatred for Rome's citizens than for her enemies. The intention was to wear out the people with army service, to give them no chance to draw breath in the City nor leisure to take thought for liberty or to gather in assembly, where from time to time they might hear the voice of a tribune discussing the reduction of interest and ways of ending their other grievances. But if the people had the spirit to recall their fathers' liberty they would not allow any Roman citizen to be assigned to his creditor nor any levy of troops to be held until there was an inquiry into debt and some method of reducing it put into action, so that every man should know what was his own and what was another's, whether his person was still free or even that was to be held in bondage.

The reward held out to sedition quickly set it in action, for many were being bound over to their creditors, and the Senate had decided to enrol new legions on hearing rumours of fighting at Praeneste. Both these operations at once began to be held up by intervention of the tribunes and combined action of the plebeians; the tribunes would not allow those bound over to be taken away, and the young men refused to enroll their names. The patricians were for the moment more immediately concerned with levying troops than enforcing the law of debt, for the enemy were reported to have already left Praeneste and taken up their position in territory of the Gabii. Meanwhile the news did not deter the tribunes, but rather served as an incentive for them to carry on the struggle they had undertaken. Nothing could calm down the violence in the City except the imminence of fighting within its very walls. 28. For when the Praenestines heard that no new army had been recruited in Rome, that there was no one definitely in command, and that patricians and plebeians were in confrontation with each other, their leaders saw that this was their chance, marched off at once, destroying the fields all the way, until they brought their standards right up to the Colline Gate. The panic in the City was unbounded; there was a call to arms and a general rush for the walls and gates. Now at last war had taken over from internal strife. Titus Quinctius Cincinnatus was made dictator, and he chose Aulus Sempronius Atratinus as his master of Horse. Once this was known (such was the dread the dictatorship inspired) the enemy immediately retreated from the walls, and the younger Romans answered the call to enlist without further refusal.

While the army was being recruited in Rome, the enemy meanwhile set up camp not far from the River Allia. From there they raided the countryside over a wide area, and boasted among themselves that they had seized a place which was ill-fated for the city of Rome: the panic and rout to come would be the same as took place in the Gallic war; for if the Romans feared the day so fraught with ill omen which they had marked with the name of that place, how much more than the Day of the Allia[36] would they dread the Allia itself, the memorial of that great disaster? They would surely see apparitions of the bloodthirsty Gauls, the sound of whose voices would ring in their ears. Such idle speculations on empty themes filled the thoughts of the Praenestines, so that they had pinned their hopes on the ill omen of the place. By contrast, the Romans were confident that wherever their Latin enemy might be, he was the same enemy they had defeated at Lake Regillus and held in peaceful submission for a hundred years; a site so memorable for disaster was more likely to rouse them to wipe out the record of their disgrace than to intimidate them into believing that any ground was inauspicious for victory. Moreover, if the Gauls themselves confronted them on that spot the Romans would fight as they once fought at Rome to recover their City, and on the day following at Gabii, when they had made sure that no enemy who had entered the walls of Rome should live to take home news of success or failure.

29. Such was the mood on either side as the Romans came up to the Allia. As they came in sight of the enemy drawn up and ready for action, the dictator called out to Sempronius: 'Do you see how they have taken their stand at the Allia, trusting to the ill fortune of the place? Events will show that the gods have given them nothing surer to rely on and no more solid assistance. You, Sempronius, put your trust in arms and morale, and charge their centre at the gallop; I will attack with the legions when their ranks are broken in confusion. Gods of the treaty, stand by us and demand the penalty due for the outrage you have suffered and the deception put upon us in your sacred name!'

The Praenestines could withstand neither horse nor foot. Ranks were scattered at the first charge and battle-cry; then, when the line could not hold anywhere, they turned and fled,

36. 18 July, cf. ch. 1.

carried even beyond their own camp in a panic-stricken mêlée, and did not check their headlong flight until they were in sight of Praeneste. There the scattered fugitives took up a position which they could hurriedly fortify, for fear that if they withdrew within the walls, their fields would immediately be fired, and then when all was plundered, their city would suffer siege. But no sooner had the Romans arrived, after sacking the camp at the Allia, than they abandoned those defence-works too, and hardly believing they would find safety behind walls, shut themselves in the town of Praeneste. There were eight other towns subject to Praeneste; the Romans took the campaign from one to another, and after capturing them in turn with no great opposition marched on to Velitrae, which they also took by storm. Then came the turn of Praeneste, the source of the war; this they captured not by force but through surrender. Titus Quinctius then returned in triumph to Rome. He had won one victory in pitched battle, captured two of the enemy's camps, taken nine towns by assault and accepted the surrender of Praeneste, and brought with him a statue of Jupiter Imperator which he had carried off from Praeneste. This he dedicated on the Capitol between the shrines of Jupiter and Minerva, with a plaque fixed below it to commemorate his exploits bearing an inscription to this effect: 'Jupiter and all the gods granted that the dictator Titus Quinctius should capture nine towns.' On the twentieth day after his appointment he resigned his dictatorship.

30. Elections were then held for military tribunes with consular powers, as a result of which patricians and plebeians came out equal. From the patricians Publius and Gaius Manlius were elected, along with Lucius Julius, while the plebeians returned Gaius Sextilius, Marcus Albinius and Lucius Antistius. The Manlii were superior in birth to the plebeians elected, and had more personal influence than Julius; they were accordingly assigned the Volscians as their sphere of action by special appointment, without any drawing of lots or previous arrangement. This they were subsequently to regret, as did the senators who made the appointment. Without any previous investigation, they sent out troops to forage, and when they supposed

these to be surrounded, on receipt of a false report, they hurried to support them. They did not even detain the author of the story, a Latin enemy, who had deceived them in the guise of a Roman soldier. They fell into an ambush, and while holding out in an awkward position through the sheer courage of the troops, fighting back as they were cut down, the Roman camp which lay in the plain was attacked by the enemy on the opposite side. In both places foolhardiness and ignorance on the part of the generals proved their undoing; what survived of the good fortune of the Roman people was saved by the soldiers' courage, which did not waver even when they had no leader to direct it. When the news reached Rome, the first thought was to appoint a dictator; but later, after it was reported that all was quiet among the Volscians and it was obvious that they had no idea how to make use of their victory and opportunity, even the army and generals already there were recalled. From then on there was peace, as far as the Volscians were concerned; the only disturbance came at the end of the year, when the Praenestines stirred up the Latin peoples to join them in a revolt.

The same year new colonists were enrolled for Setia, after complaints from the inhabitants there that their numbers were too small, and though things were not going well in the field, comfort could be found in the peaceful situation at home, secured as it was by the popularity of the plebeian military tribunes and their prestige amongst their own kind.

31. The following year started off with an outburst of serious political strife. The military tribunes with consular power were Spurius Furius, Quintus Servilius (for the second time), Licinius Menenius (for the third time), Publius Cloelius, Marcus Horatius and Lucius Geganius. Once again the subject and cause of the trouble was debt, and Spurius Servilius Priscus and Quintus Cloelius Siculus were chosen as censors to investigate this. They were prevented from doing so by a fresh outbreak of war, when first terrified messengers and then refugees from the countryside brought word that Volscian legions had crossed the border and were devastating Roman territory far and wide. In spite of general consternation, the

peril from without was far from checking the dissensions in
the City. On the contrary, the tribunes exerted their authority
all the more violently to prevent a levy of troops, until the
Senate was forced to accept their terms and agree that no one
should pay tax or pass judgement in cases of debt so long as
war continued. Once the people had obtained this relief the
recruitment was no longer held up. After new legions had been
enrolled, it was decided to divide them into two armies to be
led into Volscian territory. Spurius Furius and Marcus Horatius
went off to the right, to Antium and the coast, while Quintus
Servilius and Lucius Geganius went left, towards the mountains and Ecetra. There was no meeting with the enemy on
either route. The Romans' devastation of the land was consequently quite unlike the sporadic forays made by the
Volscians who, like bandits, relied on disagreements between
their enemies but feared their courage, and acted in nervous
haste; it was carried out by a regular army in lawful retaliation,
and did more damage because it was not pressed for time. The
Volscians had in fact limited their incursions to the frontier
regions, for fear that any minute an army might march out
from Rome. The Romans on the other hand had a further
reason for lingering in enemy territory; they hoped to provoke
the Volscians to give battle. And so they burnt down all the
farm buildings everywhere and even some of the villages, left
not a single fruit tree nor an ear of corn standing to give hope
of a harvest, took off as booty all the men and cattle outside
the town walls, and then brought both armies back to Rome.

32. The debtors had been given a short breathing-space, but
once hostilities had died down the law-courts were busy again.
There was very little prospect of reducing the interest on
former debts; in fact new debts were incurred to pay the tax
levied to build a wall of squared stones[37] which the censors had
contracted for. The plebeians were obliged to shoulder this
crushing burden because their tribunes now had no levy of
troops to obstruct, and under financial pressure from the

37. Probably the restoration of the old Servian wall. cf. F. E.
Adcock, *C A H* VII, p. 567.

nobility were also forced to elect all the military tribunes from the patricians. These were Lucius Aemilius, Publius Valerius (for the fourth time), Gaius Veturius, Servius Sulpicius, Lucius and Gaius Quinctius Cincinnatus. The patricians also used their powers to enforce action against the Latins and Volscians, who had joined forces and were encamped near Satricum. All the younger men were compelled to take the oath, without any objection raised, and three armies were enrolled. One was intended to garrison the City, another could be sent to deal with emergencies if revolt broke out in any region, and the third, which was by far the strongest, was led to Satricum by Publius Valerius and Lucius Aemilius. There they found the enemy's forces drawn up in a good position, attacked them at once, and although victory was not yet quite certain, the battle was giving good hope of success when violent gusts of wind precipitated a rainstorm and it had to be broken off. Next day fighting was renewed, and for some time the enemy stood firm, with courage and success equal to the Romans', especially the Latin legions which had been trained in Roman methods of warfare during their long association with Rome. But a cavalry charge threw their ranks into disorder, and before they could re-form, the infantry set upon them. As the Romans pushed forward the enemy were forced back from their position, and once the battle turned against them they could not hold the pressure of the Roman attack. They scattered and made for Satricum, two miles away, instead of their camp, but were cut down, largely by the cavalry; the camp was taken and sacked. On the night after the battle they fled rather than marched from Satricum and made for Antium: and though the Roman army followed hard on their heels, fear prompted greater speed than anger did. Thus the enemy entered the town before the Romans could harass or delay their rear. Several days were then spent in destroying the countryside, since the Romans lacked sufficient equipment for attacking the walls and the enemy were in no state to risk a battle.

33. A quarrel then broke out between the Latins and the people of Antium, who were exhausted by their misfortunes and worn out by a war in which they had been born and

grown old,[38] so that they were considering surrender. The Latins on the other hand were still fresh and full of spirit after a long period of peace; their revolt was only recent and made them all the more eager to carry on the war. The dispute ended when both sides realized that neither of them could be prevented by the other from carrying out their plans. The Latins departed and freed themselves from any complicity in what they saw as a dishonourable peace; the Antiates, having rid themselves of such inconvenient critics of the prudence of their policy, handed over their city and lands to the Romans. When the Latins found they could neither injure the Romans in war nor keep the Volscians in arms, their insensate fury drove them to turn on Satricum, the town which had been their first refuge after their recent defeat, and burn it to the ground. They set fire to sacred and secular buildings alike, so that none remained standing except the temple of Mater Matuta[39]; and it is said that they were kept away from this not by any religious scruple of their own or reverence for the gods, but by an awesome voice from the temple which threatened disaster if they did not remove their sacrilegious fires well away from the sanctuary. In the heat of their blind rage an impulse took them to Tusculum, furious as they were with the Tusculans for having abandoned the common council of the Latins and given themselves up to be not only allies but even citizens of Rome. They found the gates open, as their attack was unexpected, and took the town at the first battle-cry, except for the citadel. There the townspeople took refuge with their wives and children, and sent messengers to Rome to let the Senate know of their plight. An army was dispatched to Tusculum without delay, as befitted the honour of the Roman people, led by the military tribunes Lucius Quinctius and Servius Sulpicius. They found the gates of Tusculum shut and the Latins in the position of both besieged and besieger, defending the walls on the one

38. True of the Volscians generally, though not of Antium. Seventy years of war are mentioned at the end of ch. 2.

39. An ancient Italian goddess presiding over childbirth and child care and apparently especially important at Satricum. Her temple in the cattlemarket in Rome was refounded by Camillus in 396 (V.23.7).

hand and attacking the citadel on the other, as alarmed themselves as they were alarming the Tusculans. The arrival of the
Romans produced a change of heart on both sides: the
Tusculans turned from the depths of despair to the highest of
spirits, while the Latins, who had been almost completely
confident that they would soon capture the citadel, as they
already held the town, began to have small hope of even saving
themselves. The Tusculans raised a shout from the citadel
which was answered by one still louder from the Roman
army. The Latins were hard pressed on both sides; they could
neither withstand the charge of the Tusculans running downhill nor keep back the Romans as they came up to the walls
and set about breaking the bars on the gates. First the walls
were scaled and taken, then the fastenings of the gates were
broken through; the Latins were caught between two enemies,
in front and rear, and, with no strength left to fight back nor
space for flight, they were cut down where they stood, to the
last man. Having recovered Tusculum from its enemies, the
army marched back to Rome.

34. But the more settled all was abroad, thanks to the
successful campaigns that year, the more in the City the high-
handedness of the patricians and miseries of the plebeians were
increasing from day to day. The very fact that repayment of
debts was demanded immediately made it more difficult to
pay; and so, when a man no longer had property from which
to make payment, his good name and person were judicially
assigned to his creditor by way of satisfaction, and punishment
had taken the place of his being given credit to repay. Consequently not only the humblest of the people but even their
leaders were in such a state of abject submission that, far from
competing with the patricians for the office of military tribune,
for the right to which they had fought so hard, there was not
a man among them of energy and enterprise who had the spirit
to hold any of the plebeian magistracies or even offer himself
for one. The patricians appeared to have recovered possession
for all time of an office which had been only assumed by the
plebeians for a few years.

The patricians' satisfaction as a result of this would have

known no bounds had not a small event, as often happens, drastically changed the situation. Marcus Fabius Ambustus, an influential personage not only amongst men of his own class but also with the plebeians, who never felt that he looked down on them, had two daughters, the elder married to Servius Sulpicius and the younger to Gaius Licinius Stolo, a man of some distinction although of plebeian birth. The very fact that Fabius had accepted him as a son-in-law had won him the people's regard. It so happened that the two Fabia sisters were in the house of Servius Sulpicius, then a consular tribune, and were spending the time chatting, as women do, when Sulpicius was returning home from the Forum and his lictor struck the door with his rod, in the customary manner. The younger sister, unused to the custom, was much alarmed, and the elder laughed in surprise at her sister's ignorance. But that laugh rankled in the other's mind, for a woman's feelings are affected by little things. I suppose, too, that the throng of people attending Sulpicius and taking their leave made her think that her sister's marriage was a fortunate one and her own to be regretted, a misguided attitude we all share when we cannot bear to be outdone by our nearest and dearest. Her father happened to see her when she was still smarting from her wounded feelings and asked if all was well. She was reluctant to give the reason for her chagrin, as it hardly showed sisterly affection and did little honour to her own husband, but by gentle questioning he persuaded her to tell him; it was being married to someone beneath her, in a home where neither high office nor influence could come. Ambustus then comforted his daughter and bade her take heart: she would soon see the same respect paid to her own home as she saw in her sister's. From then on he began to make plans with his son-in-law, and also called in Lucius Sextius, an enterprising young man whose ambitions were thwarted only by his not being of patrician birth.

35. The opportunity for a revolution seemed to have come as a result of the crushing load of debt, from which the people could hope for no relief except through placing their representatives in the highest office. They argued that they must

prepare for battle with this end in mind. By effort and previous achievement the plebeians had already climbed to a position from which, if they continued their exertions, they could reach the top and equal the patricians in official recognition as well as in merit. For the moment they decided to get people's tribunes elected from their number, and via this office open up a way for themselves to the other magistracies. Gaius Licinius and Lucius Sextius were accordingly elected and proclaimed three bills, all aimed at breaking the power of the patricians and advancing the plebeians' interests. The first dealt with debt, and stipulated that after subtracting from the capital what had been paid in interest, the remainder should be paid off in three annual instalments of equal size. The second set a limit to land-holding and forbade anyone to possess more than five hundred *iugera*. The third abolished the election of military tribunes and ruled that one at any rate of the two consuls elected should be a plebeian. These were all measures of great importance which could not possibly be carried without a bitter struggle.[40]

Thus all the objects for which men's desire knows no bounds, land, money and advancement, were simultaneously called in question. The patricians were thoroughly alarmed at the prospect: they hurried to and fro holding public meetings and private conferences but could not think of any solution except the veto, which they had made use of in many previous confrontations. They accordingly set about getting support against the proposals from the tribunes' own colleagues. These men, when they saw Licinius and Sextius calling on the tribes to vote, came up with a bodyguard of patricians and refused to allow the reading out of the bills or any of the customary procedures prior to a plebiscite. When the assembly had thus been repeatedly summoned in vain, and the proposals were as good as rejected, 'Very well,' cried Sextius; 'as you are determined that the veto shall be so powerful, we will use that very weapon to protect the people. Come on, senators, call an

40. The Sextio-Licinian rogations of 367; cf. H. H. Scullard, *A History of the Roman World*, pp. 91–5. Licinius was later to be prosecuted for breaking his own law (VII.16.9).

assembly for the election of military tribunes. I'll see that you get no joy out of that word "veto", which now so delights your ears when you hear it from a chorus of our colleagues.' These were no idle threats; no elections were held except for the aediles and people's tribunes. Licinius and Sextius were re-elected tribunes and would not permit the election of any curule magistrates, and this dearth of magistrates continued in the City for the next five years,[41] while the people continued to re-elect these two men as tribunes and they to put a stop to the election of military tribunes.

36. Fortunately there was a respite from other wars, but the colonists of Velitrae eagerly took advantage of the peaceful situation, when they thought that the Romans had no army to check them, to make several forays into Roman territory, and set about laying siege to Tusculum. That was enough to rouse the plebeians as well as the Senate to feel deeply ashamed that the Tusculans, their old allies and now their fellow-citizens, should be begging their help. The people's tribunes relaxed their opposition, elections were held under an interrex, and Lucius Furius, Aulus Manlius, Servius Sulpicius, Servius Cornelius, and Publius and Gaius Valerius were elected military tribunes. They found the people much less amenable when it came to levying troops than they had been about the elections, and it was only with strenuous effort that they were able to enrol an army and set out. They then drove the enemy's forces away from the region of Tusculum and even shut them up within their own walls. Velitrae was then besieged much more closely than Tusculum had been. Even so, those who began the siege failed to capture the town before new military tribunes were elected. These were Quintus Servilius, Gaius Veturius, Aulus and Marcus Cornelius, Quintus Quinctius and Marcus Fabius; but even they achieved nothing memorable at Velitrae.

41. This sounds improbable, and Diodorus (XV.75.1) gives the period as one year. Livy is trying to bridge the gap between the annalists' date (390) for the Gallic Sack of Rome and the number of annual consuls on record in the *Fasti consulares*. See also the Introduction, p. 32.

At home matters took a more serious turn. For besides Sextius and Licinius, who had proposed the laws and were now re-elected people's tribunes for the eighth time, the military tribune Fabius, Stolo's father-in-law, was quite openly giving his support to the laws he had suggested; and whereas originally eight members of the college of tribunes had exercised their veto on these laws, there were now only five, and they were confused and puzzled as people usually are who have broken with their party. They could only repeat words put into their mouths and justify their veto by what they had been privately taught to say – that a great many of the plebeians were absent with the army at Velitrae, and elections should be postponed until the soldiers' return so that the whole body of people could vote on matters which were their concern. Sextius and Licinius, with some of their colleagues and the military tribune Fabius, were well versed with the experience of many years in working on the people's emotions. They started bringing leading senators forward and harassing them with questions on every point they were putting to the people. Did they dare, they asked, when there was a division of land and the plebeians were assigned no more than two *iugera* each, to demand that they should be permitted to hold more than five hundred *iugera* themselves? Was a single patrician to possess land which should be shared amongst nearly three hundred citizens, while a plebeian could scarcely find space on his land to house the necessities of life or provide a burial-place? Or did they want the people, crushed by usury, to surrender their persons to imprisonment and torture rather than pay off the capital sum they owed? Did they intend that parties of debtors, bound over to their creditors, should be hauled off from the Forum every day, to fill the houses of the nobility with chained slaves, and turn every patrician's home into a private gaol?

37. These shameful and painful accusations aroused more indignation in their hearers, who were fearful for their own safety, than in the speakers themselves, though they continued to insist that the patricians would never put a limit to their land-grabbing nor their butchery of the people with usury

until one of the two consuls elected was a plebeian, to guard the
people's liberties. The people's tribunes, they said, were now
objects of contempt, for their office was destroying its own
power by its use of the veto. There could be no question of
equal rights so long as the nobility had supreme power in their
hands, while they themselves could do no more than offer help
by intervention; unless such power was shared, the people
would never be on an equal footing in the State. Nor should
anyone think it sufficient if a plebeian were allowed to stand
as candidate in the consular elections; unless it were required
that one consul at least must be elected from the people, no
candidate would come forward. Had they already forgotten
that when the decision was taken to elect military tribunes
rather than consuls, for the express purpose of opening the
highest office to the plebeians, for forty-four years not a single
military tribune had come from the people? How could they
suppose that the patricians would voluntarily share with the
plebeians the two places which were now available, when they
had always claimed eight places at the elections for military
tribunes? Were they likely to allow the road to be opened to
the consulship when for so long they had blocked the way to
the tribunate? The law should provide what could not be
gained by popular support at the elections, and one of the two
consulships should be removed from competition and reserved
for the people, for if it remained competitive, it would always
be the prize of the more powerful party. No longer could it
be said, as used to be argued in the past, that the people could
provide no one suitable for curule magistracies. Had public
administration been less responsible and efficient since the time
of Publius Licinius Calvus, the first plebeian to be elected
tribune,[42] than it had been during those years when no one but
a patrician could be military tribune? On the contrary: several
patricians had been brought to justice after their tribuneship
but not a single plebeian. Quaestors too, like military tribunes,
had begun to be elected from the plebeians a few years ago,
and the Roman people had had no occasion to regret it. Only

42. In 400 (V.12.9).

the consulate was left for the plebeians to win, the citadel and cornerstone of freedom. If that were attained, then the Roman people would believe that the kings had really been driven from the City and their liberty set firm; for from that day the people would gain everything which gave the nobility its superiority: power and honour, military glory, birth and rank, great things for themselves to enjoy, still greater to leave to their children.

When they saw that speeches of this kind were well received, they introduced a new measure, to replace the two officials in charge of sacred rites[43] with a board of ten, composed half of plebeians, half of patricians. The voting on all these measures they postponed until the return of the army which was besieging Velitrae.

38. The year had come full circle before the legions could be brought back from Velitrae; and so the question of the laws remained in suspense and had to be deferred until new military tribunes took office. The same people's tribunes were re-elected by the commons, the two in fact who had proposed the new laws. The military tribunes elected were Titus Quinctius, Servius Cornelius, Servius Sulpicius, Spurius Servilius, Lucius Papirius and Lucius Veturius. At the very beginning of the year came the final battle over the laws. When the tribes were summoned to vote and the proposers of the laws would not accept their colleagues' veto, the patricians took fright and fell back on their two last resources – the supreme office and their supreme citizen. They voted to name a dictator, and named Marcus Furius Camillus, who chose Lucius Aemilius as his master of Horse. To meet such formidable preparations on the part of their opponents, the proposers of the laws also strengthened the people's cause by rousing immense enthusiasm for it, then summoned an assembly of the people and called on the tribes to vote.

In angry, threatening mood the dictator took his seat, surrounded by large numbers of patricians, and the proceedings

43. The keepers of the Sibylline Books; they did not take auguries and so did not impinge on the patricians' jealously guarded right; cf. ch. 41.5.

opened with the usual struggle between the people's tribunes
who were trying to get the law through and those interposing
their veto. The veto had the greater legal power, but the
popularity of the measures themselves and of their proposers
won the day, and the first tribes were voting their approval
when Camillus began to speak. 'Fellow-Romans,' he said,
'since you are now ruled by the tribunes' caprice, not their
authority, and are nullifying the right of veto, once won by
the secession of the plebs,[44] by acts of violence similar to those
which created it, for your own sake as much as in the interests
of the entire republic, I shall, as dictator, support this right and
protect with my own supreme power the safeguard you would
see overthrown. So if Gaius Licinius and Lucius Sextius yield
to their colleagues' veto, I shall not in any way intrude my
patrician office upon a plebeian assembly; but if they defy the
veto and attempt to force their laws on a city as if it were their
captive, I shall not permit the tribunes' power to destroy itself.'

The people's tribunes treated his words with contempt and
continued to carry out their operations as actively as before.
Camillus was infuriated, sent his lictors to turn the people
out of the assembly, and threatened that if they persisted he
would administer the oath to all the men of military age and
lead the army out of the City without delay. The people were
panic-stricken, but their leaders' spirit was fired rather than
damped by his threats. However, before the issue was settled,
Camillus resigned office, either because there was a flaw in his
appointment, as certain writers have held, or because the
people's tribunes proposed and the people decreed that if
Marcus Furius took any action in his capacity of dictator, he
should be fined 500,000 *asses*.[45] I am inclined to believe that
his withdrawal was due to the auspices rather than to a proposal
without precedent, for two reasons: the character of the man
himself and the fact that he was immediately replaced as
dictator by Publius Manlius – for what was the point of
electing him to deal with a crisis in which Marcus Furius had

44. The first Secession in 494 (II.32).
45. The bronze or copper *as* at this period was still measured by
weight and was equal to a Roman pound (12 ounces).

been defeated? Besides, Camillus was dictator again the following year, and surely he would not without embarrassment have reassumed the power which had been broken while he held it the previous year. Furthermore, at the time when the proposal to fine him is said to have been made, either he had the power to resist what he saw would degrade him or he lacked the power to obstruct even those measures which were the cause of the proposal to fine him. Finally, in all the confrontations between tribunes and consuls down to our own times, the dictatorship has always been out of reach of attack.

39. In the interval between the abdication of the former dictator and the assumption of office by Manlius, the new one, the tribunes took advantage of what amounted to an interregnum, and called a meeting of the people, where it became clear which of the measures proposed was preferred by the people and which by the proposers. For the voting was in favour of the bills about usury and land distribution and against the appointment of a plebeian consul, and both matters could have been settled had not the tribunes announced that they were taking the people's views on all these questions collectively. Then Publius Manlius, on becoming dictator, tipped the balance in favour of the people by naming a plebeian as his master of Horse in the person of Gaius Licinius,[46] a former military tribune. I understand that this annoyed the patricians, and that the dictator used to excuse himself by pleading his close relationship to Licinius, as well as arguing that a master of Horse had no more authority than a consular tribune.

As for Licinius and Sextius, once an assembly to elect people's tribunes had been proclaimed, they declared themselves unwilling to continue in office, while behaving in a manner calculated to put the strongest pressure on the people to give them what they pretended not to want. They said it was the ninth year they had confronted the patricians in battle, with the greatest personal danger to themselves and no general benefit to the people. Both the measures they had proposed

---

46. Not Stolo, the people's tribune of chs. 34–5, but some relative.

and all the efficacy of the tribunes' power had aged and declined with themselves. Their laws had been attacked, first by their colleagues' intercession, then when the younger men had been sent off to the war at Velitrae; finally they had been personally threatened with the thunderbolt of the dictatorship. Now the obstruction came neither from their colleagues nor from the war nor from the dictator, for he had actually foreshadowed the appointment of a plebeian consul by choosing his master of Horse from the plebs: it was the plebeians themselves who were delaying their own advancement and opportunities. The City and Forum rid of creditors, lands freed from unlawful occupation – these they could have at once if they wished. When would they ever appreciate these blessings with proper gratitude if at the moment of approving measures for their own advantage they destroyed all hope of advancement for those who were proposing them? It ill became the Roman people's self-respect to ask to be relieved of usury and settled on land which the powerful had unjustly held, while leaving the men who had won them these privileges to grow old as ex-tribunes, not only without honours but even without hope of any. So first they must make up their minds what they wanted and then state their wishes at the election of tribunes. If they wanted the measures proposed by the tribunes to be passed as a whole, that was a reason for re-electing the same men, who would see that their own proposals were carried through. But if their intention was to vote only for what would benefit each man personally, there was nothing to be gained by prolonging a term of office which had become distasteful: they could well do without the tribunate, and the people could do without the reforms proposed.

40. The other senators listened to this uncompromising speech of the tribunes in horror-struck silence, dumbfounded by its outrageous arguments, but Appius Claudius Crassus, grandson of the decemvir, is said to have come forward to challenge them, prompted more by anger and resentment than by hope of success. He spoke to the following effect: 'It would be nothing new or unexpected for me, fellow-Romans, if the one taunt always directed against our family by seditious

tribunes were now cast at me too – that the Claudian family from its very beginnings has believed nothing was of greater importance for the State than the dignity of the Senate, and that it has always opposed the interests of the common people. The former of these charges I neither deny nor seek to refute: from the day we were called on to be citizens and senators,[47] we have put all our efforts into ensuring that it could be truthfully said that the dignity of those families amongst which you wish to number us has been enhanced by us rather than diminished. As for the other charge, I venture to maintain, citizens, on my own and my ancestor's behalf, that unless anyone supposes that the welfare of the whole State is opposed to the interests of the plebeians, as though they occupied another city, we have never, either as private individuals or when in office, wittingly done anything detrimental to the people; nor could any deed or word of ours be truthfully alleged to oppose your interests, even if there have been some which did not meet your wishes. But even if I were not a Claudius nor of patrician blood but an ordinary Roman citizen, knowing only that my parents were both free born and I lived in a free State, how could I keep silence? Have Lucius Sextius and Gaius Licinius, those perpetual tribunes of ours, God help us, grown so presumptuous in the nine years of their reign that they can refuse to let you exercise your right to vote either in elections or in enacting laws?

' "There is a condition," says one of them: "that you shall re-elect us tribunes for the tenth time." Is that not tantamount to saying that "What others petition for we think so little of that we won't take it on without good reward"? But what can this reward be, which will make you our perpetual tribunes? "Your acceptance, as a whole, of all our proposals, whether you like them or not, whether they will do you good or harm." For pity's sake, you Tarquin-tribunes, imagine I am a common citizen calling out from the midst of the assembly: "With your permission, may we pick out from your proposals

47. The Claudii were Sabine in origin, traditionally said to have migrated to Rome in 504 (cf. II.16), but as a patrician *gens* must have gone back to the monarchy.

those we judge will benefit us and reject the rest?" "No, you shall not be allowed to legislate on usury and land, matters which concern you all, unless you put up with the monstrous sight of Lucius Sextius and Gaius Licinius as consuls – an outrage and abomination in your eyes. Either accept all or I propose nothing." It is as if a man were starving and someone offered poison with his food, telling him either to abstain from what is life-giving or mix with it what will bring him death. Well then, if this were a free State, wouldn't the crowd cry out, with one voice, "Clear out of here, with your tribuneships and proposals!" If you will not propose what it benefits the people to accept, does that mean there will be no one to do so? If it was some patrician, some Claudius – which they make out to be more hateful than anything – who said "Either accept all or I offer nothing", which of you Romans would put up with it? Will you never look at facts rather than at those who put them to you? Must you always give ready ear to all that "magistrate"[48] says and refuse to listen to what we are telling you?

'Certainly his language is far from suitable to a free State. But what about the proposal which, to their annoyance, you have rejected? It is no better than its language. "I propose," he says, "that you shall not be permitted to elect the consuls of your choice." For that is what it amounts to, when he lays down that in any case one consul must be elected from the plebeians, and denies you the power of choosing two patricians. If we had wars today like the Etruscan war when Porsenna occupied the Janiculum,[49] or the Gallic war a short time ago when everything here except for the Capitol and Citadel was in the hands of your enemies, if Lucius Sextius were standing for the consulship along with Marcus Furius here and any other patrician you like, could you endure it if Sextius were quite certain about his election while Camillus had to risk defeat? Is this the way to give equal opportunities for office to both parties – to allow the election of two plebeian

48. This is ironic: the people's tribune was not a magistrate.
49. Traditionally in 508; cf. II.11. Lars Porsenna was the Etruscan king of Clusium.

but not two patrician consuls? Is it obligatory for one consul
to be chosen from the plebeians when both may be passed over
if they are patrician? What sort of union and partnership is
that? Isn't it enough for you to gain a share in what you
hitherto had no share in at all, without asking for part and
making off with the whole? "I'm afraid," says he, "that if
you're allowed to elect two patricians you will not elect
anyone from the plebeians." By this he means that "Since of
your own free will you aren't likely to elect unsuitable candidates, I shall put you under obligation to elect men you don't
want." It follows that the people would get no thanks for their
support if one plebeian candidate were standing with two
patricians and could say he was elected by statute, not by their
vote.

41. 'What they are after is a way to make sure of office not
by applying for it but by using force; they intend to win the
highest positions without incurring any of the obligations even
of the lowest, and prefer to rely on snatched opportunities
rather than merit to support their application. Many a man
resents having to submit himself to inspection and appraise-
ment, thinks it right and proper that he alone shall be certain
of success while his rivals must compete for office, puts himself
outside your decision, and makes you cast your votes by
compulsion, not from choice, not as free men but as slaves. I
say nothing of Licinius and Sextius, whose years of un-
interrupted power you can count like those of the kings on
the Capitol. Is there anyone in the State today so humble that
by taking advantage of the law proposed he would not find
his way to the consulship made easier for him than it is for us
and our children? In our case you may sometimes be unable
to elect us even when you wish to, while you would be obliged
to elect those people even against your wishes.

'That will do for the indignity of this measure, for dignity
is a human concern; but what am I to say about the auspices
and religious observances, where disrespect and insult involve
the immortal gods? This City was founded under auspices, and
under auspices it conducts all its affairs in war and peace, at
home and on the battlefield, as everyone knows. Who then

controls the auspices, according to ancestral tradition? Why, the patricians, for no plebeian magistrate is elected under auspices; and the auspices are so exclusively ours that not only is it impossible for patrician magistrates elected by the people to be elected except under auspices, but also we can take auspices and appoint an interrex ourselves with no need of the people's vote. As private citizens too, we have the power to take them, which plebeians have not, even when in office. The State is therefore deprived of auspices by anyone who, by electing plebeian consuls, removes them from the patricians, when they alone can take them. These men are free now, if they like, to scoff at religious scruples: "What does it matter," they say, "if the sacred chickens will not feed and are slow to come out of the coop, or a bird gives an ill-omened squawk?" These are trivial matters, but it was because they did not scorn those trivial matters that your forefathers could build up this republic to be so great. Now we, as if we had no need of the gods' goodwill, are defiling all the sacred rites. So let pontiffs, augurs, high priests of sacrifice be chosen from the common herd; let us place the cap of the Flamen Dialis[50] on anyone's head, so long as it is a man's, and hand over the shields, shrines, gods and service of the gods to those who are excluded by divine law. Let laws be proposed and magistrates elected without taking the auspices; let neither the centuriate nor the curiate assembly receive the patricians' sanction. Let Sextius and Licinius reign in the City of Rome like Romulus and Tatius, just because they give away money and lands which are not theirs. Is it so sweet to rob others of their fortunes? Does it not occur to them that one of their laws will create vast deserts in the countryside, by driving owners from their property, while the other will make an end of men's trust in each other, and with it destroy all bonds of society? On every count I believe you should reject these proposals. May the gods prosper what you do!'

42. Appius's speech succeeded only in postponing the passing of the measures. The same tribunes, Sextius and Licinius,

---

50. The high priest of Jupiter.

were re-elected for the tenth time, and obtained the enactment of a law that half the board of ten in charge of sacred rites should be chosen from the plebeians.[51] Five patricians and five plebeians were elected, a step which seemed already to open up the road to the consulship. The people were satisfied with this victory, and accordingly allowed the Senate to elect military tribunes with no further mention of consuls for the present. Aulus and Marcus Cornelius were elected for the second time, and Marcus Geganius, Publius Manlius, Lucius Veturius and Publius Valerius for their sixth term of office.

Rome's affairs abroad were now peaceful, apart from the siege of Velitrae, the result of which was delayed though not in doubt, when a sudden report of an attack by the Gauls compelled the State to make Marcus Furius dictator for the fifth time. He named Titus Quinctius Poenus as his master of Horse. According to Claudius,[52] fighting took place with the Gauls that year near the River Anio, and this was the occasion of the famous battle on the bridge in which Titus Manlius engaged and killed a Gaul who had challenged him, and despoiled him of his torque, while the two armies looked on. I am more inclined to follow the majority of the authorities and believe that those events took place at least ten years later,[53] and that this year the dictator Marcus Furius fought the Gauls in battle on Alban territory. The Romans won a victory which was never in doubt without much difficulty, although they were in great terror of the Gauls through the recollection of their earlier defeat.

Many thousands of barbarians were killed in battle, many too when the camp was taken; the remainder dispersed, mostly making for Apulia, and were able to save themselves because their flight carried them far from the Romans and scattered them in panic all over the countryside. The dictator was voted a triumph by agreement of Senate and people.

51. cf. ch. 37.12.
52. Quintus Claudius Quadrigarius, the Roman annalist, writing in about 70 B.C.
53. The tale is told in detail in VII.9–10, and dated six years later, in 361.

Scarcely had Camillus finished off the war when he was faced by conflict at Rome even more violent than before. After fierce struggles the dictator and Senate were defeated, the measures proposed by the tribunes were adopted, and despite patrician opposition consular elections were held in which Lucius Sextius was elected as the first plebeian consul. Even that did not bring the rivalry to an end. The patricians refused to ratify the election, so that the crisis nearly ended in a secession of the plebs, with other alarming threats of civil conflicts. Then the dictator finally intervened, and differences were resolved by compromise: the nobles gave way to the plebeians on the question of the plebeian consul, and the plebeians conceded to the nobles that a single praetor should be elected from the patricians to administer justice in the City.[54] Thus after their long dispute the two orders were reconciled and in agreement at last. The Senate declared that this was a fitting occasion – and one well deserved at any time – for honouring the immortal gods by a special performance of the Great Games[55]; an extra day should therefore be added to the usual three. When the people's aediles refused this additional burden, the young patricians cried out that they would gladly organize it themselves in honour of the gods. They were thanked by the entire people, after which the Senate directed the dictator to propose for election two aediles, chosen from the patricians,[56] and decreed that the Senate should ratify all the elections of that year.

54. The *praetor urbanus*; this office was also opened to the plebeians in 337; cf. VIII.15.9.
55. Probably the *Ludi Romani,* later held annually in September.
56. The curule aediles. The rule was modified in the following year (VII.1.6).

BOOK VII

1. This year will be noteworthy as the one in which a 'new man' held the consulship, as well as for the creation of two new magistracies, those of praetor and of curule aedile. These offices the patricians sought for themselves in return for one of the two consulships which they had conceded to the plebeians. The people gave Lucius Sextius the plebeian consulship which his law had created, and the patricians used their influence at the election to secure the praetorship for Spurius Furius Camillus, son of Marcus, and the aedileship for Gnaeus Quinctius Capitolinus and Publius Cornelius Scipio, men from families ranking with their own. Lucius Sextius was given Lucius Aemilius Mamercus as his patrician colleague.

Early on in the year there was widespread rumour about the Gauls, who at first had scattered over Apulia but were now said to be gathering together, and also about defection on the part of the Hernici. As all business was being deliberately postponed, to prevent the plebeian consul from effecting anything, the general quiet and inactivity made it seem as if there was a cessation of business in the courts, though the tribunes could not let it pass in silence that in return for one plebeian consul the nobles had gained for themselves three patrician magistrates wearing the purple-edged toga and sitting like the consuls in curule chairs, while the praetor was even dealing out justice after being elected as a colleague of the consuls and under the same auspices. As a result of this the Senate felt ashamed to order that the curule aediles should be elected from the patricians. It was agreed at first that they should be taken from the plebeians in alternate years; subsequently the election was open to both classes without distinction.

Lucius Genucius and Quintus Servilius were the next consuls, and though there was peace abroad and freedom from party warfare at home, a fearful plague broke out to deny a respite from fear and dangers. It is reported that a censor, a curule aedile and three people's tribunes died in it, and a proportionately large number from the rest of the population. But what made that outbreak especially memorable was the death of Marcus Furius, which was untimely although he was ripe in years. For he was a man who was genuinely unique in every situation, and before he went into exile foremost in peace as in war. Then in exile he won even greater fame, whether through being so much missed by his fellow-citizens that they begged his help in absence after the capture of the City, or in making so successful a return to his country and restoring it along with himself. Afterwards for twenty-five years (for he survived so long) he lived up to his glorious reputation and was thought worthy to be named after Romulus as the second founder of the City of Rome.

2. The plague continued through this and the following year, when Gaius Sulpicius Peticus and Gaius Licinius Stolo were consuls. Nothing memorable happened then, except that a *lectisternium* was held, to entreat a reconciliation with the gods: this was the third occasion since the City's foundation.[1] When neither human expedient nor divine aid did anything to reduce the virulence of the epidemic, the Romans gave way to superstitious practices. Amongst their other ceremonies intended to placate divine wrath, they are said to have introduced scenic entertainments, something quite novel for a warlike people whose only previous public spectacle had been that of the circus. These began only in a modest way, as most things do, and were in fact imported from abroad. Players were brought from Etruria to dance to the strains of the pipe without any singing or miming of song, and made quite graceful movements in the Etruscan style. Then the young Romans began to copy them, exchanging jokes at the same time in crude improvised verse, with gestures to fit the words. Thus the entertainment was adopted and became established by frequent repetition. The native actors were called *histriones*,

1. The *lectisternium* or 'draping of couches' is described by Livy in V.13.6–7. Couches and reclining figures of the gods were brought out and a ceremonial feast laid before them. The first occasion was in 399, also to avert plague; the second is not mentioned by Livy.

because the Etruscan word for an actor is *ister*; they stopped bandying ribald improvised lines, like Fescennine verses,[2] and began to perform *saturae* or medleys amplified with music, the singing properly arranged to fit the pipe and movement in harmony with it.

Some years later, Livius[3] first ventured to give up the *satura* and compose a play with a plot. Like everyone else at the time, he also acted in his own dramas; and the tale is told that when he lost his voice after repeated recalls, he was given permission to place a boy in front of the pipe-player to sing the songs while he acted them himself, and did so with a good deal more vigour when not hampered by having to use his voice. From then on began the actors' practice of employing singers while they confined themselves to gesture and used their voices only for dialogue. This style of performance began to detach the play from impromptu joking to raise a laugh, and drama gradually developed into an art; the young men then handed over play-acting entirely to the professional actors and returned to the old practice of bandying jokes put into verse. This was the origin of the comic epilogues later known as *exodia*, which were combined especially with the Atellane farces[4]; they were a kind of entertainment taken over from the Oscans which the young men retained and would not allow to be debased by professional actors. That is why it is still customary for the actors of Atellane farces not to be excluded from their tribes but to serve in the army as if they had no connection with the stage.[5] Other institutions have also started in a small way, but it seemed worth while setting down how

2. Probably named after Fescennia, a place in Etruria; less probably after *fascinum*, a phallus-shaped amulet against witchcraft. cf. Horace, *Epistles* II.1.145.

3. Lucius Livius Andronicus of Tarentum, actor and dramatist, whose first comedy, adapted from Greek, was performed in Rome in 240 B.C.

4. Atella, a small Oscan town in Campania, gave its name to the stock character farces from which the Italian *commedia dell'arte* is thought to have derived.

5. Actors in general ranked as *aerarii*, the lowest class of citizen, excluded from voting and military service.

drama first originated, to show the sober beginnings of something which has now reached such a pitch of folly that a kingdom's riches could scarcely meet its wild extravagance.

3. However, the staging of plays which were first introduced to remove superstitious fears neither freed men's minds from their anxiety nor their bodies from disease. On the contrary, when the Tiber overflowed and flooded the Circus during a performance, so that the plays had to be stopped, it caused widespread panic, as if the gods were alienated and rejected what was offered to appease their anger. And so when Gnaeus Genucius and Lucius Aemilius Mamercus (for the second time) were consuls, and the people's minds were more affected by their search for a means of appeasement than their bodies were by disease, the older men remembered (so it is said) that at one time an outbreak of plague had been reduced by the dictator's hammering in a nail. Their anxiety prompted the Senate to order the appointment of a dictator for the express purpose of hammering the nail; Lucius Manlius Imperiosus was chosen and named Lucius Pinarius as his master of Horse.

There is an ancient law, recorded in archaic script and language, that on the Ides of September the chief magistrate shall hammer in a nail; the tablet was fixed on the right side of the temple of Jupiter Best and Highest, where the sanctuary of Minerva stands. This nail, it is said, served to mark the number of years at a time when there was little knowledge of letters, and the law was assigned to Minerva's shrine because number was her invention. Similar nails to mark the passage of years can be seen at Volsinii, hammered into the shrine of Nortia, an Etruscan goddess[6]: so Cincius[7] declares, and he is a scrupulous authority for records of this kind. The consul Marcus Horatius followed this law when he dedicated the temple of Jupiter Best and Highest in the year after the expulsion of the kings. Subsequently the ceremony of hammering in the nail was transferred from consuls to dictators, as

6. Of Fortune.
7. Either L. Cincius Alimentus, the Roman senator and historian, captured by Hannibal in the Second Punic War (Livy XXI.38.3), or an Augustan antiquarian of the same name.

theirs was the higher authority. Then the custom lapsed, until its celebration seemed important enough in itself to merit the appointment of a dictator. This was the reason for appointing Lucius Manlius. But he preferred to believe that he had been chosen to wage war rather than to discharge a religious duty; he set his heart on war with the Hernici and roused the opposition of the men of military age by holding a rigorous levy. Finally, when all the people's tribunes rose against him, he yielded either to force or to a sense of shame and resigned the dictatorship.

4. Nevertheless, at the beginning of the following year, in the consulship of Quintus Servilius Ahala and Lucius Genucius, Manlius was brought to trial by the people's tribune Marcus Pomponius. He was hated for the harshness of his levy, in which people had suffered not only fines but also physical cruelty, some who had not answered to their names being flogged, others led off to prison. Above all he was loathed for his violent temper and his surname, Imperiosus, which was offensive to a free State and was derived from the severity he openly paraded and exercised as much against his kindred and members of his own family as against strangers. Amongst other charges the tribune referred to Manlius's treatment of his young son, who had not been convicted of any misdeed and yet was banished from his City, home and household gods, from the Forum and public recognition, and from the companionship of young men of his own age. Instead, he was consigned to servile labour, practically in a prison or penitentiary, where this young man of noble birth and a dictator's son could learn from his daily misery how well and truly 'imperious' his father was. And what was his offence? He had some difficulty in expressing himself and was hesitant in speech. Should his father not have tried to help this natural infirmity, if he had any humanity in him, instead of castigating it and making it conspicuous by his persecution? Why, even dumb animals feed and cherish any of their young who do not do well; yet Lucius Manlius could only increase his son's hardships by adding to them, pile heavier burdens on his natural backwardness, and extinguish any spark of native

ability which might be there by confining him to a rough life and a peasant's upbringing amongst the cattle.

5. Everyone was outraged by these accusations except the young man himself; on the contrary, he was distressed at being an additional cause for his father's unpopularity and a source of further charges. With the idea of showing gods and men that he had rather help his father than his father's enemies, he formed a plan, marked, to be sure, by his ignorant, uncouth mind, and no model for civilized behaviour, but still laudable for its filial piety. Unknown to anyone, he put a knife in his belt, came to the City early one morning and quickly made his way from the city gate to the house of the tribune Marcus Pomponius. He told the porter that he must see his master at once, and ordered the man to say it was Titus Manlius, the son of Lucius. He was soon admitted, for he was expected to be furious with his father and to have come with some fresh charge or plan of acting against him. After exchanging greetings with the tribune he said he wished to speak to him without witnesses. When all present were told to go away, he drew his knife, and, standing over the tribune's couch with weapon poised, he threatened to stab him at once unless he swore in words he had formulated himself never to hold any assembly of the people for the purpose of accusing his father. The tribune was terrified, seeing the steel flash before his eyes and knowing that he was alone and unarmed, while his assailant was a powerful young man, and foolhardy in the knowledge of his strength, which was no less alarming. He took the oath in the words demanded of him, and subsequently made it known that he had been forced to give up his undertaking. Although the plebeians would have liked to have the chance of casting their votes in the case of so cruel and arrogant a defendant, yet they were not altogether displeased that a son had dared such a deed on behalf of his father; and this was all the more praiseworthy because the father's extreme harshness had not in any way diminished his son's filial loyalty. So not only was the father let off having to defend himself, but the young man also won recognition for himself from the incident. That year, when for the first time it was decided to

hold an election of military tribunes for the legions (for hitherto the generals had nominated them themselves, as they do today in the case of those called *Rufuli*[8]), he came second out of six elected, without having done anything at home or in the army to merit such popularity, seeing that he had spent his youth in the country remote from the company of his fellow-men.

6. That same year, as the result of an earthquake or some other violent upheaval, it is said that the middle of the Forum or thereabouts collapsed, leaving a huge chasm of enormous depth. The abyss could not be filled by throwing in the earth which everyone brought, until a warning from the gods started people wondering what was 'the chief strength of the Roman people': for that was what the soothsayers declared must be offered up to the place, if they wished the Roman republic to endure for ever. At this (the story goes) Marcus Curtius, a young man of great military distinction, rebuked those who doubted whether Rome had any greater asset than her arms and valour. In the silence which followed he looked up to the temples of the immortal gods which tower above the Forum and the Capitol, and stretching out his hands now to the heavens, now to the yawning gulf in the ground and the gods of the Underworld, he devoted himself to death. He then mounted a horse caparisoned with all possible splendour, and plunged fully armed into the chasm. A crowd of men and women then threw piles of offerings and fruits of the earth in after him. Curtius's Pool was named after him, it is said, and not after the Mettius Curtius[9] who was a soldier of Titus Tatius in former times. I would have spared no effort if there were any way of research arriving at the truth, but, as it is, one must stick to tradition where the antiquity of events makes certainty

8. The *Rufuli* are similarly described by the second-century grammarian Festus (ed. Müller), p. 261, who adds little to Livy's account.
9. In I.13.5 Livy seems to accept that the Lacus Curtius, a shallow pit or pool in the Forum, took its name from the Sabine Mettius Curtius, whose horse carried him into a swamp when he was fighting against Romulus. Here he prefers the heroic self-sacrifice of Marcus Curtius.

impossible; and the name of the pool is better known from the more recent legend I have just related.

After Curtius's sacrifice in expiation of this fearful portent, in the same year the Senate dealt with the question of the Hernici. Fetial priests[10] had been sent to demand redress, but to no effect, and so it was decided to submit for the people's approval on the earliest possible day a declaration of war on the Hernici. A full assembly voted for war, and the conduct of it fell by lot to the consul Lucius Genucius. He was the first plebeian consul to direct a war under his own auspices, and the City was on tenterhooks, for on the outcome of events it would be known whether or not it was a wise decision to allow offices to be open to all. As luck would have it, Genucius marched out with all speed against the enemy and fell into an ambush, where the legions were taken by surprise and put to flight in panic, while the consul was surrounded and killed unrecognized by his captors. When the news reached Rome, the patricians were not so much dismayed by the general disaster as infuriated by the unlucky effect of a plebeian in command, and filled the city with their outcry. Let them go and choose consuls from the plebs, and hand over the auspices to those for whom it was a sin to take them! They had been able to drive the patricians from office by their plebiscite; surely their unsanctioned law[11] had not prevailed on the immortal gods? No, the gods themselves had avenged the insult to their divinity and to their auspices, for as soon as these had been touched by one forbidden by law both human and divine, an army and its commander had been wiped out, as a lesson to them not to hold elections in future which would trample on the rights of patrician families. The Senate-house and Forum re-echoed with such cries. Appius Claudius had opposed the law, so he could now denounce with increased authority the outcome of a measure he had censured; with the

10. The *fetiales*, a college of twenty priests, negotiated peace treaties and delivered declarations of war. Their ancient ritual is described by Livy in I.24 and I.32.

11. Unsanctioned because the presiding tribune had no power to take the auspices.

assent of the patricians he was accordingly named dictator by the consul Servilius. A levy of troops was proclaimed and the courts suspended.

7. Before the dictator and the fresh legions could reach the Hernici, the legate Gaius Sulpicius saw his opportunity to take action and did so with remarkable success. The Hernici, grown over-confident at the consul's death, came right up to the Roman camp with every hope of taking it by storm; but the soldiers, encouraged by Sulpicius and already bursting with rage and indignation, made a sortie. The result left the Hernici far from their hopes of attacking the Roman stockade – indeed, they had to fall back with their ranks in disorder. Then when the dictator arrived, the new army joined up with the original one, so that forces were doubled. The dictator addressed the men, praising the soldiers and their commander whose courage had saved the camp, and so raised the morale of those who heard the tribute they deserved, while at the same time he spurred on the rest to rival their valour. Nor was there any delay in preparing for action on the enemy's side, for they remembered the glory they had won in the past, and being well aware of the increase in their enemy's forces began to augment their own. All who bore the name of Hernici and were of military age were called up, and eight cohorts were enrolled, each of four hundred men, selected for their fitness. These formed the pick of the younger men, and their expectations and fighting spirit had been roused by the passing of a decree which offered them double pay. They were also exempted from routine army chores, so that by being reserved for the one duty of fighting in battle they knew they must make greater efforts than those expected of ordinary men. They were even stationed outside the line of battle, so that their courage could be better displayed.

A plain extending for two miles divided the Roman camp from the Hernici, and there the battle was fought, in the middle of the plain, about the same distance from both camps. At first the issue was uncertain, and nothing came of the repeated attempts of the Roman cavalry to disrupt the enemy's line. Once the cavalry realized that their charges were largely ineffective, in spite of all their efforts, they went to the dictator for advice; and with his permission they dismounted, rushed ahead of the standards with a great battle-cry, and renewed the battle in a novel way. Nothing could have stopped them, had not the special cohorts been in their path, showing physical strength and spirit to match their own. 8. Then the issue lay between the best men of the two peoples, so that whatever the losses the common fortune of war inflicted on either side, the damage was disproportionate to the numbers involved. The rank and file of the armies let their fate depend on the others' valour, as if they had handed over the battle to their superiors. Many fell dead on both sides, and more were wounded; finally the cavalrymen began to upbraid each other, demanding to know what else remained for them if they had failed to repel the enemy when mounted and could achieve nothing decisive on foot. What third sort of fighting were they waiting for? What had they gained by dashing boldly in front of the standards to fight in a position which was not theirs? Urging each other on with words like these they attacked with renewed outcry, and first made the enemy give ground, then put them to flight, and finally routed them without a doubt. What it was that tipped the balance between forces so evenly matched is difficult to say, unless the invariable fortune of the two peoples had the power to raise or diminish their fighting spirit. The Romans pursued the fleeing Hernici right up to their camp, but did not attack it as it was late in the day. (It had taken a long time for the dictator to obtain favourable omens, which prevented him from giving the battle-signal before noon, and so the struggle had been prolonged until nightfall.) On the following day it was found that the Hernici had fled, abandoning their camp, and that only a few of their wounded had been left behind. As the column of fugitives passed under the walls of Signia the townspeople observed its scanty numbers round the standards, and so dispersed and scattered it over the countryside in panic-stricken flight. But the Romans won no bloodless victory: they lost a quarter of their soldiers, and a number of Roman cavalrymen were killed, no less serious a loss.

9. Next year the consuls Gaius Sulpicius and Gaius Licinius Calvus led an army against the Hernici and, not finding the enemy out and about in the countryside, stormed and captured their city of Ferentinum. As the Romans were returning from there, the people of Tibur closed their gates against them. Many previous complaints had been made on both sides, but this was the last straw, and the Romans decided to declare war on the people of Tibur once they had demanded reparation through the fetial priests.

It is well confirmed that Titus Quinctius Poenus was dictator that year, and that his master of Horse was Servius Cornelius Maluginensis. Licinius Macer[12] writes that the appointment was for the purpose of holding elections and was made by the consul Licinius, because his colleague was hurrying on the election before the campaign, in order to be re-elected to his consulship, and his dishonourable intention had to be thwarted. But his wish to glorify his own family makes Licinius a less reliable authority. I can find no mention of this episode in the earlier annals, so I am more inclined to think that the dictator owed his appointment to the war against the Gauls. It is certain that in this year the Gauls encamped at the third milestone on the Salt Road,[13] on the far side of the bridge over the Anio.

After announcing a suspension of the courts because of the Gallic incursion, the dictator administered the oath to all men of military age, marched out of the City with an immense army, and set up camp on the nearer bank of the Anio. A bridge separated the two armies, neither side wishing to break it down lest that should look like an indication of fear. There were frequent skirmishes for possession of the bridge, but as the strength of both forces was not known, it was uncertain

12. Gaius Licinius Macer, father of the poet C. Licinius Calvus, was a late-republican annalist mainly interested in the political significance of institutions and the sovereignty of the people. cf. Sallust, *Historiae* III.48.

13. The Via Salaria, leading from the Colline Gate into Sabine territory; so called because the Etruscans fetched their salt from the sea by it. cf. Pliny, *NH* XXXI.89.

who would take it. It was then that a Gaul of enormous size advanced on to the empty bridge and shouted as loudly as he could: 'Let the bravest man Rome has today come on and fight, so that the two of us can show by the result which race is superior in war!'

10. For a long time the young Roman nobles stood silent; they hesitated to refuse the challenge, and were reluctant to volunteer for so dangerous a risk. Then Titus Manlius, the son of Lucius, who had rescued his father from the tribune's harassment,[14] left his place and went up to the dictator. 'Without an order from you, sir,' he said, 'I would never fight out of my rank, even if I were certain of victory; but if you permit me, I want to show that monster strutting about so boldly in front of the enemy's standards that I belong to the family which threw the Gallic army down from the Tarpeian Rock.' 'Blessings on you, Titus Manlius, for your courage and loyalty to your father and country,' answered the dictator. 'Go ahead and with the gods' aid show that the name of Rome is invincible.' The young man's friends then armed him; he took up an infantryman's shield and buckled on a Spanish sword, suitable for hand-to-hand fighting. When he was armed and equipped they escorted him to the Gaul, who was fatuously delighted, and even stuck out his tongue in derision (for the ancient authorities thought even that detail worth remembering). Then his companions returned to their places, and the two armed men were left between the armies, as if they were staging a show rather than observing the rules of warfare, and not at all evenly matched, to judge by outward appearances. One was remarkable for his stature, resplendent in multicoloured clothing and painted armour inlaid with gold[15]; the other had a moderate physique for a soldier and was nothing special to look at, with armour which was suitable rather than ornate. He did not sing out war-cries, or dance about with useless brandishing of weapons, but his breast swelled with

14. cf. ch. 5.

15. Aulus Gellius (IX.13) quotes Claudius Quadrigarius as describing him as *nudus*. For an analysis of Livy's style here, see A. H. McDonald in *JRS* (1957), pp. 158-9, 167-8.

courage and silent anger; all his ferocity was held back for the critical moment of the duel.

When they took up their stand between the two armies, the hearts of the many men standing round them were on tenter-hooks of hope and fear. The huge bulk of the Gaul towered over the Roman; holding his shield in his left arm in front of himself he brought his sword down with a slashing stroke and reverberating clang on to the arms of his oncoming opponent, but to no effect. Manlius struck up the lower rim of the shield with his own, and, raising the point of his sword, slipped between his enemy's body and weapons, coming too near for any part of his person to be exposed to a wound. He gave one thrust followed immediately by another, gashed open the belly and groins of his enemy and threw him headlong to the ground to lie stretched out over a large area. He then spared the corpse any abuse,[16] despoiling it only of a torque, which, blood-spattered as it was, he put round his own neck. The Gauls stood transfixed with terror mingled with admiration, while the Romans eagerly left their position to run forward and meet their comrade, and, full of praise and congratu-lations, brought him to the dictator. Amongst the soldiers' jokes in rough rhymed form was heard the name 'Torquatus', and henceforth this was adopted as an honoured title even by later members of his family. The dictator added the gift of a gold chaplet and delivered a splendid eulogy of his fight before the assembled troops.

11. This combat had indeed great influence on the outcome of the whole war, so much so that next night the army of the Gauls left their camp in alarm and went over to the territory of Tibur. There they made a military alliance, and after being generously supplied with provisions by the Tiburtines, soon moved on to Campania. That was the reason why, in the following year, the consul Gaius Poetelius Balbus was ordered by the people to lead an army against Tibur; his colleague Marcus Fabius Ambustus had been assigned the campaign against the Hernici. The Gauls returned from Campania to

16. Gellius, again quoting, says that Manlius cut off the head.

support the Tiburtines, and the ensuing destructive raids in the neighbourhood of Labici, Tusculum and Alba were undoubtedly carried out under Tiburtine leadership. To lead an army against Tibur the State had been satisfied with a consul, but the Gallic attack required the appointment of a dictator. Quintus Servilius Ahala was appointed and named Titus Quinctius as his master of Horse. With the Senate's approval he vowed to celebrate the Great Games if the campaign ended successfully. The dictator ordered the consul's army to remain where it was, in order to confine the Tiburtines to their own field of action, and administered the oath to all the men of military age, none of whom tried to get out of serving. Not far from the Colline Gate the entire manpower of the City fought a battle in sight of their parents, wives and children. These can provide a strong incentive to courage even when soldiers are far from home, but being then in full view they stirred their menfolk's sense of honour and tender feelings. Much blood was shed on both sides, but in the end the Gauls were turned back. Their troops fled in the direction of Tibur, as though it were the stronghold of the Gallic campaign. As they scattered, the consul Poetelius rounded them up not far from Tibur, and pushed them inside the gates along with the townspeople who had come out to help them. Both dictator and consul handled the whole episode admirably. The other consul, Fabius, defeated the Hernici as well, first in minor skirmishes and finally in one decisive battle after they had brought all their forces into an attack. The dictator spoke in praise of the consuls in the highest terms, both in the Senate and before the people, even giving them the credit for his own successes, and then resigned his office. Poetelius celebrated a double triumph over the Gauls and the Tiburtines, while it was thought sufficient for Fabius to be given an ovation on his return to the City.

The Tiburtines were scornful of Poetelius's triumph. Where, they asked, had he fought a proper battle against them? A few people had gone out of the gates to look at the flight and panic of the Gauls, but when they saw they were being attacked themselves and the Romans were indiscriminately cutting down all who came their way, they went back into the

town. That was the incident the Romans thought worthy of
a triumph! They should not find creating a disturbance at their
enemy's gates such a marvellous exploit when they were going
to see a greater panic before their own walls.

12. Consequently, in the following year, when Marcus
Popilius Laenas and Gnaeus Manlius were consuls, an army
bent on attack set out from Tibur in the early hours of darkness
and reached the City of Rome. The unexpectedness of the
night alarm for people suddenly awoken from sleep was terri-
fying, and, besides, many had no idea who the enemy were or
where they had come from. But the call to arms was quickly
given, the gates were put under guard and the walls were
manned. Then when the early daylight revealed that the enemy
outside the City were in no great number and consisted only
of men from Tibur, the consuls made a sortie from two gates
and attacked them on both sides as they were approaching the
walls. It was clear that their venture depended on opportunity,
not on their courage, for they could scarcely withstand the first
shock of the Romans' assault. It was moreover generally
admitted that their coming had been a good thing for Rome,
for the fear of war so near at hand checked the dissension that
was already mounting between patricians and plebeians.

Another hostile incursion was more of a menace to the
surrounding countryside; the people of Tarquinii sent out
a raiding force which penetrated into Roman territory, especially the part bordering on Etruria. The new consuls, Gaius
Fabius and Gaius Plautius, demanded reparation, but to no
effect, and so declared war on them, at the people's bidding.
The conduct of the campaign fell to Fabius, while Plautius
took on the one against the Hernici.

There were also increasing rumours of war with the Gauls.
But amongst many causes for alarm there was comfort to be
found in the fact that peace had been granted the Latins, at their
own request, and large numbers of troops were received from
them in accordance with an ancient treaty[17] which had been
allowed to lapse for many years. These reinforcements

17. The treaty made in 493 after the capture of Corioli and described
in II.33.9 as recorded on a bronze column. cf. Cicero, *pro Balbo* 53.

strengthened the Roman position, so that there was less concern when news came that the Gauls had recently reached Praeneste and then set up camp near Pedum. It was decided to make Gaius Sulpicius dictator, and the consul Gaius Plautius was summoned to appoint him. He was then given Marcus Valerius as his master of Horse. They selected the best soldiers from the two consular armies and led them off to meet the Gauls. The campaign proceeded rather less rapidly than either side liked. First it had been only the Gauls who were bent on giving battle; then they were outstripped by the eagerness of the Roman army to rush to arms and enter the fray. But the dictator was very reluctant to risk his fortune before it was absolutely necessary against an enemy who was becoming weaker with every day he had to linger in an unfriendly country, with no previous arrangements for supplies or adequate defence works: an enemy too whose physical and mental energy depended wholly on attacking and deteriorated with every slight delay.

These considerations determined the dictator to prolong the war and were his reason for threatening severe punishment for anyone who engaged the enemy without his orders. The soldiers found it intolerable. First they grumbled about the dictator amongst themselves when they were on picket-duty or night-guard, and sometimes they all blamed the Senate for not having given the conduct of the war to the consuls. A splendid general they'd chosen, a singular commander, who believed that victory would fall from heaven into his lap without his doing a thing! Then they became quite open in these attacks and more violently outspoken, insisting that either they would fight without waiting for the general's order or march in a body to Rome. The centurions began to join up with the soldiers, and to the murmuring amongst small groups of men was now added a general clamour of voices in the central area of the camp and outside the general's tent. The crowd increased to the size of a public assembly, and on every side shouts called for an immediate confrontation with the dictator, with Sextus Tullius as spokesman for the army, as befitted his courage.

13. It was the seventh time Tullius had served as chief centurion, and there was not a man in the army, at any rate amongst the infantry, who was more distinguished for his exploits. At the head of a column of soldiers he went up to the tribunal, and addressed Sulpicius, who was less surprised to see the crowd than he was to see it led by Tullius, a soldier so obedient to authority. 'By your leave, sir,' he said, 'the entire army thinks you have condemned it for cowardice and practically deprived it of arms as a mark of disgrace, and has begged me to plead its cause with you. For my part, even if we could be reproached for abandoning our post anywhere, turning our backs to the enemy, or shamefully losing our standards, I should still think it right for you to grant what we ask, and allow us to redeem our fault by our courage and wipe out the memory of our shame by winning new glory. Even the legions which were routed at the Allia subsequently marched out from Veii and regained by their valour the very City they had lost when they panicked and fled. In our case, thanks to the gods' generosity, your own good fortune and that of the Roman people, our fortune and our glory are unimpaired; though I hardly dare to speak of glory, when the enemy keep us cowering like women behind our rampart, to be taunted with every kind of insult! And you, our general – which is harder for us to bear – think of us as an army without spirit, without arms or hands to hold them, and before you have even tested us, have such low expectations of us that you count yourself in command of an army of cripples and weaklings. What other reason can we suppose there is for you, an experienced general and one so fearless in war, to be sitting, as they say, with hands folded? For, whatever the truth of the matter, it is more likely that you should appear to have had doubts about our courage than we about yours. But if that is official policy, not your own, and some agreement between the senators and not the Gallic war is keeping us away from the City and our homes, I beg you to take what I am going to say as addressed not by soldiers to their general but by the plebeians to the patricians – and if we propose to have our own policies, as you have yours, who can blame us? I say that we serve you as soldiers,

not as your slaves, and were sent to war, not to exile; that if anyone gave the signal and led us out to battle we would fight like men and Romans; but if there is no need of our arms, we would rather spend our leisure in Rome than in an army camp. This is what we would say to the patricians. But we implore you, our general, as your soldiers, to give us a chance to fight. Victory is what we want, but, even more, to win victory led by you, to crown you with the laurel of glory, to escort you into the City in triumph, to march behind your chariot and approach the temple of Jupiter Best and Highest shouting our exultation and joy.' Tullius's speech was taken up by entreaties from the massed soldiers, who clamoured on all sides for the signal and call to arms.

14. Sulpicius thought that this was a good thing to have done, though it set a bad precedent; but he undertook to do what the soldiers wanted. In private he asked Tullius what this demonstration meant and what had prompted it. Tullius earnestly begged the dictator not to believe that he had forgotten either his military training or his own position and the respect due to his general. A mob when roused, he said, was generally like its leaders, and he had not refused to lead it for fear someone else might come forward, the sort of leader an excited crowd generally chooses: he at least would take no action against his general's wishes. But Sulpicius must also make sure that he kept the army well in hand; delay could not be imposed on feelings which ran so high, and the men would choose their own time and place for battle if he did not give these to them. While they were talking in this way a Gaul tried to drive off some pack-animals which happened to be grazing outside the rampart. Two Roman soldiers took them from him, and were stoned by the Gauls: whereupon a shout went up from the Roman guard-post and men ran forward from both sides. Soon there would have been a regular battle if the centurions had not broken up the fighting; but at least the incident strengthened the dictator's confidence in Tullius, and as the situation did not permit further delay, the order was given for a set engagement the following day.

Yet the dictator was entering a struggle in which he relied

more on his men's courage than on their strength, and so he began to cast around and work out how he could strike terror into the enemy by some ruse. His ingenuity devised a new stratagem, which many generals, both Roman and foreign, have since adopted, some even in the present day.[18] He gave orders for the pack-saddles to be taken off the mules, leaving only a couple of saddlecloths on each, and mounted the mule-teers, armed partly with captured weapons, partly with what had been taken from the sick. By this means he mustered nearly a thousand men, mixed a hundred cavalry with them, and told them to go by night up to the mountains above the camp and conceal themselves in the woods: they were not to move from there until they had a signal from him. He himself, as soon as light dawned, began to deploy his battle-line along the lower slopes, his purpose being to make the enemy take up a position facing the mountains where he had made his preparations for filling them with fear – a fear which, though groundless, would help the Romans almost more than a genuine show of strength. At first the Gallic leaders believed the Romans would not come down to the plain; then when they suddenly realized that they had descended, they rushed into battle, all eagerness themselves for the fray, and fighting began before the generals could give the signal.

15. The Gauls made their severest attack on the Roman right wing, and could not have been held if the dictator had not happened to be there, accusing Sextus Tullius by name and demanding to know if that was how he had promised the men would fight. Where was that shouting now with which they had clamoured for arms? Where were their threats that they would start the battle without their general's order? Look at their general calling on them to fight, and leading them sword in hand ahead of the standards! Was there no one to follow him from those who just now had been ready to lead – fierce fighters in camp but cowards on the field? What the men heard was no less than the truth; and shame so spurred them on that they rushed on the enemy's weapons, putting all thought of

18. e.g. Caesar at Gergovia (*De Bello Gallico* VII.45.2).

danger out of their minds. This almost crazy assault first threw the enemy into confusion; then before they could recover themselves, the cavalry charged and routed them. The dictator himself, as soon as he saw that one section of their line was giving way, turned the infantry attack on the left wing, where he saw numbers of the enemy gathering, and gave the agreed signal to those on the mountain. When a fresh battle-cry was raised from that direction and the men were seen riding obliquely down the mountain slopes in the direction of the Gallic camp, the Gauls were afraid of being cut off, broke off the battle, and made for their camp in headlong flight. There they were met by Marcus Valerius, the master of Horse, who had dispatched the Gallic right wing and was riding up to the enemy's fortifications. They turned and fled to the mountains and woods, and there great numbers of them were intercepted by the bogus cavalry formed from the muleteers, while any whose terror had carried them into the woods were horribly massacred after the battle had petered out. No one since Marcus Furius celebrated a triumph over the Gauls which was better deserved than Gaius Sulpicius. He also collected from the Gallic spoils a considerable weight of gold, which he dedicated on the Capitol, walled in with squared stones.

The consuls also campaigned in the same year, but with varying success; Gaius Plautius defeated the Hernici and forced them to submit, but his colleague Fabius engaged the men of Tarquinii in battle without proper caution or preparation. Nor were the heavy losses on the battlefield the worst result; 307 Roman soldiers were taken prisoner and massacred as an act of sacrifice by the Tarquinienses – a hideous penalty which made the humiliation of the Roman people even more marked. In addition to that disaster the Romans saw their lands laid waste by sudden incursions first from Privernum and then from Velitrae.

Also in that year, two tribes were added, the Pomptine and the Publilian[19]; the votive games were held which Marcus

19. The tribes were territorial units in which citizens were enrolled for the census, taxation and military levies. This raised the number to twenty-seven.

Furius had vowed as dictator, and for the first time a proposed law against bribery was put to the people by the people's tribune Gaius Poetelius, as authorized by the Senate. Such a measure they believed would put an end to corrupt practices, especially those of the men recently risen from the people, who had frequented markets and meeting places. 16. Less welcome to the Senate was the measure carried through the following year in the consulship of Gaius Marcius and Gnaeus Manlius by the people's tribunes Marcus Duillius and Lucius Menenius, which fixed a rate of interest at one twelfth[20]; the people voted for this with even greater enthusiasm than for the other proposal.

In addition to the new wars decided on in the previous year, the Falisci also showed themselves enemies of Rome, on two counts: their young men had fought for the Tarquinienses, and they had not returned the Romans who had taken refuge in Falerii after the Roman defeat, though requested to do so by the fetial priests. The conduct of the campaign fell to Gnaeus Manlius. Marcius led his army into the territory of Privernum, which had remained untouched during a long period of peace, and gave his soldiers their fill of plunder. His generosity added to the supply available; he put nothing aside for the public treasury and so encouraged the men to increase their personal possessions. Then when the inhabitants of Privernum had set up camp behind strong entrenchments in front of their walls, he assembled his soldiers and addressed them as follows: 'I am now giving you the enemy's camp and city to pillage, if you will promise me to throw yourselves boldly into battle and show yourselves as ready to fight as to plunder.' The men raised a great clamour for the signal and rushed eagerly into battle, their spirits high with sure hope of success. There in front of the standards was the Sextus Tullius who has been mentioned before, crying out 'Look, sir, how your army is keeping its promises!' Then he put down his javelin and

20. The exact rate of interest meant by one twelfth is much debated. One twelfth of the capital per annum gives 8⅓ per cent, which does not seem very high, whereas one twelfth per month gives the very high figure indeed of 100 per cent.

charged the enemy with drawn sword. All the front line followed Tullius and put the enemy to flight at their first charge. Then they pursued them to the town, and were already bringing up scaling ladders to the walls when it surrendered. A triumph was celebrated over the Privernates.

Nothing worth recording was accomplished by the other consul, except that he got a law passed in an unprecedented way in his camp near Sutrium by his soldiers voting in tribes. This law levied a tax of one twentieth on manumitted slaves, and had been proposed by the Senate because it brought some considerable revenue to a depleted treasury. But the people's tribunes, less disturbed by the law than by the precedent, made it a capital offence for anyone in future to hold a people's assembly outside Rome, for if that were permitted, they argued, anything, however harmful to the people's interests, could be carried through by soldiers who had taken the military oath to obey their consul.

In the same year Gaius Licinius Stolo was prosecuted under his own law[21] by Marcus Popilius Laenas and fined ten thousand *asses* for holding a thousand *iugera* of land jointly with his son, and for having evaded the law by freeing his son from paternal authority.

17. New consuls then took office, Marcus Fabius Ambustus and Marcus Popilius Laenas, both for the second time. They had two wars on their hands. One was against the Tiburtines, which presented no difficulty and was directed by Laenas, who drove the enemy into their city and laid waste their fields. The other consul was defeated by the Falisci and Tarquinienses in his first engagement, when panic spread mainly because of their priests, who advanced like Furies brandishing snakes and burning torches, and demoralized the Roman soldiers by this unexpected spectacle. At first they fled back behind their own defence works in a disorderly rabble, like men bewildered and distraught; but then when the consul, the legates and the tribunes mocked and scolded them for being frightened like children by harmless sights, however strange, shame produced

21. cf. VI.35.5; the second Licinian law limited land holding to 500 *iugera*.

a sudden change of heart and they rushed blindly against the very objects which had put them to flight. Knocking aside the enemy's useless device they attacked the real armed men, routed the whole army, and even captured the camp the same day. They returned victorious with the vast amount of plunder they had won, cracking soldiers' jokes at the enemy's set-up and even more at their own fright. Then followed a call to arms to all who bore the name of Etruscan, and, with some of the Falisci and Tarquinienses to lead them, the enemy advanced as far as Salinae. To meet that threat Gaius Marcius Rutulus was appointed dictator, the first to be chosen from the plebeians, and he named Gaius Plautius, also a plebeian, as his master of Horse. But the patricians thought it outrageous that even the dictatorship should now be open to all, and they did everything they could to prevent the dictator's obtaining any decision or preparation for carrying on the war. That made the people all the readier to vote for everything the dictator proposed. He marched out of the City and, putting his army across the Tiber on rafts, wherever he was led by reports of the enemy, he fell on a good many stragglers roaming about on both banks of the river who were raiding the countryside. He also captured the enemy's camp in a surprise attack and took 8000 prisoners, and after killing or driving out of Roman territory all the rest, he was granted a triumph by the people, though without the Senate's authorization.[22]

Because of the feeling against holding consular elections under either a dictator or a consul of plebeian origin while the other consul, Fabius, was detained on his campaign, recourse was had to an interregnum. The office of interrex was held in succession by Quintus Servilius Ahala, Marcus Fabius, Gnaeus Manlius, Gaius Fabius, Gaius Sulpicius, Lucius Aemilius, Quintus Servilius and Marcus Fabius Ambustus. During the second interregnum an argument arose because two patricians were about to be named as consuls, and when the tribunes tried to interpose their veto, the interrex Fabius declared that it was laid down in the Twelve Tables that the most recent decree

22. cf. the Senate's refusal to authorize a triumph for Horatius and Valerius in 449 (III.63.11).

of the people was the effective legal ruling, and their votes also counted as a decree. The tribunes gained nothing by their intercession but the adjournment of the elections, and two patrician consuls were elected, Gaius Sulpicius Peticus (for the third time) and Marcus Valerius Publicola. 18. They entered office that same day, in the four-hundredth year from the founding of Rome,[23] the thirty-fifth from the recovery of the City from the Gauls, thus depriving the plebeians of the office of consul which they had enjoyed for ten years.

Empulum was taken from the Tiburtines that year, though no special battle is on record: either, as some authorities say, the campaign was conducted there under the auspices of both the consuls, or the consul Sulpicius laid waste the territory of Tarquinii at the same time as Valerius led his legions against the Tiburtines.

At home things were more serious for the consuls, in their battle with the people and the tribunes. Their moral duty, they thought, as well as their sense of honour, obliged them, as two patricians, to pass on the consulship they had held to successors who would also both be patrician; they should either withdraw completely from the consulship if it were now to be a plebeian magistracy, or retain intact their possession of authority undivided, as it had been given them by their fathers. Against them the people angrily demanded what was the point of being alive or counted as citizens if they could not retain by their united efforts what had been won for them by the courage of two men, Lucius Sextius and Gaius Licinius? Better put up with kings, decemvirs, or whatever harsher regime there could be, than see both consuls patricians, no giving and receiving orders in turn but one of the parties permanently set up to command and assume that the people were born for nothing but servitude. There was no lack of tribunes to provide troublemakers, but in the general spontaneous excitement it was difficult to pick out the ringleaders. After the people had gone down to the Campus Martius several times to no purpose and many voting days had been spent in rioting, the consuls'

23. Calculated on the Roman inclusive system: the date is 355 B.C., the 399th year from the foundation, taken as 754.

perseverance finally prevailed, only to precipitate an outburst of indignation on the part of the people; so that when the tribunes shouted that liberty was done for and they ought now to leave not only the voting-place but also the City, which was held captive and subjected to the tyranny of the patricians, they found support in the plebeians' resentment. The consuls were deserted by half the voting population, but were still determined to complete the elections, despite the small number of voters present. The new consuls appointed were both patricians: Marcus Fabius Ambustus (for the third time) and Titus Quinctius. In some records I find Marcus Popilius listed as consul in place of Titus Quinctius.

19. Two campaigns were successfully carried out this year against Tarquinii and Tibur, which ended in their surrender. The city of Sassula was captured from the Tiburtines and all their remaining towns would have suffered the same fate if the entire people had not laid down their arms and put themselves under the consul's protection. A triumph was held to celebrate their defeat; otherwise the victory over the Tiburtines was a lenient one. The people of Tarquinii were treated with cruel severity: many men were killed in battle, and of the huge number of captives, 358 were chosen, all from the noblest families, to be sent to Rome. The rest of the populace were massacred. The people were equally pitiless to the prisoners who had been sent to Rome: they were all publicly flogged in the middle of the Forum and then beheaded. Such was the vengeance taken on the enemy for the Romans sacrificed in the forum of Tarquinii.[24] The success of this campaign induced the Samnites as well to apply for friendship with Rome. Their envoys were given a courteous reply by the Senate, and they were granted a treaty of alliance.

At home the Roman plebs was less fortunate than in war. Although usury had been reduced by the fixing of a rate of interest at one twelfth, the indigent still found the capital sum borrowed a crushing burden which led to their enslavement for debt. Consequently the people were prevented by their

24. cf. ch. 15.10.

personal troubles from giving their minds to the fact that both
consuls were patrician or to the conduct of elections and to
matters of state. Both consulships remained in the hands of the
patricians, and the consuls elected were Gaius Sulpicius Peticus
and Marcus Valerius Publicola, for the fourth and second times
respectively.

The City was all set for an Etruscan war (for it was rumoured
that the people of Caere had joined forces with those of
Tarquinii out of sympathy for their kindred) when envoys
from the Latins drew attention to the Volscians, who, they
reported, had levied and armed an army which was already
threatening Latium, and from there would invade and
devastate Roman territory. The Senate accordingly decided
that neither risk must be ignored, and ordered legions to be
enrolled and the consuls to be allotted their commands for
both campaigns. Before long their main concern inclined
towards the Etruscan war, after a dispatch from the consul
Sulpicius, who had drawn the command against Tarquinii,
reported that the countryside round the Roman salt-works
had been devastated and part of the plunder taken off into the
territory of Caere, whose young men had undoubtedly been
among the raiders. So the Senate recalled the consul Valerius,
who was confronting the Volscians and had his camp near the
Tusculan boundary, and ordered him to name a dictator. His
choice was Titus Manlius, the son of Lucius. He in turn
appointed Aulus Cornelius Cossus as his master of Horse and,
finding the consul's army adequate for his purpose, on the
Senate's authority and at the people's order, declared war on
Caere.

20. Then for the first time the Caerites realized that there
was a genuine threat of war, as if their enemy's words were
a surer intimation of this than their own conduct in having
challenged the Romans by their raids. They perceived that
such a conflict was beyond their strength and regretted the
destruction they had done, cursing the Tarquinienses for
having instigated their defection. No one took up arms or
made preparations for war, but each man on his own account
called for envoys to be sent to beg forgiveness for his mis-

conduct. The envoys approached the Senate but were dismissed and sent on to the people. There they implored the gods, whose sacred objects they had received and religiously cared for during the Gallic war,[25] to inspire the Romans in their prosperity with pity for their plight, such as they had formerly felt for the people of Rome in their time of trouble. Then turning to the shrine of Vesta they appealed to the hospitality by which the *flamines* and Vestals had been entertained with scrupulous piety[26]: could anyone believe that people who had been worthy of that charge could suddenly become enemies without reason? Or if they had committed any hostile act, that they had done so deliberately, and not as victims of a fit of madness which had led them to allow recent misdeeds to undo their own previous acts of kindness, especially kindness shown to such grateful friends, and make an enemy of the Roman people when prosperous and highly successful in war, though they had sought their friendship in the hour of their affliction? The name 'intention' should not be given to what should be called constraint and necessity. The Tarquinienses had led a hostile army through their territory, and though they had asked only for passage through, had taken some of the local peasants to join in the raiding of which the people of Caere were now accused. If Rome wanted those men handed over they were prepared to do so, or to see that they were punished if punishment was preferred. But Caere, sanctuary of the Roman people, resting-place of priests and refuge for Roman sacred vessels, should remain inviolate and undefiled by any charge of making war, by reason of its hospitality shown to the Vestals and reverence paid to the gods. The people were moved, not so much by the arguments now put to them as by the recollection of services received in the past, and so preferred to forget an injury rather than a kindness. Peace was accordingly granted the people of Caere, and it was agreed that a hundred-year truce should be drawn up and recorded in a senatorial decree.

The full force of the war was then directed against the

25. cf. V.40.7.   26. cf. V.50.3.

Falisci, who were guilty of the same charge, but the enemy
were nowhere to be found. The Romans ranged over their
land, destroying it as they went, but refrained from attacking
their cities; and after the legions had been brought back to
Rome, the rest of the year was spent in repairing walls and
watchtowers. A temple was dedicated to Apollo.

21. At the end of the year the consular elections were
interrupted by conflict between patricians and plebeians. The
tribunes refused to allow the elections to proceed unless they
were held in accordance with the Licinian law, while the
dictator was resolutely determined to remove the office of
consul completely from the constitution rather than to throw
it open to patricians and plebeians alike. The elections were
therefore postponed until the dictator had ended his term of
office, and once more there was an interregnum. The interreges
found the plebeians hostile to the patricians, and the political
struggle continued on to the eleventh interrex. The tribunes
continued to parade their support of the Licinian law, but the
people were more concerned about their sufferings from the
increasing interest they had to pay, and their private grievances
broke out into public brawls. These wore down the senators
until they ordered the interrex Lucius Cornelius Scipio to
observe the Licinian law at the consular elections in order to
reconcile the two parties. Publius Valerius Publicola was accordingly given Gaius Marcius Rutulus as plebeian colleague.
At the first signs of a general inclination for peace, the new
consuls tackled the questions of reducing interest as well, as this
seemed to be the sole cause of dissension; they made the
discharge of debts a public concern, and appointed five officials
whom they called state bankers, as they were to handle money.
Their impartiality and application to duty won these men
honourable mention by name in the records of all the annals;
they were Gaius Duillius, Publius Decius Mus, Marcus
Papirius, Quintus Publilius and Titus Aemilius. The matter
was extremely difficult to deal with and always brought hardship to one party and very often to both, but their administration was marked by general good sense and in particular
by proper expenditure rather than waste of public money. For

where accounts were long-standing and obstructed more by
debtors' inertia than by their lack of means, either they were
repaid by the treasury from banking tables with ready cash set
up in the Forum, after first safeguarding the interests of the
people, or they were settled by a valuation, at fair prices, of
the debtor's property. The crushing burden of debt was thus
swept away not only without injustice but also without complaints from either party.

Then fear (which proved unfounded) of war with the Etruscans, on a rumour that twelve peoples had sworn alliance,
made it necessary to appoint a dictator, and this was done in
camp, where the Senate's resolution was sent to the consuls.
Gaius Julius was named and given Lucius Aemilius as master
of Horse. 22. However, all was quiet abroad. Meanwhile at
home an attempt by the dictator to have both consuls elected
from the patricians brought about an interregnum. The two
interreges introduced were Gaius Sulpicius and Marcus Fabius,
and they succeeded where the dictator's efforts had been in
vain, now that the plebeians were more amenable as a result
of the benefit they had just gained from the relief of debt; so
that both consuls elected were patricians. They were Gaius
Sulpicius Peticus himself, the former of the two interreges, and
Titus Quinctius Poenus. (Some give Caeso, others Gaius as the
praenomen of Quinctius.) Both went off to war, Quinctius
against the Falisci and Sulpicius against the Tarquinienses; but
nowhere did they meet their enemies in battle. Consequently
their campaigns were carried on against the land, which they
burnt and plundered, rather than with men. This wore down
the tenacity of both peoples, like the debilitating effect of a
lingering disease, so that they sought a truce, first from the
consuls, and then, with their permission, from the Senate. This
was granted them for forty years.

The anxiety of two threatening wars was thus allayed, and
while there was some respite from campaigning it was decided
to hold a census; for settlement of debts meant that a good deal
of property had changed ownership. But when an assembly
was announced for electing censors, Gaius Marcius Rutulus,
who had been the first plebeian dictator, upset the harmony

between the parties by announcing that he would be a candidate for the office. It certainly seemed that he had chosen the wrong moment to do this, for both the consuls at the time happened to be patricians, and they refused to consider him as a candidate. But Rutulus stuck firmly to his intention, and the tribunes supported him with all their power, in the hope of recovering the right they had lost in the consular elections. The standing of the man himself was indeed equal to any office, however high, and besides, the people particularly wished to be called to share the censorship in the person of the man who had opened up the path to the dictatorship. There was no dissenting voice raised at the elections, and so Marcius was elected censor along with Manlius.[27]

There was also a dictator this year, not from any threat of war but to prevent the Licinian law being observed at the consular elections. Marcus Fabius was elected and given Quintus Servilius as his master of Horse. However, the dictatorship made patrician solidarity no more effective at the election of consuls than it had proved at that of censors. 23. Marcus Popilius Laenas was chosen consul from the plebeians and Lucius Cornelius Scipio from the patricians.

Fortune even allowed greater glory to the plebeian consul; for when news came that a huge army of Gauls had encamped in Latin territory, Scipio was seriously ill, and the conduct of the war was given by special enactment to Popilius. He quickly set to work levying troops, ordered all the younger men to assemble under arms outside the Porta Capena, near the temple of Mars, and told the quaestors to bring the standards there from the treasury. After fully manning four legions he handed over the remaining soldiers to the praetor Publius Valerius Publicola, and advised the Senate to enrol a second army for the State to hold in reserve against the hazards of war. Once he had completed all his preparations he marched off to meet the enemy; and in order to learn their strength before testing it in a decisive battle, he occupied a hillock, the nearest he could find to the Gallic camp, and began to fortify it. The Gauls were

27. The text is corrupt here. Livy probably refers to Gnaeus Manlius, the consul mentioned in chs. 12 and 16.

fierce people who were by nature avid for a fight, and no
sooner had they seen the Roman standards in the distance than
they spread out their line intending to join battle at once. Then
they saw that the Romans were making no move to come
down to the plain, and were protected by their position on
rising ground and still more by the rampart they were making;
so, believing them to be in a state of terror and at the same time
more open to attack at a moment when they were concentrat-
ing on their fortification work, they attacked with wild cries.
Without interrupting their work, on which the soldiers of the
third line were engaged, the Romans opened the battle with
their first and second lines who stood armed and ready for
action in front of the working-party. In addition to their
fighting spirit they had the further advantage of the rising
ground, so that their javelins and spears did not fall without
effect, as so often happens when thrown on level ground, but
were kept on course by their own weight, and all found their
mark. The Gauls were weighted down by the missiles which
either pierced their bodies or stuck in their shields and made
them very heavy to carry, and though their onrush had practically taken them up the slope facing them, first they halted,
uncertain what to do, and then when mere hesitation had
weakened their spirit and increased that of their enemy, they
were pushed back and fell one upon another, creating amongst
themselves carnage more horrible than that of the battle, for
more were trampled underfoot in the headlong rout than were
killed by the sword.

24. But the Romans were not yet sure of victory. Another
trial awaited them as they came down to the plain, for the vast
numbers of the Gauls made them impervious to such a loss,
and as if a new army had sprung up again, they were urging
on fresh troops against their enemy despite his victory. The
Roman army slowed down its advance and halted; for a
second battle had to be faced when they were tired, and the
consul had had his left shoulder practically run through by a
Gallic javelin when he was rashly moving along the front line,
and had left the battle for a short time. Now the delay had
almost lost them the victory when the consul rode back to the

front standards with his wound bound up. 'What are you stopping for, men?' he cried. 'This is no Latin or Sabine enemy you deal with, one whom you can turn into an ally when defeated in battle. We have drawn sword against wild beasts, and must either shed their blood or spill our own. You have forced them back from your camp, driven them headlong downhill to the valley, and you stand on the prostrate bodies of your foe; now cover the plains with butchered corpses as you did the hills. Don't wait for them to run away while you stand still; you must press on and attack.' Roused to further action by such stirring words, the Romans pushed back the leading maniples of the Gauls and then broke through to the main army in wedge formation. At this the barbarians broke ranks and, for lack of proper command or leadership, turned their attack on their fellows; they poured over the plain in flight, which even carried them beyond their own camp, and made for the Alban Citadel,[28] the highest point they could see in the range of hills before them. The consul did not pursue them beyond their camp, for his wound was giving him pain and he was reluctant to take his army right up to the hills occupied by the enemy. He gave his soldiers all the plunder from the camp and took his victorious army back to Rome enriched with Gallic spoils. The consul's wound delayed his triumph, and was also the reason why the Senate was anxious to appoint a dictator, so that there should be someone to hold elections while the consuls were ill. Lucius Furius Camillus was appointed dictator and given Publius Cornelius Scipio as master of Horse. He returned to the patricians their old monopoly of the consulship, and in return for that service was elected consul himself with the warmest approval of the Senate. He announced the election of Appius Claudius Crassus as his colleague.

25. Before the new consuls entered office, Popilius celebrated his triumph over the Gauls, with great acclaim from the plebeians. They began to murmur amongst themselves and ask if anyone now regretted the election of a plebeian consul; at

28. Perhaps the height now called Monte Cavo.

the same time they attacked Camillus for getting himself elected consul when he was still dictator – a reward, they said, received for his contempt of the Licinian law and one which was more disgraceful for his personal greed than for the harm it did the State.

The year was notable for many disturbances of various kinds. The Gauls came down from the Alban heights, being unable to stand the severity of the winter weather, and ranged over the plains and coastal area, destroying the countryside. Greek fleets infested the sea, the coast of Antium, the Laurentine district and the mouth of the Tiber, and on one occasion the pirates encountered the land-raiders and fought an indecisive battle, so that the Gauls returned to their camp and the Greeks to their ships, both uncertain whether they had lost or won. Meanwhile by far the greatest alarm came from the gatherings of the Latin peoples at the grove of Ferentina[29] and the categorical refusal given to the Roman demand for soldiers – the Romans, they said, should stop making demands of those whose help they needed; the Latins would rather bear arms for their own liberty than for another's dominance. Caught between two foreign wars at the same time, and worried too by the defection of their allies, the Senate realized that those who had not been bound by loyalty must be held down by fear, and ordered the consuls to exert all their powers of authority to recruit troops; for they must rely on a citizen army when their allies were leaving them. Ten legions are said to have been enrolled by conscripting men of military age everywhere, from the country as well as from the City, each legion of 4200 infantry and 300 cavalry. If anything threatened us from abroad today, it would be difficult for the present resources of the people of Rome – though the world can scarcely contain them – even if concentrated on a single aim, to raise a new army of this size; so strictly has our expansion been limited only to what we work for: wealth and luxury.

Among other gloomy events of that year was the death of one of the consuls, Appius Claudius, in the midst of prepara-

29. The centre of the Latin league, south of modern Ariccia.

tions for war. The command then reverted to Camillus, and though he was left without a colleague, the Senate decided that it would be improper to put a dictator over him, either because his standing was too high to be subjected to a dictatorship or because his surname would be a good omen in the event of a Gallic rising.[30] Camillus placed two legions to defend the City and divided the remaining eight between himself and the praetor, Lucius Pinarius. With his father's prowess in mind he took command of the war with the Gauls himself, without drawing lots, and ordered the praetor to protect the sea coast and keep the Greeks from landing on its shores. Then he came down to the Pomptine district and selected a suitable site for a permanent camp; he had no wish to come to grips with the enemy in open country unless obliged to do so, and believed that he could adequately subdue the Gauls if he prevented their raids, since necessity constrained them to subsist on plunder.

26. While the Romans were quietly passing the time on guard duty they were approached by a Gaul who was out-standing for his great size and armour. He struck his shield with his spear, thereby obtaining silence, and then through an interpreter challenged someone to do battle with him. There was a young military tribune named Marcus Valerius who thought himself no less worthy of that honour than Titus Manlius,[31] so he first made certain of the consul's wishes, then took up his arms and advanced into the space between the armies. The duel proved less remarkable for its human interest than for the divine intervention of the gods, for as the Roman engaged his adversary, a raven suddenly alighted on his helmet, facing the Gaul. The tribune first hailed this with delight, as a sign sent from heaven, and then prayed for good-will and gracious support from whoever had sent him this bird, were it god or goddess. Marvellous to relate, not only did the raven keep the perch it had once chosen, but as often as the struggle was renewed it rose up on its wings and attacked the enemy's face and eyes with beak and claws, until he was terrified at the

30. cf. V.49; his father had defeated the Gauls after their sack of Rome.
31. cf. ch. 10.

sight of such a portent; and so, bewildered as well as half-blinded, he was killed by Valerius. The raven then flew off out of sight towards the east. So far the guard posts had been quiet on both sides, but when the tribune began to strip the dead body of his enemy, the Gauls left their posts and the Romans ran even faster towards the victor. There a struggle began over the prostrate body of the Gaul, which developed into a fierce battle; and this spread from the maniples of the nearest posts to involve the legions, who came rushing in from both sides. Camillus ordered his men to move in to the battle, knowing them to be elated by the tribune's victory, elated too by the presence and assistance of the gods, and, showing them the tribune decked out in his spoils, 'Copy him, soldiers,' he cried, 'and cut down the Gallic hordes round their fallen leader!' Gods and men took part in that battle, which was fought out against the Gauls with no doubt as to its outcome; so clearly had both armies foreseen the result for themselves in the outcome of the contest between the two soldiers. Amongst those who had first entered the fray and led on the rest the battle was furious, but the remaining Gallic hordes turned tail before they came within reach of a javelin-throw. At first they scattered amongst the Volscians and in the Falernian district; from there they made for Apulia and the Lower Sea.

The consul called a military assembly, praised the tribune, and bestowed on him ten oxen and a golden crown. He himself received orders from the Senate to direct the war on the coast, and joined forces with the praetor. When the campaign there seemed to be dragging on because of inactivity on the part of the Greeks, who were reluctant to risk a pitched battle, Camillus, on the Senate's authority, appointed Titus Manlius Torquatus dictator in order to hold elections. The dictator named Aulus Cornelius Cossus master of Horse, held the consular elections, and announced amid great public rejoicing the election as consul, in his absence, of a young man of twenty-three who was the rival of his own glory: namely, Marcus Valerius Corvus – for that was his surname from then on.[32]

32. *Corvus* means 'raven'.

Corvus was given as his plebeian colleague Marcus Popilius Laenas, to be consul for the fourth time. Camillus fought no memorable action against the Greeks; they were no more warriors on land than the Romans were at sea. In the end, when they were prevented from landing and their water gave out as well as other essential supplies, they left Italy. What people or nation the fleet belonged to is quite uncertain. I am very much inclined to believe that it was sent by the tyrants of Sicily,[33] for mainland Greece at that time was exhausted by internal warfare and already lived in dread of the might of Macedon.[34]

27. The armies were disbanded, and there was peace abroad and quiet at home, thanks to the harmony between the orders; but to prevent things being too happy, plague struck the City. This compelled the Senate to order the Board of Ten to consult the Sibylline Books, and on their advice a *lectisternium* was held. In the same year the people of Antium sent a colony to Satricum and rebuilt the city which the Latins had destroyed.[35] In addition, a treaty was struck at Rome with envoys from Carthage[36] who had come seeking friendship and an alliance.

The same peace continued at home and abroad throughout the consulship of Titus Manlius Torquatus and Gaius Plautius. The rate of interest was reduced from one twelfth[37] to only one twenty-fourth, and regulations for repayment of debt made one quarter payable at once and the rest in three equal annual instalments. Some of the plebeians still found this a burden, but the Senate was more concerned with public credit than with personal hardships. The greatest relief came from the remission of tax and conscription.

Two years after the rebuilding of Satricum by the Volscians,

33. i.e. Dionysius II, tyrant of Syracuse.

34. The Third Sacred War ended only by the intervention of Philip of Macedon.

35. cf. VI.33.4.

36. Livy says nothing about the earlier treaty between Rome and Carthage, nor does Diodorus Siculus (XVI.69); but Polybius (III.22) speaks of a treaty in 509, and in IX.43.26 Livy speaks of the treaty's being renewed for the third time.

37. cf. ch. 16, note 20.

when Marcus Valerius Corvus was elected consul for the second time, with Gaius Poetelius, news came from Latium that envoys from Antium were going round the Latin peoples in order to stir up war. Valerius was therefore ordered by the Senate to attack the Volscians before others joined them, and marched on Satricum. There he was confronted by the Antiates and the other Volscians who had made their forces ready beforehand to meet any move by Rome, and, as both sides had long been bitterly hostile to each other, fighting broke out without delay. The Volscians (a race fiercer as rebels than as fighters) were defeated in the battle and fled in disorder, making for the fortifications of Satricum. But even walls gave them little confidence, for the city was encircled by Roman soldiers and was being taken by scaling ladders; so they surrendered, to the number of about four thousand soldiers besides a large number of non-combatants. The town was destroyed and burnt: only the temple of Mater Matuta[38] was saved from the fire. All the loot was given to the army, but the four thousand who had given themselves up were not counted as part of the spoils. They were marched in chains before the chariot of the consul in his triumph, and subsequently sold, bringing in a large sum of money, which he gave to the treasury. According to some writers, the men captured in such large numbers were slaves, which is more probable than that surrendered soldiers were sold.

28. These consuls were succeeded by Marcus Fabius Dorsuo and Servius Sulpicius Camerinus. War then broke out with the Aurunci, as the result of a surprise raid. It was feared that this act on the part of a single people might be the joint strategy of all who called themselves Latins, so Lucius Furius was appointed dictator – as if to deal with a Latium already under arms – and Gnaeus Manlius Capitolinus named as his master of Horse. As was customary at times of crisis, the courts were suspended and troops were levied without exemptions. Then the legions were marched off with all possible speed against the Aurunci. They were found to be more like brigands than

38. cf. VI.33, note 39.

enemies, so that the first engagement put an end to the campaign. However, as they had been the aggressors, unprovoked, and had presented themselves to do battle without holding back, the dictator had thought he should summon help even from the gods, and vowed a temple to Juno Moneta[39] during the actual fighting. Being bound by this vow on his victorious return to Rome, he resigned his office. The Senate ordered the appointment of two commissioners to construct this temple on a scale befitting the grandeur of the Roman people, and a site was chosen for it on the Citadel, on ground where the house of Marcus Manlius Capitolinus used to stand. The consuls took over the dictator's army for the Volscian war and captured Sora from the enemy by means of a surprise attack.

A year after the temple was vowed it was dedicated to Moneta when Gaius Marcius Rutulus was consul for the third time and Titus Manlius Torquatus for the second. The dedication was immediately followed by a prodigy similar to the one long ago on the Alban Mount,[40] for a shower of stones rained down and darkness spread over the sky in the daytime. The Books were consulted, and as the City was full of religious forebodings, the Senate decided to appoint a dictator to arrange a public holiday for religious observance. Publius Valerius Publicola was chosen and given Quintus Fabius Ambustus as his master of Horse. It was agreed that not only the Roman tribes but also neighbouring peoples should offer supplication, and an order was fixed for the days on which they should each do so. This year, according to tradition, severe sentences were passed by the people on moneylenders brought to trial by the aediles; and the State reverted to an interregnum, for no special reason worth recording. The result of the interregnum – so that this could seem to be its purpose – was the election of consuls who were both patricians, Marcus Valerius Corvus (for the third time) and Aulus Cornelius Cossus.

29. From now on the wars described will be of greater importance. Our enemies were more powerful, and campaigns lasted longer and were mounted in remote areas. For this was

39. cf. VI.20, note 32.   40. cf. I.31.1.

134

the year when an attack was launched against the Samnites, a
people who were strong both in resources and in arms. After
the Samnite war, which was inconclusive, Pyrrhus[41] was the
enemy, and after him the Carthaginians.[42] What a series of
momentous events! How often were we in mortal danger, to
enable us to raise up our empire to its present heights of
grandeur, where only with difficulty is it sustained!

Rome and Samnium had been united in friendship and
alliance; the cause of the war came from without and did not
arise directly between them. The Samnites had unjustly
attacked the Sidicini, simply because they were more powerful. The Sidicini were helpless, and, being forced to flee for
help to a richer neighbour, had attached themselves to the
Campanians. The Campanians had brought a reputation rather
than actual strength to protect their allies; softened by luxurious
living, they were routed in the territory of the Sidicini by a
people hardened by use of arms, and then brought the whole
weight of the war on to themselves. For the Samnites left the
Sidicini alone and directed an attack on the very citadel of their
neighbours, expecting just as easy a victory there and more
plunder and glory. They had occupied Tifata, a range of hills
above Capua, and left a strong garrison there before marching
down in battle order to the plain which lies between Capua
and Tifata. There a second battle was fought; the Campanians
were the losers and were forced within their walls, and as they
had lost the best of their fighting force and had no hope of
relief at hand, they were obliged to seek aid from the Romans.

30. Their envoys, when brought before the Senate, spoke
very much in this way: 'The people of Campania have sent us
as envoys to you, Conscript Fathers, to beg for your aid at
the present moment and your friendship for all time. If we had
sought this friendship when times were happier for us, though
this could have arisen more quickly, the ties binding us would

41. Pyrrhus, King of Epirus, invaded Italy in support of Tarentum
against Rome, and the subsequent fighting between 280 and 275 was
covered by Livy in three lost books (XII–XIV).
42. The First Punic War (264–241) was the main subject of the lost
Books XVI–XIX.

not have been so strong; for in that case we could have recalled that we had entered into friendship with you on equal terms, and though perhaps as much your friends as we are now, we should have been less obliged and beholden to you. As things are, won over by your pity, defended by your assistance in time of trouble, we must have no less at heart the benefit which we have received from you, lest we appear ungrateful and unworthy of all aid, human and divine. Nor indeed can I think that the fact that the Samnites became your friends and allies before us is any reason why we should be denied your friendship; it only gives them the advantage over us of priority and honourable status. There was in fact no provision in your treaty with the Samnites against making further treaties.

'With you it has always been a sound enough reason for friendship that when you were approached it was by someone who wished to be your friend. We Campanians, even if our present situation prevents our boasting, are not inferior to any people, except yourselves, in the grandeur of our city and fertility of our soil, and our contribution to your prosperity in becoming your friends will not, I believe, be insignificant. Every time the Aequi and Volscians, your City's perpetual enemies, bestir themselves, we shall be on their backs, and what you have done first for our preservation, we shall always do for your empire and your glory. Once these peoples who come between yourselves and us are forced to submit – and your valour and good fortune promise that this will be soon – your authority will extend unbroken as far as ourselves. For our part, the admission wrung from us by our misfortune is a bitter and pitiful one: we have reached the point, Conscript Fathers, when Campania will have to be absorbed by her friends or by her enemies. If you defend us, we shall belong to you; if you abandon us, to the Samnites. Consider then whether you prefer Capua and the whole of Campania to augment your own strength or that of the Samnites.

'Your compassion, Romans, and your aid are rightly available to all, but especially to those who in answering a call for help from others have exceeded their own resources and been reduced to our present plight. Though we fought ostensibly for the Sidicini, in actual fact it was for ourselves, since we saw our neighbours cruelly threatened by those brigands the Samnites, and knew that once the Sidicini were consumed, the flames of that fire would spread to us. For if the Samnites are on their way to attack us at this moment, it is not out of resentment for some injury but in delight at the pretext offered them. But even if this was indulgence of anger and not just a chance to satisfy their greed, is it not enough for them to have massacred our legions once in Sidicinian territory, and a second time in Campania itself? What anger is that, so bitter that the blood shed in two battles cannot appease it? Add to this the devastation of our land, the plunder they have driven off, both men and cattle, the burning and destruction of farmhouses, the total havoc wrought by fire and sword. Could all this not satisfy their anger? But it is their greed which demands satisfaction. That is what hurries them on to besiege Capua; they are bent on either wiping out this most beautiful of cities or possessing it themselves. But you, Romans, must occupy it yourselves rather than let them take it: a good deed on your part, an evil one on theirs. I am not addressing a people which refuses just wars, but even so, if you will display your troops to support us, I think you will not need to go to war. Samnite scorn extends to us, but rises no higher; and so, Romans, the shadow of your help is enough to protect us, and whatever we have, or whatever we are henceforth, we shall consider all yours. For you Campanian soil shall be tilled, for you the city of Capua shall be thronged; for us you will be numbered amongst our founders, parents, and immortal gods. No colony of yours shall there be which will surpass us in obedience and loyalty towards you.

'Give your assent, Conscript Fathers, grant the Campanians a sign of your unconquered might, and bid us hope that Capua shall be spared. What massed crowds from all classes do you suppose accompanied us when we set out? What prayers and tears did we leave at every point? In what suspense at this moment are the senate and people of Campania, and our wives and children? They are all crowded at the gates, I am sure, watching the road from Rome. What answer, Conscript

Fathers, do you bid us take back to those anxious, apprehensive souls? One reply will bring them safety, victory, light and liberty; the other – I shudder to predict what it may bring. Take thought for us, then, knowing we shall either be your future allies and friends or shall have no future existence anywhere.'

31. The envoys were then sent out while the senators were asked for their opinions. A large number of them saw that this city, the largest and wealthiest in Italy, with its exceptionally fertile territory close to the sea, would serve as a granary for the Roman people to meet fluctuations in the corn supply; yet so great an advantage carried less weight than Rome's promised word. The consul was therefore instructed by the Senate to give the following reply: 'The Senate judges you worthy of assistance, Campanians, but it would be proper for us to make a pact of friendship with you only if it did not violate an earlier friendship and alliance. The Samnites and ourselves are bound by treaty, and so we must refuse to take up arms on your behalf against them; for this would do violence to the gods before it injured men. We will send envoys to our allies and friends, as is right and just, to beg them to do you no injury.' To this the leader of the delegation replied, in accordance with the instructions they had brought from home: 'Since you refuse to take justly violent action to protect what is ours against violence and injustice, at least defend what is your own. To your authority, Conscript Fathers, and that of the Roman people, we therefore submit the people of Campania, the city of Capua, our territory, the shrines of the gods and everything else, both sacred and profane. Henceforth whatever we suffer, it will be as subjects of yours after surrender.'

At these words the envoys, with hands outstretched to the consul and eyes filled with tears, prostrated themselves in the vestibule of the Senate-house. The Fathers were deeply moved by the mutability of human fortunes, when they thought how that powerful and wealthy people, renowned for its pride and luxurious living, whose help had been sought by its neighbours a short time ago, was now so broken in spirit that of its own accord it was submitting itself and all it possessed to another's rule. Now they felt their sense of honour demanded that their subjects should not be betrayed; nor did they think the Samnites would act rightly if they attacked a city and its territory which by submission had come into the possession of the people of Rome. So it was decided to send envoys to the Samnites immediately. Their instructions were to put to the Samnites the request of the Campanians, the Senate's reply with regard to their friendship with Samnium, and, finally, the Campanians' surrender. They were to ask the Samnites, in view of their alliance and friendship with Rome, to spare Rome's subjects and to make no hostile incursion into territory which had become the property of the Roman people; and if they gained little by conciliation they were to give warning to the Samnites, in the name of the Roman people and the Senate, to keep their hands off the city of Capua and Campanian territory. This the envoys put before the Samnite council, but the reply they received was harshly uncompromising. Not only did the Samnites declare their intention of carrying on with this war, but their magistrates left the council-room while the legates were still waiting, summoned the commanders of their cohorts, and then ordered them with raised voices to march out at once and raid Campanian territory.

32. When reports of this embassy reached Rome, the Senate dropped all other business and sent the fetial priests to demand redress; then when this was not granted, war was declared in the usual ritual manner. The Senate then voted to lay the question before the people at the earliest possible moment; and, acting on the people's order, both consuls left with two armies, Valerius making for Campania and Cornelius for Samnium, and set up camp, the former near Mount Gaurus, the latter near Saticula. Valerius was the first to be confronted by the Samnite legions, for they judged that the whole weight of the war would fall in that direction; at the same time resentment impelled them to act against the Campanians, who had proved so ready first to offer them aid and then to summon aid against them. At the sight of the Roman camp everyone furiously demanded the signal for battle from his leader, and declared that the Romans would suffer the same fate when

they brought help to the Campanians as these had suffered when helping the Sidicini.

Valerius waited only a few days to test the enemy in skirmishes before giving the signal for battle. He first briefly addressed his soldiers, bidding them have no fear of a strange war or strange enemy; every advance which took them further from Rome brought them against peoples who were less and less warlike. They should not judge Samnite fighting spirit by the defeats suffered by the Sidicini and Campanians; whatever the qualities of two combatants, one of them had to be the loser. In the case of the Campanians, they had undoubtedly been defeated more by the general laxity which comes from excessive luxury and their own effeminacy than by their enemy's might. Besides, what were two wars won by the Samnites in the course of so many centuries compared with all the many achievements of the Roman people? For they could count almost more triumphs than years since the City's foundation; they had subdued by arms and now dominated all around them – Sabines, Etruscans, Latins, Hernici, Aequi, Volscians and Aurunci – and had cut down the Gauls in countless battles and finally forced them to take flight to their ships and the sea. Each one of them must go into battle with confidence in such a glorious record in war as well as in his own valour, and still more should he keep in mind under whose leadership and auspices he must enter battle – was it a man who commanded attention only as a superb orator, warlike in words but ignorant of military operations, or one who knew from his own experience how to handle arms, advance in front of the standards and take his place in the thick of the fray? 'It is my deeds, not my words, soldiers,' he said, 'which I want you to follow, and you should look to me not only for training but for an example as well. Not by means of political factions nor through the conspiracies beloved of the nobility have I won for myself three consulships and the highest praise, but by this right hand of mine. There was a time when it could have been said of me "Yes, but you were a patrician, descended from your country's liberators, and your family held the consulship in the very first year that this City had a consul at all." But today the consulship is open to all, to us patricians and to you plebeians, and is the reward not of birth, as before, but of merit. So, soldiers, fix your eyes on the highest possible honour. Though you men have given me, with the gods' sanction, this new surname of Corvinus,[43] I have not forgotten the ancient name of our family, the Publicolae,[44] the People's Friends. For my part, I have always been devoted to the Roman people and still am, in peace and in war, as a private individual and in office, whether it be high or low, as tribune and consul alike, and without interruption through all my successive consulships. Now our task is urgent: with the gods' good help, seek with me a new triumph over the Samnites, a triumph never won before.'

33. There was nowhere a commander on more friendly terms with his men. Valerius cheerfully shared all their duties with the humblest of his soldiers; in military sports too, when trials of speed and strength took place among men of the same age, he was pleasant and courteous, accepting victory and defeat with the same expression on his face, and spurning no one who offered himself as a match for him. His practical kindliness fitted every situation, his speech showed as much concern for the other man's freedom as for his own dignity, and he conducted himself in office in the same manner as when he was a candidate; nothing wins greater popularity than this. And so the entire army responded to their commander's speech with extraordinary enthusiasm and marched out of the camp.

The battle began with the same expectations and equally matched strength on both sides, as well as a self-confidence which was free from contempt for the enemy, and all to an exceptional degree. The spirit of the Samnites was raised by their recent exploits and their double victory of a few days before, that of the Romans by the glories of four centuries and

43. The same form of the name appears in ch. 40. Elsewhere Livy gives the earlier form, Corvus.

44. Publicola or Poplicola was the title given to Publius Valerius, traditionally one of the first consuls and a popular lawgiver, credited with introducing the right of appeal against a magistrate's decision; cf. II.8.1.

victories which went back to the foundation of the City. Yet
both sides were apprehensive about an enemy not previously
encountered. The fighting was proof of their determination,
for they struggled for some time without either battle-line
giving way. The consul then decided that as he could not push
back the Samnites by force, he must throw them into confusion; he therefore sent in the cavalry and tried to break up
their front ranks. But when he saw the squadrons were gaining
nothing by the confusion they caused, as they had to
manoeuvre in a confined space and could not break their way
through the enemy, he rode back in front of the legionary
standards, dismounted and cried: 'This is a job for us infantry,
soldiers! Come on, watch me, and where my sword cuts a way
through the enemy's line, each of you strike down those in
your path. All that lies before you, where raised spears are
flashing now, you will see opened up with widespread
carnage.' No sooner had he said this than the cavalry, at his
command, divided and made for the wings, leaving a free
passage for the legions to attack the centre of the line. The
consul led the charge ahead of all, cutting down any who
chanced to cross his path. Fired by this sight, on right and left
the Romans fought a memorable battle, each man pushing
forward, while the Samnites stubbornly held their ground,
though they received more wounds than they inflicted.

The battle had now lasted a long time. Though there was
fearful bloodshed round the Samnites' standards, nowhere was
there any sign of retreat, so determined were they to be
conquered only by death. The Romans then realized that their
own strength was already ebbing through exhaustion and
there was not much daylight left, and they threw themselves
on their enemy in a fury. For the first time there were signs
of a retreat and the beginning of a rout; then the Samnites were
caught and killed, and there would have been few survivors
if night had not put an end to what was now a victory rather
than a battle. The Romans admitted they had never fought
with a more tenacious enemy, and the Samnites, when asked
what it was that first changed such stubborn resistance on their
part to flight, said it was the eyes of the Romans, which

seemed to them to blaze, along with their furious expression and frenzied glare. That more than anything had caused their terror – terror which was evident not only in the outcome of the battle but in their departure during the night. On the following day the Romans took possession of the empty camp, and the whole population of Campania came streaming out there to congratulate them.

34. But this rejoicing came near to being marred by a serious reverse in Samnium. The consul Cornelius, after leaving Saticula, had rashly led his army into a wood through which ran a deep ravine that was surrounded and closely guarded by the enemy, and he failed to see the threat hanging over him until he was unable to make a safe withdrawal. While the Samnites were waiting for him to send the whole army into the depths of the valley, a military tribune, Publius Decius, espied an isolated hill which rose above the wood and dominated the enemy's camp. It was difficult of access for an encumbered army, but easy for lightly equipped men. He therefore went to the consul, who was greatly alarmed. 'Do you see, sir,' he said, 'that hilltop rising above the enemy? There lies the bulwark of our hope and safety, if we are quick to capture it, as the Samnites have been so blind as to neglect it. You need not give me more than the men in the first and second ranks of a single legion. When I have reached the top with them, move on from here without further fear, and save yourself and the army; for the enemy, once exposed to all our missiles, will not be able to stir without destroying themselves. As for us afterwards – the fortune of the Roman people or our own courage will get us out of this.'

He was warmly praised by the consul and took over the detachment of soldiers. He then made his way under cover of the wood, and came close to his objective unseen by the enemy. They were then all struck with astonishment, and when he had fixed every eye on himself, Decius gave the consul time to withdraw the army to a more favourable position, and took up his position on the top of the hill. The Samnites wheeled their standards hither and thither and lost both their opportunities; they could neither pursue the consul, except along the ravine where a short time ago they had him exposed to their missiles, nor take their army up the hill which Decius had captured above their position. But their fury spurred them on – especially against those who had snatched their chance of victory from their hands – as did, still more, the nearness of the place and the small numbers occupying it; one moment they were all for surrounding the hill with armed men, to cut Decius off from the consul, another for leaving a way open so that they could attack his men when they had come down into the ravine. Before they could decide what to do darkness fell.

Decius first had hopes of fighting the Samnites from above while they were climbing the hill; then he was amazed when they neither offered battle nor, if deterred from that plan by the disadvantages of their position, surrounded themselves with earthworks and a palisade. At that point he called the centurions to him. 'Whatever is this reluctance and ignorance of warfare?' he asked. 'How did such people ever win a victory over the Sidicini and the Campanians? You see how their standards are moving this way and that, first brought together and then deployed; and how no one starts any defensive work, though we could have had a rampart round us by now. We'll be no better than they if we linger here longer than it suits us. Come on now, follow me, and while there is still some daylight let us see if we can find out where they put their guard-posts, and where there's a way out of here.' All this he then investigated, wrapped in a common soldier's cloak and taking with him the centurions, also dressed like men from the ranks, so that the enemy should not see that the commander was in the reconnaissance party.

35. He then placed his watch guards and gave orders for word to be passed round all the other men that when the trumpet sounded the signal for the second watch they should arm and assemble round him in silence. When they had done so, quietly as they were told, he told them that they must maintain this silence while listening to him, without any of the usual soldiers' acclaim. 'When I have finished explaining my plan,' he said, 'those of you who like it will move across to my right without

a word; we shall abide by the decision of the majority. Now listen to what I have in mind. You may be surrounded here by the enemy, but you weren't driven here by running away or left through lagging behind; your own courage took the place for you and it must be your courage which gets you out of it. By coming here you have saved a splendid army for the Roman people; by breaking out from here now save yourselves. You were the right sort of men to bring help to so many, though there were few of you, and to need no one's aid yourselves. You have an enemy to deal with who couldn't bestir himself to make use of yesterday's opportunity to destroy a whole army, who failed to see a hill so strategically sited as to threaten his existence before we captured it, and, though we are so small a party and he has so many thousands of men, neither did he stop us from climbing it nor, when we held it and there was plenty of daylight left, did he hem us in with earthworks. He was wide awake and watching when you slipped through his fingers like this, so you ought to be able to fool him when he is asleep. Or rather, you have got to do so – we are in such a tight corner that I can only point out your necessity to you: I've no plan to unfold. For there is no question of discussing whether to stay here or go, now Fortune has left you nothing but arms and the spirit to make use of them, and if we fear the sword more than is proper for men who are also Romans, we must die of hunger and thirst. So our only safety lies in breaking out from here and getting away, and that we must do either in the daytime or at night. Now here's another thing, still less in doubt: if we wait for daylight, what hope have we that the enemy won't barricade us in with a continuous rampart and ditch, seeing that he has now, as you see, completely surrounded this hill with the recumbent bodies of his own men? But if night is the right time for our breakout, as it must be, this is surely the best hour of the night for it. The signal for the second watch brought you to gather here, the time when sleep lies heaviest on mortals; you will make your way between sleeping bodies, either escaping notice by keeping quiet when they are off their guard, or ready to plunge them into a state of panic by a sudden shout if they perceive you. Only follow me, as you have followed me before; I will follow the same Fortune that has led us here. Come on then, those who see the advantage of this, over to my right.'

36. They all crossed over, and then followed Decius as he made his way through the spaces left between the guard-posts. They had already got halfway through the camp when a soldier stepping over the prostrate bodies of some sleeping guards knocked his shield and made a noise which woke the sentry. He shook the man nearest to him and they both stood up and roused the others, not knowing if they heard friends or enemies, whether the Roman detachment was breaking out or the consul had captured the camp. Decius saw they were discovered and told the soldiers to raise a shout, so that on top of being stupefied with sleep the Samnites were petrified with terror, which prevented them from arming promptly, and resisting the Romans or pursuing them. Amidst the Samnites' panic and confusion the party of Romans cut down all the guards in their path and pressed on to the consul's camp.

The night had not yet ended and they now appeared to be safe, when Decius said 'All honour to your courage, Roman soldiers! Every age to come will extol your expedition and your return. But such courage needs the light of day to display it, and you deserve better than to return to camp in all your glory in silence and under cover of darkness; let us rest here and wait for the dawn.' The men fell in with his suggestion. At the first sign of light, they sent a messenger on ahead to the consul, and the camp was awakened to immense rejoicing. When word was sent round that the men who had risked their lives in certain peril for the general safety were returning unharmed, the army poured out, each man on his own account, to meet them with praise and congratulations, hailing them as their saviours, one and all. They praised and thanked the gods, and Decius they lauded to the skies. Then Decius made a triumphal entry into the camp, as he marched through to the centre with his detachment under arms; all eyes were fixed on him, and the tribune was received with every honour equal to a consul's. When he reached the praetorium the consul had the trumpet sound to call an assembly, and started to praise Decius as he deserved; but he deferred his speech when Decius himself intervened. His advice was that everything should be postponed while such an opportunity was in their grasp, and he prevailed on the consul to attack the enemy while they were still bewildered by the night alarm and were scattered around the hill in separate detachments; some of them too, he thought, would have been sent to pursue him and would be wandering about in the wood. The legions were ordered to arm and marched out of the camp; they were led in the direction of the enemy by a more open route, as the wood was now better known from reports by scouts. Their surprise attack caught the Samnites unprepared, for they were scattered far and wide, mostly unarmed, and were unable either to assemble or take up arms or withdraw inside their entrenchment. First they were driven in panic into their camp, then the outposts were overwhelmed and the camp itself was taken. The uproar re-echoed all round the hill and sent everyone running from his post, so that a great many of the Samnites gave up without meeting their enemy. Those whom terror had driven inside their ramparts (about thirty thousand in number) were all killed, and the camp was sacked.

37. After this was satisfactorily settled, the consul called an assembly and not only completed the eulogy of Publius Decius he had begun before but extended it to cover his fresh merits. In addition to other military gifts, he presented Decius with a golden crown and a hundred oxen, plus one especially fine animal, a fat white one with gilded horns. The soldiers who had been in his party were granted a double grain ration for life, and for the present received an ox each and two tunics. After the consul's presentation, the legions placed on Decius's head the wreath of grass for delivery from siege,[45] to the accompaniment of congratulatory cheers, and his own detachment crowned him with a second wreath to mark the same honour. Wearing these decorations Decius sacrificed the special ox to Mars, and presented the other hundred to the

45. This is described in Pliny, *NH* XXII.6. Traditionally it was made of grass gathered from the beleaguered site.

soldiers who had been with him on the expedition. To the same soldiers the legions contributed a pound of spelt each and a pint of wine. All this was done with immense enthusiasm, the soldiers' cheering testifying to their unanimous approval.

A third battle was fought near Suessula, for after the rout of their army by Marcus Valerius, the Samnites had called up all their best men of military age and decided to try their fortune in one last battle. From Suessula anxious messengers came to Capua to beg for help, and from there horsemen riding fast went on to the consul Valerius with the same request. The army was immediately set in motion, the baggage was left in the camp under a strong garrison, and the troops led off at a rapid pace. A site was chosen for a camp which was not far from the enemy, and though very small would do for men who had only their horses with them and none of the usual large numbers of packhorses and camp servants. The Samnite army formed up in battle-line, on the assumption that fighting would not be delayed; then when no one came forward to meet them they advanced to attack the Roman camp. When they saw the soldiers behind the rampart, and the scouts they had sent out to reconnoitre the camp from all sides reported that it was squeezed into so small an area that its numbers could be inferred to be small, the whole army began to grumble and say they ought to fill up the ditches, breach the rampart and burst into the camp. This foolhardiness would have ended the war had not their commanders curbed the soldiers' impetuosity. But because their own large numbers were a heavy drain on their supplies, and the earlier blockade of Suessula and now the delay in fighting meant that there would soon be a scarcity of everything, the Samnites decided that while the enemy was cowering in terror behind its earthworks, soldiers should be sent out to forage in the countryside. Meanwhile they argued that if the Romans took no action, as they had come without baggage, bringing with them only what corn they could carry on their backs, along with their weapons, they would soon have nothing at all.

When the consul saw the enemy dispersed around the countryside leaving the guard-posts thinly manned, he said a few words of encouragement to his men and led them out to attack the Samnite camp. This he took at the first shout and onrush, killing more men in their tents than at the gates or on the rampart, and gave orders for the captured standards to be collected in one place. He then left two legions to guard them and act as a garrison, under strict instructions not to take plunder until he had returned, and set off with his troops in close marching order, while the cavalry he had sent on ahead rounded up the scattered Samnites, like hunters with a net, and cut them down in large numbers. For in their terror they could not decide under what standard to rally together, nor whether to make for their camp or go on running further away. So urgent was their fear and impulse to escape that up to forty thousand shields were brought to the consul, though not nearly so many men were killed, while the military standards, including those captured in the camp, numbered about a hundred and seventy. The Romans then returned to the Samnite camp and there all the plunder was given to the soldiers.

38. The happy result of this action led the Falisci, who already had a truce, to ask the Senate for a treaty, and the Latins, whose armies were already prepared for action, to transfer their campaign from the Romans to the Paeligni. Nor was the renown of such a success confined to Italy; the Carthaginians also sent envoys to Rome with congratulations and the gift of a golden crown weighing twenty-five pounds to be placed in the shrine of Jupiter on the Capitol. Both consuls celebrated triumphs over the Samnites, and behind them marched Decius, conspicuous in his gifts and his glory; for the tribune's name was heard as often as the consuls' in the rough army ribaldry.

Deputations from the Campanians and Suessulani were then given a hearing, and their request was granted that they should be sent a garrison to spend the winter among them and protect them from Samnite raids.

Capua was even then a most unhealthy spot for military discipline, seducing the minds of the soldiers by all the pleasures it could provide, so that they forgot their homeland and began

to plot in their winter quarters how they could take Capua
from the Campanians by the same sort of criminal act as the
Campanians had employed to take it from its original inhabitants.[46] If their own example was turned against them, they
argued, it would not be undeserved. Why should the Campanians hold the richest land in Italy and a city worthy of the
land when they were incapable of protecting themselves or
their property, rather than the victorious army which had
expelled the Samnites by its own sweat and blood? Was it right
that men who had surrendered to them should enjoy the
delights of that fertility while they who were worn out with
campaigning had to struggle with disease-ridden, arid soil
outside Rome, or to endure inside it the deep-seated evil of
usury which went on increasing from day to day?

These schemes were still being discussed at secret meetings
and were not yet generally known to all the troops when they
were discovered by the new consul Gaius Marcius Rutulus,
who had drawn Campania as his sphere of action, while his
colleague Quintus Servilius remained near Rome. Rutulus
had learned much from age and experience, for this was his
fourth consulship, and he had also been dictator and censor,
so when he had full knowledge through the tribunes of just
what had been going on he thought he could best counteract
the soldiers' impatience for action by extending their hopes of
carrying out their plan whenever they wanted. He therefore
circulated the rumour that the garrisons would winter again
in the same towns the following year – for they had been
divided up between the cities throughout Campania, and
schemes which originated in Capua had spread to the entire
army. Once this respite was given to the conspiracies, the
disaffection died down for the present.

39. The consul brought his troops to their summer camp,
and while he was keeping the Samnites from taking action, he
decided to purge the army of its troublesome members by
discharging them; some he said had completed their term of
service, others were weighed down by years or lacking in

46. i.e. the Etruscans. cf. IV.37.2, though Livy says there that it was
the Samnites who took it then in a night massacre.

physical strength. Certain soldiers were sent away on leave,
individually at first and then by cohorts, on the grounds that
they had spent the winter far from their homes and personal
affairs; under pretext too of military requirements they were
sent in different directions, and large numbers were thus
removed. The other consul and the praetor detained a great
many of them in Rome by inventing one delay after another.
To start with, at any rate, the soldiers were unaware of the
trick played on them and were very willing to see their homes
again; later on they saw that the first to go did not return to
active service, that scarcely anyone was sent away apart from
those who had wintered in Campania, and that the choice
from these fell particularly on the leading troublemakers.
They were surprised at first, and then seized with definite fears
that their schemes were discovered and that soon they would
have to face inquiries, denunciations, executions in secret of
each in turn, along with the cruel, unbridled tyranny which
consuls and senators exercised over them. Such were the
rumours spread secretly by the soldiers in the camp when they
realized that the consul's stratagem had plucked the heart out
of the conspiracy.

One cohort which was stationed not far from Anxur took
up a position near Lautulae, in a narrow pass between the
mountains and the sea, in order to intercept the soldiers whom
the consul was dismissing, for one reason or another, as has
been told before. They were soon a very large party, and
lacked nothing but a commander to form themselves into a
regular army. As it was, they straggled on as they pleased,
pillaging as they went, until they reached Alban territory,
where they encamped and entrenched themselves under the
ridge of Alba Longa. Once the work was finished they spent
the rest of the day arguing about the choice of a general, for
they had little confidence in any of those present. But whom
could they summon from Rome? What patrician or plebeian
was there who would knowingly expose himself to such
danger? Who could properly be entrusted with the cause of
an army maddened by its grievances? The same question was
being discussed the following day, when some of the men

roving about for plunder reported they had heard that Titus
Quinctius[47] was working on his farm near Tusculum, with no
thought of the City or honours. This man belonged to a
patrician family and had had an army career of great distinction, but when this was cut short after a wound in one foot
had made him lame, he decided to live in the country, far from
the Forum and political strife. The soldiers knew who he was
as soon as they heard his name and demanded that he should
be sent for, hoping that all would go well; but as there was
small prospect that he would do anything of his own accord,
they agreed to use force and intimidation. And so when those
who had been sent for this purpose entered his farmhouse at
dead of night and surprised Quinctius sound asleep, they told
him he had no alternative between command with honour and
death – and when he held back, they threatened death unless
he came with them. They took him off to the camp, where
he was promptly hailed as general on arrival, presented with
the insignia of office in spite of his bewilderment at the strange
suddenness of what had happened, and ordered to lead them
to the City. Thereupon, acting more on their own impulse
than by any decision of their commander, they tore up the
standards and marched off, ready for action, as far as the eighth
milestone on what is now the Appian Way; and they would
have gone straight on to the City had they not heard that an
army was coming to confront them and that Marcus Valerius
Corvus had been named dictator to deal with them, with
Lucius Aemilius Mamercus as his master of Horse.

40. As soon as the armies came in sight of one another and
recognized each other's arms and standards, they were all
immediately reminded of their homeland, and their anger died
away. They were not yet hardened to shedding the blood of
their fellow-citizens, they knew none but foreign wars, and
they believed that madness could go no further than defection
from their own people. And so on both sides commanders and
soldiers soon sought how to meet and talk together; Quinctius
had had enough of fighting, even on behalf of his country, and

47. Titus Quinctius Poenus, consul in 351; cf. ch. 22.3, where Livy
says his *praenomen* is also given as either Caeso or Gaius.

much less did he intend to fight against it; Corvinus's affection extended to all his fellow-citizens, particularly to the soldiers, and to his own army above all. He came forward to parley, and, once he was recognized, his adversaries as much as his own men showed their respect for him and immediately granted him silence to speak.

'Soldiers,' he said, 'as I left the City I prayed to the immortal gods, who are both yours and mine, and humbly begged them to grant me not a victory over you, but the honour of bringing about a reconciliation. There have been enough occasions, and will be more, to provide glory in war; this is the time to seek for peace. The petition I begged of the immortal gods as I made my vows you can enable me to obtain yourselves, if you are willing to remember that you are not encamped in Samnium or amongst the Volscians but on Roman soil, that the hills you see are those of your homeland, that this army is made up of your fellow-citizens, and that I am your consul under whose leadership and auspices last year you twice routed the Samnite legions and twice took their camp by storm. I am Marcus Valerius Corvus, soldiers, whose nobility you have recognized yourselves through the benefits, not the injuries you have received. I have not instigated any repressive law against you or any harsh senatorial decree, and in all my commands I have been stricter with myself than with you. Yet if any man's origin, his merit, dignity and honours have ever been able to inspire pride in him, my birth, the proof I gave my character, and the early age at which I held the consulship were such that when elected consul at the age of twenty-three[48] I could have treated not only the plebeians but the patricians too with equal insolence. But was any deed or word of mine when consul harder to bear than what you heard from me as tribune? In the same spirit I carried out the duties of two subsequent consulships, the spirit that I shall bring to my present dictatorship with all its powers; so that I shall be no more indulgent towards these soldiers who are mine and belong to their country than to you who are – I shudder to

48. cf. ch. 26.12.

say it – our enemies. You then will draw sword on me before I draw it on you; it will be on your side that the trumpets give the signal, that the war-cry will first be raised and the attack be launched, if fighting there must be. Steel your hearts then to do what your fathers and grandfathers never did – neither those who seceded to the Sacred Mount nor those who later encamped on the Aventine.[49] Wait until each of you sees, as once Coriolanus saw, your mothers and wives pouring out of the City to meet you, tearing their hair.[50] On that occasion the Volscian legions, because they had a Roman general at their head, ceased action; but you, a Roman army, refuse to give up your wicked war! Titus Quinctius, whatever place you occupy over there, whether willingly or against your will, if we must fight, you at least should go back to the rear; it would even be more honourable to flee and turn your back on your fellow-citizens than to fight against your country. Alternatively, if you intend to offer peace, you will hold your place in the front line with credit and honour, and speak for your side in this parley that good may come of it. Make requests which are just and you shall have them granted; yet it would be better to put up with injustice than for us to shed all sense of patriotic duty and fight each other.'

Titus Quinctius was moved to tears as he turned to his followers. 'In me too, soldiers,' he said, 'if I am any use to you at all, you will find a better leader towards peace than to war. For it was no Volscian or Samnite who spoke those words just now but a Roman, your consul and your general, soldiers. You have proved the value of his auspices on your behalf; do not try to prove their worth against yourselves. The Senate had other commanders who could make war on you more ruthlessly; but they chose one who would show most mercy to you, his soldiers, one who would best win your confidence as your general. Peace is the desire even of men well able to conquer; what then should our own desire be? Should we not forget hope and anger, those treacherous counsellors, and entrust ourselves and all our interests to the integrity we know?'

49. cf. II.32.2 and III.50.13.
50. cf. II.40.

41. There were loud cries of approval everywhere as Titus Quinctius stepped in front of the standards and declared that the soldiers would accept the dictator's authority. He begged him to take on the cause of his unhappy fellow-citizens and, having done so, to defend it with all the integrity he had brought to his handling of state affairs. For himself, he said, he needed no personal assurance, for he wished to rest his hopes on nothing but his own innocence. But the soldiers must have the assurance that in their forebears' time had been given once to the people and a second time to the legions: that their defection should not do them injury.

After congratulating Quinctius and bidding the other soldiers to be of good heart, the dictator returned at the gallop to Rome, and there on the Senate's authority he met the people in the Peteline Wood and put the proposal that none of the soldiers should suffer for their defection. He also begged them, as Roman citizens, to do him the favour of not reproaching anyone for what he had done, either in jest or in earnest. A military *lex sacrata*[51] was also passed, forbidding the name of any enrolled soldier to be erased without his consent,[52] and an additional proviso forbade anyone to be a chief centurion in a legion where he had previously served as military tribune. This clause was demanded by the conspirators because of Publius Salonius, who in almost unbroken succession was one year military tribune and next year first centurion, or *primipilus*, as it is now called. He was much disliked by the army because he had always opposed their subversive schemes, and had fled from Lautulae so as not to be associated with them. And so when this was the sole item to which the Senate would not agree, out of regard for Salonius, he implored the Conscript Fathers not to put any consideration for his position before harmony in the State, and induced the Senate to pass this too. Another demand was equally insolent – that the cavalry should have their pay reduced (at that time it was triple that of the

51. i.e. a law the breaking of which made a man *sacer*, outlawed and devoted to the gods of the Underworld. cf. IX.39.5.
52. Because a man on active service could not have his goods seized as a debtor or be denied his share of gains from the campaign.

legionaries) on the grounds that they had opposed the conspiracy.

42. As well as these incidents, I find that, according to certain authors, one of the tribunes of the people, Lucius Genucius, put the proposal to the plebeians that lending money at interest should be forbidden: while other plebiscites stipulated that no one should hold the same office twice within ten years, nor two offices in one year, and that it should be permissible to elect both consuls from the plebeians. If the people gained all these concessions, evidently the revolt had considerable influence. Other annals have recorded that Valerius was not made dictator but the whole affair was carried out by the consuls, and that it was not before they came to Rome but actually when in Rome that this band of conspirators was incited to armed revolt; that the night attack was not made on the farmhouse of Titus Quinctius but on the town house of Gaius Manlius, and it was he who was seized by the conspirators to be their leader. In this account they reached the fourth milestone and established themselves in a position they had fortified. No suggestion of reconciliation was made by the commanders, but the two armies had actually gone forward under arms to do battle when suddenly they hailed each other, and the soldiers began to mix together, clasping hands and embracing each other in tears, so that the consuls had seen that the men were in no mood to fight and were obliged to put before the Senate proposals for restoring harmony. Thus there is no agreement between the ancient authorities on any point, apart from the fact that there was a revolt, and it was settled.

The report of this revolt, along with the gravity of the war which the Romans had taken on against the Samnites, turned several peoples against alliance with Rome. The Latins had long been disloyal to the treaty, and now even the Privernates, in a surprise raid, laid waste the neighbouring Roman colonies of Norba and Setia.

BOOK VIII

1. The consuls were now Gaius Plautius (for the second time) and Lucius Aemilius Mamercus, when messengers from Setia and Norba arrived at Rome with news that the Privernates were in a state of revolt, as well as with complaints of a defeat their own people had suffered. It was also reported that a Volscian army, led by people from Antium, had encamped near Satricum. The conduct of both wars fell by lot to Plautius. He first marched on Privernum, where he fought a battle immediately in which the enemy were defeated without much of a struggle. The town was captured and given back to its inhabitants, after a strong garrison had been put in it, but two thirds of their territory were taken from them. The victorious army was then taken on to Satricum to confront the Antiates. There the fighting was fierce, with heavy losses on both sides, and was interrupted by a storm before either army could realize its expectations. The Romans were in no way weakened by so indecisive a struggle and prepared to do battle on the following day, but when the Volscians had counted up the men they had lost on the battlefield they were not at all eager to run into danger a second time, and marched off apprehensively to Antium during the night like defeated men, leaving their wounded and part of their baggage behind. A great quantity of arms was found, not only amongst the enemy's dead but also in their camp. The consul announced that he was dedicating these to Mother Lua,[1] and proceeded to lay waste the enemy's territory as far as the sea coast.

Aemilius, the other consul, entered Sabine territory, but came upon no Samnite camp or army anywhere. He was destroying the countryside with fire and sword when he was approached by Samnite envoys begging for peace. He referred

1. i.e. as a burnt offering. Lua Mater was a consort of Saturn who expiated blood shed in battle. In XLV.33 Livy describes captured spoils being burnt in dedication to her along with Mars and Minerva.

them to the Senate. There they were granted permission to
speak and, dropping their truculent attitude, they besought the
Romans to grant them peace and the right to make war on
the Sidicini. Their requests, they said, were the more reasonable
because they had entered into friendship with the Roman
people when their own fortunes were flourishing and not, like
the Campanians, when everything was against them. Moreover, they were asking to take up arms against the Sidicini,
who were always their enemies and never friendly to Rome,
who had never, like the Samnites, sought friendship in peace
or, like the Campanians, asked for help in time of war, and
who were not under the protection of the Roman people or
subject to them. 2. These requests were put to the Senate by
the praetor Titus Aemilius, and when the senators voted that
the Samnites should be granted a treaty, the praetor gave the
Samnite envoys their reply: it was no fault of the Roman
people that friendly relations had been interrupted, but since
the Samnites had themselves grown tired of a war for which
they were to blame, the Romans would raise no objection to
restoring friendly relations. As for the Sidicini, the Romans
would not interfere with a free decision of the Samnite people
whether to be at peace or war. A treaty was agreed, the envoys
went home, and the Roman army was withdrawn at once,
after receiving a year's pay and a three months' corn ration,
which the consul had fixed to cover the period of truce until
the envoys had returned.

The Samnites marched out against the Sidicini with the
same forces they had used in the war with Rome, and were
confidently hoping they would speedily capture the enemy's
city, when an attempt was made by the Sidicini to forestall this
by surrendering to the Romans. Then when the Senate rejected
this offer, as it came too late and was wrung from them only
by the direst necessity, they offered to surrender to the Latins,
who had already risen in arms on their own account. Even the
Campanians were prepared to join in the fighting – so much
more vivid was their recollection of the wrongs they had
received from the Samnites than of kindness shown them by
Rome. From all these peoples a single huge army was formed

under Latin leadership which entered Samnite territory and
created more havoc by pillaging raids than in battle; and
although the Latins came off best in their encounters, they
were quite glad to leave enemy territory and not to have to
fight further. That gave the Samnites time to send envoys to
Rome. When these appeared before the Senate, they complained that they were receiving the same treatment now they
were allies as they had when they had been enemies, and most
humbly besought the Romans to rest content with having
snatched from the Samnites a victory over their Campanian
and Sidicinian foes, and not to let them actually be defeated
by the most cowardly of peoples. If the Latins and Campanians,
they said, were subject to the Roman people, then the Romans
should exercise their authority to keep them out of Samnite
territory; but if these peoples rejected that authority, they
should be restrained by force of arms. To this plea they were
given an ambiguous reply; for the Romans disliked having to
admit that they no longer had the Latins under their control,
and were afraid of provoking them to disaffection if they
censured them. The Campanians, they said, were on a different
footing, because they had come under Roman protection by
surrender, not by treaty, and should therefore maintain peace,
whether they wanted to or not; but there was nothing in their
treaty with the Latins which enabled the Romans to prevent
their making war on anyone they liked.

3. This reply sent the Samnites away quite uncertain of
Roman intentions, while it alarmed and alienated the Campanians, and emboldened the Latins by suggesting that there
was now no concession the Romans were not willing to make.
And so the Latin leaders, under pretext of preparing a campaign against the Samnites, called frequent councils and in all
their deliberations began secretly to plot war against Rome.
The Campanians also took part in this war against their pro-
tectors. But although all their preparations were deliberately
concealed, for they wanted to shake the Samnite enemy off
their backs before the Romans were alerted, information
about the conspiracy still leaked out and reached Rome
through certain people who were connected by personal ties

of hospitality and kinship. The consuls were ordered to resign office before their time was up, and to speed up the election of new consuls in order to cope with so serious a war, but there were then religious scruples about elections being held by those whose authority had been cut short; and so there was an interregnum. There were two interreges, Marcus Valerius and Marcus Fabius; the latter named as consuls Titus Manlius Torquatus (for the third time) and Publius Decius Mus.

It is generally thought that this was the year in which Alexander, King of Epirus,[2] brought a fleet to Italy, and if his attack had had a more successful beginning, it would undoubtedly have spread to reach the Romans. This was also the time of the exploits of Alexander the Great, the son of this man's sister, who was destined to be cut off in his youth by sickness, in another part of the world,[3] though in war he had proved invincible.

But though the defection of their allies and all who called themselves Latins was not in doubt, the Romans still behaved as if concerned for the Samnites and not for themselves, and summoned to Rome ten leading men from the Latins to receive such orders as they wanted to give. Latium at the time had two praetors, Lucius Annius of Setia and Lucius Numisius of Circeii, both from Roman colonies; through their influence the Volscians (apart from Signia and Velitrae, which were also Roman colonies) had also been incited to take up arms. It was decided to summon these men by name. It was quite clear to everyone why they were sent for, and so before setting out for Rome, the praetors called a council, explained that they had been summoned by the Roman Senate, and asked for instructions on what answers to give to the questions they expected would be put to them.

4. While different suggestions were being made, Annius spoke. 'Though I asked you myself for instructions on what to reply, I still think that how we should act will affect the

2. Alexander was King of Molossia in Epirus from 342 to 330 B.C. His campaign in south Italy at the request of Tarentum and his death are described in ch. 24, but here are dated some ten years too early.

3. In 323, at the age of nearly thirty-three, at Babylon.

main issue more than what we should say. It will be easy to find words to fit our actions once we have set our plans in order. For if we are able to endure slavery even now when we have a pretence of a fair treaty, doesn't that mean that we are as good as abandoning the Sidicini, obeying the bidding of the Samnites as well as of the Romans, and answering the Romans that we will lay down our arms whenever they give the word? But if at last we feel the painful stirrings of a longing for liberty, if treaties and alliances mean true equality of rights, if we may now glory in our kinship with the Romans, of which we were once ashamed, if by "allied army" they mean one which, when added to their own, doubles its strength, one which they would not wish to make its own separate decisions on starting and ending war, why is there not equality in everything? Why is not one consul provided by the Latins? Where strength is shared, there should also be sharing of authority.

'In itself this can be no great honour for us, since we accept that Rome is the capital of Latium, but we have made it seem one by putting up with the situation so long. But if ever at any time you have wanted a chance to share authority and win your freedom, now is your moment, granted you by your own valour and the gods' good-will! You have tried their patience by refusing them troops; who doubts that they were furious when we broke the tradition of two hundred years? Yet they swallowed their resentment. We fought a campaign on our own account against the Paeligni; those who previously withheld from us the right to protect even our own territory by ourselves did not intervene. They have heard how we took the Sidicini under our protection, how the Campanians have left them to join us, and how we are preparing armies against the Samnites, their allies under treaty; but they have not bestirred themselves to leave the City. Where does this excess of restraint on their part spring from if not from an awareness of our strength in comparison with their own? I have it on good authority that when the Samnites complained of us, the reply they received from the Roman Senate made it quite clear that even the Romans no longer required Latium to be under

Roman authority. All you have to do is to take up in your demands what they are tacitly conceding. If anyone is inhibited by fear from saying this – why, I declare in the hearing not only of the people and Senate of Rome, but of Jupiter himself who dwells on the Capitol, that I will say it myself: if they want us to adhere to the treaty of alliance, they must accept from us one of the consuls and a proportion of the Senate.' This bold advice and confident assurance were received with a unanimous shout of approval, and Annius was authorized to act and speak in accordance with the best interests of the Latin League and with his own honour.

5. When the Latins arrived in Rome they were given an audience by the Senate in the Capitol. There the consul Titus Manlius, on the senators' instructions, tried to persuade them not to make war on the Samnites, who were allies by treaty with the Romans; but Annius spoke out as if he were a conqueror who had taken the Capitol by storm, not like any envoy under protection of the law of nations. 'It was high time, Titus Manlius, and you, Conscript Fathers,' he said, 'that you stopped treating us as in any sense your subjects, when you can see that Latium, by favour of the gods, is so flourishing in men and arms, with the Samnites defeated in war, the Sidicini and Campanians received as allies, and now even the Volscians as well. You can see too that even your own colonies have preferred Latin to Roman rule. But since you have no intention of putting an end to your tyranny, we must act. Though we are well able to set Latium free by force of arms, we will make this concession to our kinship with you: we offer terms of peace which shall be equally fair to both of us, since the immortal gods have willed that we shall be equal in strength. One consul ought to be chosen from Rome, the other from Latium; the Senate must be drawn equally from both peoples, and there must be one nation and one State; and so that there may be the same seat of authority and the same name for all, as one side must make necessary concessions from which both sides may benefit, by all means let this be our mother-city, and let us all be called Romans.'

It so happened that the Romans had in their consul Titus

Manlius a match for Annius's outspokenness. He was far from suppressing his anger; in fact he openly declared that if the Conscript Fathers were so crazy as to allow a Latin from Setia to impose laws he would gird on his sword, enter the Senate, and kill any Latin he saw in the Senate-house with his own hand. Then, turning to the statue of Jupiter, 'Listen to these wicked words, Jupiter,' he cried, 'and you listen too, Justice and Right! Are you to behold alien consuls and an alien Senate in your dedicated temple, to witness your own overthrow and enslavement? Are these the treaties, Latins, which Tullus, King of Rome, made with the Albans, your forefathers, which Lucius Tarquinius afterwards made with you?[4] Don't you remember the battle at Lake Regillus?[5] Have you so completely forgotten your old defeats and our generosity to you?'

6. The consul's words were taken up by the general indignation in the Senate. Tradition relates that above the repeated appeals to the gods, whom the consuls called on again and again as the witnesses to treaties, the voice of Annius was heard rejecting the godhead of Roman Jupiter. It seems certain that when he rushed at top speed out of the temple entrance, beside himself with rage, he slipped on the steps and hit his head so hard on the bottom stone that he lost consciousness; but as the authorities do not all say that he was killed, I too may leave the question open, as also the tradition that while the senators were calling the gods to witness that treaties were broken, there was a violent thunder-clap and whirlwind. Such things may well be true, or they may be invented as aptly portraying the wrath of the gods. Torquatus was sent by the Senate to dismiss the envoys, and when he saw Annius lying there he cried out in a voice audible to both people and senators: 'It is well: the gods have started a righteous war. There *is* a heavenly power, and you do exist, great Jupiter; not in vain did we consecrate you in this seat. Why do you hesitate, men of Rome, and you, Conscript Fathers, to take up arms with the gods to lead you? I shall cut down the legions of the Latins to lie as you see their envoy lying here.' The consul's speech was

4. cf. I.24 and I.52.
5. cf. II.19–20; VI.2.3 and note 7.

acclaimed by the people, and created such excitement that the departing envoys were shielded from the violence and fury of the crowd more by the protection of the magistrates bidden by the consul to escort them than by the law of nations. The Senate also agreed on war, and the consuls enlisted two armies and marched off through the territory of the Marsi and Paeligni. They were joined by an army of Samnites and set up camp near Capua, where the Latins and their allies had already assembled.

There in the stillness of night, both consuls, it is said, were visited by the same apparition, that of a man of superhuman stature and majesty, who told them that the general on one side and the army on the other were due as an offering to the gods of the Underworld and to Mother Earth; if either army's general should devote to death the enemy's legions and himself in addition to them, victory would fall to the people on his side. When the consuls had compared these nocturnal visions, they decided to slaughter victims in order to avert the wrath of the gods, and, at the same time, if the signs indicated by the entrails coincided with what they had seen in their dream, then one or other of the consuls should fulfil his destiny. The soothsayers' reports agreed with the unspoken conviction already in their minds; and so they summoned the legates and tribunes and publicly announced the gods' commands, hoping thereby that the army in the field would not be alarmed by a consul's voluntary death. They then agreed together that on whichever flank the Roman army started to give way, the consul in command there should sacrifice himself on behalf of the nation and citizens of Rome. It was also argued in the council that if ever at any time a war had been conducted under strict command, now was the moment to recall military discipline to its former ways. Their anxiety was more acute because they had to make war on Latins, who were the same as themselves in language, customs, type of arms, and above all in military institutions; soldiers had intermingled with soldiers, centurions with centurions, tribunes with tribunes as equals and colleagues in the same garrisons and often in the same maniples. To prevent the men committing some blunder on account of this, the consuls issued the order that no one was to leave his position to fight the enemy.

7. It happened that amongst the squadron leaders in the cavalry, who had been sent off to reconnoitre in all directions, was the consul's son, Titus Manlius. He had managed to ride with his cavalry beyond the enemy's camp until he was hardly a spear throw from their nearest outpost. There the Tusculan cavalry were stationed under the command of Geminus Maecius, whose reputation was high amongst his fellows for his exploits as much as for his noble birth. He recognized the Roman cavalry, and amongst them the conspicuous figure of the consul's son, riding at their head (for they were all known to each other, especially the nobility). 'Do you Romans,' he cried, 'intend to make war on the Latins and their allies with a single squadron? What will your consuls and your two consular armies be doing meanwhile?' 'They'll be here in good time,' replied Manlius, 'and with them will be Jupiter himself, who has more power and might than they, as witness of the treaties violated by you. If we gave you your fill of fighting at Lake Regillus, here too we shall certainly see that you get little joy out of our fighting force and a clash with us.' At this Geminus rode out a little in front of his men: 'Then will you fight me yourself, while waiting for that great day to come when you all make a mighty effort to get your armies moving? The outcome of a duel between you and me will show how much better a Latin cavalryman is than a Roman.'

The young man's bold spirit was roused, whether by anger, by shame at the thought of refusing the challenge, or through the invincible power of destiny. And so, forgetting his father's supreme authority and the consuls' order, he threw himself headlong into a fight where it mattered little whether he won or lost. The rest of the cavalry were made to stand back, as if to watch a riding display, and the two men rode their horses hard at each other across the empty space between them. But when they met with spears levelled for attack, Manlius's spear glanced off his enemy's helmet, while Maecius's passed over the neck of the other's horse. Then when they wheeled their horses round, Manlius was the first to collect himself for a second blow and pricked Maecius's horse between the ears with his spear-point. The horse reared when it felt the wound and shook its head so violently that it threw its rider; and as Maecius was trying to get up after the heavy fall, leaning on his spear and shield, Manlius ran through his throat so that the spear came out between his ribs and pinned him to the ground. Gathering up the spoils, Manlius rode back to his men, and then made for the camp, accompanied by their shouts of triumph. He went straight to his father's headquarters, not knowing what fate and future awaited him, or whether praise or punishment were to be his desert.

'Father,' he said, 'so that all men may proclaim me your true son, I am bringing you these cavalryman's spoils, taken from the enemy I killed after accepting his challenge.' On hearing this, the consul promptly turned away from his son and gave orders for a trumpet to summon an assembly. When this had filled up, he spoke as follows: 'Titus Manlius, you have respected neither consular authority nor your father's dignity; you have left your position to fight the enemy in defiance of my order, and, as far as was in your power, have subverted military discipline, on which the fortune of Rome has rested up to this day; you have made it necessary for me to forget either the republic or myself. We would therefore rather be punished for our own wrongdoing than allow our country to expiate our sins at so great a cost to itself; it is a harsh example we shall set, but a salutary one for the young men of the future. As far as my own feelings are concerned, they are stirred by a man's natural love for his children, as well as by the example you have given of your courage, even though this was marred by a false conception of glory. But since consular authority must either be confirmed by your death or annulled for ever by your going unpunished, I believe that you yourself, if you have any drop of my blood in you, would agree that the military discipline which you undermined by your error must be restored by your punishment. Go, lictor, bind him to the stake.'

All were transfixed with horror by this dreadful command; every man saw the axe as if raised against himself, and it was fear, not obedience, which held them in check. So they stood rooted to the spot in silence, as if lost in amazement; then when the blood gushed from the severed neck, suddenly their voices broke out in agonized complaint so unrestrained that they spared neither laments nor curses. They covered the young man's body with his spoils, built a pyre outside the earthworks, and burnt it with all the honours that can attend any military funeral. The 'commands of Manlius' not only caused a shudder at the time but were a grim warning in the future. 8. However, the brutality of the punishment made the soldiers more obedient to their commander, and not only was better attention given everywhere to guard-duties, night watches, and picket-stationing, but in the final struggle too, when the army went into battle, that stern act of discipline did them good. The fighting was in fact like nothing so much as that in civil war, so little did the Latins differ from the Romans in anything except temperament.

The Romans had formerly used round shields; then, after they began to serve for pay, they changed from round to oblong shields; and their previous formation in phalanxes, like those of the Macedonian army, afterwards began to be a battle-line formed in maniples, with the troops in the rear drawn up in several ranks. The first line, the *hastati*, consisted of fifteen maniples stationed with short gaps between them; each maniple had twenty light-armed soldiers, the rest of its number being men with oblong shields: 'light-armed' was applied to those carrying only a spear and javelins. This front line contained the pick of the young men who were just reaching the age for service. Behind them came the same number of maniples formed from men who were stronger and more mature; these were called the *principes* and all carried oblong shields and had especially fine arms. The whole thirty maniples combined were called the *antepilani* because immediately behind the standards were placed another fifteen companies, each one of which was divided into three sections, the first section of each being named the *pilus*. A company consisted of three sections or *vexilla*, and a single *vexillum* comprised sixty soldiers, two centurions and one *vexillarius* or standard-bearer, so that

altogether there were 186 men.[6] The first standard led the
triarii, veteran soldiers of proven courage, the second the
rorarii, younger and less experienced men, the third the *accensi*,
who were the least reliable group and so relegated to the
rearmost line. When an army had been drawn up in this order,
the *hastati* were the first to open the battle. If they failed to
dispatch the enemy, they slowly withdrew and were received
through the gaps between the *principes*. Then the fighting was
taken up by the *principes*, with the *hastati* behind them, and the
triarii knelt under their standards, with their left legs stretched
forward and shields resting against their shoulders, holding
their spears fixed in the ground and pointing forwards so that
the line seemed to bristle with a protective palisade. If the
principes too fought with no success, they gradually fell back
from the front line to the *triarii*: hence the common saying
when things go badly, 'to have reached the *triarii*'. Once the
triarii had allowed the *principes* and *hastati* through the gaps
in their line they rose up and quickly closed their ranks,
blocking the lanes, so to speak, and then, with no reserves to
rely on behind them, fell upon the enemy in one unbroken
force. That was particularly alarming for the enemy who had
followed up men they believed defeated only to see a new line
suddenly rising up, with increased numbers. There were
usually about four legions enlisted, each with 5000 foot soldiers, and 300 horse to each legion.

A second contingent of the same size used to be levied from
the Latins, who were now enemies of Rome and had drawn
up their army for battle in the same formation. They knew that
not only must section meet section in battle, the whole line of
hastati face *hastati*, *principes* face *principes*, but the centurions
must confront each other if the ranks were not broken. In each
army the chief centurion or *primipilus* took up his position
amongst the *triarii*. The Roman was not physically particularly
powerful but was an active man and experienced soldier, while
the Latin was immensely strong and a first-class fighter. They
knew each other very well, having always led companies of

6. The figure is correct if the *vexillarius*, or standard-bearer, is
included. cf. G. Webster, *The Roman Imperial Army*, pp. 21 ff.

similar rank. The Roman was uncertain of his own strength, and had already obtained permission from the consuls before he left Rome to choose whom he wanted for his deputy centurion, to protect him against the one marked out as his opponent; this young man met the Latin centurion in battle and defeated him.

The engagement was fought not far from the foot of Mount Vesuvius, where a road led to the River Veseris.[7] 9. Before they led their men into battle, the Roman consuls offered sacrifices. It is said that the soothsayer pointed out to Decius that the head of the liver was cut where it had special reference to his family, but that otherwise the victim was acceptable to the gods; and that Manlius's sacrifice had been very successful. 'If my colleague's sacrifice went well,' said Decius, 'that should be all right.' The ranks were formed as described above and the army advanced on to the battlefield; Manlius commanded the right, Decius the left wing. To begin with, the two forces were equally matched and fought with the same eagerness and spirit; then when the Roman *hastati* on the left wing could not withstand the Latins' pressure, they fell back to the *principes*. In this moment of consternation the consul Decius cried aloud to Marcus Valerius: 'We need the gods' help, Marcus Valerius. Come now, you are a state pontiff of the Roman people – dictate the formula whereby I may devote myself to save the legions.'[8] The priest bade him put on the purple-edged toga, veil his head, and with one hand protruding from the toga to touch his chin, stand on a spear laid under his feet and repeat these words[9]: 'Janus, Jupiter, Father Mars, Quirinus, Bellona, Lares, New Gods, Native Gods, deities who have power over us and our enemies, and gods of the Underworld: I supplicate and revere you, I seek your favour and beseech you, that you prosper the might and victory of the Roman people, the Quirites, and afflict the enemies of the Roman people, the

7. Or 'in the direction of Veseris': town and river had the same name. cf. Cicero, *de Officiis* III.31.112 and *de Finibus* I.23.

8. Evidently a member of the college of *pontifices* accompanied the army to preside on ritual occasions.

9. For the invocation, cf. Macrobius, *Saturnalia* III.9.

Quirites, with terror, dread and death. As I have pronounced the words, even so on behalf of the republic of the Roman nation of Quirites, and of the army, the legions and auxiliaries of the Roman nation of Quirites, do I devote myself and with me the legions and auxiliaries of our enemies to the gods of the Underworld and to Earth.'

After reciting this prayer he ordered the lictors to go to his colleague Titus Manlius and tell him without delay that he had devoted himself for the good of the army. Then he girded up his toga in the Gabine manner,[10] leaped fully armed on to his horse, and rode into the midst of the enemy – a sight to admire for both armies, almost superhuman in its nobility, as if sent from heaven to expiate all anger of the gods and deflect disaster from his own people to the Latins. Thus the terror and panic in every form which Decius brought with him first threw the line of standards into confusion and then penetrated deep into the entire Latin army. This was quite clear to see, because wherever he rode, men shrank away as though struck by some death-dealing star; and when he finally fell beneath a rain of missiles, from that moment there was no doubt that the Latin cohorts were thrown into complete confusion and had emptied the battlefield to scatter far and wide in flight. At the same time the Romans, their spirits freed from religious uncertainty, rallied and started the battle afresh as if they had only then been given the signal for the first time: for the *rorarii* had run forward between the *antepilani* and reinforced the *hastati* and *principes*, while the *triarii* were kneeling on their right knees waiting for the consul to give the sign for them to rise.

10. Then as the struggle continued, with the Latins gaining in some parts of the field by weight of numbers, the consul Manlius heard of his colleague's end, and paid to so memorable a death the well-merited tribute of tears as well as praise, as justice and piety demanded. For a little while he was uncertain whether the time had come for the *triarii* to rise to their feet; then he decided it was better to keep them fresh for the final testing time, and ordered the *accensi* from the rearmost line to

10. A ceremonial manner of wearing the toga to leave both arms free; cf. V.46.2 and X.7.3.

move forward in front of the standards. No sooner had they moved up than the Latins called in their own *triarii*, supposing that their opponents had done the same. These fought savagely for some time until they had exhausted themselves and broken or blunted their spears, but they continued to push the Romans back, believing that the battle was won and they had reached the last line. At that moment the consul called to the *triarii*: 'Get up now: you are fresh and face troops who are tired: remember your country, your parents, wives and children; remember your consul, who lies dead to bring you victory.' As soon as the *triarii* rose to their feet, arms gleaming bright and ready for the fray, a fresh army unexpectedly sprang up; they let the *antepilani* retire between the gaps in their ranks and, raising a shout, threw the Latins' front ranks into confusion. Thrusting spears into their faces they cut down the best of the fighting men and went through the other maniples almost unscathed, as if these were unarmed, and broke up their enemy's formation with such slaughter that they left scarcely a quarter of their opponents alive. The Samnites too, who were drawn up some way off at the base of the mountain, struck terror into the hearts of the Latins.

But of all the citizens and allies, the consuls won the greatest glory in that war. One of them drew all the threats and dangers from the gods above and below on to himself alone, while the other displayed such courage and wise tactics on the field that it is readily agreed amongst Romans and Latins alike who have handed down to posterity a record of this battle that whichever side had been led by Titus Manlius would undoubtedly have been victorious. The Latins fled and reached Minturnae. Their camp was captured after the battle, and many men, mostly Campanians, were taken alive and killed. Night overtook those searching for the body of Decius, so that it could not be found that day; but next day it was found, covered with missiles under a great pile of dead bodies, and was given burial by Manlius in a style befitting his colleague's death.

Here I think it should be said that when a consul, dictator or praetor devotes the legions of his enemy he need not necessarily devote himself, but may choose any citizen he likes from an enlisted Roman legion. If the man who has been devoted dies, it is assumed that all is well. If he does not die, then an effigy of him is buried seven feet deep or more in the ground and a propitiary sacrifice is made; Roman magistrates are banned from climbing on to the mound under which the effigy is buried. But if someone chooses to devote himself, as Decius did, and does not die, he cannot perform any religious act either on his own account or for the people without defiling it, whether it be by sacrificial victim or by anything else he chooses. He who has devoted himself has the right to dedicate his arms to Vulcan or to any other god he chooses. The spear on which the consul has stood to offer his prayer must not be allowed to fall into the hands of the enemy; if it does, expiation must be made to Mars with the ritual sacrifice of a pig, sheep and bull. 11. These details I have thought it appropriate to repeat, in the very words in which they were formulated and handed down, although the memory of every practice, religious and secular, has been effaced by our preference for all that is new and foreign in place of what is native and traditional.

In certain authorities I find that it was not until the battle was over that the Samnites came up to support the Romans, for they waited to know the outcome of the fighting. The Latins too were already defeated when help eventually began to be sent them from Lavinium, where time was lost in considering what to do; and then when the leading standards and part of the army had already passed out through the gates, news was brought of the Latin defeat, and the army wheeled round and marched back into Lavinium. Their commander Milionius is reported as saying that they would have to pay the Romans heavily for this short march. The Latins who survived the battle scattered in many directions; when they had reassembled they found refuge in the city of Vescia. In meetings held there Numisius, their commander, addressed them, declaring that the fortunes of war were surely the same for both armies and had destroyed both with equal bloodshed. The Romans, he said, could claim only nominal victory, and in every other respect shared the fate of the vanquished; both the consular headquarters were polluted, one by the murder of a son, the other by the death of the consul who devoted himself. The entire army had been cut to pieces, the *hastati* and *principes* slaughtered, before the standards and behind them was equally a bloodbath; in the end it took the veteran *triarii* to restore the situation. Even though the Latin forces had been equally cut to pieces, still, for recruiting more men, either Latium or Volscian territory was nearer than Rome. So, if they thought fit, he would quickly summon fighting men from the Latin and Volscian peoples, would return to Capua with an army ready for war, and by his unexpected arrival would strike terror into the hearts of the Romans, who were now looking for anything rather than a battle. Misleading letters were dispatched around Latium and Volscian country, and since those who received them had not been present at the battle they were readier to believe them without question. Troops were hurriedly assembled from all quarters and speedily enlisted.

The consul Torquatus met this army near Trifanum, a place between Sinuessa and Minturnae. Without waiting to find sites for camps, both sides piled up their baggage and fought a battle which ended the war, for the losses of the enemy were so great that when the consul led out his victorious army to plunder their lands, the Latins all gave themselves up, and their surrender was followed by that of the Campanians. Latium and Capua were made to give up their territory. The Latin land, plus that belonging to Privernum and the Falernian land as well (which had belonged to Campania) as far as the River Volturnus, was divided out amongst the Roman plebeians. The share for each man was two *iugera* in Latium supplemented by three quarters of a *iugerum* from land belonging to Privernum, or three *iugera* in Falernian territory, with an additional quarter to compensate for the distance from Rome. The Laurentians and the Campanian knights were exempted from the punishment meted out to the Latins, because they had not been guilty of disloyalty; instructions were issued that the treaty with the Laurentians should be renewed, and from that time it has been renewed annually, on the tenth day after the

Latin festival. The Campanian knights were granted Roman citizenship, and to commemorate this a bronze tablet was attached to the temple of Castor in Rome. In addition, the Campanian people were ordered to pay an annual tax of 450 *denarii*[11] a head, and they numbered 1600. 12. After settling the war and apportioning rewards and punishments in accordance with individual deserts, Titus Manlius returned to Rome. It is generally agreed that only the older men went to meet him as he approached the City, and that the younger men loathed and abominated him then and afterwards throughout his life.

The Antiates raided the lands of Ostia, Ardea and Solonium. As the consul Manlius was unable to carry out a campaign against them because of ill health, he appointed as dictator Lucius Papirius Crassus, who happened to be praetor at the time; and he named Lucius Papirius Cursor master of Horse. The dictator achieved nothing remarkable against the Antiates, although he had a permanent camp in their land for several months.

This year was remarkable for the victory over so many powerful nations, as well as for the glorious death of one of the consuls and the exercise of the other's supreme authority which, though brutally harsh, was renowned through the ages. The next one saw Tiberius Aemilius Mamercinus and Quintus Publilius Philo as consuls, men who lacked similar opportunities for action and were besides more taken up with their own or their party's concerns than with their country. The Latins took up arms again out of resentment for the loss of their land, but they were defeated on the Fenectane Plains[12] and their camp was sacked. While Publilius, under whose direction and auspices the campaign had been conducted, stayed there to receive the surrender of the Latin peoples whose fighting men had been killed, Aemilius led his army against Pedum.

The Pedani were supported by the peoples of Tibur, Praeneste and Velitrae, and auxiliary troops had also come

11. The silver *denarius* was not in fact struck until 211 B.C.
12. Site unknown.

from Lanuvium and Antium. Though the Romans showed their superiority in battle they still had the task of dealing with the city of Pedum and the camp of the allied peoples adjoining it. Then the consul heard that his colleague had been decreed a triumph, promptly broke off the campaign before it was finished, and returned to Rome to demand a triumph for himself as well, though victory was not yet won. The Fathers were outraged by his greed and refused him a triumph unless Pedum was either captured or surrendered; this caused a breach between Aemilius and the Senate, and henceforward his behaviour in office was like that of a tribune making trouble. For as long as he was consul he never ceased to complain of the Senate to the people, while his colleague raised not the slightest opposition, being himself of plebeian birth. The ground for his accusations was the niggardly distribution amongst the plebeians of the land in Latin and Falernian territory. When the Senate wished to terminate the consul's authority and ordered the appointment of a dictator to deal with the Latin revolt, Aemilius, who was holding the fasces,[13] named his colleague dictator, and he in his turn named Junius Brutus master of Horse. Publilius's dictatorship was a popular one, both for the accusatory speeches he made against the Senate and because he introduced three laws which were highly advantageous to the plebeians and unfavourable to the nobility: one, that a people's decree should be binding on every Roman citizen; two, that the Senate should ratify measures proposed at the *comitia centuriata* before voting began; three, that one censor at least must be elected from the plebeians, since they had already gone so far as to permit both to be plebeian. In the senators' opinion, the damage done at home that year by the consuls and dictator outweighed the increase in empire resulting from their victory and management of the campaigns abroad.

13. In the following year, when Lucius Furius Camillus and Gaius Maenius were consuls, in order to make more pointed criticism of Aemilius (the consul of the year before) for his

13. The rods of supreme authority in the City, held by each consul for a month in turn.

negligence in office, the Senate clamoured for arms and men and every kind of force to be used against Pedum, to bring about its capture and destruction. The new consuls were obliged to give this priority over everything else, and set out from Rome. The situation in Latium was already one where peace and war were equally intolerable: the Latins lacked the means to make war, and rejected peace because they were still aggrieved about the confiscation of their land. They decided to adopt a middle course and remain in their towns, so that the Romans would be under no provocation to find a pretext for war; and, if any town was reported to be under siege, to send aid to the besieged from all the surrounding peoples. All the same, the communities which gave help to Pedum were very few. The forces sent from Tibur and Praeneste, whose lands were near by, reached Pedum; but those from Aricia, Lanuvium and Velitrae were suddenly attacked by Maenius and routed while they were joining up with Volscians from Antium near the River Astura. Camillus fought the very powerful army from Tibur in the neighbourhood of Pedum; the struggle was harder, but the result equally successful. During the battle a sudden sally of the townspeople created very great confusion. Camillus directed part of the army against them, and not only drove them back behind their walls but, after he had disheartened them and their allies, even took the town by scaling ladders that very day. Roman morale and courage were already raised by the capture of this one city, so the consuls then decided to take the victorious army round Latium and make a complete conquest. This continued without respite until by storming each city in turn or receiving its surrender the Romans had put down the whole of Latium. Garrisons were then stationed amongst the towns they had taken over, and the consuls departed for Rome and the triumph unanimously awarded them. As well as the triumph they were granted the honour (rare in those days) of having their equestrian statues set up in the Forum.

Before the elections were held to appoint consuls for the following year, Camillus addressed the Senate on the subject of the Latin peoples, and spoke as follows: 'Conscript Fathers, the task we had to perform in Latium by armed warfare has now reached conclusion by favour of the gods and the bravery of our soldiers. The enemy's armies were cut to pieces at Pedum and on the Astura: all the Latin towns and Antium in Volscian territory have either been taken by storm or have offered surrender, and are now held by your garrisons. It remains to consider, since the Latins harass us so often by renewing hostilities, how we can keep them quiet and continuously at peace. The immortal gods have put you in control of the situation, so that the decision whether Latium shall exist in future or not is left in your hands; as far as the Latins are concerned, therefore, you have the power to create a permanent peace for yourselves by exercising either cruelty or forgiveness.

'Do you choose to adopt harsh measures against men who have surrendered or suffered defeat? You may destroy the whole of Latium, and create vast deserts out of the places from where you have often drawn a splendid allied army to make use of in many a major war. Or do you want to follow the example of your ancestors and extend the State of Rome by admitting your defeated enemies as citizens? The material for such increase is there in abundance, with glory to be won of supreme kind. Certainly by far the strongest government is one to which men are happy to be subject. But whatever you decide to do, you must make haste; you are keeping so many peoples in suspense, between hope and fear. You must resolve your own doubts concerning them as soon as possible, and while their minds are benumbed with apprehension, give them either the certainty of punishment or generous treatment. It was our duty to give you the power to make decisions about everything; it is yours to decide what is best for yourselves and for the State.'

14. The leading members of the Senate praised the consul's treatment of the main point at issue, but said that as the Latins were not all in the same position, his advice could best be carried out if the consuls would put proposals about the different peoples by name, so that a settlement could be reached according to their individual deserts. The Latins were accord-

ingly dealt with under separate decrees. The Lanuvini were given citizenship and their temples were restored to them, with the proviso that the temple and grove of Juno the Deliverer should be owned jointly by the burghers of Lanuvium and the people of Rome. The Aricini, Nomentani and Pedani were received as citizens on the same terms as the Lanuvini. The Tusculans retained the citizenship which they already had, and the charge of renewing the war was laid against a few ringleaders without injury to the community. The Veliterni, Roman citizens of long standing, were savagely penalized for having rebelled so many times: their walls were pulled down, their senate deported, and its members ordered to live on the far side of the Tiber on the understanding that if one of them were caught on the near side, his ransom should be no less than a thousand pounds of bronze and his captor should not release him from bondage until the money was paid. Colonists were sent to occupy the senators' land, and when they were enrolled Velitrae recovered its previous appearance of having a large population. A new colony was dispatched to Antium too, on the understanding that the Antiates, if they wished, should be allowed to be enrolled as colonists themselves. Their warships were taken from them and their people were forbidden access to the sea; they too were granted citizenship. The Tiburtines and Praenestini had their land confiscated, not only because of the fresh charge of rebellion which they incurred along with the other Latins, but because they had once joined forces with the Gauls,[14] a race of savages, out of disgust with Roman rule.

The rest of the Latin peoples were deprived of their rights to intermarry and trade with each other and to hold councils amongst themselves. The Campanians were granted citizenship without the vote as a tribute to their knights who had refused to revolt with the Latins, and so were the Fundani and Formiani for having always allowed a safe and peaceful passage through their territories. It was decided to grant the people of

14. The Tiburtines are explicitly said to have allied with the Gauls in 361; cf. VII.11.1. In VII.12.8 it is implied that Praeneste had welcomed a Gallic army in 358.

Cumae and Suessula the same rights and terms as those enjoyed by Capua. Some of the ships from Antium were laid up in the dockyards at Rome, while the rest were burnt, and it was decided to use their prows or beaks to decorate a platform set up in the Forum; this sacred place was named the Rostra, or The Beaks.

15. In the consulship of Gaius Sulpicius Longus and Publius Aelius Paetus a general peace was maintained, thanks to the good-will which the Romans had gained from their acts of generosity no less than to their power, until war broke out between the Sidicini and the Aurunci. The Aurunci had surrendered in the consulship of Titus Manlius[15] and had given no trouble since then, so they had better reason for seeking help from the Romans. But before the consuls could lead an army from Rome – for the Senate had ordered them to defend the Aurunci – a report came that the Aurunci had taken fright and abandoned their town to take refuge with their wives and children in Suessa, the town now called Aurunca, which they had fortified; their ancient walls and city had been destroyed by the Sidicini. This news made the Senate angry with the consuls for delaying and so betraying their allies, and they ordered the appointment of a dictator. Gaius Claudius Inregillensis was nominated, and he named Gaius Claudius Hortator as master of Horse. Then some religious problem cast doubt on the dictator, and when the augurs declared that there appeared to have been a flaw in his appointment, both he and the master of Horse resigned office.

That year the Vestal Minucia first attracted suspicion by her dress, which was more elegant than was proper, and was subsequently charged before the pontiffs on the evidence of a slave. She was ordered by their decree to abstain from performing sacred rites and to retain her household slaves in her power[16]; after sentence was passed she was buried alive near the Colline Gate, to the right of the paved road, in the Polluted Field – a place so named, I believe, from her unchastity.

15. 340 B.C.
16. If freed the slaves could not have been legally questioned under torture.

The same year Quintus Publilius Philo was elected praetor, the first to be chosen from the plebeians.[17] His election was opposed by the consul Sulpicius, who declared that he would refuse to consider him, but as the Senate had not been successful in rejecting plebeians for the highest offices, it felt less strongly about the praetorship.

16. The following year, when Lucius Papirius Crassus and Caeso Duillius were consuls, was noteworthy for a war which was novel rather than serious. This was with the Ausones who inhabited the city of Cales. They had joined forces with their neighbours, the Sidicini, and when their combined army had been defeated in a single – and by no means memorable – battle, it was all the readier to take to flight, as the two cities were close at hand, and it found greater safety in running away. Nevertheless the senators continued to feel concerned about this war, because the Sidicini had so often started a war themselves, or had given support to others who did so, or had been the occasion of hostilities; and so they threw all their efforts into electing Marcus Valerius Corvus, the greatest soldier of the day, to his fourth consulship. He was given Marcus Atilius Regulus as his colleague, and so that nothing should chance to go wrong, the consuls were requested to allow Corvus to take on the command without drawing lots. He took over the victorious army from the former consuls and set out for Cales, where the fighting had started.

His first battle-cry and charge routed the enemy, who had not got over their fears after their earlier engagement, and he proceeded to attack the walls of the town itself. His soldiers were indeed so eager that they wanted to bring the scaling ladders up to the walls straightaway, and insisted that they could climb them. But that was not going to be easy, and Corvus preferred to make a successful attempt by putting his men to work rather than endangering them. He therefore had a mound built and protective sheds constructed, and brought his siege towers up to the wall; but before these were used a chance piece of luck made it unnecessary. A Roman prisoner,

17. cf. VI.42.11 for the election of the *praetor urbanus* only from the patricians.

Marcus Fabius, broke his bonds when his guards were careless on a feast-day, let himself down the wall hand over hand on a rope he had tied to a battlement, and landed among the Roman siege works. He prevailed on the general to attack the enemy while they were half-asleep after drinking and feasting, and so the Ausones and their city were taken with no more effort than it had cost to defeat them in battle. A vast amount of booty was captured, a garrison established in Cales, and the legions brought back to Rome. The consul held a triumph,[18] by decree of the Senate, and, to give Atilius his share of glory, both consuls were ordered to lead an army against the Sidicini.

Before they left, on the Senate's orders, they appointed Lucius Aemilius Mamercinus dictator so that elections could be held; he named Quintus Publilius Philo as master of Horse. At the elections held by the dictator the consuls chosen were Titus Veturius and Spurius Postumius. Half the war – with the Sidicini – still remained, but in order to anticipate the wishes of the plebeians by doing them a kindness, the consuls introduced a measure for sending a colony to Cales. The Senate passed a resolution that 2500 men should be enrolled for this, and appointed Caeso Duillius, Titus Quinctius and Marcus Fabius as a commission of three to conduct the colonists to Cales and divide the land amongst them.

17. The new consuls then took over the army from their predecessors, entered the enemy's territory and reached their city walls, destroying the land as they went. The Sidicini had raised a huge army themselves and looked likely to put every effort into a battle which would be their last hope; it was also reported that the Samnites were mustering their forces for war. That was the moment for the Senate to authorize the consuls to appoint a dictator. Publius Cornelius Rufinus was chosen, with Marcus Antonius as master of Horse. Then religious doubts were raised about a possible flaw in their election, they resigned office, and when this was followed by an outbreak of plague it was supposed that all the auspices were affected by the irregularity, and the State reverted to an interregnum.

18. His third; cf. VII.27.8 and VII.38.3.

The fifth interrex from the start of the interregnum, Marcus Valerius Corvus, finally got Aulus Cornelius (for the second time) and Gnaeus Domitius elected as consuls. The general situation was peaceful when a rumour of a Gallic war had the effect of a rebellion in deciding the Senate to choose a dictator. Marcus Papirius Crassus was elected, with Publius Valerius Publicola as master of Horse. While they were holding a levy, more stringently than they would have done for a war against neighbouring peoples, scouts were sent out and returned to report that all was quiet amongst the Gauls. Samnium also had been suspected for the last two years of being rife with schemes for revolution, and consequently the Roman army had not been brought back from Sidicinian territory. But a campaign launched by Alexander of Epirus diverted the Samnites to Lucania, and the two peoples fought a pitched battle with the King as he was marching up from Paestum. Alexander was the victor in the engagement and made a peace treaty with the Romans. How honourably he intended to keep this if everything else had gone equally well for him is uncertain.

A census was held the same year, and new citizens were assessed. The Maecian and Scaptian tribes were added on their account, the names of the censors responsible being Quintus Publilius Philo and Spurius Postumius. The people of Acerrae were made Romans under a law proposed by the praetor Lucius Papirius which gave them citizenship without the right to vote. These were the events of that year at home and abroad.

18. The following year (when Marcus Claudius Marcellus and Gaius Valerius were consuls) was a horrible one, whether because of the inclement weather or the treachery of man. I find that the surname of Valerius is given in the annals as either Flaccus or Potitus, but the truth of this is not important. There is one thing I should very much like to think was falsely put on record (not all the authorities mention it) – namely, that those whose death made this year notorious for the plague were in fact killed by poison; but I must set down the affair as it has come down to us, lest I destroy confidence in any of my authorities. When leading citizens showed symptoms of the same disease which resulted in nearly every case in their

death, a certain serving-maid approached the curule aedile
Quintus Fabius Maximus and declared that she could disclose
the cause of the general epidemic if he would assure her that
her testimony would do her no injury. Fabius immediately
referred the matter to the consuls, and the consuls to the
Senate, and with its agreement the informer was given the
assurance she sought. She then revealed that the City was
suffering from the treachery of its women, and that the poisons
were being brewed by married women who could be caught
in the act if her hearers were willing to follow her at once.
They followed their informant and found certain women
brewing poisons, and other potions that were stored away.
These were brought to the Forum, and up to twenty matrons
in whose houses they had been found were served an official
summons to appear there. Two of the women, Cornelia and
Sergia, both of patrician families, argued that these were
wholesome remedies, but when their informer disproved this
and told them to drink if they wanted to prove she had
invented false charges, they took time to confer, and then
when the crowd had been dismissed, put the question to the
others. These like themselves did not refuse to drink, so that
all swallowed down the potion and died by their own evil
practices. Their attendants were arrested at once, and informed
against a large number of matrons, of whom as many as 170
were found guilty.

Before that day there had never been a public inquiry into
charges of poisoning in Rome. The case was regarded as an
ill omen, and it appeared likely that the women's minds were
possessed rather than depraved. It was then recalled from the
annals how once at the time of the secession of the plebs[19] a
nail had been hammered in by the dictator, and how the
people's minds, which had been driven to distraction by dissension, regained their self-control as a result of that act of
propitiation. It was therefore decided to appoint a dictator for
the purpose of hammering the nail. Gnaeus Quinctilius was

19. Livy does not mention this ceremony in connection with the
Secession of the plebs but describes it in VII.3.4 as being performed
to relieve a plague. cf. IX.28.6.

chosen, and he named Lucius Valerius as master of Horse. The nail was duly hammered in and they resigned office.

19. The consuls elected were Lucius Papirius Crassus (for the second time) and Lucius Plautius Venox. At the beginning of their year of office, Volscian envoys from Fabrateria and Lucania came to Rome asking to be granted protection and promising that if they were defended against Samnite attacks they would be loyal and obedient subjects of the Roman people. Envoys were then dispatched by the Senate to warn the Samnites to refrain from doing violence to the territories of those peoples, and they succeeded in their mission not so much because the Samnites wanted peace as because they were not yet prepared for war.

In the same year began the war with Privernum. The inhabitants had the people of Fundi as allies and even a Fundanian commander, a man named Vitruvius Vaccus who enjoyed some distinction not only in his home town but in Rome as well, where he had a house on the Palatine; after his house was demolished and the land confiscated, the area was known as the Meadows of Vaccus. He was effecting widespread destruction in the territory of Setia, Norba and Cora when Lucius Papirius marched out against him and took up a position not far from his camp. Vitruvius had neither the good sense to stay behind his rampart when confronted by a more powerful enemy nor sufficient courage to fight further away from his camp. He had scarcely deployed the whole of his army outside the camp gates, and his soldiers were thinking more of flight than of battle or the enemy, when he went into action, but without plan or forcefulness. It needed little effort to defeat him decisively, but as the area was so restricted and retreat was easy when his camp was so near, he was able to save his men from serious bloodshed without much difficulty. Scarcely anyone in fact was killed in the actual fighting, and only a few late-comers died in the general confusion as the men rushed into the camp. As soon as darkness fell they made for Privernum in a state of panic, to find protection for themselves behind walls instead of ramparts.

After destroying the land in all directions and driving off the cattle, the other consul, Plautius, led his army into the territory of Fundi. As he crossed the border he was met by the Fundanian senate, who said they had come to plead not for Vitruvius and his followers but on behalf of the people of Fundi. Vitruvius himself, they said, had decided they were not to be held responsible for the war when he chose to seek refuge in Privernum and not in his native city. Privernum, then, was where they should seek out and punish the enemies of the Roman people, who had broken simultaneously with Fundi and with Rome, with no thought of loyalty to either. At Fundi there was peace, sentiments which were Roman, a grateful recollection of the citizenship they had received. They begged the consul not to make war on an innocent people and declared that their lands, their city, their own persons and those of their wives and children were subject to the power of the Roman people and would remain so. The consul warmly praised the Fundanians, sent off a dispatch to Rome to say that Fundi was loyal, and marched away to Privernum. Claudius[20] writes that before Plautius left he executed the ringleaders of the plot and dispatched up to 350 of the conspirators in chains to Rome, but the Senate did not accept their surrender, judging that the people of Fundi wanted to get off with a punishment appropriate to the humbled and needy.

20. While the two consular armies were laying siege to Privernum, one of the consuls was recalled to Rome to hold the elections. This year for the first time starting stalls were built in the Circus.

The war with Privernum was not yet finally settled when a gloomy report reached Rome of a Gallic rising, news which the Senate scarcely ever ignored. Without delay the new consuls, Lucius Aemilius Mamercinus and Gaius Plautius, were accordingly ordered, on the very day (the first of July) they entered office, to divide the commands between them. Mamercinus, who had been allotted the Gallic war, was told to enlist an army without allowing any exemption; indeed, it is said that this included a mob of craftsmen and mechanics

20. Q. Claudius Quadrigarius, the annalist; cf. VI.42, note 52.

who were called up, types quite unsuitable for military service. An immense army was assembled at Veii, from where the campaign was to be mounted against the Gauls; but it was decided not to go further afield lest the enemy should slip past unnoticed by another route in an advance on Rome. A few days later it was quite clear that all was quiet amongst the Gauls at that time, and the whole army was diverted to Privernum.

From this point the tradition is divided. Some say that the town was taken by storm and Vitruvius was taken prisoner alive; others that before the final assault the inhabitants came out bearing a herald's staff and gave themselves up to the consul, and that Vitruvius was handed over by his own people. The Senate was consulted about Vitruvius and the Privernates, and ordered the consul Plautius to raze the walls of Privernum and leave a strong garrison there, then to return for a triumph. Vitruvius was to be held in prison until the consul's arrival and then be flogged and executed; his house on the Palatine must be demolished and his property dedicated to Semo Sangus.[21] From the bronze money his goods realized discs of bronze were made which were placed in the shrine of Sangus next to the temple of Quirinus. As for the senate of Privernum, it was decreed that any of its members who had remained in Privernum after its defection from Rome should live on the far side of the Tiber under the same restrictions as the Veliterni living there.[22] Once these decrees were passed nothing more was said about the people of Privernum until Plautius had held his triumph. After this Vitruvius was executed along with his partners in crime, and the consul then thought it safe to make mention of the Privernates in the hearing of men who had already had their fill of punishment of the guilty. 'Now that the ringleaders of revolt,' he said, 'have received the punishment they deserved from the immortal gods and from you, Conscript Fathers, what do you wish to be done with the main body of innocent men? For my part, although my position demands that I should be seeking opinions rather

21. Semo Sangus or Sancus was a Sabine god of oaths identified with Dius Fidius.
22. cf. ch. 14.6.

than offering one, when I see that the people of Privernum are neighbours of the Samnites, with whom our peaceful relations are at present highly precarious, I should like there to be as little bad feeling as possible remaining between us and them.'

21. The question in itself was not easy to answer, as the arguments for severity or leniency rested on the senators' individual inclinations, and the whole issue was further confused by the behaviour of one of the envoys from Privernum who was more conscious of the position to which he had been born than of the urgency of his present plight. When asked by someone advocating a harsher sentence what punishment he thought the Privernates deserved, he answered: 'The punishment deserved by those who think themselves worthy of freedom.' Seeing that this arrogant reply was increasing the hostility of those who were already opposed to the cause of Privernum, the consul put a kindlier question which he hoped would elicit a more tactful response. 'Suppose we let you off punishment,' he said, 'what sort of a peace may we hope to have with you?' 'If you grant us a good one,' was the answer, 'it will be loyally kept and permanent. If a bad one, it will not last long.' At this some cried out that the man was threatening them, and in no uncertain terms: peoples already settled in peace could be stirred to revolt by utterances like those. But the better senators put a more favourable interpretation on his words, and said that the voice they heard was that of a man, and a man free-born. Was it credible, they asked, that any people, or indeed any individual, would remain longer than was necessary in a situation that was painful? A peace was loyally kept when its terms were voluntarily accepted; loyalty could not be expected from those on whom they wished to impose servitude.

The consul himself did more than anyone to press for support for this view by repeatedly addressing the ex-consuls, who came first in expressing their opinions, loudly enough for many others to hear him; only those, he said, who took thought for nothing except freedom were worthy of becoming Romans. And so they won their case in the Senate, and with its approval the proposal was put to the people to confer citizenship on the Privernates.

In this same year three hundred colonists were dispatched to Anxur, where they each received two *iugera* of land.

22. The following year, when Publius Plautius Proculus and Publius Cornelius Scapula were consuls, was not distinguished by any event either domestic or military, apart from the fact that a colony was sent out to Fregellae (the land had once belonged to the people of Signia and subsequently to the Volscians) and a distribution of meat was made to the people by Marcus Flavius at his mother's funeral. Some saw this as using the honour due to his mother as a pretext for paying off the debt he owed the people, because he had been acquitted when brought to court by the aediles on the charge of seducing a married woman. Though the meat was distributed on account of the favour previously shown him at his trial, it was also the cause of his gaining office; and at the next elections for people's tribune he was chosen in absence, in preference to those who were canvassing for votes.

The town of Palaepolis was not far from the present site of Neapolis. Both places were inhabited by the same people, who had originally come from Cumae, while the Cumani trace their origin from Chalcis in Euboea. Thanks to the fleet which had brought them from their native place, they exercised considerable influence along the coast of the sea by which they lived, having first landed on the islands of Aenaria and the Pithecusae[23] and then ventured to transfer their settlements to the mainland. Relying on their own strength and still more on the unreliability of the Samnite alliance with the Romans, or else putting their trust in the plague which was reported to have attacked the City of Rome, these people committed many acts of hostility against the Roman settlements in Campanian and Falernian territory. Consequently when Lucius Cornelius Lentulus and Quintus Publilius Philo (for the second time) were consuls, the fetial priests were sent to Palaepolis to demand reparation; and when a sharp reply was

23. Islands in the Bay of Naples, one the modern Ischia.

brought back from the Greeks, a race more vigorous in speech than in action, the people acted on the motion put to them by the Senate and ordered war to be declared on Palaepolis. In the division of command between the consuls it fell to Publilius to direct the fighting against the Greeks, while Cornelius with another army took up a position where he was ready to meet the Samnites if they showed any signs of movement. As it was rumoured that they were watching for a revolt on the part of the Campanians as a signal to bring up their army, that seemed the best place for Cornelius to set up a permanent camp.

23. Both consuls told the Senate that there was small hope of peace with the Samnites. Publilius reported that two thousand soldiers from Nola and four thousand Samnites had been given entry to Palaepolis, though this was forced on the Greeks by the Nolani rather than by their own wish. Cornelius said that the Samnite officials had proclaimed a levy, that the whole of Samnium was up in arms, and the neighbouring cities of Privernum, Fundi and Formiae were undoubtedly under pressure to give their support. In view of this the Senate voted to send representatives to the Samnites before declaring war, but the answer brought back was defiant. The Samnites gratuitously accused the Romans of unlawful conduct, and were even more determined to clear themselves of the charges levelled against them. The Greeks, they said, were not receiving any official advice or support from them, nor were they trying to win over Fundi and Formiae; in fact they were perfectly satisfied with their own resources, if they decided to go to war. But they could not disguise the annoyance of the Samnite nation when the Roman people had restored Fregellae, which the Samnites had captured from the Volscians and destroyed, and planted a colony in Samnite territory to which the Roman settlers gave the same name; this was an outrage and insult, and if it was not removed by those responsible, they would use every means to get rid of it themselves. When the Roman envoy invited them to discuss the situation with friends and allies of both parties, the Samnite spokesman replied that this only confused the issue. 'Our differences, Romans,' he said, 'will be resolved neither by

parleying between envoys nor by any man's arbitration, but by the plain of Campania where we must meet in battle, by the sword and the common fortune of war. Let us then pitch camp facing each other between Capua and Suessula and determine whether Samnites or Romans shall dominate Italy.' The Roman envoys replied that they would go where their own generals led them, not where bidden by their enemies and . . .[24]

Publilius had already occupied a convenient site between Palaepolis and Neapolis, and had deprived the enemy of the mutual sharing of assistance which they had made use of as one place or the other was in difficulties. And so as the date of the elections was imminent, and it was not in the public interest that while Publilius was threatening the enemy's walls he should be called away from his expectations of taking a city any day, the Senate arranged with the tribunes that they should propose to the people that when Quintus Publilius Philo had ended his term as consul he should continue to conduct the campaign with consular powers until the war with the Greeks was ended.

Lucius Cornelius had already entered Samnium, so that the Senate was equally unwilling to recall him from active prosecution of the war; he was therefore sent a letter bidding him name a dictator to conduct the elections. He chose Marcus Claudius Marcellus, who named Spurius Postumius as his master of Horse. However, the elections were not held by the dictator, because the regularity of his appointment was questioned. The augurs were consulted and declared that the dictator's nomination appeared irregular. This opinion the tribunes discredited and made suspect by their accusations; they pointed out that the flaw could not have been easily detected, since the consul had risen in the night and made the appointment in silence. He had not written to anyone either officially or privately about it, nor was there any man alive who could say that he had seen or heard anything to invalidate the auspices; neither could the augurs sitting in Rome have

24. The gap in the MSS accounts for the end of the embassy to the Samnites and start of hostilities.

been able to divine what obstacle the consul had met with in camp. Surely everyone could see that what seemed an irregularity to the augurs was no more than the dictator's plebeian origin? These and other objections raised by the tribunes had no effect; the State reverted to an interregnum, and the elections were postponed for one reason or another until finally the fourteenth interrex, Lucius Aemilius, appointed as consuls Gaius Poetelius and Lucius Papirius Mugillanus. In other annals I find the name of Cursor.

24. The foundation of Alexandria in Egypt is recorded in the same year,[25] and also the murder by a Lucanian exile of Alexander, King of Epirus, whose fate fulfilled the oracle of Jupiter of Dodona. When summoned to Italy by the people of Tarentum he had been given a warning by the oracle to beware of the water of Acheron and the city of Pandosia, for there he was fated to meet his end. He therefore made all the more speed to cross over to Italy and be as far away as possible from the city of Pandosia in Epirus and the River Acheron, which flows from Molossis into the Infernal Marshes and thence into the Thesprotian Gulf. But a flight from fate often plunges one headlong into it. When he had several times routed the Bruttian and Lucanian armies, taken Heraclea, a Tarentine colony, from the Lucanians, as well as Sipontum and the Bruttian towns of Consentia and Terina, then more towns belonging to the Messapians and Lucanians, and had sent three hundred noble families to Epirus to be held as hostages, he took up a position near the city of Pandosia, close to the borders of Lucania and Bruttium, on three hills which are a short distance apart from each other; from there he intended to direct attacks on enemy territory in all directions. He had around him some two hundred Lucanian exiles whom he believed trustworthy, though their loyalty was apt to veer with changes of fortune, a natural characteristic in general of that people.

Continuous rain had flooded all the plains and prevented the three sections of the army from giving mutual support to each other. The two camps which were not the King's were over-

25. Livy dates both these events about five years too late.

whelmed by a surprise attack from the enemy, and when they were wiped out, the entire force concentrated on blockading Alexander himself. The Lucanian exiles then sent messengers to their own people, promising to hand over the King alive or dead if they were assured of their safe return. But Alexander, by a fine feat of daring, broke out with a picked band of men through the midst of the enemy, and cut down the Lucanian general in a hand-to-hand engagement. Then, rallying his men, who were scattered in flight, he reached a river, where the fresh ruins of a bridge broken down by the force of the flood showed the way. As his party was crossing by a hazardous ford, a soldier, exhausted with fear and the hard struggle, cursed the river's ill-omened name. 'You're well named Acheros!'[26] he cried. The King caught the words, immediately thought of the fate promised him and halted, uncertain whether to cross. At this Sotinus, one of the royal pages in attendance on him, asked why he was hanging back in such a perilous situation, and pointed out that the Lucanians were seeking a place for an ambush. The King looked back, and, when he saw them some way off coming up in large numbers, drew his sword and rode his horse into mid-stream. He had already gained shallow water when a Lucanian exile cast a javelin at long range which transfixed him. He fell with the weapon still sticking in his lifeless body, and the current carried him down to the enemy's guard-posts. There his body was horribly mutilated. They cut it in two down the middle, sent half to Consentia, and kept the other half to make a mock of, standing back to attack it with stones and javelins, until a solitary woman pushed her way through the raging mob, hardly human in its fury, and besought the men to hold off a while. Through her tears she told them that her husband and children were held captive by the enemy, and she hoped to redeem them with the King's body, however maltreated. That put a stop to the mutilation. What was left of the corpse was buried at Consentia, in the sole care of this woman, and the

26. The word seems to be a byform of Acheron, the river of the Underworld, and the soldier was probably thinking of Greek *achos*, 'pain'.

bones dispatched to the Greeks at Metapontum, then taken by
sea to Epirus to the King's wife Cleopatra and his sister
Olympias, one of whom was the mother, the other the sister,
of Alexander the Great. This brief account of the sad end of
Alexander of Epirus must be given here because of his campaigns in Italy, though fortune held him back from making
war on Rome.

25. This same year a *lectisternium*[27] was held in Rome, the
fifth time since the foundation of the City, to propitiate the
same gods as before. Then the new consuls, at the people's
bidding, sent fetial priests to declare war on the Samnites and
began to make general preparations themselves on a larger
scale than they had done against the Greeks; they also received
new support, quite unlooked-for at the time. For the Lucanians
and Apulians, nations who up to that moment had had no
dealings with the Roman people, sought protection, with
promises of men and arms for the war, and were accordingly
granted a treaty of friendship. At the same time the campaign
in Samnium was successful. Three towns – Allifae, Callifae and
Rufrium – fell into Roman hands, and land elsewhere was
devastated far and wide at the first appearance of the consuls.

While this war was making such a successful start, the other
one, in which the Greeks were being besieged, was also coming
to an end. For in addition to the fact that part of the enemy
had been cut off from the rest by the barrier of the Romans'
earthworks, the sufferings of the people of Palaepolis within
the city walls were far greater than anything they had to fear
from their attackers. They were already having to submit to
outrageous treatment even of their own wives and children,
as if they were the prisoners of their own defenders, and to
endure all the final horrors of a captured city. And so when
reports came that reinforcements were on the way both from
Tarentum and from the Samnites, they felt that there were
already more Samnites than they wanted in their city, but,
being Greeks, they looked forward to the arrival of their
fellow-Greeks, the young men from Tarentum, hoping this

27. cf. VII.2, note 1.

would help them to resist the Samnites and Nolani no less than their Roman enemies. In the end they decided that surrender to the Romans was the least of the evils before them. Charilaus and Nymphius, two leading citizens, laid their plans together and decided what part each should play in bringing this about: one was to go over to the Roman general, the other to stay and prepare the city for acceptance of their plan. Charilaus was the one who came to Publilius Philo and told him that he had decided to hand over the city's defences, praying that this would be good, favourable and propitious for Palaepolis and for the Roman people. Whether he would appear to have betrayed or served his country by what he had done depended on the honourable conduct of the Romans. For himself, he said, he neither stipulated nor requested anything personal; for his people he requested, without making stipulations, that if his attempt were successful the Roman people should bear in mind how eagerly and at what risks the Palaepolitans had resumed friendly relations, rather than how foolish and rash they had been in failing in their obligations. He was warmly praised by the general and given three thousand soldiers to capture the part of the city which the Samnites occupied; the military tribune Lucius Quinctius was put in command of the troops.

26. At the same time Nymphius had also diplomatically approached the Samnite commander, and, by pointing out that the entire Roman army was either encircling Palaepolis or else in Samnium, prevailed on him to agree that Nymphius should take a fleet and sail round to Roman territory, where, he said, he would raid not only the sea coast but also the neighbourhood of Rome itself; but if he were to get away unperceived, he must leave at night and the ships had to be taken down to the water's edge immediately. To speed these preparations, all the Samnite fighting men, apart from those needed to garrison the town, were sent to the beach. While Nymphius was killing time in the dark and deliberately issuing conflicting orders to confuse the men, whose large numbers were also proving a hindrance, Charilaus was let into the city by his fellow-conspirators as arranged, and after occupying the

citadel with Roman soldiers, ordered them to raise a cheer. Hearing this, the Greeks stayed quiet, as instructed by their leaders, but the Nolani rushed out of the city in the opposite direction by the road which leads to Nola. The Samnites, being cut off from the town, had the advantage of an easier escape but one which appeared in a more disgraceful light once the danger was over. Unarmed, with everything abandoned to the enemy, they returned home destitute, stripped of all they had, a laughing stock to their own people as well as to strangers.

I am aware of the alternative tradition, whereby the betrayal of Palaepolis is ascribed to the Samnites, but have chosen to follow the more reliable authorities; furthermore, the treaty with Neapolis[28] – where the Greeks transferred their centre of administration from then on – makes it seem more probable that they renewed their friendship with Rome of their own accord. Publilius was decreed a triumph, because it was generally believed that the enemy had been forced to submit to Roman protection as a result of the siege he had conducted. He was the first to enjoy these two distinctions: an extension of his command, which was unprecedented, and a triumph after his term of office had ended.

27. This war was followed at once by another outbreak, this time with the Greeks of the eastern coast. For when the Tarentines, who had for some time been bolstering up the situation at Palaepolis with unfulfilled promises of support, learned that the Romans had taken possession of the city, they rounded on the Palaepolitans as if they had been let down themselves instead of being the ones who had failed their fellow-Greeks. They were consumed with rage and jealousy against the Romans, all the more when they heard that the Lucanians and Apulians had submitted to Rome; for an agreement had been drawn up that year with both those peoples. Soon their turn would come, they argued, and already things had reached the point when they must choose between having

28. It is not clear that Palaepolis was ever a separate place. It could have been the area in Neapolis which housed the 'old settlers' from Cumae. See F. E. Adcock, *CAH* VII, p. 595.

the Romans as enemies or as masters. The Samnite war and its outcome would undoubtedly prove the turning-point of their own affairs; the Samnites were the only people still holding out, and their position was none too strong since the defection of the Lucanians, though it was possible that these could still be won back and forced to break off their agreement with Rome if a little guile were applied to sowing discord.

Once these arguments found favour with the Tarentines, eager as they were to adopt new schemes, some young Lucanians who were conspicuous among their fellows rather than of good character were bribed to come to the city. There they beat each other with rods and then returned to display their naked bodies at a gathering of their fellow-Lucanians, crying out that because they had ventured to set foot in the Roman camp they had been flogged by the consuls and narrowly escaped the axe. The sight was ugly in itself, and was taken as a proof of injury without thought of deception; the excited populace clamoured for their magistrates to call a meeting of their senate. At this some crowded round the assembled senators, demanding war against the Romans, while others rushed off to rouse the peasants to arms, until even sensible men lost their heads in the general uproar, and it was decided to renew the alliance with the Samnites. Envoys were then sent off to arrange this, but the offer was too unexpected, and prompted by no apparent motive, for it to carry conviction. The Lucanians were therefore compelled by the Samnites both to surrender hostages and to admit garrisons inside their fortified positions; none of this they refused, blinded as they were by anger and deception. After a while, when the men who had brought false charges had removed themselves to Tarentum, the fraud began to come to light; but by then the Lucanians had lost all power to act independently and nothing was left for them but vain regrets.

28. In that year the liberty of the Roman people had as it were a second birth, with the abolition of enslavement for debt. The change in the law was made as a result of the exceptional lust and cruelty of a single man who had lent

money.[29] This was Lucius Papirius, to whom Gaius Publilius
had bound himself for a debt owed by his father. The debtor's
youth and beauty, which might have won him mercy, only
inflamed the other's lust and violence. Treating the boy's
youthful prime as an additional bonus for the loan, he first tried
to seduce him with indecent suggestions, then, when he turned
a deaf ear to any shameful proposal, threatened and terrified
him with frequent reminders of his position. Finally, when he
saw that the boy thought more of his honour than of his
present plight, he had him stripped naked and flogged. Bleeding from the lash, Publilius rushed out into the street, bewail-
ing his creditor's lust and cruelty, and a great number of
people, moved with pity for his youth and indignation at the
shameful treatment he had suffered, and no less with concern
for their own situation and that of their children, hurried to
the Forum and then in a massed crowd to the Senate-house.
The consuls, caught unawares by the commotion, were forced
to convene the Senate, and as its members entered, the crowd
fell at the feet of each one of them, and showed the young
man's bleeding back. On that day, as the result of one individual's outrageous treatment, a powerful bond of credit was
broken, and the consuls were told to put the proposal to the
people that no one should be held in fetters or in prison while
awaiting punishment except those who deserved it for an
offence committed, and that, to repay money lent him, a
debtor's property could be seized, but not his person. Those
in bondage were accordingly set free, and enslavement for
debt was forbidden in future.

29. In the same year, though the senators had anxiety enough
over the Samnite war alone, along with the sudden revolt of
the Lucanians and the Tarentines who had been responsible for
it, the Vestini added to their worries by allying themselves
with the Samnites. The problem was widely discussed in
private conversations rather than officially debated during that
year, but the consuls of the year following, Lucius Furius
Camillus (for the second time) and Junius Brutus Scaeva,

29. cf. Cicero, *de Republica* II.34.

decided it was too serious not to be given priority in matters
to be put before the Senate. Although this was no news to
them, the senators' disquiet was enough to make them equally
afraid of taking action and of doing nothing. They feared that
if the Vestini were left unpunished, it might encourage their
neighbours to insolence and arrogance, while if penalties were
enforced after a war, resentment and fear of approaching
danger would have a similar disturbing effect. Indeed, the
Vestini as a whole were fully equal to the Samnites in matters
of war, comprising as they did the Marsi, Paeligni and
Marrucini, all of whom must be counted as enemies if the
Vestini were attacked. Nevertheless, the day was carried by the
party which at the time could have seemed stronger in courage
than in wisdom; but the outcome showed that fortune favours
the brave. At the Senate's direction the people declared for war
against the Vestini, the command of which fell by lot to
Brutus, while Camillus was assigned the war with the
Samnites. Armies were led off in both directions and the
enemy were prevented from joining forces in their concern to
protect their frontiers. But one of the consuls, Lucius Furius,
on whom the heavier responsibility had been laid, had the
misfortune to fall seriously ill and withdrew from the campaign. He was ordered to appoint a dictator to carry on in his
command, and named Lucius Papirius Cursor, who was by far
the most distinguished soldier at the time; he in his turn named
Quintus Fabius Maximus Rullianus[30] as his master of Horse.
The pair were famous for their successes in office, but more
so for the dissension between them, which almost reached the
pitch of mortal combat.

The other consul conducted a campaign amongst the Vestini
which took many forms, though everywhere meeting with
uniform success. For he destroyed their land, and, by pillaging
and burning their houses and crops, forced them out to give
battle against their will. Then he broke their power in a single
action, though not without casualties amongst his own men,
so that the Vestini first took refuge in their camp and then,

30. Called Rullus in XXIV.9.8; the grandfather of Fabius
Cunctator.

losing confidence in palisades and entrenchments, dispersed amongst their towns with the intention of defending themselves by the siting of their cities and their walls. Finally the consul set about storming the towns as well, and thanks to the fighting fury of his men, in resentment for their wounds, as scarcely any of them had come out of the battle unscathed, he scaled and captured first Cutina and then Cingilia. The plunder from both cities he gave to the soldiers, because neither gates nor walls of the enemy had held them back.

30. The auspices were doubtful for the march on Samnium, and the flaw in them had effect not on the outcome of the campaign, which was conducted successfully, but on the violent jealousy and personal animosity of the commanders. The dictator Papirius set out for Rome in order to repeat the taking of auspices, acting on the advice of the keeper of the sacred chickens; as he left he warned the master of Horse not to leave his post or engage the enemy in his own absence. After the dictator had gone, Quintus Fabius learned through scouts that things were generally as relaxed on the enemy's side as if there were not a single Roman in Samnium, and whether because his youthful high spirits were fired with indignation that all initiative should apparently be in the hands of the dictator, or because he was carried away by the opportunity for achieving success, he marshalled his troops in readiness for action, and marched on a place called Imbrinium, where he engaged the Samnites in a pitched battle. This went so well, as it happened, that nothing could have offered greater success had the dictator been present; the commander did not fail his men nor the men their commander. The cavalry too, when they failed to break the enemy's line after several charges, at the command of Lucius Cominius, one of the military tribunes, took off their horses' bridles and spurred them on so hard that nothing could check their advance. They cut down arms and men along a broad front; the infantry followed up the cavalry charge and attacked the demoralized enemy, who are said to have lost twenty thousand men that day. Some authorities, I find, say that two engagements were fought in the dictator's absence, with two outstanding victories, but only this one

battle is mentioned by the earliest historians, while in some
records the episode has been omitted altogether.

After carnage on such a scale the master of Horse took
possession of extensive spoils. He piled up the enemy's arms
in a great heap, set fire to them and burnt them all. This was
either to carry out a vow made to one of the gods, or (if we
like to believe Fabius[31]) it was done to prevent the dictator's
taking the credit for his own glory, and having the arms
inscribed with his name and carried in his triumph. Furthermore, a dispatch reporting the victory which was sent to the
Senate, not the dictator, was an indication that Fabius had no
intention of sharing any congratulations with him. That is
certainly how Lucius Papirius received the news, showing
every sign of annoyance and dissatisfaction while others were
rejoicing in the victory won. He therefore hastily adjourned
the Senate and hurried out of the Senate-house, repeatedly
declaring that if the master of Horse should be allowed to defy
authority with impunity, his victory in battle had overthrown
and destroyed the dictator's sovereign power and military
discipline no less than the Samnite legions. And so he set out
for the camp, breathing threats and fury, but although he
pressed on by the longest stages he could manage, he was
unable to forestall the news that he was coming; for messengers
had left the City ahead of him to report that the dictator was
on the way, thirsting for vengeance and praising with nearly
every other word the deed of Titus Manlius.[32]

31. Fabius quickly summoned his soldiers to a meeting and
exhorted them to call on the same courage they had shown in
defending the State against its bitterest enemies to protect the
commander – under whose leadership and auspices they had
won their victory – from the uncontrollable fury of the dictator. Papirius was on his way, he said, raging with insensate
jealousy against the courage and good fortune of another man;
he was beside himself because his country had gained conspicuous success in his own absence, and if he had the power

31. Quintus Fabius Pictor, the Roman senator and historian, who
took an active part in the Second Punic War.
32. i.e. in executing his son; cf. ch. 7.

to contrive a change of fortune he would prefer a Samnite victory to a Roman one. He kept saying that his authority was defied, as if the same spirit had not prompted his veto on fighting as his indignation that a battle was fought! On that occasion jealousy had made him want to obstruct another man's enterprise, and he would have snatched arms from the most eager of his soldiers to prevent their using them in his absence. Now he was consumed with anger and resentment simply because his men had not lacked arms and hands to use them when Lucius Papirius was not with them, and Quintus Fabius had conducted himself as master of Horse and not as the dictator's orderly! What would he have done if the hazards of war and common lot of battle had meant that the engagement ended in defeat, seeing that when the enemy was overcome, and the State so well served that it could not have fared better even under his own unrivalled leadership, he now had only threats of punishment for the master of Horse in his hour of victory? In fact he was no more hostile to the master of Horse than to the military tribunes, the centurions and the men in the ranks, and had it been possible, he would have vented his fury on all alike; as it was not, one man was the target for his violence. 'Jealousy like lightning seeks out the heights,' he cried. 'He is aiming at your leader in counsel, your commander, and if he succeeds in destroying me along with the glory of my achievement, then as if lording it over a defeated army, he will be emboldened to visit on the troops all he got away with in the case of the master of Horse.' He urged them to defend the liberty of all by supporting his cause. If the dictator saw that the same united spirit they had shown in battle was applied to defending their victory and that the safety of one man was the common concern of them all, he would turn his mind to a more merciful judgement. He ended by entrusting his life and fortunes to their loyalty and courage. 32. The cry rose from the whole assembly that he should be of good heart: no one should do him violence while all was well with the Roman legions.

Soon after this the dictator arrived, and a trumpet call summoned an assembly without delay. Then a herald obtained

silence and named Quintus Fabius, the master of Horse, who
had no sooner mounted the tribunal from his position below
it than the dictator addressed him as follows. 'Tell me, Quintus
Fabius, since the power of a dictator is supreme and the consuls
obey him, though theirs is the authority of kings, as do the
praetors, who are elected under the same auspices as the
consuls: do you think it right or not that a master of Horse
should also obey his command? And I put this further question
to you: when I knew that I had left home under ambiguous
auspices, should I have put the public safety at risk when our
religious duties were in a state of confusion, or take the auspices
again, so as to avoid action when the gods' will was in doubt?
I should also like to know whether a master of Horse could
possibly feel unrestricted and free to take action in matters
where a dictator has been prevented by religious scruple. But
why do I put these questions? Even had I left without a word,
your thoughts should still have been directed towards inter-
preting my wishes. Answer me now: did I forbid you to take
action in my absence? Did I forbid you to engage the enemy?
But you flouted my authority; the auspices were ambiguous,
our religious duties were in confusion, yet you presumed to
defy military precedent, our fathers' teaching and the gods'
divine power – to do battle with the enemy. Answer the
questions put to you; but take care not to utter a word besides!
Stand by, lictor.'

It was not easy for Fabius to answer these charges separately.
Now he protested that he had the same man acting as his
accuser and judge on a capital charge, then cried out that his life
could more easily be taken from him than the glory of his
deeds; he switched from self-justification to wild accusations,
until Papirius in a fresh burst of fury gave orders to strip
the master of Horse and make ready the rods and axes. As the
lictors tore off his clothing Fabius escaped, calling on the
loyalty of his men, and took refuge amongst the *triarii,* who
were already spreading riot.

At this, uproar arose throughout the whole assembly, with
entreaties and threats to be heard on all sides. Those who
happened to stand nearest to the tribunal and could be recog-

nized be being under the general's eyes implored him to spare
the master of Horse and not condemn the army with him. The
furthest ranks and the crowd round Fabius upbraided the
dictator for his severity and came near to mutiny. Even the
tribunal was involved; the officers standing round the consul's
seat begged him to postpone the matter until the following
day, and allow time for consideration and for his anger to cool.
Fabius's youth had suffered sufficient reproof, they said, and
his victory was discredited enough. Papirius should not push
punishment to its extreme or bring disgrace upon a young man
of such merit, his distinguished father and the whole Fabian
family. As they made little impression with pleas and argument, they bade him look at the commotion in the assembly:
when the soldiers were so excited, surely a man of his age and
discretion should not add fire and fuel to the flames of mutiny!
No one would find fault with Quintus Fabius for trying to
avert his own punishment, but the dictator would be blamed
if in his blind fury he provoked the crowd's hostility against
himself by this perverse confrontation. Finally, he should not
suppose that they acted thus out of personal obligation to
Fabius; they were prepared to swear on oath that it did not
appear to be in the public interest that Quintus Fabius should
be punished at that moment.

33. By these words the officers roused the dictator's hostility
against themselves rather than reconciled him with the master
of Horse, and they were ordered to descend from the tribunal.
Papirius tried to gain silence through the herald, but without
success, and since neither his own voice nor his attendants'
could be heard for the shouting and uproar, nightfall put an
end to the struggle as it does to a battle.

The master of Horse was ordered to appear next day, but
when everyone told him that Papirius would be more violently
hostile, provoked and exasperated as he was by the very fact
of having met opposition, he slipped out of the camp unseen
and fled to Rome. There, with the support of his father,
Marcus Fabius, who had been three times consul and also
dictator, he immediately summoned the Senate and made his
complaint to the senators. He was actually dealing with the

violence and injustice shown him by the dictator when a sudden disturbance was heard outside the Senate-house as the lictors moved people away, and Papirius himself arrived in a fury; for he had followed with a company of light-armed horse as soon as he heard that Fabius had left the camp. The battle was on again, and Papirius ordered the arrest of Fabius. Both the leading senators and the Senate as a whole tried to make him relent, but he remained obdurate and persisted in his intention. At this the young man's father, Marcus Fabius, spoke out: 'Since neither the Senate's authority nor my own advanced age – which you are preparing to bereave – means anything to you, nor do the courage and noble birth of the master of Horse whom you appointed yourself, nor even the pleas which have often pacified an enemy and can appease the wrath of the gods, I call on the people's tribunes and appeal to the people. You shun the judgement of your own army and the judgement of the Senate; the people then shall be your judge – a judge that alone has more power and authority than your own dictatorship. Let me see whether you will yield to an appeal to which a Roman King, Tullus Hostilius, submitted!'[33]

From the Senate-house they repaired to the Rostra, which the dictator mounted with a few supporters, while the master of Horse was accompanied by the whole body of leading senators. Papirius ordered Fabius to be removed from the Rostra to stand below it, and his father followed him, saying 'Very well, order our removal, but we can still speak as private citizens from where we stand.' At first continuous speeches were not to be heard so much as angry arguments on both sides; then the elder Fabius raised his voice in indignation to quell the din, as he attacked the arrogance and cruelty of Papirius and reminded him that he had been a dictator at Rome himself, but no one – not even a plebeian, centurion or soldier – had suffered at his hands. Papirius, he said, claimed victory and triumph over a Roman general as if over enemy commanders. What a difference there was between the self-

33. At the trial of Horatius for murdering his sister, recounted by Livy in I.26.

restraint of the ancients and this new kind of arrogance and
cruelty! When Quinctius Cincinnatus was dictator and had to
rescue the consul Lucius Minucius from blockade, he showed
his anger only by leaving Minucius in command of the army
as his legate, not as consul.[34] Marcus Furius Camillus, when
Lucius Furius had scorned his advanced age and authority and
fought a battle with fearful consequences, not only controlled
his anger at the time, so as not to say anything against his
colleague in his dispatches to the people or Senate, but on his
return, when the Senate gave him permission to choose someone to share his command, picked Furius from all the consular
tribunes as his choice of colleague.[35] Why, even the people,
who held supreme power over everything, had never vented
their indignation on those who had lost armies through rashness or inexperience with anything worse than a fine; capital
punishment for a defeat in war had never been demanded of
any general up to that day. Now the commanders of the
Roman people, whom it was a sin to punish even after defeat,
were being threatened with rods and axes despite their victories
and well-merited triumphs. Whatever would have happened
to his own son had he lost an army, had he been defeated, put
to flight, driven from his camp? To what further lengths could
Papirius's fury and violence have gone than to order flogging
and execution? Was it right and proper that the State should
be rejoicing in victory with supplications and thanksgivings,
all because of Quintus Fabius, while he, on whose account the
shrines of the gods were thrown open, while their altars
smoked with sacrifices and were piled high with offerings to
do them honour, should be stripped and scourged by the rods
in full sight of the Roman people, as he looked up to the
Capitol and Citadel and the gods whose aid he had twice
invoked in battle, and never in vain? What would be the
reaction of the army, which had won victory under his leadership and auspices? What grief there would be in the Roman
camp, what rejoicing among the enemy!

All this he said mingling reproof with complaint, and call-

34. cf. III.26–9, especially 29.2.
35. cf. VI.22.5.

ing for the protection of gods and men as he embraced his son amid floods of tears. 34. On his side were ranged the powerful authority of the Senate, the good-will of the people, the support of the tribunes, the memory of the absent army. His opponent countered with the invincible authority of the Roman people, military discipline, the order of a dictator, which had always been revered as the gods' will, the precedent of Manlius,[36] and the way he put the general good before his love for his son, as Lucius Brutus, the founder of Roman liberty, had done before him in the case of his two children.[37] Today (Papirius argued) fathers were easy-going and older men unconcerned about the flouting of another's authority, ready to find excuses for the young when military discipline was subverted, as if it were a matter of little importance. But he would continue in the course he had undertaken and remit nothing of the proper punishment for a man who had fought a battle against his orders, when the auspices were ambiguous and religious duties in confusion. Whether the majesty of absolute authority were to continue was not in his power to decide; but Lucius Papirius would do nothing to diminish it. His earnest desire was that the tribunes would not use their power, itself inviolate, to violate Roman authority by their intervention, and that the people would not destroy the lawful effectiveness of the dictatorship at the very time he held office. If they did so, it would not be Lucius Papirius but the tribunes and the perverted judgement of the people which posterity would censure − but in vain. For let military discipline once be dishonoured, and soldier would not obey centurion, nor centurion tribune, nor tribune legate, nor legate consul, nor master of Horse dictator. No one would have respect either for men or for the gods; neither edicts of generals nor auspices would be regarded; without leave of absence soldiers would roam around in peaceful or hostile territory alike; with no thought of their oath they would discharge themselves by their own permission when they liked; the standards would be abandoned through lack of numbers to guard them; the army

36. ch. 7.18–19.   37. cf. II.5.

would not muster to order, and would fight regardless of day or night, good or bad position, order or prohibition of their general, keeping neither to ranks nor formation, so that army life would become a blind and casual kind of brigandage instead of a long-established and dedicated service. 'On these charges, tribunes of the people, you must allow yourselves to stand trial in all ages to come! Your heads must bear the guilt if Quintus Fabius goes unpunished for doing as he pleases.'

35. The tribunes stood aghast, more concerned now on their own account than for him on whose behalf their help was sought, but were relieved of their responsibility when the Roman people turned as one man to the dictator, begging and imploring him to listen to them and remit the punishment of the master of Horse. The tribunes too fell in with the prevalent mood of entreaty, and set about beseeching the dictator to make allowances for human weakness and for the youth of Quintus Fabius, who, they said, had been punished enough. Next the young man himself, and after him his father Marcus Fabius dropped all thought of further argument, and flung themselves at the dictator's knees in an attempt to avert his anger. Then the dictator, calling for silence, spoke as follows: 'Very well, Romans. Military discipline and the majesty of authority have prevailed, despite the risk that this day would be their last. Quintus Fabius retains his guilt for the crime of going into battle against his general's orders, but having been found guilty he is offered as a gift to the people of Rome and to the power of the tribunes, which has helped him through entreaties instead of in proper legal form. Live, Quintus Fabius, more fortunate in this united wish of your fellow-citizens to preserve you than in the victory which was your proud boast a short time ago! Live, though you dared to commit a crime which even your father, had he been in my own position, would not have forgiven you. With me you can resume good relations when you please; for the Roman people to whom you owe your life you need do no more than show that you have learned the lesson which this day has taught you – that in war and in peace you are able to bow to lawful authority.' Then after declaring that he would not detain Fabius further,

he came down from the Rostra; the joyful Senate and still more joyful people gathered round and escorted them off with congratulations on all sides for both the master of Horse and the dictator. It appeared that military discipline was strengthened as much by the peril of Quintus Fabius as by the lamentable punishment of the young Manlius.

It so happened that year that every time the dictator left the army there was enemy movement in Samnium. But with the example of Quintus Fabius before his eyes, the legate Marcus Valerius, who was in command of the camp, feared the grim wrath of the dictator as much as any attack from the enemy. And so when a forage party was caught in an ambush and killed while fighting in a difficult position, it was generally believed that it could have been rescued by Valerius had he not been so nervous at the thought of those harsh commands. Fear of his anger also lost the dictator the support of the army, already hostile because he had been so implacable towards Quintus Fabius, and had granted the Roman people the concession which he had refused to their own pleas.

36. When the dictator had given Lucius Papirius Crassus authority over the City and forbidden the master of Horse, Quintus Fabius, to make use of his official powers in any way, he returned to the camp. His arrival gave little pleasure to the Romans and caused no alarm at all among their enemies; for on the following day, whether unaware of the dictator's coming or not caring whether he was there or not, the Samnites approached the camp in full battle order. But so decisive an influence on events had one man, in the person of Lucius Papirius, that if the soldiers had been willing to act upon their general's plans, it was held to be certain that the war with the Samnites could have ended on that day: so well did he dispose his forces and strengthen their position with military tactics of every kind. Yet the men held back and deliberately prevented a victory in order to deny their commander the credit for it. There were more Samnites killed, but more Romans wounded. Experience made the dictator realize what had barred his way to victory; he saw that he must moderate his ways and temper his natural severity with a more genial

manner. So he summoned his legates and made the round of
his wounded soldiers in person, putting his head into their
tents, asking them in turn how they were, and committing
each one by name to the care of the legates, tribunes and
prefects. This in itself was a popular thing to do, and he carried
it out with such tact that in the process of healing their bodies
Papirius won his soldiers' hearts long before recovery; in fact
nothing helped them to regain health more effectively than the
grateful spirit in which they accepted these attentions. When
the army was restored he met the enemy, confident of the
result, as were his soldiers, and so completely defeated and
scattered the Samnites that this was the last day they ever
joined battle with him. The victorious army then marched off
wherever hope of plunder led them, and traversed enemy
territory without encountering any arms or resistance either
open or from ambush. The soldiers were the more eager for
having been promised all the plunder, spurred on by hopes of
personal gain as much as by general resentment against the
enemy. Their losses drove the Samnites to ask the dictator for
peace, and they agreed with him to give each soldier a garment
and a year's pay. He ordered them to go before the Senate, to
which they replied that they entrusted their cause to the
honour and integrity of none but himself, and would follow
him there. The army was accordingly withdrawn from
Samnium.

37. Lucius Papirius entered the City in triumph, and as he
wished to resign his dictatorship, before doing so he held an
election for consuls by order of the Senate, at which Gaius
Sulpicius Longus (for the second time) and Quintus Aemilius
Cerretanus were elected. The peace treaty could not be concluded while its terms were still under discussion, so the
Samnites left the City under a truce for a year. Even this was
broken when they failed to honour their promises, so much
were they encouraged to make war when they heard that
Papirius had resigned office.

In the consulship of Gaius Sulpicius and Quintus Aemilius
(some of the annals call him Aulius), the Samnites were in
revolt and a new war also broke out in Apulia. Armies were

sent in both directions; the drawing of lots gave the Samnites to Sulpicius and the Apulians to Aemilius. Some records say that war was not made on the Apulians but fought in defence of the people allied to Apulia against Samnite wanton aggression; but the circumstances of the Samnites, who at the time were hardly able to repel an attack on themselves, make it unlikely that they invaded Apulia. More probably both Apulians and Samnites were at war with Rome simultaneously, However, there was no engagement worth mention; Apulia and Samnium were laid waste by the Romans without any encounter with the enemy in either region.

At Rome a night alarm suddenly roused the City from sleep in a panic, and the Capitol and Citadel, walls and gates were crowded with armed men. But after all the rushing about and calls to arms in every quarter, at daybreak no one could be found to have started the alarm nor any reason for it.

In the same year the Tusculans were brought to trial before the people in accordance with the proposed Flavian bill. The people's tribune, Marcus Flavius, had proposed that the Tusculans should be punished for having given support and advice to the Veliterni and Privernates in their war with Rome. The people of Tusculum, with their wives and children, came to Rome in a large crowd, changed their clothing to make them look like men under accusation, and went the round of the tribes, clasping the knees of every citizen in supplication. In this way pity did more to gain them remission of punishment than argument to clear them of the charges. All the tribes rejected the proposal except the Pollian, which voted that the adult men should be flogged and put to death and the women and children sold as slaves under the laws of warfare. The memory of the anger aroused in the Tusculans against the proposers of so cruel a punishment is known to have lasted down to our fathers' day, and scarcely any candidate from the Pollian tribe ever got support from the Papirian.[38]

38. The following year, when Quintus Fabius and Lucius

38. The Tusculans were eventually enrolled in the Papirian tribe, where their numbers dominated it.

Fulvius were consuls, fear of a more serious war in Samnium – where the Samnites were said to have assembled an army of mercenary soldiers from their neighbours – led to the appointment of Aulus Cornelius Arvina as dictator, with Marcus Fabius Ambustus as master of Horse. They recruited an excellent army by means of a strict levy, and led if off to meet the Samnites. They took no precautions over setting up camp in hostile territory, as if the enemy were far away, when suddenly Samnite legions appeared and boldly entrenched themselves next to a Roman outpost. Night was already drawing on, and this stopped them from attacking the fortifications, but they did not conceal their intention of doing so at dawn next day. The dictator saw that the battle would be upon him sooner than he had expected and he did not wish his soldiers' morale to suffer from their position; so he left a number of fires burning to deceive the enemy and silently led the legions out. However, the camps were too close for him to escape notice. The Samnite cavalry pursued him at once, but though they followed close upon the marching army they refrained from attacking until day began to dawn. As for the Samnite infantry, they did not even leave their camp before daybreak. When at last it was light, the cavalry ventured to attack the Romans, and, by harassing the rearguard and pressing hard on the army at places where it was difficult to find a crossing, they stopped its advance. Meanwhile the infantry had joined up with the cavalry and the Samnites threw all their forces into an attack. The dictator saw that he could not move forward without a lot of trouble and therefore gave orders to measure out a site for a camp where he had halted. But with Samnite cavalry surrounding them on all sides it was impossible for the men to collect stakes and start the work.

So, when he saw that he had no chance of moving on or staying, the dictator had the baggage moved out of the way of his men and drew them up for battle. The enemy too formed up against him, his equals in spirit and in strength. Their spirits were high mainly because they were unaware that the Romans had retreated from a difficult position and not from them, and believed that it was their own formidable

pursuit which had scattered them in terror. That held the
balance even for a while, although the Samnites had long been
unused to withstanding the battle-cry of a Roman army.
Indeed, the outcome of the battle on that day, from the third
hour until the eighth, is said to have been so uncertain that no
second cry was raised after the one at the first clash of arms;
the standards were neither moved forward nor taken back; and
nowhere did either side give ground. Every man stood firm
in his place, as the armies pressed forward with their shields and
fought without pausing to take breath or look behind. The
continuous din and unchanged course of the battle looked as
though only nightfall or utter exhaustion would call a halt.
Now men were losing strength, their swords lacked thrusting
drive, the commanders' tactics failed them, when the Samnite
cavalry heard from one of their companies which had forged
ahead that the Romans had left their baggage some distance
away from the army, where it was lying without a guard or
palisade to protect it, and made a sudden dash to get it in their
greed for plunder. But when a frightened messenger told the
dictator of this, his reply was 'Just leave them to hamper
themselves with loot.' Then more and more men came up,
calling out that everywhere the soldiers' fortunes were being
plundered and carried off. At this Cornelius called to the
master of Horse: 'Marcus Fabius, do you see how the enemy's
cavalry have left the battle? They are mixed up and encumbered with our baggage. Attack them while they are scattered,
as any large group of men must be when they are out for loot
– you will find few still mounted, few with sword in hand –
and while they load their horses with plunder, cut them down
unarmed and make their looting bloody for them! I'll take care
of the legions and the infantry battle; let glory for the cavalry
be yours!'

39. The Roman cavalry, drawn up in the best possible
formation, fell on their scattered and encumbered enemy and
butchered them right and left. Amongst the packs hastily
thrown down, which lay under the hooves of the terrified
horses and hindered their escape, the Samnites were powerless
either to fight or to run away, and were massacred. Then when

the cavalry was almost wiped out, Marcus Fabius wheeled the two wings of his horsemen to come close together and attacked the line of infantry from the rear. The fresh noise of battle which now broke out struck terror into the hearts of the Samnites, and the dictator saw that the men in their front line were looking round, the standards were in disorder, and the whole battle-line was beginning to waver. He shouted to his men, then urged them on, and called on the tribunes and centurions by name to renew the battle with him. The battle-cry was raised again, the Romans pressed on to attack, and as they advanced they could see that the Samnites were in growing confusion. Now the cavalry was actually within sight of the front ranks; Cornelius looked back at the maniples of soldiers and showed them as far as he could with hand and voice that he could see the shields and banners of his own men. This was no sooner heard than the cavalry was seen. The army quickly forgot their wounds and the struggle they had endured for nearly the whole day, and hurled themselves at the enemy like men who had come fresh from camp and had just been given the signal for battle. The Samnites could withstand the shock of the cavalry and fierce pressure of the infantry no longer. Some were cut down in the mêlée, others scattered in flight. The infantry surrounded those who held out and killed them off, while the cavalry butchered the fugitives, among whom was the Samnite general himself.

This battle finally broke the Samnites, so much so that in all their councils men grumbled that it was no wonder if they had no success in a sacrilegious war started in violation of a treaty,[39] where the gods had more right than man to be hostile to them. A heavy price would have to be paid to expiate this war and atone for it; the only question was whether they should pay the penalty with the blood of the guilty few or of the innocent many. Some even ventured at this point to name those responsible for their taking up arms. One name in particular could be distinguished, as all clamoured for Papius Brutulus, an influential noble who had undoubtedly been

39. ch. 2.1–4; cf. ch. 22.7.

responsible for breaking the most recent truce. The praetors were obliged to report on his case, and it was decreed that Papius Brutulus should be handed over to the Romans and sent to Rome with all the Roman plunder and prisoners, and that everything the fetial priests had sought to recover under the terms of the treaty should be returned, as was just and proper. The fetial priests were dispatched to Rome, in accordance with this resolution, taking with them the dead body of Papius Brutulus, who had escaped punishment and ignominy by voluntary suicide. It was agreed that his possessions should be handed over with his body. The Romans, however, would accept none of these things except the prisoners and any pieces of plunder they recognized as their own; the surrender of everything else came to nothing.[40] The dictator celebrated a triumph voted him by the Senate.

40. Some authorities claim that this war was fought by the consuls and that the triumph over the Samnites was theirs. They say that Fabius even advanced into Apulia and took off a great deal of booty. It is not disputed that Aulus Cornelius was dictator that year; what is uncertain is whether he was appointed to conduct the war or so that there should be someone to give the starting signal for the chariot races at the Roman Games, since the praetor, Lucius Plautius, happened to be seriously ill at the time; and whether after discharging this duty, which certainly demands no particularly memorable exercise of authority, he resigned his dictatorship. It is not easy to choose between the facts or the authorities. The record has been falsified, I believe, by funeral eulogies and fictitious inscriptions on portrait busts, when families try to appropriate to themselves the tradition of exploits and titles of office by means of inventions calculated to deceive. This has undoubtedly led to confusion both in individual achievements and in public records of events. Nor is there extant any writer contemporary with those times to provide the firm basis of a reliable authority.

---

40. Evidently the Romans wished to impose revised and harsher terms.

BOOK IX

1. This year was followed by the Caudine Peace, the notorious outcome of a Roman catastrophe. The consuls were Titus Veturius Calvinus and Spurius Postumius.[1] The Samnites had as general that year Gaius Pontius, whose father Herennius was outstanding for his wise foresight, while the son was unrivalled in military ability and leadership. When the envoys who had been sent to Rome to make restitution returned without having been granted peace, Pontius spoke to the Samnites as follows: 'You should not think that this mission has achieved nothing. Any anger we incurred from the gods by breaking a treaty[2] has been expiated. I am certain that whatever gods wished us to be forced to make restitution of what was demanded of us under the terms of the treaty, it was not their wish that our attempts at reparation should have been so contemptuously rejected by the Romans. For what more could have been done to placate gods and appease men than what we did? The enemy's property which we captured as booty, and believed to be ours by right of war, we returned; those responsible for the war, as we could not hand them over alive, we surrendered after they had met their end, and their possessions we carried to Rome, lest any guilt should linger amongst us from contact with them. What more do I owe you, Romans, what more do I owe the treaty or the gods who witnessed it? Whom can I offer you to judge between your anger and the punishment I deserve? I reject no one, neither people nor individual. But if no common justice is left to the weak when dealing with the powerful, I can still turn to the gods who exact vengeance for intolerable pride, and beg them to direct their wrath against those who are satisfied neither by the restoration of their own property nor by its increase from what belongs to other men; whose savage fury will not be

1. They had been consuls together before, in 334 (VIII.16.12).
2. The treaty described in VIII.2.1, made in 341.

sated by the death of the guilty, and surrender of their lifeless bodies, nor by the owners' property following on that surrender, unless we give them our blood to drink and our vitals to tear. War is just, Samnites, when it is necessary, and arms are righteous for those whose only hope remains in arms. Since, then, it is of the greatest importance in men's affairs whether what they do has the favour or the disfavour of the gods, rest assured that you fought your previous wars against gods rather than men, but you will fight this one now threatening you with the gods themselves for your leaders.'

2. With these prophetic words, no less true than they were encouraging, he led out his army and set up camp near Caudium with the greatest possible secrecy. From there he sent ten soldiers disguised as shepherds in the direction of Calatia, where he kept hearing that the Roman consuls were already encamped, with orders to scatter and graze their flocks not far from the Roman outposts. Whenever they came upon raiding parties they were all to tell the same story – that the Samnite legions were in Apulia, were besieging Luceria with their entire forces, and were on the point of capturing it. This rumour had already been deliberately spread abroad and had reached the ears of the Romans, but the prisoners strengthened their belief in it, especially as they all gave similar accounts. The Romans had no hesitation about going to the aid of the people of Luceria, who were their good and loyal allies, and at the same time they wished to forestall the defection of the whole of Apulia in the face of imminent danger; their deliberations were only on the route to be taken.

Two roads led in the direction of Luceria, one along the coast of the Upper Sea, which was open and accessible, but though safer was proportionately longer, while the other, through the Caudine Forks, was shorter, but the nature of the site is like this: two deep defiles, narrow and wooded, are linked by an unbroken chain of mountains on either side. Between them lies an enclosed open area which is fairly extensive, grassy and well watered, with the road running through the middle; but before you come to it, you have to enter the first ravine and then either go back the same way you came in, or if you go on, you can get out only by the other defile, which is narrower and more obstructed.[3]

The Romans sent their army into this plain by one road through the rocky gorge, but when they went on to the second defile they found it blocked by trees which had been felled and a pile of huge boulders lying in their path. The enemy's plot was now apparent, and at the same moment their troops were seen at the head of the pass. The Romans then hurried back and tried to regain the road by which they had made their entry, but that too they found blocked with its own barricade and armed men. At this they halted, without any word of command, all of them stupefied and gripped by a strange sort of paralysis, as they looked at each other, everyone supposing that his neighbour was more capable of thought and decision than himself. Thus they remained for a long time, without moving or speaking. Then when they saw the consuls' tents being put up and some soldiers getting out their entrenching tools, although they realized that it would be ludicrous to dig themselves in when their situation was desperate and all hope was abandoned, they did not want to incur blame on top of their misfortune; so they turned to digging, each man for himself with no word of encouragement or command, and entrenched a camp close to the water. They even joked among themselves with pitiful candour about their useless work and effort, while all the time the enemy jeered contemptuously at them. The wretched consuls did not even call a council, since the situation permitted neither advice nor aid, but the legates and tribunes assembled before them unbidden, and the soldiers gathered round the headquarters and begged their leaders for help – though this the immortal gods could hardly have given them.

3. Night overtook them lamenting their plight rather than consulting on action, each man giving voice to his woes as his nature prompted him. 'Let us push through the barriers on the roads,' said one, 'cross the mountains confronting us, penetrate the forests, go wherever we can carry arms, if only we can get

3. See Map 4 for the most generally accepted site.

at the enemy we have been defeating for nearly thirty years.[4] Every road will be level and easy for a Roman fighting a treacherous Samnite.' 'Where can we go or how?' asked another. 'Are we aiming at shifting mountains from their seat? So long as these ridges tower over us, how can you reach the enemy? Armed and unarmed, brave men and cowards, we are all equally trapped and defeated. The enemy will not even draw his sword, to grant us death with honour. He will finish the war by sitting still.' The night was spent in exchanges of this kind, without a thought of food or sleep.

Even the Samnites had no plan for making use of such good fortune, and so they unanimously agreed to send a letter to Herennius Pontius, the father of their general, asking his advice. He was already bowed down with years and had retired from civil as well as military duties; but despite his frail body his mind and judgement had lost none of their vigour. Once he learned that the Roman armies were trapped between the two passes at the Caudine Forks and was asked for guidance by the messenger from his son, his advice was that the Romans should all be sent away unharmed as soon as possible. When this opinion was rejected and the same messenger returned to seek further advice, he declared that they should all be put to death, down to the last man. On receiving these replies, as conflicting as the ambiguous responses of an oracle, his son was among the first to believe that his father's mind had aged along with his enfeebled body, but gave way to the general wish that he should be fetched for consultation in person. The old man raised no objection (the story goes); he was brought to the camp in a wagon and invited to a council, where what he said showed no change in his opinion but merely added his reasons for it. His first advice, he said, which he thought the best, would establish lasting peace with a very powerful people by conferring on them an immense benefit; the second would postpone war for many generations during which the Romans would not easily recover their strength after the loss of two armies; there was no third alternative. His son and the other

4. In fact there had been peace between 341 and 325.

leading men pressed him to tell them what would happen if they took a middle course and let the Romans go unhurt, but imposed terms on them as defeated men according to the laws of war. 'That is an idea of yours,' he said, 'which neither wins friends nor removes enemies. Just try saving the men you have exasperated by humiliation! The Roman people is one which does not know how to lie down under defeat. Whatever brand of shame they undergo in their present straits the wound will always rankle in their hearts and will not let them rest until they have made you pay for it many times over.' Neither of his opinions was accepted, and Herennius was taken home from the camp.

4. In the Roman camp, when many unsuccessful attempts had been made to break out and by now all essentials were scarce, the army had to yield to necessity and send envoys, who were first to seek a fair peace and, if they failed to obtain one, to challenge the enemy to fight. Pontius thereupon replied that the war was already fought and won; and since the Romans did not admit their plight even when defeated and taken prisoner, he would send them under the yoke unarmed, with a single garment each. In other respects terms of peace would be fair for both vanquished and victors. If the Romans would evacuate Samnite territory and withdraw their colonies,[5] then Romans and Samnites should live under their own laws henceforth on equal terms. On these conditions he was prepared to conclude a treaty with the consuls, but if anything in them was rejected, the envoys were not to come back to him. When the results of the delegation were made known in the Roman camp, there was an immediate outcry on every side and distress so great that it looked as though the Romans would take it no harder if they were told that they must all die where they stood.

For a long time there was silence, while the consuls were unable to utter a word either for a treaty so shameful or against one so necessary. Finally Lucius Lentulus, who was at the time

5. e.g. Cales, founded in 336 and resented by the Sidicini (VIII.16.13), and Fregellae, founded in 328 (VIII.22.2), both in contravention of the treaty of 341.

foremost among the legates in character and official record,[6] made this speech. 'I have often heard my father recall that he was the only man on the Capitol who did not advise the Senate to buy off the City from the Gauls with gold;[7] he argued that the Romans were not shut in with ditch and rampart by their enemies, who were always very slow about starting an entrenchment and fortification, and it was possible to break out without inevitable disaster, if not without great danger. They had the chance then of running down from the Capitol bearing arms against their attackers, as the besieged have often enough broken out against their besiegers; and if we too could only find a way to grapple with our enemies, whether the ground be favourable or not, I should show that I have inherited something of my father's spirit in the advice I offer. Death for one's country I admit is a glorious thing, and I personally am ready either to devote myself for the legions and people of Rome or to hurl myself into the midst of the enemy. But it is here that I see my country, here all that is left of the Roman legions, and unless they are prepared to rush to their death on their own behalf, what have they to save by dying? The roofs and walls of the City, someone may say, and the great numbers who inhabit it. But all these are surely betrayed, not saved, if this army is wiped out. For who will protect them then? The common mob, I suppose, unwarlike and unarmed — just as much as it defended the City against the onset of the Gauls! Or will they beg for an army from Veii and a Camillus to command it?[8] Here is where all our hopes and resources rest, and if we save these we save our country; but by giving them up to death, we abandon it. You will say that surrender is shameful and humiliating. But our country is so dear that we will save it, if need be, by our humiliation as much as by our death. Let us then submit to that indignity, however great it

6. He had been consul in 328 (VIII.22.8); some of his descendants were to take the name Caudinus.

7. cf. V.48, though Lentulus's father is not mentioned.

8. In V.38.5–10 more than half the Roman army defeated at the battle of the Allia are said to have escaped to Veii, to be led back by Camillus.

be, and bow to necessity, over which not even the gods can prevail. Go, consuls, buy back the City by giving up your arms, as your forebears bought it back by gold.'

5. The consuls then went off to confer with Pontius, but when their conqueror proposed a treaty, they replied that this was impossible without orders from the Roman people, and also without the fetial priests and the other customary ceremonial. Consequently the Caudine Peace was not made by treaty, as is generally believed and is actually stated by Claudius,[9] but by guarantee.[10] For what need would there have been either of guarantors or hostages in the case of a treaty, where negotiations conclude with a prayer that the people responsible for not keeping to the recited terms may be smitten by Jupiter just as the pig is smitten by the fetials? The guarantors were the consuls, legates, quaestors and military tribunes, and the names of all these guarantors are extant, whereas if the settlement had been made by treaty, only the names of the two fetials would have been preserved; and because of the inevitable postponement of a treaty, six hundred Roman cavalry were demanded as hostages, who would forfeit their lives if the terms were not kept. A time was then fixed for delivering the hostages and sending the army under the yoke after arms were laid down.

The return of the consuls caused a fresh outburst of lamentation in the camp. The men could scarcely keep their hands off those whose foolhardiness, so they said, had led them to that place and through whose cowardice they were now to depart more disgracefully than they had come. The consuls had lacked guides and scouts, and like wild beasts had been sent blindly into a trap. The men stared at each other, eyeing the arms they must soon give up, the right hands which would be weaponless and the bodies which were to be at the enemy's mercy. Each one in his mind's eye saw the enemy's yoke, the jeers of the victors, and their scornful faces. They pictured their passage, unarmed, through the armed ranks, then the wretched

9. Q. Claudius Quadrigarius, the annalist; cf. VI.42, note 52.
10. *Sponsio,* a verbal pledge made by responsible officials who then became guarantors of its being kept.

journey of a disgraced army through their allies' cities, and their return to their own City and their parents, who, like their ancestors before them, had often returned in triumph. They alone had been defeated without a wound, without a weapon, without a battle. They had been denied the chance to draw a sword and come to grips with the enemy; arms, strength and spirit had been granted them – but all in vain.

As they made these protests the fated hour of their humiliation arrived, one which would go beyond all their expectations in the bitterness of experience. To start with they were ordered to come outside the rampart, each clad in a single garment and unarmed; and first the hostages were handed over and led off into custody. Then the lictors were told to move away from the consuls, who were stripped of their generals' cloaks, a sight which stirred so much pity in the men who only recently had cursed them, and had declared that they ought to be handed over and tortured, that everyone forgot his own plight and averted his eyes from the outrage to so noble an office, as from a scene of horror. 6. The consuls, pretty well half-naked, were the first to be sent under the yoke, then their officers were humiliated, each in order of rank; then the legions one by one in turn. The enemy stood round under arms, taunting and jeering at them; many were threatened with swords, and some were wounded or killed if the expressions on their faces showed too much resentment at their intolerable position and annoyed their conquerors.

Thus they were sent under the yoke and, what was almost harder to bear, in full view of their enemies. When they came out of the pass, they seemed like men brought back from the dead, seeing the light for the first time; yet the real light which showed them their ranks so disgraced was grimmer than any death. And so, though they could have reached Capua before nightfall, being doubtful of their allies' loyalty and held back by shame, they threw themselves on the ground by the roadside not far from the town, with nothing to supply their needs. When this was reported at Capua, the natural sympathy of allies overcame Campanian inborn arrogance. Without delay the Capuans generously sent insignia of office to the consuls,

along with arms, horses, clothing and provisions for the men,
and as the army approached Capua, the entire senate and
people came out to meet it, and performed all the proper duties
of hospitality, both official and private. Yet the kind courtesy
of their allies and their friendly looks and words were quite
unable either to get a word out of the Romans or even to make
them raise their eyes or look their sympathetic friends in the
face: to such an extent did their feeling of shame, over and
above their misery, constrain them to shun talk and meetings
with their fellow-men.

The following day, when the young nobles sent from Capua
to escort the Romans to the borders of Campania had returned
and were summoned to the senate-house to be questioned by
their elders, they reported that they had found the army much
more dejected and low-spirited than before; the column had
moved on in total silence, almost as if dumb. The old Roman
spirit lay prostrate, the men's courage cast down with their
arms. They returned no greeting, and no one could open his
mouth for apprehension, as if they still bore on their necks the
yoke under which they had been sent. The Samnites, they said,
had won a victory which would be lasting as well as glorious,
for what they had overpowered was not the City of Rome,
as the Gauls had done before them, but something which
demanded far more warlike effort: the Roman courage and
fighting spirit.

7. Such was the account given and heard, and the name of
Rome had almost been given up for lost in the council of her
loyal allies, when (it is said) Aulus Calavius, son of Ovus, a man
of distinguished birth and achievements, who was also respected for his age, declared that the truth was very different:
that stubborn silence, eyes fixed on the ground, ears deaf to any
word of comfort, that shrinking from looking at the light were
indications of the stirring of a deep-seated powerful resentment. Either he knew nothing of the Roman character or that
silence would soon draw from the Samnites doleful cries and
groans, and the Caudine Peace would be a much more painful
memory for the Samnites than for the Romans. Each people
would continue to show its own native spirit, wherever they

might come to grips, but for the Samnites there could not be everywhere a Caudine Pass.

By this time news of the shameful disaster had also reached Rome. The first report was that the army was trapped; then came grimmer news, not so much of danger as of a humiliating peace. At the rumour of a blockade the City had started to hold a levy, but when it was known that there had been so disgraceful a surrender, all preparations for bringing help were abandoned, and without any official sanction the people as one man took to every form of mourning. The shops round the Forum were shut and business in the Forum was suspended spontaneously before proclamation was made. Broad-striped tunics and gold rings were discarded, and the citizens were almost more grief-stricken than the army. Not only were they incensed against the generals and those who had instigated and guaranteed the peace, but their hatred was roused against the innocent soldiers, and they declared their intention to ban them from the City and their homes. These outbursts of fury were dispelled by the arrival of the army, for which even angry men could feel only pity. For they were not like men returning home in safety after losing hope of doing so. They entered the City late in the day, looking and behaving like prisoners; each man hid himself away in his own house, and on the next and following days none of them wanted to look at the Forum or the streets. The consuls shut themselves up in their homes and carried out none of their official duties, except when it was required of them by senatorial decree to appoint a dictator to hold elections. They named Quintus Fabius Ambustus and Publius Aelius Paetus as master of Horse: but as there was a flaw in their election they were replaced by Marcus Aemilius Papus as dictator and Lucius Valerius Flaccus as master of Horse. Even they did not hold elections, and as the people were disgusted with all the magistrates of that year, the State reverted to an interregnum, with Quintus Fabius Maximus and Marcus Valerius Corvus as interreges. Quintus Publilius Philo and Lucius Papirius Cursor (for the second time) were elected as consuls, with the evident approval of the citizens, who felt that there were no leaders more distinguished at that time.

8. The consuls took up office on the day of their election, as the Senate had required, and after dealing with routine resolutions of the Senate brought up the subject of the Caudine Peace. Publilius held the fasces[11] and called on Spurius Postumius to speak. He rose to his feet, with the same look on his face as when he had been sent under the yoke. 'I am well aware, consuls,' he said, 'that I have been called on to rise and speak first not as an honour but because of my humiliation: not as a senator but as one guilty of an ill-starred campaign and an ignominious peace. However, you have not raised the question of our offence or of our punishment; so I will offer no defence, though it would not be very difficult to do so in the hearing of those who have knowledge of men's fortunes and constraints. I will confine myself to a brief statement of opinion on the subject you have raised. This statement will bear witness whether it was myself or your legions that I spared when I bound myself by a guarantee which may have been disgraceful or forced upon me, but is not binding on the Roman people, since it was made without orders from them; and by its terms the Samnites are owed nothing except our own persons. Let the fetial priests hand us over, naked and bound; let us release the people from religious obligation, if we have laid any upon them, so that no obstacle, divine or human, shall prevent a renewal of a just and righteous war. Meanwhile I propose that the consuls shall enrol and equip an army and lead it out, but not enter enemy territory before all the proper details of our surrender have been completed. To you, immortal gods, I address this prayer and plea: if it was not your wish that the consuls Spurius Postumius and Titus Veturius should be successful in their war on the Samnites, rest content now you have seen us sent under the yoke, have seen us bound by an infamous guarantee, and see us now handed over to the enemy naked and bound, receiving on our own heads all the resentment of our foes. May you grant that new consuls and the Roman legions will make war on the Samnites in the way that all wars were carried out before our consulship.'

11. cf. VIII.12, note 13.

When he had finished speaking such a wave of astonishment mingled with sympathy for the man swept through the senators that one minute they could scarcely believe that this was the same Spurius Postumius who had been responsible for so shocking a peace, and the next they were filled with pity at the thought of such a man having to undergo no ordinary punishment at the hands of an enemy infuriated by the breaking of the peace. When they were all moving over to vote for his motion, with nothing but praise for its proposer, the people's tribunes, Lucius Livius and Quintus Maelius, made a brief attempt to interpose their veto. They argued that the people could not be released from their religious obligation by the surrender of themselves (the tribunes), unless the Samnites were returned all the advantages they had had at Caudium; that they deserved no punishment for having saved the army of the Roman people by acting as guarantors of the peace; nor, finally, could they be handed over to the enemy or violated, as their persons were sacrosanct.

9. To this Postumius replied: 'Then meanwhile surrender us, who are unconsecrate persons, as you can do without breaking your religious obligations. Later on, when they have retired from office, you shall surrender those individuals who are now sacrosanct, but if you will listen to me, before doing so, you will have them beaten with rods here in the Comitium, by way of interest on the punishment they have deferred. For when they argue that the people cannot be freed from religious obligation by our surrender, there can be no one so ignorant of fetial law as not to know that they say so in order not to be surrendered rather than as a true statement of fact. Yet I am not denying, Conscript Fathers, that guarantees just as much as treaties are sacred in the eyes of those for whom honour amongst men ranks with our duty to the gods. What I do deny is that any sanction can be given which shall be binding on the people if it is not authorized by them. Why, if the Samnites had forced us to pronounce the correct form of words used by those who surrender cities, with the same high-handedness they showed when they wrung from us that guarantee – would you tribunes declare that the Roman people had been surrendered,

and that this City, its temples, sanctuaries, territories, and waters were now Samnite property? No more of surrender! The question at issue is that of a guarantee. What if we had guaranteed that the Roman people would abandon this City? Set fire to it? Give up having magistrates, a senate and laws? Submit to the rule of kings? "The gods forbid," you say. But humiliating conditions do not reduce the binding power of a guarantee; if the people can be put under obligation for one thing, it can for all. Nor does it even matter, as perhaps some people suppose, whether consul or dictator or praetor gave the guarantee. This was evidently what the Samnites thought, when they were not satisfied with consuls alone as guarantors and insisted on having legates, quaestors and military tribunes as well.

'Now let no one ask me why I gave this guarantee, when it was one which not even a consul had the right to give, and I could neither have guaranteed a peace to the Samnites when it was not in my power to do so nor done so on your behalf when you had given me no mandate. Nothing, Conscript Fathers, was done at Caudium by man's counsel; the immortal gods destroyed the wits, both of your own and of the enemy's commanders. On our side we took inadequate precautions in the campaign; on theirs, they threw away their ill-won victory in their haste to seize arms on any terms from those born to use them. Would it have been difficult for them, had they been in their right minds, to summon older men from home for consultation, and meanwhile to dispatch envoys to Rome? To negotiate terms of peace and a treaty with the Senate and people? It was a three-day journey for anyone travelling light, during which there could have been a truce to fighting, until the envoys returned from Rome bringing them either positive victory or a peace. That and that only would have been a guarantee which we could have given under instructions from the people of Rome. But neither would you have voted this guarantee nor would we have given it. Nor did heaven permit any other ending to the affair than for the Samnites to be deceived by a dream too rosy for their comprehension, and for us to have our army extricated by the same fortune which trapped it: for an empty victory to be rendered useless by an emptier peace, and for a guarantee to be offered which would bind no one but the guarantor. Was there any discussion with you, Conscript Fathers, or with the Roman people? Can anyone appeal to you or say you have deceived him? Can an enemy or a citizen? You gave no guarantee to the enemy, you instructed no citizen to act as guarantor on your behalf; so you have no concern either with us, to whom you gave no mandate, nor with the Samnites, with whom you have had no dealings. The Samnites have in us adequate and responsible guarantors for what is ours to give, what we can make over to them, namely our persons and our lives. On these let them vent their fury, against these let them sharpen their swords and their anger. As for the tribunes, you must decide whether their surrender can be carried out immediately or should be postponed to an appointed day; meanwhile let us, Titus Veturius, and you others, offer these worthless heads of ours in fulfilment of our guarantee, and by our suffering liberate the Roman arms.'

10. Both subject and speaker much impressed the senators and everyone else, including the people's tribunes, who declared themselves ready to bow to the Senate's authority. They then resigned office at once and were handed over to the fetial priests to be taken with the others to Caudium. Once action had been taken on this motion a new light seemed to dawn for the City. The name of Postumius was on everyone's lips: he was lauded to the skies and his conduct compared with the self-sacrifice of the consul Publius Decius[12] and with other famous deeds. The State (it was said) had emerged from a slavish peace by his counsel and efforts; he was giving himself up to torture at the hands of a resentful enemy, to be a sacrificial victim on behalf of the Roman people. People looked only to war and arms; would the time *ever* come, they asked, when they might confront the Samnites weapons in hand?

In a City ablaze with anger and hatred a levy was made up

12. cf. VIII.9.4.

almost wholly of volunteers. The same soldiers were re-
enrolled into new legions and the army marched off towards
Caudium. The fetials went ahead, and when they reached the
town gate gave orders for the guarantors of peace to be
stripped and have their hands bound behind their backs. Out
of respect for Postumius's high position the attendant was
tying him loosely when he said 'No, pull the thong tight, for
a proper surrender.' Then when they came before the
Samnites' assembly and the tribunal of Pontius, the fetial priest
Aulus Cornelius Arvina spoke these words: 'Whereas these
men have acted as guarantors for a treaty when they had no
orders from the Quirites, the people of Rome, and by so doing
have inflicted an injury: so that the Roman people may be
absolved from an impious crime, I surrender these men to
you.' As the fetial spoke, Postumius drove his knee into the
other's thigh with all the force he could, and loudly declared
that he was a Samnite citizen[13] and had profaned the sanctity
of an envoy in violation of the law of nations; this would give
the Romans a better right to make war.

11. Pontius replied: 'I will not receive this surrender, nor
will the Samnites accept it as valid. And you, Spurius
Postumius, if you believe in the existence of the gods, why not
reject the whole negotiation or stand by your agreement? The
Samnite people is entitled to all those it had in its power or to
peace in their place. But why do I appeal to you, when you
are returning yourself as a prisoner to your conqueror, with
what honour you can? I appeal to the people of Rome: if they
regret the guarantee they gave at the Caudine Forks, let them
return the legions to the defile where they were surrounded.
Let no one have deceived anyone; let everything be as if
nothing had happened. Let the Romans resume the arms they
handed over under agreement; let them return to their camp;
let them recover all they had on the day before the conference;
that will be the time for them to vote for war and bold
measures and to reject the guarantee and the peace. Let us carry
on the war in the same circumstances and in the same positions

13. As a prisoner of war he would be the property of the Samnites,
but hardly a Samnite citizen.

we were in before there was mention of peace; let the Roman people make no complaint of the consuls' guarantee nor we of the Roman people's sense of honour. Will you never lack a reason for not keeping to your word in defeat? You gave hostages to Porsenna, and then withdrew them by a trick.[14] You bought back your City from the Gauls with gold – and while they were accepting the gold you cut them down.[15] You agreed with us on a peace, so that we should return you the legions we had captured; now you have nullified that peace. And you always give your fraud some semblance of legality. Does the Roman people not approve of preserving its legions by a shameful peace? Then let it keep its peace, and return the captured legions to the victor; this would have been something worthy of its honour, its treaties, its fetial ceremonies. If you gain what you sought by your agreement, that is, the safety of all these citizens, while I do not gain the peace which was my stipulation when I returned them to you, is this the justice which you, Aulus Cornelius, and you, fetial priests, proclaim to the world?

'As for me, I neither accept those whom you pretend to be surrendering, nor do I hold that they are surrendered. Neither do I hinder their return, despite the anger of the gods whose divinity they have slighted, to the City which is committed by their guarantee. Go to war then, since Spurius Postumius has just now struck at an envoy with his knee! So shall the gods believe that Postumius is a Samnite citizen, not a Roman, that a Roman envoy has been violated by a Samnite, and because of this that you have made a just war on us! To think that you are not ashamed to bring this mockery of religious duty into the light of day, and, old men and consulars as you are, to search for evasions whereby to break your word, evasions which are hardly worthy of children! Go, lictor, free the Romans from their fetters, and let no one hinder them from departing when they please.' The guarantors accordingly

14. Evidently a reference to the famous escape of Cloelia and the girls with her, who swam the Tiber to get back to Rome (II.13.6). For Porsenna, cf. VI.40.17 and note 49.

15. cf. V.48–9.

returned from Caudium to the Roman camp unscathed – possibly released from the nation's pledge and certainly from their own.

12. The Samnites now realized that instead of an insolent peace they faced the renewal of a highly dangerous war, the future consequences of which were not only in their thoughts but in their mind's eye. Too late and all in vain they praised the policies of the aged Pontius, alternatives between which they had fallen, thereby exchanging the victory which was already theirs for an uncertain peace. They had let slip the opportunity of doing good and of doing harm, and now had to fight with men whom they could either have got rid of permanently as their enemies or made their permanent friends. There had been no fighting since the Caudine Peace to give either side advantage; yet there was such a change of heart that Postumius won more fame amongst the Romans for his surrender than Pontius did amongst the Samnites for his bloodless victory. The Romans felt that the very fact that the war could now continue was a definite victory, whereas to the Samnites it seemed that the Romans had at the same moment both renewed the war and won it.

Meanwhile the Satricans defected to the Samnites, who took the colony of Fregellae during the night in a surprise attack with the support, apparently, of men from Satricum. Mutual fear then kept both sides from further action until daybreak, when the dawning light saw the start of a battle in which for some time the people of Fregellae managed to keep on fighting on equal terms, because they were battling for their altars and hearths, and were also supported from the housetops by large numbers of citizens who were not under arms. Then a ruse tipped the balance, when they allowed the voice to be heard of a herald who promised safety to anyone who laid down his arms. Hope of this weakened their determination to fight on, and on all sides they began to throw down their arms. The more tenacious of them kept their weapons and broke out by a gate in the rear, finding more safety in their bold enterprise than the others did in their foolish credulity born of their fears. The Samnites ringed them round with fire, as they vainly appealed to the gods and Samnite honour, and burnt them to death.

The consuls divided the spheres of duty between them, and Papirius then made his way into Apulia towards Luceria, where the Roman cavalrymen handed over as hostages at Caudium were under guard, while Publilius remained in Samnium to confront the troops returning from Caudium. The Samnites were accordingly in two minds what to do; they dared not go off towards Luceria, for fear of enemy attack from the rear, nor stay where they were, lest meanwhile they lost Luceria. The best plan seemed to trust their luck and fight it out with Publilius; and so they led out their troops to battle.

13. The consul Publilius was ready to fight them, but thinking he should first address his army, he gave orders for an assembly to be called. The men came running up to the praetorium all eagerness, but not a word of the general's exhortation could be heard for the clamour of those demanding battle. However, everyone had his own spirit and memory of humiliation to encourage him. Thus they rushed into battle, urging on the standard-bearers, and, so as not to delay the encounter while javelins were cast and swords drawn, they discarded their javelins as if at a given signal, and sword in hand swept headlong against the Samnites. No tactics on the part of their commander were needed for positioning ranks or reserves; the soldiers' fury carried all before them in their half-crazy onrush. As a result, not only were the enemy routed but, not daring to check their flight even at their own camp, they scattered and made for Apulia; however, by the time they reached Luceria they had re-formed themselves into a single marching column. The same fury which swept the Romans straight through the enemy lines also carried them into the Samnite camp. There there was more bloodshed and slaughter than in the battle, and the greater part of the plunder was destroyed in anger.

The other army, led by the consul Papirius, marched along the coast as far as Arpi. Everything was peaceful on the way, more through the wrongs done by the Samnites and consequent hatred of them than from any benefits received from the Roman people; for the Samnites, who at that time lived in mountain villages, used to plunder the plains and coastal districts, despising the farmers for their softer character, which, as often happens, resembled their countryside, while the Samnites themselves were rough mountain people. If this region had been loyal to the Samnites, either a Roman army would have been unable to reach Arpi or it would have been cut off from its supplies and destroyed on its way by the totally barren state of the countryside. Even so, when they had moved on towards Luceria, both besiegers and besieged suffered equally from lack of food. All the supplies for the Romans were brought from Arpi, but in meagre amounts, for while the infantry were engaged in mounting pickets and guards and digging themselves in, the cavalry would bring small bags of corn to the camp from Arpi, but from time to time they would meet the enemy and be forced to throw the corn off their horses and fight. The besieged, before the arrival of the other consul with his victorious army, had got in their provisions from the mountains of the Samnites, and additional troops as well. The arrival of Publilius made everything more difficult; handing over the siege to the care of his colleague he was free to range the country and generally endangered the movement of the enemy's supplies. As a result the Samnites encamped near Luceria lost all hope of being able to endure the shortage of food if the siege continued, and they were compelled to rally their forces from all quarters and engage Papirius in battle.

14. At that moment, when both sides were preparing for battle, envoys from Tarentum arrived and told both Samnites and Romans to desist from war. Whichever army should be responsible for preventing an end to hostilities, they declared, they would fight themselves on behalf of the other. After hearing these envoys, as if he were persuaded by what they had said, Papirius replied that he would confer with his colleague. He sent for Publilius, but spent the whole interval completing his preparations; then when he had discussed with him the situation (about which there was no doubt) he displayed the signal for battle. The two consuls were engaged in matters both religious and practical, as is usual before a set engagement,

when the Tarentine envoys approached them, hoping for an answer. 'Tarentines,' said Papirius, 'the keeper of our chickens reports that the auspices are favourable, and the omens from the sacrifice are also excellent, so, as you see, the gods are behind us as we go into action.' He then gave the order to advance the standards and led out his troops, expostulating on the folly of a people which was incompetent to manage its own affairs because of internal strife and discord, but yet thought fit to prescribe limits to peace and war for others.

The Samnites on their side had dismissed from their minds any interest in continuing the war, either because they genuinely desired peace or because they thought it expedient to pretend they wanted it in order to win over the Tarentines. So when they saw the Romans suddenly drawn up for battle they cried out that they would abide by the wishes of the Tarentines, and would neither march on to the field nor carry arms outside the camp; they had been deceived, but they would rather suffer whatever fate awaited them than appear to have rejected the Tarentines and their counsels of peace. The consuls replied that they welcomed the good omen and prayed that the enemy would keep to their intention of not even defending their ramparts. Then they divided the troops between them, advanced on the Samnite earthworks, and attacked them simultaneously on all sides. Some began to fill in the trenches, others to tear down the stakes and throw them into the trenches, their spirit fired not only by their native courage but by anger and the rankling thought of their humiliation. They burst into the camp, every man crying out that here were no Forks, no Caudium, no trackless passes where guile had insolently trampled over error, but Roman valour which neither rampart nor trench could keep off. Indiscriminately they cut down those who resisted and those who fled, the armed and unarmed, slaves and free men, adults and children, men and animals; nor would any living creature have survived if the consuls had not given the signal to withdraw and forced the bloodthirsty soldiers out of the camp with commands and threats. The men were furious at the interruption to their sweet revenge; the consuls therefore quickly

harangued them to explain that their commanders had stood
second to none of them in hatred of the enemy, nor did they
intend to do so. On the contrary, they would have led them
as in war, to exact punishment without measure had their
intentions not been curbed by the thought of the six hundred
cavalry who were held as hostages in Luceria, for fear that if
the enemy despaired of quarter they might be driven blindly
to execute their prisoners, deciding to kill them off before they
were killed themselves. The soldiers applauded, declared themselves glad that their rage had been held in check, and admitted
it was better to endure anything rather than hazard the lives
of so many of Rome's leading young men.

15. The assembly was then dismissed and a council of war
held to decide whether to concentrate all the troops on the
siege of Luceria or to send one army and its general to test the
attitude of the Apulians in the surrounding area, as they were
a people whose intentions were uncertain. The consul Publilius
set out to traverse Apulia, and in a single expedition either
reduced or by granting terms received as allies a considerable
number of Apulian tribes. Papirius too, who had stayed behind
to carry on the siege of Luceria, soon found his hopes were
realized in the turn of events. For after he had blocked all the
roads by which supplies were brought in from Samnium, the
Samnite garrison in Luceria was driven by hunger to send
envoys to the Roman consul to ask him to raise the siege if
they returned the cavalrymen who were the cause of the war.
Papirius told them that they should have asked Pontius, son
of Herennius, on whose instructions they had sent the Romans
under the yoke, what he thought the vanquished ought to
suffer; but since they preferred their enemies to fix fair terms
for them rather than propose anything themselves, he told
them to take orders to Luceria to leave arms, baggage, pack-
animals and all non-combatants within the town; the soldiers,
he said, he would send under the yoke, each clad in a single
garment – this would inflict on them nothing new, but would
avenge the humiliation imposed on the Romans. No objection
was made. Seven thousand soldiers were sent under the yoke
and a vast amount of booty was captured at Luceria; all the

standards and arms lost at Caudium were retrieved, and greatest joy of all was the recovery of the Roman cavalry whom the Samnites had handed over to Luceria to be kept under guard as security for the peace. Scarcely any other victory of the Roman people is more glorious for its sudden reversal of fortune; especially if it is true, as I find in certain records, that Pontius, son of Herennius, the Samnite chief commander, was sent under the yoke with the rest to expiate the humiliation suffered by the consuls.

However, I am not unduly surprised that there is some doubt about the identity of the Samnite commander who was surrendered and disgraced. More astonishing is the uncertainty whether it was the dictator Lucius Cornelius with Lucius Papirius Cursor as his master of Horse who led the campaign at Caudium and afterwards at Luceria, and by his unparalleled retribution for the Roman disgrace enjoyed a triumph which in my opinion was the most highly deserved of any down to that time, second only to that of Furius Camillus,[16] or whether the glory should go to the consuls, and to Papirius in particular. This doubt brings in another: whether at the next elections Papirius Cursor had his term of office extended in recognition of his success at Luceria and was elected consul for the third time, along with Quintus Aulius Cerretanus, consul for the second time; or whether it was Lucius Papirius Mugillanus who was elected, and a mistake was made in the matter of the last name.

16. It is generally agreed that from then on the remainder of the war was effectively dealt with by the consuls. Aulius finished off the campaign against the Ferentani in a single successful battle, and after demanding hostages received the surrender of the town itself, where the defeated army had taken refuge. The other consul was equally fortunate in action against the Satricans, who (in spite of being Roman citizens) had gone over to the Samnites after the disaster at Caudium and had allowed a Samnite garrison into their city. For when the Roman army moved up to the walls of Satricum the

---

16. For his victory over the Gauls in 390 (V.49).

townspeople sent envoys to beg and pray for peace, only to receive a stern reply from the consul: if they did not execute or hand over the Samnite garrison they were not to come back to him again – words which struck more terror into their hearts than an armed attack. The envoys then went on to press the consul to say how he thought they could use force on such a strong and well-armed garrison when they were weak and few in number, but were told to ask advice from those at whose instigation they had admitted the garrison into the city. The envoys therefore departed and returned to their people, after obtaining with difficulty the consul's permission to consult their own senate on the matter and come back to him with its reply.

The Satrican senate was divided into two factions, one led by the instigators of the revolt from Rome, the other consisting of loyal citizens; however, both parties were equally eager to do the consul a service in order to regain peace. One party, observing that the Samnite garrison intended to slip out the following night (for they were quite unprepared to withstand a siege) thought it sufficient to inform the consul at what hour of the night and by what gate the enemy would leave, and which road they intended to take. The other, which had been against going over to the Samnites, actually opened a gate for the consul that same night and let the army into the city unknown to the Samnites. As a result of this double betrayal the Samnite garrison was taken by surprise and overwhelmed by ambushes planted in the wooded area around their road, while from the city filled with Romans a shout went up, and in the brief space of a single hour the Samnites were killed, the Satricans captured, and everything was in the consul's hands. He then held an inquiry to find who was responsible for the defection, and had those found guilty scourged and beheaded. The Satricans had their arms taken from them and were put under a strong garrison.

Papirius Cursor then left for Rome and his triumph, according to the authorities who say that it was under his command that Luceria was recovered and the Samnites sent under the yoke. He was indeed a man who undoubtedly deserved every military honour, outstanding as he was both in mental vigour and physical strength. He was exceptionally fleet of foot (hence his name of Cursor[17]) and is said to have outstripped all his contemporaries at running, whether because of his natural strength or of intensive training. It is also said that he had a great capacity for food and drink, and that, because no effort could physically exhaust him, military service was harsher for infantry and cavalry alike under him than under any other commander. Indeed, a story is told how his cavalrymen once ventured to ask him to let them off some task in return for a duty well performed and he told them that, to stop their saying they had been let off nothing, he would excuse them from patting their horses' backs on dismounting. Then too he possessed a great power of command over allies and citizens alike. A praetor of Praeneste who was nervous had been rather slow in bringing up his men from the reserve to the front rank. Papirius was walking by and ordered the man to be summoned before his tent, and the lictor to make ready his axe. The praetor stood transfixed at those words, but Papirius said to the lictor 'Come along, cut out this root – it gets in the way when people are walking.' Then he fined the man and sent him off, overwhelmed with fear of a death sentence. There is no doubt that in his generation, which produced more fine qualities than any other, there was no single man who gave such staunch support to the State of Rome. People even consider that he would have been a match for Alexander the Great in generalship, had Alexander turned his arms against Europe after his conquest of Asia.

17. Nothing can be thought to be further from my intention at the beginning of this work than to diverge unduly from the true order of events and by introducing various embellishments to attempt to provide my readers with enjoyable digressions and myself with mental relaxation. Yet the very mention of this great king and commander evokes certain thoughts on which I have often brooded in silence, and prompts me to inquire what would have been the result

17. But in ch. 34.20 it is also given as his grandfather's name.

for the fortunes of Rome if there had been war with Alexander.[18]

It seems that the most important elements in war are the numbers and courage of the soldiers, the talents of the commanders, and luck, which is a powerful influence on all the affairs of men and particularly in warfare. These factors, whether taken separately or jointly, readily suggest that the power of Rome would not have been conquered by Alexander any more than by other kings and peoples. First of all, to begin by comparing generals, I certainly do not deny that Alexander was an outstanding commander, but his fame was increased by the fact that he stood alone, and died as a young man on a rising tide of success, before he had time to experience a reverse of fortune. To say nothing of other famous kings and generals, all noteworthy examples of change in the affairs of men, what else but his long life exposed Cyrus,[19] whom the Greeks single out for high praise, to a change of fortune? The same applies in recent times to Pompey the Great. Shall I go through the names of the Roman generals – not all nor of every age but those consuls or dictators with whom Alexander would actually have had to fight – Marcus Valerius Corvus, Gaius Marcius Rutulus, Gaius Sulpicius, Titus Manlius Torquatus, Quintus Publilius Philo, Lucius Papirius Cursor, Quintus Fabius Maximus, the two Decii, Lucius Volumnius and Manius Curius?[20] And there are great men immediately after those, if he had concentrated on war with Carthage first, and afterwards with Rome, and had crossed over to Italy at a later age. Any one of these was gifted with the same qualities of courage and natural ability as Alexander was, and, moreover, the military training which had been handed down from generation to generation ever since the early days of the City had by now developed into a systematic discipline based on a

18. For the relevance of this rhetorical digression on Alexander the Great, see the Introduction, pp. 16–17.

19. The elder Cyrus, defeated and killed in Scythia in 529 B.C.

20. L. Volumnius defeated the Samnites (cf. Book X *passim*); M', Curius Dentatus ended the Third Samnite War in 290 and defeated Pyrrhus at Beneventum in 275.

series of precepts. In this manner the kings had made war, and
after them, in the same way, the Junii and Valerii who expelled
the kings, and then in turn the Fabii, Quinctii and Cornelii,
and Furius Camillus, who had been seen as an old man in their
youth by those who would have had to fight with Alexander.

In actual performance of a soldier's duties by fighting in
person – where Alexander is thought to have shown himself
no less distinguished – are we to suppose that Manlius
Torquatus or Valerius Corvus, though renowned as soldiers
before they became commanders, would have had to yield to
Alexander had they met him in hand-to-hand combat? Or
would the Decii, who dedicated their persons and then rushed
on the enemy, or Papirius Cursor, for all his physical and
mental vigour? And the designs of a single youth would
doubtless have mastered that Senate – to name no individual
members – which was called an assembly of kings by one[21]
who had a true conception of the Roman Senate! Then I
suppose there was a danger that Alexander would show greater
ingenuity than any one of those I have named in choosing a
camp site, organizing supplies, guarding against ambush,
deciding on a time for battle, drawing up his army and
strengthening it with reserve troops. Surely he would
have said it was no Darius[22] he had to deal with, trailing along
with him a crowd of women and eunuchs, weighed down by
the gold and purple trappings of his rank, an easy prey rather
than an enemy, to be defeated without bloodshed, simply by
daring to scorn empty display. Far different from India,
through which he riotously advanced at the head of a drunken
army, would Italy have appeared to him, as he looked on the
passes of Apulia and mountains of Lucania, and the
recent traces of that disaster to his family in which his uncle
Alexander, King of Epirus, not long before had lost his life.[23]

18. And we are speaking of an Alexander who was not yet
overwhelmed by success, which no one has ever been less able

21. Cineas, envoy of Pyrrhus; cf. Plutarch, *Pyrrhus* 19.5.
22. Darius III, the last king of Persia, defeated by Alexander at
Gaugemela in 331 B.C.
23. cf. VIII.24.

to sustain. For judged in the light of his new fortune and what I may call his new character, which he assumed after his conquests, he would have been more like Darius than Alexander by the time he reached Italy, leading an army which had already forgotten its Macedonian origins and was adopting degenerate Persian habits. I am reluctant in the case of so great a king to mention his ostentation in altering his attire, his desire for prostration as a form of adulation (something which would have been distasteful to Macedonians even in defeat, and much more so when they were conquerors), his horrible punishments and butchery of his friends as they drank and feasted, and the vainglory of his lies about his origin. What when his love of wine became daily more consuming, as did his fiery outbursts of violent temper? I refer to nothing which is in doubt amongst historians. Are we to think those faults in no way damaging to a general's good qualities? There was, I suppose, the danger – which the most irresponsible of the Greeks,[24] who set the reputation even of the Parthians against the name of Rome, are always quoting – that the Roman people could not have withstood the majesty of the name of Alexander, though I believe he was unknown to them at the time even by repute; and that out of all the Roman nobility not a single one would have raised a voice freely against him, although in Athens, after the city's defeat by Macedonian arms, at the very moment when the smoke could almost be seen rising from the ruins of Thebes, men dared to speak out against him freely in public, as the records of their speeches bear witness.[25]

However impressive we find the great reputation of this man, the fact remains that it is the great reputation of a single individual built up from the successes of little more than ten years, and those who sing its praises on the grounds that the Romans have been defeated in many battles, even if they have

24. A possible reference to the Alexandrian historian Timagenes, brought to Rome in 55 B.C. and known for his prejudices against Augustus and Romans generally.
25. Notably the *Philippics* of Demosthenes, though these were delivered before the destruction of Thebes.

never lost a war, whereas Alexander's good fortune never failed him in a single battle, do not understand that they are comparing one man's achievements – and those of a young man too – with the exploits of a nation now in its eighth century of warfare. Should it be surprising, then, if on one side more generations are counted up than years on the other, that there have been more vicissitudes of fortune over so long a period of time than in the space of thirteen years?[26] Ought you not to compare men with a man, generals with a single general, their fortunes with his? How many Roman generals could I name whose fortune in battle never turned against them? In the annals and lists of magistrates you can run through pages of consuls and dictators whose fine qualities and fortune never gave the people of Rome a single day's regret. And what makes them more remarkable than Alexander or any king is this: some were dictators for no more than ten or twenty days, and no one held the consulship for more than a year; their levies were obstructed by the people's tribunes; they were late going to war and were recalled early to hold elections; in the midst of their endeavours the year came full circle; the rashness or irregularity of their colleague was a hindrance or did positive harm; they succeeded to a situation mishandled by their predecessors; they took over an army of raw recruits or one which was undisciplined and badly trained. Kings, on the other hand, are not only free from all hindrances but are masters of times and circumstances; their decisions determine and are not dependent on events. Therefore an undefeated Alexander would have made war on undefeated generals and hazarded the same stakes of fortune; indeed, he would have run greater risks than they would, seeing that the Macedonians had only a single Alexander, who was not only exposed to many dangers but also placed himself in their way, while there would have been many Romans who could have been his match in glory or in the magnitude of their exploits, each one of whom could have lived and died as his own destiny ruled, without endangering the State.

26. Those of Alexander's career.

19. It remains to compare the forces on each side, whether in number, or type of soldier, or the size of their auxiliary contingents. In the five-yearly census of the period, the population was put at 250,000.[27] Thus to meet a general revolt of the Latin allies, ten legions were enlisted from a levy based almost entirely on the City. Often in those years four or five armies were on active service in Etruria, Umbria (where the Gauls joined their enemies), Samnium and Lucania. The whole of Latium, along with the Sabines, the Volscians and Aequi, all Campania and part of Umbria and Etruria, as well as the Picentes, Marsi and Paeligni, Vestini and Apulians, together with the coast of the Lower Sea occupied by the Greeks from Thurii as far as Neapolis and Cumae, and then the Samnites up to Antium and Ostia, would later on have been found by Alexander to be either powerful allies of the Romans or their defeated enemies. He himself would have crossed the sea with his veteran Macedonians, no more than thirty thousand infantry and four thousand cavalry, mostly from Thessaly, for this comprised his main strength. If he had added Persians, Indians and other nations he would have found them more of an encumbrance to drag around with him than a help.

Then consider that the Romans were on home ground, with reinforcements ready to hand, while Alexander was fighting in a foreign land and would have watched his army melt away, as Hannibal did at a later date. His men would have been armed with the round shield and long Macedonian lance; the Romans with the oblong shield, a better protection for the body, and the Roman javelin, which is much more effective on impact when thrown than the spear. The troops on both sides were heavily armed, keeping to their ranks, but whereas the Greek phalanx did not vary and its soldiers were all of the same type,[28] the Roman line was more open and formed of several units, easy to divide wherever it was necessary, and easy to join up. Furthermore, what soldier can equal the Roman

27. Perhaps a round figure; in the previous census recorded by Livy for 459 (III.24.10) a precise total is given of 117,319, and again in 292 a total of 262,321 (X.47.2).

28. This ignores Alexander's reliance on cavalry.

in performance or is better at standing up to fatigue? Alexander, if defeated in a single battle, would have been defeated in the war, but what army could have beaten the Romans, unbeaten by Caudium and Cannae?[29] There would certainly have often been occasions – even if things went well for him at the start – when Alexander would have wished to confront Persians and Indians and unwarlike Asians, and would have admitted he had hitherto been at war with women – as Alexander, King of Epirus, is related to have said when mortally wounded, comparing the kind of campaign in Asia fought by this same young man with what had been his own lot. Why, when I remember how we fought the Carthaginians at sea for twenty-four years in the First Punic War, it seems to me that Alexander's whole life would have been hardly long enough for that single war. And in view of the fact that the Punic state had been linked with the Roman by ancient treaties,[30] and the fear both felt could have joined the two cities most powerful in men and arms against their common enemy, Alexander might perhaps have been destroyed by simultaneous attacks from Carthage and Rome. The Romans have indeed had experience of the Macedonians in war, admittedly not when they were led by Alexander and their fortunes still stood high, but in the Roman campaigns against Antiochus, Philip and Perses,[31] and not only without any defeat but even without danger to themselves. If my presumption may be forgiven (and may civil wars keep silence!), never have we been endangered by hostile cavalry, never by infantry, never in open battle, never on even, or at any rate on favourable, ground. For arrows, impassable defiles, regions with no roads to carry supplies can well cause fear amongst heavily armed troops, but Rome has driven back a thousand armies more

29. The major catastrophe of the Second Punic War, in 216, described by Livy in Book XXII.

30. cf. VII.27, note 36.

31. Antiochus the Great, defeated by Scipio Asiaticus at the battle of Magnesia; Philip V of Macedon, defeated by Flamininus at Cynoscephalae; Perses (or Perseus), his son, defeated by L. Aemilius Paullus at Pydna.

dangerous than those of Alexander and Macedon, and this she will still do, provided that the love of peace which rules our lives and our concern for domestic concord continue unbroken.

20. Marcus Folius Flaccina and Lucius Plautius Venex were the next consuls elected. In that year envoys from the populous Samnite states sought a renewal of the treaty, and prostrated themselves before the Senate, thereby stirring the senators' sympathy, but when they were referred to the people their pleas were not nearly so effective. Consequently they were refused a treaty, but after they had spent several days importuning individuals with their requests, they succeeded in obtaining a two-year truce. In Apulia too, the people of Teanum and Canusium, being exhausted by the raids on their land, gave hostages to the consul Lucius Plautius and offered submission. In the same year prefects first began to be appointed and sent to Capua, after the praetor Lucius Furius had given the Capuans laws; both changes were made at their own request as a remedy for the hardship caused by internal dissension. In Rome two additional tribes were formed, the Ufentina and the Falerna.[32]

Once affairs in Apulia had taken this turn, the people of Apulian Teate[33] also approached the new consuls, Gaius Junius Bubulcus and Quintus Aemilius Barbula, to ask for a treaty, and took on the responsibility of guaranteeing peace to the Roman people throughout Apulia. This bold promise gained them their treaty, though one which did not grant them equal terms but made them subject to Roman authority. Once Apulia was completely in Roman control (for Junius had also gained possession of the powerful town of Forentum), the campaign moved on to Lucania, where Nerulum was stormed and captured on the unexpected arrival of the consul Aemilius. And once the news had spread throughout the allies that Capua's affairs were firmly settled by Roman discipline, the

32. Bringing the total to thirty-one.
33. Teate is the same place as Teanum, mentioned with Canusium above; Livy has drawn on two sources and made two episodes out of one.

people of Antium also complained that they were living without fixed laws or magistrates. The Senate then appointed patrons[34] for the colony, to draw up laws for it, and the power not only of Roman arms but of Roman law began to be widely felt.

21. At the end of the year the consuls (Gaius Junius Bubulcus and Quintus Aemilius Barbula) handed over their legions not to the consuls Spurius Nautius and Marcus Popilius, over whose election they had presided, but to a dictator, Lucius Aemilius. He had attempted to make an assault on Saticula, with the support of Lucius Fulvius, his master of Horse, thereby giving the Samnites a pretext for revolt. Thus the Romans had double cause for alarm; on the one hand the Samnites, with the large army they had assembled to raise the siege of their allies, were encamped not far from the Roman camp; on the other the Saticulans suddenly flung open their gates and made a violent rush attack on the Roman outposts. Both parties then pressed heavily on the Romans, each relying more on expectation of help from the other than on any strength of their own, and soon a regular battle began. Although the fighting was on two fronts, the dictator's forces were protected on both sides, for he had taken up a position where he could not easily be surrounded and made his lines face different ways. However, he concentrated his fiercer attack on the sallying party, and drove them back behind their walls without much of a struggle; then he turned his whole force to face the Samnites. There he met with more resistance, but though victory was slow to come it was definite and complete. The Samnites were routed and forced back into their camp; during the night they put out their fires and marched silently away, having given up hope of saving Saticula. They then turned to laying a siege themselves and attacked Plistica, a town allied to Rome, by way of retaliation on their enemy.

22. As the year came full circle, the dictator Quintus Fabius took on the conduct of the war immediately. The new con-

34. Patrons of Italian or foreign towns were chosen from influential Romans who agreed to protect the interests of their clients.

suls[35] stayed in Rome as their predecessors had done, and
Fabius arrived at Saticula with reinforcements to receive the
army from Aemilius. The Samnites had not remained near
Plistica, but had called up fresh troops from home and, relying
on their numbers, pitched camp on the same site as before and
were trying to provoke the Romans to battle in an attempt
to divert them from the siege. That only made the dictator
intensify his attack on the walls, for in his view the whole
campaign rested on the siege of Saticula. He showed himself
largely indifferent to the Samnites' movements, apart from
placing outposts to prevent any attack on his camp. At this the
Samnites became even bolder; they kept riding up to the
ramparts and gave the Romans no peace. They were nearly
within the camp gates when Quintus Aulius Cerretanus, the
master of Horse, without consulting the dictator, collected all
his squadrons of cavalry and charged out full tilt to drive the
enemy off. At this point, although the battle was not at all the
kind to be bitter and lasting, Fortune intervened so as to bring
about remarkable losses on both sides, including the glorious
deaths of the commanders themselves. First the Samnite
general, annoyed at being routed and put to flight from the
position he had so boldly taken, prevailed on his cavalry by
pleas and exhortation to renew the struggle. He was conspicuous amongst his men as he pressed them into battle, and
the Roman master of Horse rode at him with levelled spear
so hard that he was knocked off his horse and killed with a
single blow. The rank and file were not so much dismayed as
infuriated by their leader's death, as often happens, and all
those round him hurled their javelins at Aulius as he rashly
rode through the Samnite squadrons. But the gods granted the
special glory of avenging the Samnite general to his brother.
Filled with grief and fury he dragged Aulius off his horse in
his moment of victory and killed him; and indeed the Samnites
very nearly seized possession of the body as it had fallen in the
midst of their own troops. But the Romans immediately
dismounted, and the Samnites were forced to do the same;

35. Surprisingly, their names are omitted; they were L. Papirius
Cursor and Q. Publilius Philo, both consuls for the fourth time.

lines were hastily drawn up and a battle started round the bodies of the leaders, in which the Romans certainly had the better. They recovered the body of Aulius and bore it back triumphantly to their camp, with mixed feelings of joy and sorrow. For their part the Samnites, after losing their commander and hazarding their strength in a cavalry engagement, abandoned Saticula, since they felt nothing was gained by defending it, and returned to besieging Plistica. Within a few days Saticula surrendered to the Romans and the Samnites captured Plistica by storm.

23. The seat of war was now moved, and the legions were transferred from Samnium and Apulia to Sora, which had gone over to the Samnites after killing its Roman colonists. The Roman army got there first by forced marches in order to avenge the slaughter of their fellow-citizens and to recover their colony. But when the scouts dispersed along the roads reported one after another that the Samnite legions were following and were not far away, the Romans marched out to meet the enemy, and a battle was fought near Lautulae which proved indecisive. It was not the losses or the flight of either side which broke off the battle but nightfall, leaving them uncertain whether they had lost or won. In some authorities I find that the battle went against the Romans and that it was there that Quintus Aulius, the master of Horse, was killed.[36] Gaius Fabius was appointed master of Horse to replace Aulius, and arrived from Rome with a new army. After consulting the dictator by means of messengers sent on ahead about where and when he should halt and where he should attack the enemy, once he was sufficiently informed about the plans for every contingency, he halted where his army could not be seen. For several days after the battle the dictator had kept his men within their ramparts, more like one besieged than a besieger; then suddenly he put out the signal for battle and, thinking he could rouse the spirits of brave men more effectively if he left none of them any hope except in himself, he said nothing to the soldiers about the arrival of the master

36. This is the version given by Diodorus Siculus (XIX.72.8), who names the place Laustulae.

of Horse and his new army, and spoke as if their only chance was to force their way out.

'Soldiers,' he said, 'we are caught in a trap with no way out unless victory can open one for us. Our permanent quarters are sufficiently protected by fortification but still unsafe through lack of supplies; for every place round about from which provisions could have been brought up has revolted, and even if people wished to help us, the locality is against it. So I am not going to mislead you by leaving a camp here where you can retreat if you fail to win a decisive victory, as you did last time. Entrenchments must be secured by arms, not arms by entrenchments. Those with time to prolong a war can have a camp and retire to it. For our part, we must refuse to contemplate anything but victory. Forward, then, against the enemy! And once we are all outside the rampart, those under orders shall set fire to the camp. Your losses, soldiers, shall be made good out of the plunder from all the rebel peoples round us.' Fired by the dictator's speech – an indication of the dire straits they were in – the soldiers fell upon the Samnites. A mere backward glance at their burning camp was an increased incentive, although only the parts nearest to them had been set alight, as the dictator ordered. And so they attacked like madmen, breaking up the enemy's ranks in their first assault; and in the very nick of time the master of Horse, who had seen the blazing camp from afar – the signal agreed on – attacked the enemy in the rear. Thus surrounded, the Samnites took to flight, in different directions, each man for himself; a huge crowd clung together in terror, blocking each other's way in the confusion, and were cut down between the lines. The Samnite camp was taken and plundered; then the dictator led his army back to the Roman camp, laden with booty, and rejoicing not so much in their victory as in the fact that, contrary to their expectations, they found everything there intact apart from a small area damaged by the fire.

24. The Romans then returned to Sora. The new consuls, Marcus Poetelius and Gaius Sulpicius, took over the army from the dictator Fabius, dismissed a great many of the veterans, and brought in new cohorts to make up the numbers.

But when no very definite plan of attack was being formed, as the town was awkwardly situated, and victory would mean either long waiting or danger if hurried, a Soran deserter slipped out of the town unseen, made his way to the Roman sentinels, and told them to take him to the consuls. Once escorted there he offered to betray his city. He was asked how he would carry out his promise, and when he told his inter-rogators, it was clear that his proposal was feasible. He then prevailed on the Romans to move their camp from where it almost touched the walls of Sora to a position six miles from the town, explaining that the guards posted day and night would then be less strict in keeping watch over the city. The following night he ordered certain cohorts to occupy the wooded area below the town, while he himself took with him ten picked soldiers over steep and practically trackless ground up to the citadel.[37] Here he had assembled a great many missiles, out of all proportion to the number of men involved; besides which there were the rocks which happened to be lying about, as usual on rough ground, as well as those which the townsfolk had deliberately piled up for the better protection of the place.

There he stationed the Romans, and showed them a steep, narrow path leading from the town up to the citadel. 'Three armed men would be enough,' he said, 'to keep back any number of men from an ascent like this; you are ten, and what is more, you are Romans and Romans of the greatest courage. You will have the advantage of position and darkness, which makes everything loom larger to frightened men where noth-ing is certain. I am off to spread terror everywhere; you keep watch and hold the citadel.' Then he ran down, making all the noise he could, as he shouted 'To arms! Help, help citizens! The enemy has taken the citadel! Come, defend it!' This he called as he knocked on the doors of the leading citizens, to those he met and to those who ran out in terror into the streets, until the panic started by one man spread widely through the city. The magistrates were alarmed, sent men up to investigate, and

37. Here, apparently, an unfortified height above the *oppidum*.

when they received exaggerated accounts of the weapons and the armed men holding the citadel, they gave up any hope of regaining it. The whole town thought of nothing but flight, and while the gates were being broken open by men who were still half-asleep and for the most part unarmed, the Roman detachment, roused by the uproar, burst through one of them and cut down the terrified townsfolk as they ran through the streets. Sora was already taken when the consuls arrived at dawn and accepted the surrender of those whom Fortune had allowed to survive the rout and carnage of the night. From these, 225, who by general consent were picked out as the ringleaders of the revolt and of the shocking massacre of the colonists, were sent to Rome in chains; the majority who remained were left at Sora with a garrison over them. All those who were sent to Rome were flogged and beheaded in the Forum, to the vast delight of the common people, who were the most closely concerned for the general safety of the numbers sent out to one or other of the colonies.

25. The consuls left Sora, and proceeded to campaign against the lands and cities of the Ausones[38]; for everything had been thrown into confusion by the arrival of the Samnites, when the battle was fought at Lautulae, and plots were formed in various places in and around Campania. Even Capua did not escape accusation; indeed, investigations actually extended to Rome and, what is more, to certain leading citizens there. But the Ausonian people were brought to submission by the betrayal of their cities, as was the case with Sora. From Ausona, Minturnae and Vescia, twelve young nobles who had conspired to betray their cities came to the consuls, explaining that their people had long been eagerly awaiting the arrival of the Samnites, and as soon as they heard of the battle at Lautulae had taken it as a Roman defeat and assisted the Samnites with fighting men and arms; but then since the Samnites were routed they had been living in a doubtful sort of peace, not shutting their gates against the Romans, for fear of provoking action against themselves, but all the same determined to shut

38. The Greek name for the Aurunci.

251

them if an army approached. In that uncertainty of mind they could be surprised and overcome. On these men's advice the Roman camp was moved nearer, and soldiers were sent round to the three towns simultaneously. Some of them, wearing armour, were to take up positions unseen close to the town walls, while others, in civilian dress, concealing swords under their clothing, were to enter the cities just before daybreak when the gates were opened. These started to kill the watchmen and at the same time gave the signal to the men in armour to run in from their hiding-places. Thus the gates were captured, and the three towns taken within the same hour by the same stratagem; but because the attack was made in the absence of the commanders, there was no limit to the bloodshed, and the Ausonian people were wiped out as if they had been fighting a war to the death, although it was not even quite certain that they were guilty of revolt.

26. In the same year Luceria fell into the hands of the Samnites after betraying the Roman garrison to the enemy; but the traitors did not go long unpunished for the deed. There was a Roman army not far away, which captured the city (situated as it was in a plain) at the first assault. The inhabitants of Luceria and the Samnites were all annihilated, and resentment ran so high that even in Rome, when the Senate was debating whether to send colonists to Luceria, there were many who voted for the destruction of the town. Hatred was extremely bitter against people who had twice been subdued, and, in addition, the remoteness of the place made the Senate recoil from the idea of banishing citizens to an exile so far from home and amongst such hostile peoples. Nevertheless the motion to send colonists was carried, and 2500 were dispatched.

In the same year, one of complete breakdown of loyalty to the Romans, there was secret plotting amongst the nobility even at Capua. When this was reported to the Senate, serious action was taken; investigations were voted and it was decided to appoint a dictator to hold them. Gaius Maenius was chosen, and he nominated Marcus Folius as master of Horse. The office of dictator was a cause of great alarm, and so, whether through fear or consciousness of guilt, the two Calavii, Ovius and Novius (the leaders of the conspiracy), before the dictator could be given information against them, escaped trial by deaths which were undoubtedly self-inflicted.

After this there were no further grounds for an inquiry in Campania and the proceedings were transferred to Rome, on the theory that the investigation ordered by the Senate was not specifically into the activities of individuals in Capua but generally into all who had ever combined or conspired against the State; and that cabals formed for the purpose of obtaining magistracies were contrary to public interest. The field of the inquiry widened in regard both to charges and to persons involved, and the dictator was not unwilling for his inquiry to be unlimited in its judicial powers. Some of the nobles were accordingly summoned for trial, and on appealing to the tribunes found no one to help them by preventing their names being entered on the lists. Then the nobles – not only those at whom the accusation was aimed, but all of them jointly – argued that the charge did not apply to the nobility, for whom the path to office was open unless fraudulently obstructed, but to plebeian parvenus, and added that in fact the dictator and the master of Horse could be more suitably put on trial themselves for this charge than hold an inquiry into it – which they would discover as soon as they resigned office.

At this point Maenius, more concerned now for his reputation than for his authority, came forward and addressed the assembly as follows: 'Roman citizens, you are all well aware of how my past life has been spent, and the office conferred on me itself bears witness to my innocence. It was necessary to choose as dictator to conduct these investigations not a highly distinguished military man, as often on other occasions when a critical situation in the State demanded it, but one who had spent his life furthest removed from cabals of this kind. Yet certain members of the nobility – for what reason it is more fitting that you determine yourselves than that I, in my official capacity, should pronounce on anything that I have not fully ascertained – have in the first place made every effort to put a stop to these very investigations; and then, when they were not sufficiently powerful to evade answering the charge against them, they took refuge (patricians though they are) in the protection offered by their adversaries, the appeal, that is, and the help of the tribunes. Finally, when repulsed in that quarter they have directed an attack on us – so much do they think to find greater safety in anything rather than in trying to vindicate their innocence – and though they hold no official position they have felt no shame in demanding the prosecution of a dictator. In order, then, that gods and men may know that those men are attempting the impossible to avoid having to account for their lives, whereas I am prepared to meet their accusation and offer myself to my enemies for trial, I hereby resign my dictatorship. You, consuls, if you are entrusted with this matter by the Senate, I ask first to direct your inquiries against me and against Marcus Folius here, so that it shall be evident that we are safe from those accusations by reason of our innocence, not because of the high dignity of the office we hold.' He then resigned his dictatorship, and immediately after him Marcus Folius resigned as master of Horse. They were the first to appear on trial before the consuls,[39] whom the Senate put in charge of the case, and were splendidly acquitted against the evidence of the nobles. Publilius Philo, too, who had repeatedly held the highest offices and performed many notable deeds at home and in war, but was nevertheless unpopular with the nobility,[40] was put on trial and acquitted. But the inquiry throve on the distinguished names of those accused only so long as its novelty lasted, as often happens; then it began to fall off as it came to people of much less importance, until it was finally suppressed by the cabals and factions it had been set up to oppose.

27. The rumour of these events, but even more the hope of a Campanian rising, which had been the object of the conspirators, recalled the Samnites from concentration on Apulia to Caudium, with the idea of being close at hand to seize Capua from the Romans if any disturbance gave them the

39. i.e. not before a dictator.
40. In 339 he had introduced three laws to benefit the plebeians (VIII.12.14).

opportunity. There the consuls came with a powerful army. To begin with, both forces waited in the neighbourhood of the pass, since the road was too difficult for either side to make any advance; then the Samnites made a short detour through open country and led their troops down into the plain, where for the first time each set up camp in full view of the other. After that there was some skirmishing of cavalry more often than of infantry, as each side tested its strength. The Romans were not displeased with the results or with the delay prolonging the campaign, whereas to the Samnite leaders it seemed that their strength was being whittled away by minor daily losses and declining as the fighting was deferred.

The Samnites therefore formed up for action, with their cavalry divided between the wings, under orders to concentrate on watching the camp to prevent any attack on it rather than entering the battle; the infantry would hold the line. Of the two consuls, Sulpicius stationed himself on the right, Poetelius on the left wing. The right section was extended over a fairly wide area; there the Samnites too had taken up their position with their ranks spread out, intending either to turn the Romans' flank or to prevent their own from being turned. On the left the Roman troops were stationed in much closer formation, and had also had their strength reinforced by a sudden decision on the part of the consul Poetelius when he sent immediately into the front line the auxiliary cohorts, which were usually held in reserve so as to be fresh in the event of a prolonged battle. With these combined forces he forced the enemy back at the first attack. When the Samnite infantry was dislodged their cavalry entered the battle to support them, but as these wheeled round and rode into the gap between the two armies, the Roman cavalry charged them at full gallop, throwing the ranks and formations of infantry and cavalry into confusion, until they put the entire Samnite army to flight from this position. Sulpicius as well as Poetelius was present on that wing to give encouragement, for he had left his own men, who had not yet joined battle, and ridden in the direction of the shouting as soon as it broke out on the left. There he saw victory was assured and rode back with twelve hundred men to his own wing, where he found a very different situation, with the Romans forced from their position and the victorious enemy charging their broken ranks. But the arrival of the consul quickly changed everything. The soldiers took heart again at the sight of their commander; the help brought was not to be measured by numbers, and the news, soon followed by the sight, of the victory on the other flank restored the battle. In a short time the Romans began to win all along the line, while the Samnites gave up the fight and were cut down or taken prisoner, except for those who fled to Maleventum, the city now called Beneventum.[41] According to tradition some thirty thousand Samnites were killed or captured.

28. After their remarkable victory the consuls led off the legions straightaway in order to besiege Bovianum; and there they stayed in winter quarters until the new consuls, Lucius Papirius Cursor (for the fifth time) and Gaius Junius Bubulcus (for the second time), nominated Gaius Poetelius dictator, with Marcus Folius as his master of Horse, and he took over command of the army. When he heard that the citadel of Fregellae had been captured by the Samnites he broke off the siege of Bovianum and made for Fregellae, which he recaptured without a struggle, as the Samnites had fled in the night. Leaving a strong garrison in the town he returned to Campania, mainly for the purpose of recovering Nola by force of arms. Just before his arrival all the local Samnites and the farming population of Nola had taken refuge within the town walls. After surveying the position of the city the dictator set about opening up an approach to the walls by setting fire to all the buildings immediately below them, which were densely populated. Not long after this Nola was taken, either by Poetelius himself or the consul Gaius Junius; the tradition is divided between the two. Those who give the honour of capturing Nola to the consul go on to say that Atina and

41. Malventum or Maleventum had its name changed, as it sounded ill-omened, when a Roman colony was settled there in 268; but the name was not derived from Latin *male* but from Greek *mēlon* or *malon*, meaning 'sheep' (or possibly 'apple').

Calatia were also taken by him, but that Poetelius was made dictator on an outbreak of plague for the purpose of hammering in a nail.[42]

In the same year colonies were set up at Suessa and Pontiae. Suessa had belonged to the Aurunci, while the Volscians had inhabited Pontiae, an island within sight of their own coast. The Senate passed a resolution that Interamna Sucasina should also be colonized, but it was left to the succeeding consuls, Marcus Valerius and Publius Decius, to elect the three commissioners and send out four thousand colonists.

29. The war with the Samnites was nearly ended, though the Roman senators were still anxious about it, when rumour sprang up of war with the Etruscans. At the time there was no other nation (apart from the Gauls when they invaded) more formidable under arms, because of the proximity of their territory and also of the size of their population. While the other consul stayed in Samnium to finish off what was left of the war, Publius Decius (who had remained in Rome, seriously ill) at the Senate's instigation accordingly appointed Gaius Junius Bubulcus dictator. He administered the oath to all of military age, as the gravity of the situation required, and applied all his energies to getting ready arms and everything else needed to meet the crisis. But he was not carried away by the magnitude of his preparations to think of an offensive war, doubtless intending to take no action unless the Etruscans first made an attack. However, the Etruscans adopted the same plan of preparing for war and at the same time holding back from starting it; so neither side moved beyond their own frontiers.

That year also saw the famous censorship of Appius Claudius and Gaius Plautius, though for later generations the name of Appius was of happier memory because he built a road and brought a water supply into the City.[43] He was solely respon-

42. cf. VII.3.4.
43. The Via Appia ran from Rome to Capua and later to Brundisium. The Aqua Appia of 312 B.C., the first of Rome's aqueducts, ran west from near Gabii to supply water to the Circus Maximus and the low-lying district round it.

sible for these achievements because his colleague had resigned office, out of shame at the shocking and invidious manner in which Appius had filled up the senatorial list.[44] Appius then displayed the obstinacy which had characterized his family since earliest times, and continued to hold the censorship alone. It was Appius too who authorized the Potitian *gens,* for whom the priesthood of Hercules at the Ara Maxima was hereditary,[45] to instruct the public slaves in the forms of the holy ritual in order to delegate this service to them. According to tradition, something remarkable then happened which could well create a religious objection against disturbing the lawful order of sacred rites. There were twelve families of the Potiti at the time, including up to thirty adult men, but within a year they were all wiped out, root and branch, and not only did their name die out but even the censor[46] was struck blind within a few years by the ever-mindful wrath of the gods.

30. Accordingly the consuls of the year following, Gaius Junius Bubulcus (for the third time) and Quintus Aemilius Barbula (for the second time), as soon as they took office complained to the people that the senatorial order had been degraded by irregular revision of the list, whereby men who were better than several of those chosen had been passed over. They said they refused to recognize a list which had been drawn up with no distinction between right and wrong, and dictated by partiality and caprice. They then immediately read out the senatorial roll in the order it had been before the censorship of Appius Claudius and Gaius Plautius.

In that year also two spheres of command, both of them military, began to be assigned by the people: one, the election by the people of sixteen military tribunes for distribution amongst the four legions, whereas previously these had been almost exclusively in the gift of the dictators and consuls,

44. cf. ch. 46.10, where Appius is said to have filled vacancies from sons of freedmen.

45. The origin of this privilege is described in I.7.3–15.

46. i.e. Appius himself. As an explanation of his surname Caecus ('blind') this is not very plausible, as Appius was afterwards both consul and dictator and commanded an army in 296.

except for a very few places which were left to the people's vote; two, the appointment by the people of two naval commissioners to be in charge of equipping and refitting the fleet. This measure was proposed by the people's tribune Marcus Decius, and the first one by the tribunes Lucius Atilius and Gaius Marcius.

I should have omitted an episode of the same year as being scarcely worth mentioning did it not seem to concern religious duties. The pipe-players were angry at having been forbidden by the last censors to hold their feast in the temple of Jupiter, according to ancient custom, and marched off to Tibur in a body, with the result that there was no one in the City to play the pipes at sacrifices. The Senate was seized with pious misgivings about the incident, and sent delegates to Tibur to request the citizens to do their best to return the men to Rome. The Tiburtines courteously promised to do so, and first summoned the pipers to their senate-house and urged them to go back to Rome. Then, when they found that persuasion achieved nothing, they dealt with the men by a ruse nicely in tune with their nature. On a public holiday various citizens invited parties of pipers to their homes on the pretext of celebrating the feast with music, and sent them to sleep by plying them with wine, for which men of their kind are generally greedy. In that condition they dumped them, heavily asleep, in carts and carried them off to Rome. The carts were left in the Forum and the pipers knew nothing until daylight surprised them there, still very drunk. The people quickly gathered round them and prevailed on them to stay. They were given permission on three days a year to roam the City in fancy dress, making music and enjoying the licence which is now customary, and those of them who played pipes at sacrifices had their right to hold a feast in the temple restored.[47] These events occurred at a time of general concern for two very serious wars.

47. The tale of the pipe-players' strike is also told by Ovid, *Fasti* VI.561 ff., and by Plutarch, *Quaestiones Romanae* 55. The three days during which the pipers' guild celebrated their festival of the *Quinquatrus minores* were 13–15 June.

31. The consuls divided the commands between them; lots were cast, Junius drawing the Samnites and Aemilius the new war with Etruria. In Samnium the Roman garrison at Cluviae,[48] which it had proved impossible to take by direct attack, was starved into surrender under siege, but in spite of this the Romans were savagely flogged by the Samnites and put to death. Infuriated by this brutality, Junius thought it his first duty to launch an attack on Cluviae. He took the town by storm on the very day he attacked the walls, and killed all the adult males. From there he took his victorious army on to Bovianum, the capital of the Pentrian Samnites, which was by far the wealthiest of their towns and the richest in both arms and men. There the troops had not the same fury to spur them on, but they captured the town in hope of plunder. Consequently they dealt less savagely with the enemy, while the amount of plunder carried out almost exceeded what had been taken at any time from the whole of Samnium; and it was all generously handed over to the soldiers.

Now that the Roman superiority in arms could not be withstood by any battle-line, camp or city, the Samnite leaders all eagerly turned their attention to looking for a place for an ambush, in the hope that the Romans might be scattered in unchecked pursuit of plunder and could be intercepted and surrounded. Certain deserters from the peasants and prisoners who fell into the consul's hands, some by chance, some deliberately, all gave the same account, which was in fact true, that vast numbers of cattle had been collected in a remote forest clearing; thus they persuaded him to take the legions there, lightly equipped, to drive them off. There a great army of Samnites had blocked the tracks unperceived; when they saw the Romans inside the clearing, they rose up with shouts and uproar, and attacked them unawares. At first the unexpectedness of the attack threw the Romans into confusion, while they were seizing their arms and piling their packs in the middle, but later on, when each man had got rid of what he was carrying and armed himself, they began to gather from

48. Site unknown.

all sides round their standards. As the result of a long military training they knew their positions in the ranks, and began to draw up a fighting line of their own accord without anyone's giving them the command. The consul rode up to the place where the fighting was most critical, leapt from his horse and called on Jupiter, Mars and the other gods to witness that he had come there seeking not glory for himself but booty for his men, and that he could be blamed only for being too eager to enrich them at the enemy's expense. Nothing could save him from such disgrace but his soldiers' courage. Let them all only make a combined effort to launch an attack on an enemy who was already defeated in battle, stripped of his camp, deprived of his cities, and now as his last hope attempting the treachery of an ambush, trusting to his position, not to his arms. But what position was there now which could withstand an attack from Roman valour? He reminded them of the citadels of Fregellae and Sora and all the places where they had won victories though the site did not favour them.

Fired by these words the soldiers advanced on the enemy's line which threatened them, without a thought of the difficulties in their path. They had some trouble while they were moving up the slope, but as soon as the front ranks reached the level ground at the top and the army saw that the position they held was now no longer at a disadvantage, it was the turn of those who had laid the ambush to panic; they threw down their arms, scattered, and fled to the hiding-places where they had concealed themselves a short while before. But the ground they had chosen to be difficult for their enemy now caught them in their own trap; and so very few found a way of escape. Up to twenty thousand Samnites were killed, and the victorious Romans ran hither and thither rounding up for plunder the cattle which the enemy had given them.

32. During these events in Samnium all the peoples of Etruria, apart from the Arretini, had taken up arms and started a large-scale war by an attack on Sutrium, a city which was allied to Rome but, as it were, the gateway to Etruria. The other consul, Aemilius, came up with an army to raise the siege of his allies, and as the Romans arrived the people of Sutrium

readily brought supplies to the camp which was set up in front of their town. The Etruscans spent the first day deliberating whether to hurry on the war or to prolong it; on the following day, when their leaders had decided on the speedier course in preference to the safer, the signal for battle was displayed at sunrise, and their army took the field armed for battle. As soon as this was reported to the consul he ordered the word to be passed round that the men should breakfast, and arm only after they had built up their strength with food. His order was obeyed, and when he saw them armed and ready he ordered the standards to be carried outside the rampart, and drew up his battle-line not far from the enemy. For some time both sides stood watching each other closely, waiting for their opponents to raise a shout and start the battle. Midday passed and the sun began to sink before a missile was thrown from either side; then the Etruscans, not wanting to leave the field with the issue unsettled, raised a battle-cry and sounded their trumpets as they charged forward. The Romans were no less eager to start fighting, and the two sides clashed in a furious encounter. The Etruscans were superior in numbers, the Romans in courage. The issue hung in the balance, and many fell on both sides, including all the bravest; nor was the result settled until the second Roman line came up fresh to the fight, to relieve the exhausted men in the first line, and the Etruscans, who had no fresh reserves to support their front line, all fell in front of their standards and around them. There would never have been less running away or more slaughter in any battle, had not nightfall protected the Etruscans when they were determined to die, with the result that the victors put an end to the fighting before the vanquished. The signal for retreat was sounded after the sun had set, and in the night both armies returned to their camps.

After this nothing was done at Sutrium that year which is worth recording. In the Etruscan army the whole of the front line had been wiped out in a single engagement, leaving only the reserves, which were hardly sufficient to garrison their camp, while the Romans had suffered such heavy casualties that more men died of their wounds after the battle than fell in the fighting line. 33. Quintus Fabius, the next year's consul, took over the war at Sutrium, and was given Gaius Marcius Rutulus as colleague. Fabius also brought up replacements from Rome, while a new army was recruited in Etruria and arrived to reinforce the Etruscans.

For a good many years there had been no rivalry between the patrician magistrates and the people, but now strife broke out through that family which was apparently fated to quarrel with tribunes and people. The censor Appius Claudius had completed the eighteen months which was the time limit for the censorship laid down by the Aemilian law,[49] but when his colleague Gaius Plautius had resigned office, nothing could prevail on him to resign as well. One of the people's tribunes, Publius Sempronius, had already started proceedings to confine the censorship within its legal period, an action which was no less just than popular, and as welcome to the aristocrats as to the common people. After Sempronius had repeatedly quoted the Aemilian law and extolled its promoter, the dictator Mamercus Aemilius, for having set a limit of a year and a half to an office which had hitherto been held for five years and was proving tyrannical because of its length of tenure, he addressed Appius Claudius directly, demanding to know what he would have done if he had been censor at the time when Gaius Furius and Marcus Geganius had held the censorship.[50] Appius denied that the tribune's question had much relevance to his own case, for even though the Aemilian law was binding on those censors during whose term of office it had been passed, because it had been enacted by the people after their election to the censorship, and the latest enactment was the effective law, yet neither he himself nor any of the censors elected subsequently to the passage of the law could have been bound by it.

34. As Appius found no one to support these quibbling arguments, Sempronius spoke again: 'There, men of Rome, you see the descendant of the Appius who was elected decemvir for a year, then elected himself for a second year, and in a third

49. In 434; cf. IV.24.5.
50. i.e. at the time when the *Lex Aemilia* was passed.

year, though he was a private citizen, elected neither by himself
nor by anyone else, retained the fasces and supreme authority,
and did not relinquish his unbroken term of office until he was
destroyed by his ill-gotten, ill-administered and ill-retained
powers.[51] This is the same family, Romans, whose violence
and injustice forced you to banish yourselves from your native
city and occupy the Sacred Mount,[52] the same against which
you provided yourselves with tribunes to help you,[53] the same
on whose account two of your armies were stationed on the
Aventine,[54] the same which always opposed any laws restricting usury and redistributing land,[55] the same which broke off
marriages between patricians and plebeians, the same which
blocked the path of the plebeians to curule offices.[56] This is a
name which is far more inimical to your liberty than that of
the Tarquins. Can it really be the case, Appius Claudius, that
in the hundred years since Mamercus Aemilius was dictator,
when we have had so many censors, all high born and cour-
ageous men, not one of them has looked at the Twelve Tables?
Has none of them known that the people's latest enactment
was the law? Why, of course they all knew it; and they
followed the Aemilian law in preference to the ancient law
whereby censors were first elected precisely because it was the
latest enactment of the people, and because, where two laws
are at variance, the new law always supersedes the old.

'Or are you saying, Appius, that the people are not bound
by the Aemilian law? Or that they are bound, but you alone
are above the law? The Aemilian law was binding on those
violent censors, Gaius Furius and Marcus Geganius, who
showed what damage the office you hold could do in the State,
when in their fury at the curtailment of their power they
reduced Mamercus Aemilius, the foremost man of his day

51. For Appius Claudius the decemvir of 451, see III.33–58. He was
the censor's great-great-grandfather.
52. In 494, (II.32.2).
53. cf. II.33.1–3.
54. In 449 (III.50.13 and III.51.10).
55. cf. II.44.2 and VI.40.11.
56. cf. IV.1.6 and IV.6.7.

both in war and in peace, to the lowest grade of citizen; it was
binding on all subsequent censors for a period of a hundred
years; it is binding on your colleague Gaius Plautius, who was
elected under the same auspices with the same rights as yourself. Or did the people not elect him to be censor with the
fullest rights? Are you the sole exception for whom this holds
good, as a unique and special privilege? Who will be elected
'king' for performing sacrifices[57] if he is going to seize the title
of monarch and declare that his election means he is elected
with fullest rights to be king of Rome? Who do you think will
be content with six months as dictator or five days as interrex?
Whom will you be rash enough to appoint as dictator for
hammering in a nail or holding games? How dull and stupid
you must think men look to Appius, when they resign their
dictatorship within twenty days after highly successful achievements, or withdraw from office because of a flaw in their
election! I need not draw examples from times long past; only
recently, within the last ten years,[58] the dictator Gaius Maenius
held an inquiry which was stricter than was safe for
certain powerful individuals, and was accused by his enemies
of being tainted with the crime he was investigating, so that
he resigned the dictatorship in order to meet the charge against
him as a private citizen. It is not my wish to ask for that kind
of self-restraint from you; you need not fall below the dom-
ineering standards of your family! Resign your office not a
day, not an hour sooner than is necessary; only see that you
do not go beyond the time limit. Would it be enough to add
a day or a month to his censorship? "Three years," he says,
"and six months beyond the time allowed by the Aemilian law
will I hold the censorship, and I will hold it alone." Surely this
already looks like monarchy!

'Or will you substitute another colleague, though sub-
stitution to fill the place even of a dead man is forbidden by
divine law? For it is not sufficient for you to have made
scrupulous use of your position as censor to degrade a cult of

57. The *rex sacrorum*; cf. II.2.1–2.
58. In ch. 26 Livy dates the dictatorship of Maenius to 314, but the
Fasti capitolini put it in 320.

the greatest antiquity, the only one instituted by the very god in whose honour it is observed, from the level of a priesthood held by men of the noblest blood to that of service by slaves; not sufficient that a family whose history goes back beyond the origins of this City, a family hallowed by its hospitality to the immortal gods, has been exterminated within a year, root and branch, because of you and your censorship; no, you must involve the whole State in an impious act, the consequences of which the mind shudders to predict. The City was captured[59] in that five-year period when, to avoid having to vacate his office on the death of his colleague Gaius Julius, Lucius Papirius Cursor appointed Marcus Cornelius Maluginensis as substitute. And how much more moderate, Appius, was his ambition than yours! He neither held his censorship alone nor prolonged it beyond the legal term; yet he found no one thereafter to follow his initiative; all subsequent censors have resigned office on the death of a colleague. But nothing restrains you – neither the expiry of your term of censorship nor the resignation of your colleague, neither the law nor any sense of propriety; you measure worth in terms of arrogance, audacity and contempt of gods and men.

'For my part, Appius Claudius, out of consideration for the majesty of the office you have held and the reverence it inspires, I wish I could spare you not only personal arrest but even any word you might think harsh, but your obstinacy and pride have forced me to speak as I have done so far, and, unless you obey the Aemilian law, I shall order you to be taken to prison. Moreover, since our forefathers established that, in the election of censors, unless both candidates obtain the legal vote one must not be declared elected and the elections must be postponed, I will not allow you, who cannot be elected sole censor, to hold the censorship alone.'

Having said these words and others to the same effect, he gave orders for the arrest and imprisonment of the censor. Six tribunes upheld the action of their colleague, while three gave their support to Appius on his appeal and, to the great

59. By the Gauls; cf. V.31.6.

indignation of all the social orders, he carried on as sole censor.

35. During these events in Rome, Sutrium was already under siege by the Etruscans, and as the consul Fabius was leading his army at the foot of the mountains with the intention of bringing relief to the allies and attacking the enemy's earthworks, if it were at all possible, he was confronted by the Etruscans drawn up for battle. The wide plain at the base of the hills revealed that they were there in enormous numbers, and so, in order to give his own limited force the advantage of position, he slightly changed course and led his men up the hills, which were rough and strewn with boulders, then turned to face the enemy. The Etruscans, with no thought for anything but their numbers, on which alone they had relied, rushed into battle in such eager haste that they threw away their missiles in order to come to grips the sooner, and charged their enemy sword in hand. By contrast the Romans started to hurl first their javelins, then the rocks, which the place itself provided in plenty, with the result that those of the Etruscans who were not wounded were thrown into disorder when these came raining down on their shields and helmets. It was difficult for them to move up to fight at closer quarters, and they lacked missiles for a battle at long range; so they stood exposed to the attack without any adequate protection until some of them began to move back and the line wavered unsteadily. Then the Roman first and second lines raised another cheer, and charged them with drawn swords. The Etruscans could not withstand this assault; they wheeled round and fled headlong, towards their camp. But when the Roman cavalry, riding obliquely across the plain, barred their flight, they gave up trying to reach their camp and made for the mountains. From there they moved on in a body, practically unarmed and distressed by their wounds, into the Ciminian Forest. The Romans killed many thousand Etruscans, captured thirty-eight military standards, and also took possession of the enemy's camp with a vast amount of plunder. Then they began to think about pursuit.

36. At this time the Ciminian Forest was more impenetrable

and fearful than the wooded ravines of Germany were in recent times,[60] and no one, not even a trader, had approached it. Hardly anyone was bold enough to set foot in it except the commander himself; for all the rest, the memory of the Caudine disaster had not yet faded from their minds. Amongst those who were present at the time was the consul's brother (some give his name as Marcus Fabius, others as Caeso Fabius, and others again call him Gaius Claudius, a son of the same mother as the consul), who offered to investigate and bring back definite information about everything in a short time. He had been educated in the home of friends at Caere, and was consequently well informed about Etruscan literature and had a good knowledge of the Etruscan language. I have authority for believing that at that time Roman boys in general used to be grounded in Etruscan literature as they are in Greek today; but it seems more likely that there was something special in the man to make him move amongst the enemy by so bold a feint. It is said that as sole companion he took a slave who had been brought up with him and therefore also knew Etruscan. On setting out they wanted only a summary account of the nature of the region they had to enter and the names of the chief men of the various peoples, to avoid being detected in conversation by being at a loss over some well-known detail. They went dressed as shepherds, armed with rustic weapons, sickles and a couple of javelins each. But neither their familiarity with the language nor the nature of their clothing and weapons gave them such protection as the fact that it was beyond belief that any stranger would enter the Ciminian Forests. They are said to have made their way as far as Camerinum in Umbria, where the Roman ventured to say who they were. He was then led into the senate and opened negotiations in the consul's name on an alliance and friendship. He was afterwards hospitably entertained and told to return to the Romans with the message that thirty days' provisions would be ready for their army if it entered that region, and

60. The campaigns of Drusus in 12–9 B.C. are too late a date; Livy must have published his first decade before then. Caesar had crossed the Rhine in 55 and 53, and so had Agrippa in 38.

that the Umbrian Camertes of military age would be armed
and waiting for their orders.

When this was reported to the consul, he sent the baggage
on ahead, at the first watch, and ordered the legions to follow
the baggage. He himself stayed behind with the cavalry, and
at dawn on the following day rode up to the enemy's outposts,
which had been stationed outside the pass. Having held the
enemy's attention long enough he returned to his camp,
then left it by the opposite gate and caught up with the army
on the march before nightfall. At daylight next day he was
occupying the heights of the Ciminian mountain, from where
he could look down on the rich ploughlands of Etruria, and
sent out his men to plunder them. The Romans had already
made off with a large amount of booty when some improvised
bands of Etruscan peasants, hurriedly called up by the leading
men of the district, encountered them, but with such lack of
discipline that in trying to recover the spoils they nearly
became spoils themselves. The Romans killed them or put
them to flight, and after devastating the countryside over a
wide area, they returned to camp victorious and enriched with
all kinds of supplies. There, as it happened, they found five
envoys with two people's tribunes who had come to convey
to Fabius the Senate's instructions that he was not to go
through the Ciminian Forest. They were delighted to find
they had come too late to be able to hold up the campaign,
and returned to Rome with news of victory.

37. This expedition of the consul's, instead of bringing the
war to an end, had extended it further afield, for the area lying
at the foot of the Ciminian mountain had suffered devastation,
and this roused the indignation both of the peoples in Etruria
and of those in the neighbouring parts of Umbria. And so at
Sutrium they assembled an army which was larger than ever
before, and not only moved their camp out of the forest, but
in their eagerness to fight even came down to the plain in battle
formation as soon as they could. At first when drawn up they
remained in their positions and left the Romans space to draw
up opposite; then on finding that their enemy refused battle
they moved right up to the rampart. When they found that

even the outposts had been withdrawn within the earthworks, they quickly clamoured for their leaders to give orders that their rations for the day should be sent out to them from their camp: they would remain there under arms, they said, and launch an attack on the Roman camp either in the night or certainly at daybreak. The Roman army was no less restless, but was held back by the consul's authority. It was about the tenth hour when he gave the order for the soldiers to have a meal, and instructed them to be armed and ready for whatever hour of the day or night he gave the signal. He briefly addressed his troops, making the most of the Samnite wars and belittling the Etruscans. There was no comparison, he said, between the two as enemies, nor between their numbers; he had, besides, another secret weapon, which they would know about in due course; meanwhile they must say nothing about it. By these vague hints he tried to insinuate that the enemy was being betrayed, in order to restore the spirits of his soldiers, who had been dismayed by the large numbers confronting them; and his insinuations seemed true enough because the Etruscans had settled down without entrenching themselves.

Refreshed with food the soldiers relaxed and slept, and at about the fourth watch were awakened noiselessly to arm themselves. Picks were handed out to the camp-servants so that they could demolish the rampart and fill up the trenches. The army was drawn up within the defences and selected detachments were stationed at the exits by the gates. Then the signal was given shortly before dawn, which on summer nights is the time of deepest sleep, and the Romans in battle order burst out over the levelled rampart and attacked their enemies, who were spread about over a wide area. Death overtook some before they could stir and others who were half-awake where they lay, but the largest number were caught reaching for their arms in haste and confusion. Few were given time to arm themselves, and even these, with no definite standard or leader to follow, were overcome by the Romans, and pursued as they fled. They scattered, making for the camp or the woods. The woods gave them safer refuge, for the camp set up in the plain was captured the same day.

Orders were issued that any gold or silver was to be brought to the consul, while the rest of the plunder went to the soldiers. About sixty thousand of the enemy were killed or captured on that day.

Some authorities say that this famous battle was fought on the other side of the Ciminian Forest, near Perusia, and that there was great alarm at Rome for fear the army should be cut off in those dangerous forests and overwhelmed by a general rising of Etruscans and Umbrians. But, wherever it was fought, the Romans won the victory. Envoys accordingly came from Perusia, Cortona and Arretium, which at the time were probably the chief cities of the Etruscan peoples, to seek peace and a treaty from the Romans. They were granted a truce for thirty years.

38. During these events in Etruria the other consul, Gaius Marcius Rutulus, attacked and captured Allifae from the Samnites.[61] Many other forts and villages were either destroyed during hostilities or came into the possession of the Romans intact.

At about the same time Publius Cornelius, whom the Senate had put in command of the sea coast, brought a Roman fleet to Campania and put in at Pompeii. From there the sailors went off to plunder the territory of Nuceria, and after a quick foray into the nearest places from where they could return to their ships in safety, they were carried away by the delight of looting, as often happens, went on too far and brought out the enemy. Nobody came across them when they were spread out over the fields and could have been completely wiped out, but as they came trooping back, with no thought of danger, they were overtaken not far from the ships by peasants, who despoiled them of their plunder and even killed some of them; the survivors of the attack were driven back to the ships in disorder.

The march of Quintus Fabius through the Ciminian Forest which caused so much alarm in Rome gave no less delight to the enemy in Samnium at the rumour that the Roman army

61. The previous capture of Allifae is mentioned in VIII.25.4, but not its recapture by the Samnites.

was cut off and besieged. They recalled the Caudine Forks as an example of disaster; by the same foolhardiness, they said, a people always greedy for further advances had been led into trackless forests, to be hemmed in more by the difficulties of the terrain than by the arms of their enemy. Already their joy was tinged with a kind of envy, because, they supposed, Fortune had diverted the glory of a war with Rome from the Samnites to the Etruscans. So they hurried to put all their armed strength into crushing the consul, Gaius Marcius, with the intention of making for Etruria immediately through the territory of the Marsi and Sabines if he gave them no opportunity for an encounter. The consul met them, and a battle was fought fiercely on both sides, the result of which was uncertain; yet, although it was doubtful which side had more casualties, the main rumour was that the Romans had suffered a reverse; they had lost certain members of the equestrian order, some military tribunes and one legate, and, worst of all, the consul himself had been wounded.

As a result of these reverses, which as usual were exaggerated in reports, the Senate was seriously alarmed and resolved to name a dictator. No one doubted that the choice should fall on Papirius Cursor, who was regarded as foremost in military matters, but the senators were uncertain whether a messenger could get through to Samnium in safety when there was hostility everywhere, and also whether the consul Marcius were alive. The other consul, Fabius, had a personal grudge against Papirius, and the Senate feared that this ill feeling might do public harm. They therefore voted to send a deputation of ex-consuls to him in the hope that their personal influence combined with official authority would persuade him to forget his animosity in his country's interests. The envoys went to Fabius and delivered the Senate's resolution, with a speech in accord with their instructions. The consul kept his eyes on the ground and retired without a word, leaving the envoys uncertain of his intentions. Then in the silence of the night, as the custom is, he appointed Lucius Papirius dictator. When the envoys thanked him for nobly overcoming his feelings, he maintained an obstinate silence, dismissing them without any

reply or mention of what he had done, so that it was quite clear
what strong resentment his great spirit was suppressing.

Papirius named Gaius Junius Bubulcus as master of Horse,
but as he was proposing to the curiate assembly the law
confirming his authority,[62] a sinister omen cut short the proceedings. The first vote reported was that of the Curia Faucia,
which was notorious for two disasters, the capture of the City
and the Caudine Peace, both of which events had happened
in a year when it had made the first return. (Licinius Macer[63]
makes the Curia Faucia ill-omened for a third disaster as well,
that at the River Cremera.[64]) 39. On the following day the
dictator took the auspices again and carried the law through.
He then set out with the legions recently recruited on account
of the fear aroused by the army's march through the Ciminian
Forest, and arrived outside Longula, where he took over the
veteran troops from the consul Marcius and led his army out
to battle. The enemy too appeared ready to fight; then, when
both armies were drawn up and ready armed but neither was
willing to make the first move, night overtook them. For some
time after that they stayed quietly in the permanent camps they
had pitched near each other, neither lacking confidence in their
own strength nor despising their opponents. ⟨Meanwhile
things were going well in Etruria,⟩ for a battle was fought
against an army of Umbrians in which they were routed rather
than killed, because they had not been able to withstand the
fierce start of the battle[65]; and near Lake Vadimo the Etruscans
under a *lex sacrata*[66] had raised an army in which each man had
chosen another, and set to with greater forces and also with

62. The old curiate assembly retained its function of ratifying the
elections of magistrates.

63. See VII.9, note 12.

64. The river where the Fabian *gens* was virtually wiped out by a
force from Veii in 477; cf. II.50.

65. There is confusion between Livy's sources here, as elsewhere
(ch. 41.8) the Umbrians are said not to have been previously involved
in fighting. But see R. M. Ogilvie, *Yale Classical Studies* 23 (1973),
pp. 166–8.

66. cf. VII.41.4 and note 51.

greater spirit than ever before. The battle was fought with such rivalry of fury that not a missile was thrown by either side. The fighting began with swords, and after a furious start increased in intensity as the struggle continued, since for some time neither side had the advantage; it seemed as though the Romans had to contend not with the Etruscans they had so often defeated but with some new race. There was no sign of flight on either side. As the advance troops fell, the second line replaced the first so as not to leave the standards undefended. Then men were brought from the last resort, the reserves, and such extremes of distress and danger did the Romans reach that the cavalry dismounted and made their way over arms and bodies to the front rank of the infantry. Like a fresh line risen amongst the weary soldiers they threw the Etruscan ranks into confusion; next the remainder of the army, in spite of their exhaustion, followed up the attack and finally broke through the enemy's lines. At last, Etruscan tenacity began to break down, some of the companies gave way, and when once these had turned tail, all the others more definitely took to flight. That day for the first time broke the power of the Etruscans which had long flourished in their good fortune. Their strength was cut down on the battlefield, and their camp was taken and sacked in the same attack.

40. Immediately afterwards, war broke out in Samnite country, which was equally hazardous and equally glorious in its result. In addition to their other preparations for war the Samnites had made their battle-line glitter with new splendour in their arms. There were two armies; the shields of one were inlaid with gold, of the other with silver, and the shape of the shields was this: the upper part was quite broad where it protected the breast and shoulders and had a smooth rim, while the base was rather tapering, for easy handling. A corslet made of sponge covered the breast, and the left leg was protected by a greave. Helmets were plumed, to give an impression of greater stature. The tunics of the gilded soldiers were multi-coloured, and of the silver-plated of dazzling white linen. [The latter had silver scabbards and silver baldrics, the former had golden scabbards and baldrics, and their horses gold-

embroidered saddle-cloths.[67]] These were assigned the right
wing; the others were stationed on the left. The Romans had
already been told of this splendid armour and taught by their
commanders that a soldier ought to be rough-looking, not
inlaid with gold and silver but trusting to courage and the
sword; indeed, those were not arms so much as spoils of war,
gleaming bright before action but unsightly amongst blood
and wounds. A soldier's ornament was his manly courage;
everything else went with victory, and a rich enemy was the
prize of the victor, however poor he might be.

With these words Cursor roused his men and led them out
to battle. He took up his position on the right wing, and entrusted the left to the master of Horse. From the first moment
of the engagement there was a fierce struggle with the enemy,
and a struggle no less keen between the dictator and the master
of Horse to determine which wing should initiate victory. It
so happened that Junius was the first to dislodge the enemy,
with his left wing against their right, where the soldiers had
dedicated themselves in the Samnite manner and for that
reason were prominent in shining white clothing and armour
equally shining. Declaring that he offered these men as a
sacrifice to Orcus,[68] Junius charged, broke their ranks and
definitely forced the line back. When the dictator saw this, he
cried out: 'Shall victory start on the left wing, and the right
one, the dictator's division, follow on another's attack and not
carry off the greatest share of victory?' This spurred on his
men; the cavalry displayed no less courage than the infantry,
and the legates showed themselves as eager as the generals.
Marcus Valerius on the right and Publius Decius on the left,
both men of consular rank, rode out to the cavalry posted on
the wings, urged them to join them in seizing a share of glory,
then made a charge obliquely upon the Samnite flanks. With
the addition of fresh terror sweeping through the line on either
side and the pressure of the Roman legions with renewed
shouts as they saw the enemy's alarm, the Samnites began to

67. These words are not in extant M S S. of Livy, though some are
quoted by later historians.
68. Orcus (Pluto) was god of the dead.

flee. Soon the fields were strewn with heaps of dead bodies and gleaming armour. At first the terrified Samnites took refuge in their camp, but then could not hold even that; and before darkness fell it was taken, sacked and set on fire.

The dictator celebrated a triumph, in accordance with the Senate's decree. In this by far the most spectacular sight was that of the captured armour. So magnificent was its appearance that the shields with gold inlay were shared out amongst the owners of the banking-houses, to be used for decorating the Forum. This is said to be the origin of the decorating of the Forum by the aediles when the state carriages of the gods were taken through it. Thus the Romans made use of the splendid arms of their enemies to do honour to the gods; while the Campanians in their pride, out of hatred for the Samnites, equipped the gladiators who provided entertainment at their banquets with similar armour and gave them the name of Samnites.[69]

In the same year the consul Fabius fought an engagement with the remnants of the Etruscan armies near Perusia, one of the cities which had broken the truce,[70] and won a decisive victory with little trouble. His success brought him right up to the walls, and he would have taken the town itself if envoys had not come out to hand it over. After putting a garrison in Perusia and sending on ahead of himself to the Senate in Rome the Etruscan delegations which came seeking friendship, the consul rode in triumph into the City. He had won a victory more outstanding even than that of the dictator; for a large part of the glory of defeating the Samnites went to the legates, Publius Decius and Marcus Valerius, who at the next elections were returned as consul and praetor respectively by the people with immense acclamation.

41. In recognition of his brilliant conquest of Etruria Fabius's consulship was prolonged, and he was given Decius as colleague. Valerius was elected praetor for the fourth time. The

69. One of the four standard types of gladiator; cf. Pliny, *NH* VII.81.
70. The truce only recently granted; cf. ch. 37.12.

consuls shared out the spheres of command: Decius drew Etruria and Fabius Samnium, and Fabius marched out against Nuceria Alfaterna. There he rejected the people's petition for peace, because they had not wished to avail themselves of it when offered them, besieged the town and forced it to surrender. A pitched battle was fought with the Samnites, in which the enemy were defeated without much of a struggle; nor would the engagement have been remembered had it not been the first occasion that the Marsi had made war on the Romans. The Paeligni copied the Marsian revolt and met with the same fate.

Decius too, the other consul, enjoyed success in war. After he had frightened the people of Tarquinii into providing corn for his army and applying for a forty-year truce, he stormed and captured several fortresses belonging to Volsinii. Some of these he destroyed to prevent the enemy taking refuge there, and by extending his campaign far and wide he made himself so dreaded that all who counted themselves Etruscans begged him to grant them a treaty. This was flatly refused, but they were given a year's truce. They were required to supply a year's pay for the Roman army and two tunics for each soldier: that was the price paid for the truce.

The peace which now prevailed in Etruria was disturbed by a sudden revolt of the Umbrians, a people who had been quite untouched by the disasters of war except when their land had suffered the passage of an army through it.[71] They had called up all their men of fighting age and put pressure on a large number of Etruscans to rebel; thus they had assembled so large an army that they could speak in exaggerated terms of themselves and in open contempt of the Romans, boasting that they would leave Decius behind them in Etruria and march off to launch an attack on Rome. When a report of their intention reached the consul Decius, he hurried from Etruria to the City by forced marches and encamped in the region called Pupinia, keenly awaiting news of the enemy. At Rome too, no one made light of war with the Umbrians. Their very

71. Not mentioned elsewhere.

threats had aroused the fears of those who had learned from the Gallic disaster how unsafe was the City they lived in. Envoys were therefore dispatched to the consul Fabius to tell him to take his army into Umbria with all haste, if there were any slackening off of the Samnite war. Fabius obeyed the order, and moved by forced marches towards Mevania, where the Umbrian forces were gathered.

The sudden arrival of the consul, whom they had believed to be occupied with another war in Samnium, far away from Umbria, so alarmed the Umbrians that some thought they should withdraw to their fortified cities, while others were for abandoning the war altogether; only one district, which they themselves call Materina, not only kept the rest under arms but quickly brought them to battle. They attacked Fabius while he was entrenching his camp. As soon as he saw them rushing wildly over his earthworks, he recalled the soldiers from their work and drew them up, as well as time and the nature of the terrain allowed. After he had encouraged them with a faithful account of the honours they had won in Etruria or in Samnium, he told them to finish off this petty appendix to the Etruscan war, and wreak punishment on the foe for his impious threat to attack the City of Rome. The soldiers heard this with such enthusiasm that they interrupted their general with their spontaneous cheering. Then, before the command was given, the horns and trumpets rang out, and they rushed headlong at the enemy. The attack did not seem to be on armed men, or on men at all, but (marvellous to tell) they began by first wrenching the standards from the bearers' hands, and then went on to drag the bearers themselves to the consul and to bring armed men over from the Umbrian side to their own. Where they met with opposition, they dealt with it by using their shields rather than swords, pushing hard with their shoulders and shield-bosses to throw the enemy down. There were more prisoners taken than men killed, and throughout the Umbrian lines with one voice the call was raised to lay down arms. Thus, while fighting was still going on, surrender was made by the men who first instigated the war. On the following and successive days the rest of the Umbrian peoples

gave themselves up, and Ocriculum was admitted to friendship under guarantee.

42. After his victory in this action fought in his colleague's
province, Fabius took his army back to his own area of command. In recognition of his successes the Senate extended his
command into the coming year, just as the people had continued his consulship the year before. The consuls were Appius
Claudius and Lucius Volumnius; Appius strongly opposed the
extension of Fabius's command.

I find in certain annals that Appius was a candidate for the
consulship while censor, and that the elections were held up
by the people's tribune Lucius Furius until he resigned the
censorship. After his election, his colleague was assigned the
command in a new campaign against the Sallentini, and
Appius remained in Rome, to strengthen his power by statecraft, as the chance of winning military glory was taken out
of his hands.

Volumnius did not regret his assignment; he fought many
successful battles and took several of the enemy's cities by
storm. He was liberal in sharing out plunder, and enhanced his
generosity, which was popular in itself, by his friendly manner
– thereby making his men avid for hard work and danger.

The proconsul Quintus Fabius fought the Samnite army in
a regular battle near Allifae, the result of which was not in any
doubt. The enemy were routed and driven into their camp,
and could not have held that had there not been so little
daylight left. Even so the camp was surrounded before darkness fell, and guards were posted in the night to prevent
anyone's escaping. Next day the surrender began before it was
properly daylight, those who were Samnites stipulating that
they should be allowed to come out with a single garment
each; they were all sent under the yoke. No special provision
was made for the allies of the Samnites, about seven thousand
of whom were sold into slavery. All those who claimed citizenship as Hernici were kept apart in custody, and sent by Fabius
to the Senate in Rome.[72] After an inquiry to find whether they

72. The Hernici had been subdued in 358 (VII.15.9) and had been
at peace with Rome ever since.

had been conscripted or had fought voluntarily for the Samnites against the Romans, they were handed out amongst the Latin peoples to be kept under guard, and the new consuls, Publius Cornelius Arvina and Quintus Marcius Tremulus – for these men had already been elected – were instructed to refer the matter afresh to the Senate. That annoyed the Hernici, and at a council of all their peoples held by the inhabitants of Anagnia in the circus which they call the Maritime Circus, all the Hernici except those from Aletrium, Ferentinum and Verulae declared war on the Roman people.

43. In Samnium too, Fabius's departure had led to fresh outbreaks of unrest. Calatia and Sora, with the Roman garrisons in occupation, were stormed and captured, and the soldiers taken prisoner were treated with savage fury. Publius Cornelius was therefore sent there with an army. Marcius was assigned the new enemies, for war had already been declared on the people of Anagnia and the rest of the Hernici. At the start the enemy occupied all the strategic points between the consuls' camps with such success that even a messenger travelling light could not get through. For several days neither consul knew anything definite about the general situation, and each was uncertain how the other was faring. The anxiety even spread to Rome, and became so serious that the oath was administered to all the men of military age, and two regular armies were enlisted to meet any sudden emergency. But the war with the Hernici was in no sense proportionate to the present alarm, nor to that people's high reputation in the past. They ventured nothing to speak of at any time, and after being driven out of three camps were granted a thirty-day truce in which to send envoys to the Senate in Rome, at a cost of two months' pay and corn and a tunic for every soldier. The Senate returned the envoys to Marcius after passing a decree giving him a free hand to deal with the Hernici, and he received their unconditional surrender.

In Samnium the other consul was superior in strength to the enemy, but was more hampered by the terrain. The Samnites had blocked all the roads and seized the practicable passes, to make it impossible for supplies to be brought up by any route; but the consul could not draw them out to fight, although he marched out in battle order every day. It was quite clear that the Samnites would not submit to an immediate confrontation, nor the Romans put up with any prolongation of the war. The arrival of Marcius, who had hurried to the support of his colleague as soon as he had settled the Hernici, put an end to the enemy's delaying tactics. For since they had not believed themselves equal to a battle with even one army, now that they had allowed two consular armies to unite they thought there was no hope left for them, and so they attacked Marcius as he was approaching in loose marching formation. The Romans hurriedly threw down their baggage and formed up round it, as well as time permitted. The noise of shouting was the first thing to reach Cornelius's camp; then the sight of dust rising in the distance threw his men into an uproar. He ordered them to arm and quickly led them out to battle, charging the enemy's flank cross-wise when they were taken up with another struggle, and crying out that it would be a monstrous shame if his men allowed the other army to win both victories and did not claim for themselves the honours of their own campaign. He burst through the enemy's line wherever he attacked and went on to capture their camp, which was empty of defenders, and set it on fire. When Marcius's soldiers saw the blaze and their enemies looked round and saw it too, that was the moment for the flight of the Samnites to become general; but everywhere was blocked by slaughter, and nowhere was there a safe refuge.

Thirty thousand of the enemy had already been dispatched, and the consuls had sounded the signal for withdrawal and were gathering their forces together amid mutual rejoicing and congratulation when suddenly new detachments of Samnites, who had been levied as reinforcements, were seen in the distance, and the slaughter was renewed. The victorious Romans fell on them without waiting for any signal or order from the consuls, calling out that Samnite recruits must start with a harsh lesson. The consuls gave the eager men their head, being quite confident that the enemy's recruits, when amongst veterans who were already put to flight, would hardly be up to even an attempt at fighting, and they were proved right. All the Samnite forces, old and new, fled to the nearest mountains, up which the Roman army went after them. There was no place of safety there for the defeated; they were sent running down from the heights they had occupied, and then with one voice all begged for peace. They were ordered to supply three months' corn, with a year's pay and a tunic for each soldier, and their envoys were sent to the Senate to ask for terms of peace.

Cornelius was left in Samnium, while Marcius returned to enter the City in triumph over the Hernici. He was decreed an equestrian statue, which was set up in front of the temple of Castor.[73] The three tribes of Hernici belonging to Aletrium, Ferentinum and Verulae were duly allowed to retain their own laws, because they preferred them to Roman citizenship, and they were also given permission to intermarry with each other – a privilege which for some time they were the only Hernici to enjoy. The people of Anagnia and any others who had taken up arms against the Romans were granted citizenship without voting rights; they were no longer allowed to hold councils or to intermarry, and were forbidden to have any magistrates except those in charge of religious rites.

In the same year the censor Gaius Junius Bubulcus let out the contract for the building of the temple of Safety,[74] which he had vowed as consul during the Samnite war. He and his colleague, Marcus Valerius Maximus, also built roads through the countryside at public expense. In this year too the treaty with Carthage was renewed for the third time,[75] and their ambassadors who had come to arrange this were courteously presented with gifts.

44. The same year saw a dictator, Publius Cornelius Scipio, with Publius Decius Mus as his master of Horse. They held consular elections, the purpose for which they had been ap-

73. That of the Dioscuri, vowed at the battle of Lake Regillus (II.20.12).

74. On the Quirinal, vowed in 311.

75. See VII.27, note 36.

pointed, as neither consul had been able to absent himself
from war. The consuls elected were Lucius Postumius and
Tiberius Minucius. Piso[76] puts these consuls immediately after
Quintus Fabius and Publius Decius, leaving out the two years
in which we have recorded the consulship of Claudius and
Volumnius, followed by that of Cornelius and Marcius.
Whether they escaped his memory when he was arranging his
annals or he deliberately left out two pairs of consuls, believing
them not to be genuine, is not certain.

Also in that year the Samnites carried out raids on the
Stellate region in Campania, and accordingly both consuls
were sent to different areas of Samnium; Postumius made for
Tifernum and Minucius to Bovianum. Fighting first broke out
at Tifernum, where Postumius was in command. Some say
that the Samnites were undoubtedly defeated and twenty
thousand of them were taken prisoner, others that the armies
left the battlefield on equal terms, and that Postumius feigned
fear and led his troops secretly into the mountains by night.
There the enemy followed him, entrenched a camp themselves
and settled in it two miles away. The consul wanted it to
appear that he had chosen a site which was both secure and well
supplied, as indeed it was – so he strengthened the camp with
earthworks and provided it with all sorts of useful equipment.
Then he left a strong garrison in it and led his legions, travelling light, by the nearest route to his colleague, who was also
encamped opposite another army. There Minucius, encouraged by Postumius, engaged the enemy and, when the
battle had continued late into the day without result, Postumius with his fresh legions made an unexpected attack on the
Samnite army, which was already exhausted. Their fatigue
and wounds prevented them even from running away, and so
they were completely annihilated. The Romans captured
twenty-one standards and then made their way to Postumius's
camp, where the two victorious armies attacked the Samnites,
who were already dismayed by the news they had heard,
overwhelmed them and put them to flight. Twenty-six mili-

76. L. Calpurnius Piso Frugi, consul in 133 B.C., wrote annals
covering the period from the foundation of Rome to his own day.

tary standards were captured, along with the Samnite commander, Statius Gellius, and many other people, as well as both
the camps. Next day the Romans began to lay siege to the city
of Bovianum, which was soon taken, and the consuls celebrated a triumph for their glorious achievements. Some
authorities say that Minucius was seriously wounded and
brought back to his camp, where he died. They add that
Marcus Fulvius was appointed consul to replace him, and after
he was sent to take over Minucius's army, it was he who captured Bovianum.

That year Sora, Arpinum and Cesennia were recovered
from the Samnites. The great statue of Hercules was set up and
dedicated on the Capitol.

45. During the consulship of Publius Sulpicius Saverrio and
Publius Sempronius Sophus, the Samnites sent a deputation to
Rome to negotiate a peace, in an attempt either to end or to
postpone the war. The reply given to their humble request was
that if the Samnites had not often sought peace while preparing
for war, negotiations for peace could have been carried on by
mutual discussion; but as matters stood, there had been
nothing but empty words so far, and the Romans must take
their stand on facts. The consul Publius Sempronius would
soon be in Samnium with an army, and he was not one they
could deceive about whether their inclinations were for war
or for peace. He would make a full investigation and report
back to the Senate, and when he left Samnium their
envoys should attend him. The Roman army marched all over
Samnium, and as they found everything peaceful and the
people very willing to provide supplies, the Samnites had their
old treaty[77] restored to them that year.

The Romans then turned their arms against the Aequi, their
old enemies, though they had been quiet for many years[78]
under cover of a peace not reliably maintained. The reason for
Roman action was the fact that, so long as the Hernici remained unsubdued, the Aequi had joined them in repeatedly

77. That granted in 354 (VII.19.4) and renewed in 341 (VIII.2.1)
at the end of the First Samnite War.
78. Since 388; cf. VI.4.8.

sending help to the Samnites, and after the Hernici were put down the Aequi had defected to the enemy almost to a man, without any disguising of their policy. Then when the fetial priests had come to them demanding reparation, after the treaty with the Samnites had been drawn up in Rome, they kept saying that this was an attempt to intimidate them into becoming Romans by threat of war; and how desirable *that* was the Hernici had shown, when those permitted had chosen their own laws in preference to Roman citizenship, while those allowed no option were to have citizenship enforced on them as a punishment.[79] It was because of such remarks, openly expressed in the assemblies of the Aequi, that the Roman people ordered war to be declared. Both consuls set out for the new campaign and took up their position four miles from the enemy's camp.

The Aequi had fought no war on their own account for a great many years; their army looked like an emergency levy, without definite leaders or supreme command, and was in a state of confusion. Some were all for marching out to battle, others for guarding the camp. Most of them were concerned about the devastation their lands would suffer and the subsequent destruction of their cities, which they had left only lightly garrisoned. So among the proposals made one was heard which disregarded the general interest and turned every man's thoughts to his own possessions; at the first watch they should leave the camp and go off in different directions, to bring their property from the fields into the cities where they could defend themselves behind walls. This was unanimously accepted with loud applause. The Aequi were scattered about the countryside when at daybreak the Romans left their camp and took up their positions for battle; then, when no one confronted them, they moved off rapidly to the enemy's camp. There they found neither sentries at the gates nor anyone on the rampart; and, hearing none of the usual sounds of a camp, they were disturbed by the unnatural silence and halted, fearing an ambush. Then when they scaled the rampart

79. cf. ch. 43.23–4.

and found everything deserted, they tried to follow the enemy's tracks, but these led equally in all directions, as they would when men had dispersed and scattered. This perplexed them at first, but later on, when they learned through scouts of the Aequi's intentions, they carried their campaign to the towns one after another, and captured thirty-one[80] within fifty days, all by direct attack. Most of these were razed and burnt, and the Aequian name was almost completely wiped out. A triumph was celebrated over the Aequi, and the example of their destruction acted as a general warning, so that the Marrucini, Marsi, Paeligni and Frentani sent deputations to Rome to plead for peace and friendship. These peoples were granted a treaty in answer to their request.

46. In the same year a government clerk, Gnaeus Flavius, son of Gnaeus, was curule aedile.[81] He had been born in humble circumstances, his father being a freedman, but was an able man and a good speaker. In certain annals I find that when he was in attendance on the aediles and saw that the tribal vote would elect him aedile had his candidature not been unacceptable because he was recording the proceedings,[82] he threw away his writing-tablet and took an oath that he would make no record. However, Licinius Macer[83] declares that he had ceased to be a recording clerk some time previously, and had already been a people's tribune and member of a commission of three on two occasions, once in charge of the night watch,[84] and once for the purpose of founding a colony. At any rate there is no difference of opinion about the stubborn determination with which he battled against the nobles, who looked down on his humble birth. He published the forms of civil law

80. Diodorus (XX.101.5) gives the number as forty-one.

81. With this account compare Pliny, *NH* XXXIII.17–19, and Gellius VII.9, quoting the annalist Piso, from whom Livy probably took his details.

82. He was a paid civil servant and could not hold a magistracy unless he first resigned his post.

83. See VII.9, note 12.

84. The *tresviri capitales*, police commissioners whose duties included superintendence of the night watch, though they were not a regular institution until later.

which had been hidden away amongst the secret archives of
the pontiffs, and posted the official calendar on white notice-
boards around the Forum, for the dates to be generally known
when a legal action could be brought. He dedicated a temple
of Concord in the precinct of Vulcan, greatly to the annoyance
of the nobility, and the chief pontiff, Cornelius Barbatus, was
compelled by the united wishes of the people to dictate the
formula of dedication to him, although he insisted that by
ancestral custom no one but a consul or a general could
dedicate a temple. As a result of this, acting on the Senate's
proposal, the people passed the measure that no one should
dedicate a temple or an altar without the authorization of the
Senate or of a majority of the people's tribunes. (I will relate
an incident not in itself worth mentioning, did it not provide
evidence of the people's assertion of their liberty against the
arrogance of the nobles. Flavius had come to visit a sick
colleague, and the young nobles sitting by the man's bedside
by general consent did not rise to their feet at his entrance. He
ordered his curule chair to be brought in, and from his official
seat sat looking at his enemies, who were much annoyed and
embarrassed.) But Flavius had been elected aedile by a faction
of the Forum, which had gained power from the censorship
of Appius Claudius. Claudius had been the first to lower the
standard of the Senate by filling up its list of members from
the sons of freedmen, and when no one accepted his selection
and he failed to obtain the political influence he sought in the
Senate-house, he distributed the lower-class tradesmen and
artisans throughout all the tribes, with damaging effect on the
Forum and Campus.[85] And so great was the indignation
roused by the election of Flavius that the majority of the nobles
discarded their gold rings and military decorations. From then
on the citizens were divided into two parties; the honest men
who supported and upheld right principles took one view, and
the rabble of the Forum another, until Quintus Fabius and
Publius Decius were elected censors and Fabius, partly to

85. This was in fact a necessary extension of the franchise to those
who had hitherto been denied the right of membership of the assembly and the power to vote because they were not landowners.

establish harmony and partly to prevent the elections being in
the hands of the lowest of the low, weeded out all the Forum
mob and deposited them in four tribes, to which he gave the
name of Urban tribes. This is said to have been so gratefully
received that Fabius won for his settlement of the orders the
surname of Maximus which all his many victories had not
brought him. It is said too that it was Fabius who instituted
the annual parade of the knights on every fifteenth of July.

BOOK X

1. During the consulship of Lucius Genucius and Servius Cornelius there was almost a complete respite from foreign wars. Colonies were taken out to Sora and Alba: six thousand settlers were enrolled for Alba, which was in Aequian territory, while Sora had been in Volscian land but occupied by the Samnites; it received four thousand colonists. In this year too, citizenship was granted to Arpinum and Trebula. Frusino was stripped of a third of its land because it was discovered that its people had influenced the Hernici, and after an investigation conducted by the consul, at the Senate's behest, the ringleaders of the plot were flogged and beheaded. But so that the year should not pass without any warlike activity, a minor expedition was led into Umbria because of reports that armed forays were being made on farmland from a certain cave. The soldiers carried their standards into the cave and there in the darkness received a good many wounds, mainly from stones thrown at them, until they found the other mouth of the cavern (for there was a way through), blocked both openings with heaped-up wood, and set them on fire. In this way up to two thousand armed men died in the cave from the smoke and heat, for they ended by running into the actual flames in their attempts to escape.

War with the Aequi was renewed during the consulship of Marcus Livius Denter and Marcus Aemilius. The Aequi resented the colony planted like a fortress in their midst and launched a violent attack on it, only to be repelled by the colonists themselves. But this caused so much alarm in Rome – for it was hardly believable that the Aequi should have rallied to start a war unaided when their fortunes were so reduced – that Gaius Junius Bubulcus was appointed dictator to cope with the insurrection. With Marcus Titinius as his master of Horse he set out and forced the Aequi to submit at the first encounter, returning to the City in triumph a week later. He then dedicated as dictator the temple of Safety which he had vowed as consul, and for which he had placed the contract as censor.

2. In the same year a Greek fleet under the command of Cleonymus the Spartan arrived off the Italian coast and captured the city of Thuriae[1] in the territory of the Sallentini. The consul Aemilius was dispatched against the Greeks, routed them in a single battle, and forced them back to their ships. Thuriae was restored to its former inhabitants and peace established in Sallentine country. (In certain records I find that it was the dictator Junius Bubulcus who was sent amongst the Sallentini, and that Cleonymus left Italy before he had to come into conflict with the Romans.)

Cleonymus rounded the promontory of Brundisium and was driven on by the winds in the Adriatic gulf, exposed to the perils of the harbourless Italian coast on his left, and the Illyrians, Liburnians and Istrians on his right, savage tribes and most of them notorious for their acts of piracy. He kept on until he reached the shore of the Veneti. He sent a few men ashore to reconnoitre, and learned that there was a narrow beach in front of them and, after it was crossed, lagoons behind which were flooded by the sea tides; then not far away flat land could be seen, with hills visible further off, and the mouth of a deep river (the Mediacus) where the ships could be brought round into safe harbourage. He then gave orders for the fleet to sail in and move upstream. But the river channel would not take the heaviest ships, so large numbers of armed men transferred to lighter boats and went on until they came to inhabited fields, where the river bank was occupied by three shore settlements of the Patavini. There they landed and, leaving a few men on guard over the ships, they sacked the villages, burnt the houses, carried off men and cattle, and, lured on by the sweets of plunder, went further and further away from their ships.

When news of this reached the Patavini, who were kept perpetually under arms because of the proximity of the

1. If the text is correct, the site is unknown. The Sallentini lived in the heel of Italy.

Gauls, they divided their fighting force into two parts. One of these was led to the area from where came the reports of widespread raids, and the other, by another route, so as not to meet any of the marauders, to where the ships were moored, fourteen miles from the town. The men on guard were caught unawares and killed, the ships were attacked, and their terrified sailors forced to take them over to the other bank of the river. On land the battle against the struggling raiders was equally successful, and the Greeks who tried to escape to their landing place found their way blocked by the Veneti. In this way the enemy were caught between the two parties and cut down. Some who were taken prisoner revealed that the main fleet and King Cleonymus were three miles away. The captives were then handed over to the custody of the nearest village, and an armed force of Veneti embarked, some on their river-craft, which were constructed with flat bottoms, designed for sailing on the shallow water of the lagoons, others on the boats they had captured. They made for the fleet and surrounded the unwieldy ships, whose occupants feared unknown water more than an enemy, and were more eager to escape to deep water than offer resistance. The Veneti pursued them as far as the mouth of the river, and, after capturing and setting fire to some ships which had run aground in the general confusion, returned victorious. Cleonymus departed with barely a fifth of his ships undamaged, and with no success in his attempts on any part of the Adriatic coast. The ships' prows and Laconian spoils were nailed to the walls of the old temple of Juno; and there are many people still living in Patavium[2] who have seen them. In commemoration of the naval battle, a battle of ships is regularly staged every year in the centre of the town, on the day it was fought.

3. Also in this year a treaty was made at Rome with the Vestini in answer to their request for friendship. Then alarms broke out in several places. It was reported that Etruria was in revolt, as a result of disturbances at Arretium, where a movement had begun to force out the all-powerful family of the

2. Patavium (Padua) was Livy's home town.

Cilnii, because of the envy aroused by their wealth. At the
same time the Marsi forcibly defended their territory against
the planting of the colony at Carseoli,[3] for which four
thousand men were enrolled. To deal with these outbreaks
Marcus Valerius Maximus was appointed dictator and chose
Marcus Aemilius Paulus for his master of Horse. I find this
more credible than that Quintus Fabius, at the age he had
reached and after the offices he had held, was made subordinate
to Valerius, though I would not deny that the error could have
arisen out of the surname Maximus. The dictator set out with
an army and defeated the Marsi in a single battle. He then
drove them into their walled cities, captured Milionia, Plestina
and Fresilia within a few days, fined the Marsi by confiscating
part of their territory, and renewed the treaty with them. Then
operations were directed against the Etruscans; and the dictator
left for Rome to take the auspices again. During his absence
the master of Horse went out foraging and was ambushed. He
lost several standards, his men were disgracefully put to flight
and slaughtered, and he was forced back into his camp. Something so dreadful is most unlikely to have happened to Fabius,
not only because if in anything he lived up to his surname it
was in his military reputation, but also because he would not
have forgotten the harsh judgement of Papirius[4] and could
never have been induced to engage in battle without an order
from the dictator.

4. The news of this calamity caused greater alarm at Rome
than the situation warranted; a cessation of legal business was
ordered, guards posted at the gates, night watches called out
along the streets, and arms and missiles piled up against the
walls. All men of military age were summoned to take the
oath, and the dictator was sent off to the army, where he found
everything quieter than he expected and in good order in the
hands of the master of Horse. The camp had been moved back
to a safer position, and the cohorts which had lost their stan-

3. But in ch. 13.1 Livy dates the foundation of Carseoli about four
years later.
4. cf. VIII.30–35.

dards were left outside the rampart without tents.[5] The army
was avid for battle, to wipe out its disgrace the sooner. He
therefore quickly moved the camp forward into the district of
Rusellae. There the enemy followed him, and although, as a
result of their recent triumph, they had the highest expectations of their superiority even in an open battle, they also
attempted an attack by ambush, as they had successfully done
before. Not far from the Roman camp were the half-ruined
buildings of a village which had been burnt when the countryside was laid waste. There they hid armed men, and drove up
cattle in full view of a Roman guard-post, which was commanded by the legate Gnaeus Fulvius. As none of the Romans
fell for the bait or moved from his post, one of the herdsmen
came right up to the earthworks and called out to the rest, who
were driving the cattle rather hesitantly from the ruins of the
village, to know why they were holding back when they could
safely drive them straight through the Roman camp. When
some men from Caere translated this to the legate, an indignant outcry ran through all the maniples of soldiers, though
none of them dared to move without an order. The legate told
those who knew the language to listen carefully and see
whether the herdsmen's speech sounded more like that of
country or of city people. When they reported that the accent,
dress and general appearance were too refined to belong to
peasants, 'Then go and take them,' he cried, 'to uncover the
ambush they have laid in vain; for the Romans know all and
cannot be captured by guile any more than they can be defeated by arms.' As soon as this message was received and
conveyed to the men lying in ambush, they immediately
jumped up from their hiding-place and advanced for battle in
the plain, which was open to view on all sides. The legate
judged their numbers to be too great for his own detachment
to withstand, and hurriedly sent to the dictator to summon
help; meanwhile he held the enemy's attacks himself.

5. On receiving the message the dictator gave orders to
advance the standards and for his men to arm and follow them.

5. As a punishment.

But everything was almost sooner done than bidden; standards and arms were hurriedly snatched up and the soldiers could hardly be restrained from charging the enemy full tilt. Anger at the reverse they had lately received spurred them on, and even more did the shouts which met their ears in rising intensity as the battle developed. So they urged each other on and pressed the standard-bearers to go faster. The more the dictator saw them hurrying on, the more anxious he was to hold them back, and he commanded them to advance more slowly. The Etruscans, on the other hand, had been called out at the start of the fighting and were there with all their forces; and as one messenger after another told the dictator that all the Etruscan legions were engaged in the battle and his own men could not hold out any longer, from his position on higher ground he could see for himself the peril the troops were in. Yet he was fairly confident that the legate was capable even now of keeping up the struggle and that he himself was not too far away to rescue him in a crisis, and he wanted to tire the Etruscans as much as possible so that he could bring fresh forces in to attack them when exhausted. But though the Romans were advancing slowly, there was already only a small space for a charge, at any rate for the cavalry. In the van advanced the legions' standards, so the enemy had not to fear any hidden or sudden attack, but Valerius had left gaps between the files of infantry to give wide enough space to let the horses through. The legions raised a cheer, and at the same moment the cavalry were released and charged the enemy at an unchecked gallop, overwhelming them in immediate panic, as they were quite unprepared for a cavalry attack. So although help had nearly come too late for the men who were already almost surrounded, they were all now given a respite. The fresh troops took over the battle, which did not last long; nor was its issue in doubt. The enemy retreated to their camp in disorder, and as the Roman standard-bearers bore in on them, they gave way and huddled into the furthest corner of the camp. Fugitives choked the narrow exits at the gates, and large numbers climbed the earth rampart and palisade to see if they could either defend themselves from a higher position or climb over somewhere and escape. It happened that in one place the rampart had been badly pressed down, so that it collapsed into the trench with the weight of those standing on it, and thus they got out, crying that the gods had opened them a way of escape; but more of them left without arms than with them.

In this battle the power of the Etruscans was broken for the second time.[6] They agreed to supply a year's pay for the army and a two months' supply of corn, and were then permitted by the dictator to send envoys to Rome to negotiate terms of peace. Peace was refused them, but they were granted a truce for two years. Valerius returned to the City in triumph. (I find some authorities saying that peace was established in Etruria by the dictator without any memorable battle, only by settling the disturbances at Arretium and reconciling the family of the Cilnii with the people.) After resigning his dictatorship, Marcus Valerius was elected consul. Some records say that he was elected without seeking office, and even without being present, and that the election was held by an interrex; one thing anyway is not in doubt, that he held his consulship with Quintus Apuleius Pansa as colleague.

6. During their consulship, affairs abroad were quite peaceful: the Etruscans were kept quiet by their defeat in war and by the truce, and the Samnites were subdued by their reverses over many years and were not yet dissatisfied with the renewal of their treaty.[7] In Rome too the dispatch of large numbers to the colonies kept the plebeians quiet. However, so that peace might not be universal, the people's tribunes, Quintus and Gnaeus Ogulnius, stirred up dissension amongst the leading citizens, both patrician and plebeian. They had sought opportunities everywhere for maligning the senators in the hearing of the commons, and when all their other attempts were unsuccessful, they embarked on a course of action calculated to arouse not the lowest of the plebeians but actually their leaders – those plebeians in fact who had held consulships and triumphs, and to complete their official titles needed only

6. The first time is described in IX.34.11.
7. cf. IX.45.4.

the priesthoods, which were not yet open to all. The tribunes
therefore proposed the following measure: since at the time
there were four augurs and four pontiffs, and it was desired to
increase the number of priests, four pontiffs and five augurs
should be added, all to be taken from the plebs. How the
college of augurs could have been reduced to four members,
unless by the death of two, I cannot discover; since it is well
established amongst the augurs that their number should be
uneven, so that the three ancient tribes, the Ramnes, Titienses
and Luceres, should each have its augur, or, if more are needed,
they should increase the number of priests in the same proportion – as in fact they were increased when five were added to
the four to make up the number of nine and give each tribe
three. But because the extra priests were to come from the
plebeians, the senators were as enraged by the proposal as they
were when they saw the consulship thrown open. They pretended that it was the gods' concern rather than their own: the
gods would see that their rites were not defiled, while their
own desire was only that no calamity should befall the State.
Yet they did not offer much resistance, as they were now
accustomed to being the losers in conflicts of this kind; and
they were used to seeing their adversaries no longer aspiring
to high offices which in the past had been almost beyond their
hopes, but already in possession of everything for which they
had fought with doubtful expectations of success – repeated
consulships, censorships and triumphs.

7. However, tradition relates that there was a violent confrontation between Appius Claudius and Publius Decius Mus
on the passage or rejection of the law. After they had brought
up nearly the same arguments about patrician and plebeian
rights as had been used previously for and against the Licinian
law, when the plebeians were seeking the consulships, it is said
that Decius recalled the scene (witnessed by many who were
present at the assembly) of his father wearing his toga in the
Gabine manner and standing on a spear, as he had looked when
he devoted himself on behalf of the people and legions of
Rome.[8] On that occasion, he declared, the immortal gods had

8. cf. VIII.9.5–9 and note 10.

accepted Publius Decius the consul as an offering just as pure
and holy as if it had been his colleague Titus Manlius who
devoted himself. Then could not that same Publius Decius
have been duly chosen to perform the official rites of the
Roman people? Or was there a risk that the gods would hear
his own prayers less willingly than those of Appius Claudius?
Did Appius perform his private devotions more piously and
worship the gods more devoutly than he did himself? Who
was there who regretted the vows on the State's behalf made
by so many plebeian consuls and so many dictators, either on
going out to their armies or during their campaigns? They
should count up the generals of those years since campaigns
were first mounted under the leadership and auspices of
plebeians, and count up the triumphs. Even on the question of
their noble birth, the plebeians had now nothing to regret. It
was quite certain that if any sudden war broke out, the Senate
and Roman people would pin their hopes no more on patrician than on plebeian generals.

'Since this is so,' he said, 'what god or man can think it
unbecoming if men whom you have honoured with curule
chairs, the purple-edged toga, the palm-embroidered tunic,[9]
and with the decorated toga, the triumphal crown and laurel
wreaths,[10] whose houses you have marked out from the rest
by the enemy's spoils fastened to their walls – if such men add
the insignia of pontiffs and augurs? Shall the man resplendent
in the robes of Jupiter Best and Highest, who has been carried
through the City in a gilded chariot to ascend the Capitol, not
be seen with sacrificial cup and augur's crook[11] when with
covered head he slaughters the victim or receives an augury
from the Citadel? If in the inscription below a man's
portrait the words consulship, censorship and triumph can be
read with equanimity, cannot the reader's eyes bear to see
mention of the offices of augur or pontiff? Speaking for myself
– with the gods' permission – I hope that thanks to the Roman

9. The dress of a curule magistrate.

10. The insignia worn when celebrating a triumph.

11. The *lituus*, described by Livy in I.18.7 as a crook or crozier made
from wood without a knot in it.

people we are now in a position to confer on the priesthoods, through the esteem in which we are held, as much honour as we draw from them and, more on the gods' account than on our own, to seek permission to worship officially the objects of our private devotions.

8. 'But why have I been arguing so far as if the patrician case for retaining the priesthoods has not yet been questioned, and we are not already in possession of one most honourable priesthood? We see that plebeians are already members of the Board of Ten for performing sacred rites, interpreters of the Sibylline oracles and the destinies of our people, and they are also priests serving the ritual of Apollo and of other ceremonies. Yet surely no wrong was done to the patricians at the time when the two officials performing the sacred rites had their number increased on account of the plebeians, and today our brave and enterprising tribune has proposed to add five augurs' posts and four pontiffs', to which plebeians may be appointed, not with any intention of ousting you patricians, Appius, but to give you the assistance of men of plebeian rank in administering divine matters, as they give it to the best of their ability in all other, human affairs. You should not blush, Appius, to have a colleague in the priesthood whom you could have had as fellow-consul or censor, or whose master of Horse you could have been, just as he could have been yours if you were dictator. A Sabine alien, Attius Clausus or Appius Claudius, as you prefer, the first to ennoble your family, was accepted as one of them by the patricians of past times; so do not think it demeans you to admit us to the number of priests. We bring with us many distinctions, all of them in fact the same as those which have made you so proud. Lucius Sextius was the first plebeian consul, Gaius Licinius Stolo the first master of Horse, Gaius Marcius Rutulus the first to be both dictator and consul, Quintus Publilius Philo the first praetor. Always we have heard the same thing from you – that the auspices belong to you, that you alone are of noble birth, you alone have supreme power of command and the right to take auspices at home and on the battlefield. But these powers have flourished equally well in both plebeian and patrician hands up

to now, and they will do in the future. Why, have you never heard tell how the first patricians were not created from beings descended from heaven but were those who could name their fathers – that is, they were free-born men and nothing more? I can already name a consul as my father, and my son will be able to name one as his grandfather. The fact is, Romans, that everything is denied us at first, but we obtain it in the end. All the patricians want is a contest of wills, and they care nothing for the outcome of these conflicts. I say that this law should be approved as proposed, and may it prove good, happy and fortunate for you and for the State!'

9. The people immediately ordered the tribes to be summoned, and it seemed that the law was accepted; however, no progress could be made that day because of a veto. Next day the tribunes were deterred from further action, and the law was passed with great acclamation. The following were elected pontiffs: the proposer of the law, Publius Decius Mus, Publius Sempronius Sophus, Gaius Marcius Rutulus and Marcus Livius Denter. Five augurs were also chosen from the plebeians: Gaius Genucius, Publius Aelius Paetus, Marcus Minucius Faesus, Gaius Marcius and Titus Publilius. Thus the number of pontiffs was raised to eight and of augurs to nine.

In the same year the consul Marcus Valerius proposed a law of appeal which should have stricter sanctions. This was the third time since the expulsion of the kings that such a law had been proposed, each time by a member of the same family.[12] The reason for its having been brought up more than once was, I think, simply the fact that the wealth of the few was more powerful than the liberty of the people. Yet the Porcian law alone seems to have been introduced in order to protect the persons of the citizens, as it laid down a heavy penalty for flogging or killing a Roman citizen.[13] The law proposed by Valerius forbade that anyone who had appealed should be scourged with rods or beheaded, but if the law was disregarded on either point it did no more than term it 'a wicked deed'.

12. cf. II.8.2 and III.55.4.
13. The Porcian law was not passed until 198, when the elder Cato was praetor, or less probably in 195, when he was consul.

Such was the sense of shame amongst men at that time that
this, I suppose, was thought to impose a legal sanction which
would be sufficiently binding. Today hardly anyone would
seriously utter such a threat.

Valerius also led a campaign of no importance against the
Aequi, who were in revolt, although all that was left them
from their former fortunes was their fighting spirit. The other
consul, Apuleius, besieged the town of Nequinum in Umbria.
The approach was steep and on one side precipitous, so that
it could not be taken by assault or by siege-works. (The site
is now occupied by Narnia.) The operation was therefore still
unfinished when it was taken over by the new consuls, Marcus
Fulvius Paetus and Titus Manlius Torquatus.

Licinius Macer and Tubero[14] record that all the centuries
wanted to name Quintus Fabius consul for that year, though
he was not a candidate, and that he himself was responsible for
postponing his consulship to a year when there would be more
fighting. He argued that he would be of more service to the
State in the current year if he held an urban magistracy, and
so, without concealing his preference, though not seeking
election, he was made curule aedile[15] with Lucius Papirius
Cursor. I am unable to state this with any certainty because
Piso,[16] one of the older annalists, says that the curule
aediles for that year were Gnaeus Domitius Calvinus, the son
of Gnaeus, and Spurius Carvilius Maximus, son of Quintus. I
believe that there was a mistake over the aediles arising out of
the surname Maximus, and that a legend was afterwards
developed to fit in with the error by coalescing the two
elections of aediles and consuls. That year too the lustral
sacrifice[17] was performed by the censors Publius Sempronius
Sophus and Publius Sulpicius Saverrio, and two tribes were

14. For Licinius Macer, see VII.9, note 12. Quintus Aelius Tubero,
jurist and annalist, was probably the father of the consul of 11 B.C.;
see the Introduction, p. 21.

15. He had held this office before, in 331; cf. VIII.18.4.

16. For Piso see IX.44, note 76.

17. The *suovetaurilia,* the ritual sacrifice of a pig, a sheep and a bull,
first mentioned by Livy in I.44.2.

added, the Aniensis and the Terentina. So much for affairs at Rome.

10. Meanwhile at the town of Nequinum time passed and the siege dragged on, until two of the townspeople, whose houses were built up against the wall, dug a tunnel through and made their way unseen to the Roman outposts. From there they were taken to the consul, and assured him they would conduct a party of soldiers inside the town's fortifications and walls. The offer was apparently not to be scorned, but at the same time not to be rashly trusted. Two scouts were sent through the tunnel with one of the men, while the other was retained as a hostage; and when they had made satisfactory investigations, three hundred armed men led by the deserter entered the city by night and captured the nearest gate. Once this was broken down the Roman consul and his army took possession of the city without meeting resistance. Thus Nequinum came under the sovereignty of the Roman people. A colony was sent there to be a check on the Umbrians, which was called Narnia after the river.[18] The army was brought back to Rome laden with plunder.

The Etruscans also chose this year to prepare for war in contravention of the truce, but were diverted from their purpose for a little while by a huge army of Gauls which crossed their borders when they were busy with other things. They then tried to convert the Gauls from enemies to allies, relying on the money which gave them power, in order to fight the Romans with the two combined armies. The barbarian Gauls did not refuse an alliance; it was only a question of the price. This was agreed on and the money changed hands, but when the Etruscans had finished all the rest of their preparations for war and ordered the Gauls to follow them, the Gauls denied that the agreed payment was for making war on the Romans; anything they had received had been in return for not destroying Etruscan land and interrupting its cultivation by armed raids. However, they were willing to take up arms if the Etruscans really wanted them, but only on condition that they

18. The Nar. The later Via Flaminia crossed the river here.

were admitted to a share in Etruscan land where they could at last settle in some definite home. Many councils of the people of Etruria were held to consider this request without reaching any decision, not so much out of reluctance to allow any reduction of territory but because everyone dreaded having men of so savage a race as his neighbour. The Gauls were accordingly dismissed, and went off with an enormous amount of money which they had acquired without effort or risk. At Rome the rumour of a Gallic rising in addition to an Etruscan war caused much alarm, and speeded up the conclusion of a treaty with the people of Picenum.[19]

11. The command in Etruria fell to the lot of the consul Titus Manlius. He had scarcely entered enemy territory and was taking part in a cavalry exercise when he was thrown while wheeling his horse round after a rapid gallop, and almost died on the spot; the third day from the accident brought his life to an end. The Etruscans took this as an omen for the war, declaring that the gods had opened battle on their side, and their spirits rose. For the Romans the news was a bitter blow. Not only had they need of the man but his death came at an inconvenient moment. An election was held to appoint a substitute for the consul, and this turned out as the leading senators wished; all the centuries voted for Marcus Valerius as consul, so that the Senate did not have to call for a dictator, with the intention of naming Valerius. They then told him to leave for Etruria at once to join the legions. His arrival was a set-back for the Etruscans, so much so that none of them dared venture outside their fortifications, and their fears had the same effect on them as a siege. Nor could the new consul entice them out to battle by destroying their lands and burning their buildings, though the smoke rose everywhere from numerous villages as well as farmhouses.

While this war dragged on longer than expected, reports of another began to come in, from information given by the Picentes, the Romans' new allies. This gave grounds for justifiable alarm, in view of the many reverses both sides had suffered

19. The coastal area north-east of the Apennines, not previously mentioned.

in the past. The Picentes reported that the Samnites were looking to arms and rebellion and had asked for their help. They were thanked, and the Senate's attention was largely switched from Etruria to the Samnites.

The high price of grain was also a cause for public anxiety, and, according to those authorities who believe that Fabius Maximus was aedile that year, the most serious scarcity would have developed if the great man had not brought the same application he had so often devoted to military affairs to bear this time at home on distributing the food supply, and on providing and transporting grain.

This year there was an interregnum, for which no reason is recorded. The interreges were Appius Claudius, followed by Publius Sulpicius, who held a consular election in which Lucius Cornelius Scipio and Gnaeus Fulvius were elected consuls.

At the beginning of this year representatives of the Lucanians came to the new consuls to lodge a complaint against the Samnites, who, they said, had invaded and destroyed their territory with a hostile army, and by this act of aggression were forcing them to go to war, because Samnite inducements had been unable to persuade them into an armed alliance. The Lucanians, they admitted, had erred more than enough in the past, but now their minds were made up, and they thought it easier to bear and endure anything rather than ever again to offend the Roman nation.[20] They begged the senators to take the Lucanians under their protection and shield them from the violence and aggression of the Samnites, and although their siding with the Samnites had necessarily involved disloyalty to the Romans, they were nevertheless now prepared to give hostages.

12. The Senate did not take long to discuss the request; opinion was unanimous that a treaty should be made with the Lucanians and reparation demanded from the Samnites. The Lucanians were given a friendly answer and granted a treaty. Fetial priests were sent to order the Samnites to withdraw from

20. Lucania had been granted a treaty in 326 (VIII.25.3) but was afterwards persuaded to join the Samnites (VIII.27.9–10) and was invaded by a Roman army in 317 (IX.20.9).

country belonging to Roman allies and to remove their army from Lucanian territory, but they were met on the way by messengers from the Samnites who warned them that if they approached any Samnite council they would not depart unscathed. When this was known at Rome, the Senate called for war on the Samnites and the people confirmed it.[21]

The consuls divided the commands between them. Scipio drew Etruria and Fulvius the Samnites, and both set out for their respective battle-fronts. Scipio expected the campaign to move slowly like that of the previous year, but was confronted near Volaterrae by the enemy, who were prepared for action while on the march. The fighting lasted most of the day and both sides suffered heavy losses; darkness fell when it was still uncertain whose was the victory. Daylight revealed victor and vanquished, for the Etruscans had left their camp at dead of night. The Romans marched out to battle and, when they saw that the enemy had conceded victory by his departure, advanced to the camp. Finding it empty, they took possession of it along with a vast amount of plunder, for it had been a permanent post and was hastily abandoned. Scipio then led his men back into Faliscan territory, left the baggage under adequate guard in Falerii, and set off with the army in light marching order to raid Etruscan territory. The whole area was destroyed with fire and sword, and plunder collected from all quarters. The enemy was left with the bare earth, and even fortresses and villages were burnt down; but the Romans stopped short of attacking the walled towns where the terror-stricken Etruscans had been forced to take refuge.

The other consul, Gnaeus Fulvius, fought a famous battle in Samnium, near Bovianum, in which his victory was in no sense in doubt. He then attacked and took Bovianum by storm, and soon afterwards Aufidena.

13. In that year too a colony was planted at Carseoli[22] in territory of the Aequicoli, and the consul Fulvius celebrated his triumph over the Samnites.

As the consular elections approached, the rumour arose that

21. Generally known as the Third Samnite War.
22. Contrast ch. 3.2 and note 3.

the Etruscans and Samnites were enlisting huge armies, and
that in all their councils the Etruscan leaders were openly
abused for not having brought the Gauls into the war, whatever the terms, while the Samnite magistrates were blamed
for having opposed the Romans with an army which had
been raised to meet a Lucanian enemy. Thus, it was said,
the enemies of Rome were preparing for war with all their
own might and that of their allies, and would have to be met
on far from equal terms. There were distinguished candidates
for the consulship, but the general state of alarm made everyone turn to Quintus Fabius Maximus. He was not a candidate
in the first place, and then, when he saw the direction the
people's inclinations were taking, he positively refused to
stand. Why must they trouble him, he asked, an old man now
who had done with toil and toil's rewards? Neither physically
nor mentally had his vigour remained as it used to be, and he
even dreaded Fortune herself, lest one of the gods might think
she had already shown him too much favour and stood by him
more constantly than they liked for mortal men. He himself
had risen to the glory of his elders and he was happy to see
others coming on to reach his own fame. There was no lack
of high positions at Rome for the bravest men, or of brave
men to fill them.

Such self-restraint on his part only served to intensify the
justifiable eagerness of the people and, thinking this must be
curbed by reverence for the laws, Fabius ordered a public
reading of the law prohibiting re-election of the same man to
the consulship within ten years.[23] The law was scarcely audible
for the uproar which ensued, and the people's tribunes declared
that there was nothing to prevent his election, for they would
propose a measure to the people that he should be exempt
from the law. But Fabius persisted in his refusal. What was the
point of making laws, he asked, if even the lawmakers were
going to evade them? Rule of law was now become rule over
law. Nevertheless the people started to vote, and each century,

23. If Fabius had not been consul since 308 (IX.41.1) this ruling did
not apply, but the episode may perhaps have originally belonged to
the election described in ch. 9.10.

as it was called into the enclosure, clearly named Fabius consul. Only then did he yield to the unanimous wish of his fellow-citizens. 'May the gods approve,' he cried, 'of what you are doing, Romans, and what you intend to do. But as you are going to get your way with me, in the matter of my colleague you must grant me a favour – I ask you to elect, as consul with me, Publius Decius, a man I know well as a good friend in office, and one who is worthy of you and of his father.'[24] The recommendation seemed a proper one, and all the remaining centuries voted for Quintus Fabius and Publius Decius.

In that year several people were brought to court by the aediles for possessing more than the legal limit of land. Practically no one was cleared of the charge, and heavy restrictions were imposed on their immoderate greed.

14. While the new consuls (Quintus Fabius Maximus for the fourth time and Publius Decius Mus for the third) were planning together how one of them should take on the Samnites and the other the Etruscans, what forces would be sufficient for their respective commands and who would be more suitable to lead one or the other campaign, representatives from Sutrium, Nepete and Falerii arrived with reports of a council of Etruscan peoples met to discuss how they could seek peace. The whole weight of the war was accordingly directed against Samnium. The consuls set out, Fabius taking his troops via Sora, and Decius through Sidicinian territory, in order to increase their sources of supply and to keep the enemy guessing where to expect an attack. As soon as they reached enemy territory, both consuls sent their men out raiding over a wide area. However, they scouted further afield than they plundered, and consequently it did not escape the army's notice that the Samnites were drawn up in a remote valley near Tifernum,[25] from where they were preparing to attack the Romans from above once they had entered it. Fabius had the baggage removed to a safe place and put a small force to guard it; then he warned the troops about the coming battle

24. The elder Decius had devoted himself in 340; cf. VIII.9.4 ff. The son had been Fabius's colleague in 308 (IX.41.1).

25. A Samnite town, on or near the mountain Tifernus.

and led them in square formation right up to the place where, as mentioned before, the enemy lay hidden. The Samnites had to abandon hope of a surprise assault and, in view of the fact that the outcome would have to be settled once and for all in an open confrontation, also preferred to fight a regular engagement. So they came down to level ground and committed themselves to Fortune with more courage than hope; yet, whether because they had put together the manpower of all the Samnite peoples or because a struggle on which the whole issue depended intensified their will-power, they caused some alarm amongst the Romans even in an open battle.

When Fabius saw that the enemy was nowhere giving ground, he told his son Maximus[26] and Marcus Valerius, the military tribunes with whom he had hurried to the front line, to go to the cavalry and urge them on – to say that if they remembered any occasion when the State had ever been supported by cavalry aid, this was the day for them to put out every effort to keep their glory undimmed: in the infantry struggle the enemy were still standing firm, and the only hope left was a cavalry charge. Addressing both the young men by name with equal warmth of feeling, he heaped praise and promises upon them. But as there was a risk that even their energy and drive might prove inadequate, he thought he should proceed with a stratagem, in case strength was not enough. He told his legate Scipio to withdraw the *hastati* of the first legion from the battle and to take them round as unobtrusively as possible to the nearest mountains, which they were then to climb by a route hidden from sight, and suddenly to show themselves behind the enemy's rear.

The cavalry, led by the tribunes, caused little more disturbance among the enemy than among their own infantry, as they rode out unexpectedly in front of the standards. The Samnite line held firm against the charging squadrons and could nowhere be pushed back or broken; and when the cavalry failed in their attempt, they retired behind the lines and left the battle. This put new heart into the enemy, and the

26. Q. Fabius Maximus Gurges, aedile in 295 (ch. 31.9) and consul in 293 (ch. 47.5).

Roman front ranks could not have withstood so long a struggle and the violence which increased with the Samnites' self-confidence if the second line had not relieved the first at the consul's command. Their fresh strength checked the Samnites as they were already pressing forward, and at that moment the sight of the party coming down from the mountains and the sound of the cheer they raised greatly alarmed the Samnites, more indeed than the true facts warranted; for Fabius called out that his colleague Decius was coming, and the soldiers, wild with delight, all shouted that the other consul and the legions were there. This mistake served the Romans well, by filling the Samnites with panic and dread, for there was nothing they feared so much as the arrival of the second army, fresh and intact, to overwhelm them in their exhausted state. They scattered far and wide in flight, so that the bloodshed was less than to be expected in so great a victory. 3400 were killed, about 830 taken prisoner and twenty-three standards were captured.

15. The Apulians would have joined up with the Samnites before the battle had not the consul Publius Decius set up camp near Maleventum to prevent this and then drawn them out to battle and defeated them. Here too there was more flight than slaughter, and only two thousand Apulians were killed. Despising such an enemy, Decius led all his legions into Samnium. There the two consular armies ranged over the land in different areas and destroyed everything within four months. There were forty-five sites in Samnium where Decius had set up camps, and the other consul had encamped in eighty-six places. Not only traces of their earthworks and ditches were left, but much more prominent records of destruction than these in the devastation of the surrounding countryside. Fabius also took the city of Cimetra. 2900 armed men were taken prisoner there, and about 930 killed fighting.

Fabius then set out for Rome to hold the elections, and lost no time in doing so. All the centuries first called on were voting for Quintus Fabius as consul when Appius Claudius, who was a candidate for the consulship and a forceful and ambitious man, though no more anxious for the honour on his own account than for the patricians to recover two consular seats, exerted all his own influence and that of the entire nobility to make them elect him consul with Fabius. Fabius at first refused, using practically the same arguments about himself as he had done the year before. The nobles all gathered round his chair and begged him to lift the consulship out of the plebeian mire and restore both to the office and to the patrician families the dignity of former times. Fabius called for silence, and then calmed down the general excitement by a moderately worded speech. He would have done as they wished, he said, and accepted the nomination of two patricians, if he had seen someone other than himself elected consul. As things were, he would not accept his own nomination at an election, since that would be illegal and would set a very bad precedent. Lucius Volumnius, a plebeian, was accordingly elected consul with Appius Claudius; the two had also been paired in an earlier election.[27] The nobility taunted Fabius with having avoided Appius Claudius for a colleague, evidently as his superior in eloquence and statecraft.

16. Once the elections were over, the old consuls were ordered to continue with the war in Samnium, with an extension of their command for six months. Similarly in the following year, when Lucius Volumnius and Appius Claudius were consuls, Publius Decius, who had been left by his colleague in Samnium when consul, continued as proconsul to destroy the farm lands until he finally compelled the Samnite army (which would not risk a battle anywhere) to leave the region. After their forced retreat they made for Etruria, where they demanded a council of Etruscan leaders, thinking that, by means of so great a number of armed men and a mixture of threats and entreaties, they would obtain more effectively what their envoys had often tried to achieve without success. When the council assembled, the Samnites explained how for many years they had been fighting the Romans for their freedom; how they tried everything to see if they could bear the heavy brunt of the war by their own

27. In 307; cf. IX.42.2.

unaided strength, and had also made trial of help from their
neighbours, which had proved of little use. They had sought
peace from the Roman people when they could not keep on
with the war, and turned to war again because peace with
servitude was harder to bear than war with liberty. The only
hope left them lay with the Etruscans: them they knew to be
the richest people in Italy, in arms, men and money, and they
had for neighbours the Gauls, a race born to the clash of arms,
fierce not only by nature but also in their hatred of the people
of Rome – of whose defeat and ransom for gold[28] they could
tell, making no empty boast. If the Etruscans still had the spirit
which fired Porsenna[29] and their forebears, there was nothing
to prevent their driving the Romans out of the whole region
north of the Tiber, and forcing them to fight not to maintain
their intolerable tyranny over Italy but for their own self-
preservation. The Samnite army was there ready for them; it
had come fully armed and paid, prepared to follow at once
even if the Etruscans led them to attack the city of Rome itself.

17. During all this boasting and intrigue in Etruria, the
Roman campaign was beginning to harass their people at
home. Once Publius Decius learned from scouts that the
Samnite army had departed, he called a council of war. 'Why
are we roaming round the countryside,' he asked, 'carrying
war from village to village? Why don't we attack cities and
walled towns? There is no army now to protect Samnium –
they have crossed their borders and gone into self-inflicted
exile.' With the men's acclaim, he led them to launch an
attack on Murgantia, a powerful town; and so keen were the
troops, out of affection for their leader, combined with hope
of more plunder than could be got by raiding the country, that
they took the city by storm in a single day. 2100 Samnites were
surrounded there and captured as they fought, and an immense
amount of plunder was seized. As Decius was anxious for his
marching force not to be burdened with heavy baggage, he
called a meeting and addressed his men. 'Are you going to

28. In V.49 Livy follows the tradition that the gold was recovered
by Camillus.
29. Lars Porsenna, the Etruscan king of Clusium; cf. II.9 ff.

content yourselves with this as your only victory or with only
these spoils?' he asked. 'Don't you want your expectations to
match your courage? All the cities of the Samnites and the
wealth abandoned in them are yours, now you have finally
driven from their land the legions you have defeated in so
many battles. Sell what you have there, and tempt traders to
follow your march through their love of gain; leave it to me
to provide a regular supply of what you can sell! Let us go on
from here to the city of Romulea, where no greater effort
awaits you, only greater plunder!'

The booty was sold off, and the soldiers marched on to
Romulea, urging on their general of their own accord. There
too there was no need of siege-works or engines; as soon as
they came up to the walls nothing could force them away.
They quickly set up ladders at the nearest points and scaled the
battlements. The town was captured and sacked; as many as
2300 men were killed and 6000 taken prisoner. The troops
seized a huge amount of plunder, which, as before, they were
made to sell, and then marched on with the greatest alacrity
– though they were given no chance to rest – to Ferentinum.
However, that proved more difficult and dangerous: the walls
were defended with the utmost fury and the place was
naturally protected as well as being fortified. But every
obstacle was overcome by an army grown accustomed to
plunder. About three thousand of the enemy were killed
around the walls; the booty went to the soldiers.

In certain annals, the greater part of the glory for the assaults
on these towns is assigned to Fabius Maximus; records say that
Murgantia was taken by Decius, but Ferentinum and Romulea
by Fabius. Others give the credit to the new consuls, some not
to both but to one of them, Lucius Volumnius, who, they say,
drew Samnium as his sphere of command.

18. During these operations in Samnium (whoever it was
who held the command and took the auspices), preparations
were set on foot in Etruria by a Samnite, Gellius Egnatius, for
a massive campaign against the Romans in which many
peoples were involved. Nearly all the Etruscans had decided
on war; the contagion had spread to bring in their new neigh-

bours in Umbria, and the Gauls were being offered pay in
return for their support. The joint forces were massing at the
Samnite camp. When news of this sudden rising reached
Rome, the consul Lucius Volumnius had already left for
Samnium with the second and third legions and 15,000 allied
troops, and it was decided to send Appius Claudius to Etruria
as soon as possible. Two Roman legions followed him, the first
and fourth,[30] and 12,000 allies. They encamped not far from
the enemy.

But more was achieved by Appius's speedy arrival, whereby
fear of the name of Rome checked certain peoples of Etruria
who were already contemplating taking up arms, than by his
leadership, which was marked by no special skill or good
fortune. Many engagements with the enemy were fought at
awkward times and places, so that their hopes mounted every
day and made them more formidable, while the Roman
army's confidence in their general was already beginning to
fail, as his was in them. In three annalists I find it recorded that
a letter was sent to summon his colleague from Samnium, but
I am reluctant to put it down as certain, when that very point
was disputed by the consuls of the Roman people, who were
now holding office for the second time. Appius denied that he
had sent a letter, while Volumnius maintained that he had been
summoned by a letter from Appius.

Volumnius had already taken three fortresses in Samnium
in which up to three thousand of the enemy had been killed
and about half as many taken prisoner and, with the full
approval of the patricians, had put down risings in Lucania,
instigated by impoverished plebeian leaders, by dispatching
Quintus Fabius there as proconsul with an experienced army.
Volumnius left it to Decius to destroy the land, and went
himself with his own troops to join his colleague in Etruria.
His arrival was received with general delight; what Appius felt
I think only he could know. If he had written no letter he had
every reason to be angry, but if he had needed help and was
now concealing the fact, his reaction was mean and un-

30. The consuls each led one legion, and the two legions of the
previous year were still serving.

312

gracious. He came out to meet his colleague, and greetings were scarcely exchanged, when 'Are you all right, Lucius Volumnius?' he demanded. 'How are things in Samnium? What has brought you out of your own province?' Volumnius replied that everything was going very well in Samnium, and he had come in answer to Appius's summons; but if the letter was a forgery and he was not needed in Etruria, he would turn round at once and march off. 'Be off then,' said Appius; 'no one is stopping you. It is quite improper for you to boast of having come here to help others when maybe you are hardly able to cope with your own war.' Volumnius replied that he could only hope it would turn out for the best – he would rather have taken trouble for nothing than have anything happen to make one consular army insufficient for Etruria.

19. As the consuls parted, the legates and tribunes from Appius's army gathered around them. Some begged their general not to scorn his colleague's help, which he should have sought of his own accord and was now offered voluntarily, while larger numbers stood in the path of Volumnius, as he made to go, and implored him not to betray the State through an unseemly quarrel with his colleague – if any disaster should follow, the deserter would be more to blame than the deserted. Things had come to such a pass that the entire credit or disgrace for a success or reverse in Etruria would to to Lucius Volumnius; no one would ask about the words used by Appius, only about the fortunes of his army; Volumnius was being dismissed by Appius, but retained by the republic and the army; he had only to test the will of the soldiers.

With warnings and pleas such as these they practically dragged the reluctant consuls to the assembly place. There they spoke at greater length to much the same effect as they had argued with only few to hear them. When Volumnius, besides having the better cause, even showed himself to be no mean orator when confronted by the exceptional eloquence of his colleague, Appius mockingly remarked that *he* should be given the credit for the fact that they now had a consul who could express himself instead of one who was speechless and tongue-tied, seeing that in his former consulship, at any rate

in the early months, Volumnius had been incapable of opening
his mouth, but was now composing popular speeches. 'I would
much prefer that you had learned from me how to take
vigorous action,' said Volumnius, 'instead of my having
learned how to speak well from you!' In the end he put
forward a proposition to determine not which of them was the
better orator, for that was not what the country needed, but
the better general.[31] Etruria and Samnium, he said, were the
two fields for action, and Appius should choose which he
preferred; he himself was prepared to campaign with his own
army either in Etruria or in Samnium.

At this point the soldiers began to clamour for both to tackle
the Etruscan war together. Seeing they were all agreed on this,
Volumnius said to them: 'Since I was wrong in my interpretation of my colleague's wishes, I shall make sure there is no
doubt about what you want. Give a shout to show whether
you want me to stop or go.' Then indeed a shout rang out,
so loud that it brought the enemy out of their camp. Snatching
up arms they came down and formed their line of battle.
Volumnius too gave orders for the signal to sound and the
standards to be carried out of the camp. Appius, it is said, was
uncertain what to do, realizing that, whether he joined in the
fighting or kept out of it, the victory would belong to his
colleague; then, fearing that his own legions would also follow
Volumnius, he too gave his men the signal they were demanding.

Neither side was adequately deployed: for the Samnite
commander, Gellius Egnatius, had gone foraging with a few
cohorts of cavalry, and his soldiers were entering battle more
on their own impulse than under anyone's leadership and
command, while the two Roman armies were not led out
together nor had there been enough time to arrange their
formation. Volumnius was engaged before Appius reached the
enemy, and so the battle opened on an uneven front, and, as
if lots had been cast and changed the usual matching of opponents, the Etruscans confronted Volumnius, and the Samnites,

31. In their previous joint consulship Appius had held no military
command; cf. IX.42.5.

after hesitating a little in the absence of their commander, met Appius. It is said that at the height of the battle Appius was seen amongst the foremost standards raising his hands to heaven and uttering a prayer: 'Bellona, if you grant us victory today, then I vow you a temple.' After this prayer, as if the goddess were urging him on, his courage matched that of his colleague, and his army kept pace with their general. The soldiers indeed kept up with their leaders' achievements and strove to prevent victory's coming first to the other army. Thus they routed and scattered the enemy, who could not easily withstand a larger force than they usually met in battle, and by pressing hard as they gave ground and pursuing them as they fled, the Romans drove them to their camp. There the battle was briefly renewed on the appearance of Gellius and his Sabellian cohorts, but these too were soon put to flight and the victorious troops began their attack on the camp. While Volumnius personally led a charge against the gate and Appius repeatedly called on Bellona, as goddess of victory, to fire the spirit of his men, they burst through the rampart and the trenches. The camp was taken and sacked; a great deal of plunder was seized and handed over to the army. 7800 of the enemy were killed and 2100 taken prisoner.

20. While both consuls and the entire might of Rome were mainly directed towards the Etruscan war, fresh armies rose up in Samnium to raid the lands under Roman rule, crossed over to Campania and Falernian territory by way of Vescia, and took possession of large spoils. Volumnius was returning to Samnium by forced marches (for the prolongation of command granted to Fabius and Decius was now coming to an end) when a rumour about the Samnite army and its destructive raids on Campanian territory made him change course in order to protect Rome's allies. As he approached Cales he saw for himself fresh traces of the havoc wrought by the enemy, and the Caleni told him that the Samnites were already taking so much plunder with them that they were having difficulty in keeping their army on the march; their leaders were now saying openly that they must go back at once to Samnium, leaving the booty there, and return to carry on their raids, not

subject an army so heavily burdened to the risks of battle. All this sounded true enough, but Volumnius thought he ought to find out something more definite; and so he sent out parties of horsemen to intercept any roving plunderers who might be scattered about the countryside. From these he found on questioning that the enemy was encamped at the River Volturnus, and would set out at the third watch on their way back to Samnium.

Once he was satisfied with his investigations, Volumnius set out and encamped just far enough from the enemy for his arrival not to be known by his being too near, but near enough to be able to attack as they left their camp. A little before dawn he drew closer and sent on men who knew the Oscan language to find out what was happening. They mingled with the enemy, as was easy in the darkness and confusion, and discovered that the standards had been carried out with only a small number of armed men accompanying them, that the plunder and its guards were just setting out, but that the main army could not be got moving, as everyone was struggling for himself without any common agreement or definite command. It seemed the best time for an attack, and day was already breaking; so Volumnius gave orders to sound the signal for battle and charged the enemy's column. The Samnites were encumbered with their spoils and few of them carried arms; some quickened their pace and drove the cattle in front of them, some stood still, uncertain whether it would be safer to push on or go back to the camp. While they hesitated they were overpowered; the Romans were already over the rampart, and the camp was filled with bloodshed and commotion. The Samnite army was wholly disorganized, not only because of the confusion caused by the Romans, but by the sudden break-out of the prisoners, some of whom were not bound and were releasing those who were, while others seized the weapons tied together in the soldiers' packs and, mixed up with the army as they were, caused havoc more alarming than the actual battle. Then they achieved a memorable success: they rushed at the Samnite general, Staius Minatius, as he rode along the ranks shouting encouragement, scattered his escort of cavalry, surrounded him, and led him off as their prisoner, still mounted on his horse, to the Roman consul. The uproar this caused brought back the Samnite vanguard to renew the battle, which was already nearly over, and could not be continued for long. Up to 6000 men were killed, 2500 taken prisoner (amongst them four military tribunes), and thirty military standards were captured. What most delighted the victors was the recovery of 7400 prisoners as well as a vast amount of plunder taken from the allies. The owners of this were summoned by proclamation to identify and reclaim their property on an appointed day; everything without an owner was handed over to the soldiers, who were compelled to sell their spoils, so as not to be distracted from further fighting.

21. The raids on Campanian country had caused great alarm in Rome, and at the same time, as it happened, news came from Etruria that after Volumnius had withdrawn his army there had been a general call to arms, that Gellius Egnatius, the Samnite general, and the Umbrians were being invited to join the revolt, and a high price was offered to win over the Gauls. Terrified by this report, the Senate ordered the courts to be closed and the conscription of every category of men. Not only were free-born citizens of military age obliged to take the oath, but cohorts were also formed of older men, and freedmen were assigned to centuries. Plans were discussed for the defence of the City and supreme command was given to the praetor Publius Sempronius. However, the Senate's anxiety was partly relieved by a letter from the consul Lucius Volumnius giving the news of the slaughter and dispersal of the raiders in Campania. The senators therefore decreed a day of thanksgiving for the victory in the consul's name, and ended the suspension of legal business, which had lasted for eighteen days. The thanksgiving was a particularly happy one.

Next they began to discuss protective measures for the region raided by the Samnites, and decided to settle two colonies in Vescinian and Falernian country: one, which was named Minturnae, at the mouth of the River Liris, the other in the woodlands of Vescia which adjoin Falernian territory, where the Greek city of Sinope is said to have been, afterwards called Sinuessa by the Roman settlers. The people's tribunes were given the task of obtaining a plebiscite to order the praetor Publius Sempronius to nominate three commissioners to take out the colonists to these places, but it proved difficult to find men who would enter their names, as they believed they were being sent not to settle on the land but to provide what would amount to a perpetual outpost in a hostile area.

The Senate's attention was diverted from these worries by the increasing gravity of the war in Etruria, and by frequent dispatches from Appius warning them not to make light of the disturbance there. Four races, he said, were combining their armed forces, the Etruscans, Samnites, Umbrians and Gauls; already their camp was divided in two, as one place could not hold such large numbers. For this reason, and also because of the elections (the time of which was already approaching), the consul Lucius Volumnius was recalled to Rome. Before he called on the centuries to vote, he summoned the people to an assembly and addressed them at length on the magnitude of the Etruscan war. Even at the time when he was there himself, he told them, campaigning alongside his colleague, the war had been too intensive for one commander and one army to conduct it, and since then it was said that the Umbrians had joined in as well as an enormous army of Gauls. They must bear in mind that there were four peoples to be confronted by the consuls whom they were choosing that day. For his own part, were he not confident that the Roman people would unanimously agree to offer the consulship to the man who was considered to be the foremost of all commanders of their day, he would have immediately named him dictator.

22. No one had any doubt that Fabius would be unanimously elected for the fifth time; and indeed, the centuries privileged to open the voting[32] and all the centuries who were called on immediately afterwards chose him for consul along with Lucius Volumnius. Fabius then made a speech similar to that of two years before, but when he had to bow to the general will, he ended by asking to have as colleague Publius

32. The *centuriae praerogativae*, the eighteen centuries of knights.

Decius, who would be a support for his old age. In both the censorship and the two consulships they had held together, he found that nothing could give the republic such sound protection as harmony between colleagues. At his age he would now hardly be able to accustom himself to a new associate in authority; it would be easier for him to share his counsels with someone whose character he knew. The consul supported his plea, with well-merited praise of Publius Decius. He also recalled the benefits which resulted from harmony between consuls in the administration of military affairs, and the damage which could be done by discord between them, with a reminder of how a near-fatal crisis had recently arisen out of the dissension between himself and his colleague. Decius and Fabius, he went on to say, were of one heart and one mind; they were, moreover, men born for war, great in their deeds but unskilled in battles of the spoken word. Their gifts fitted them for the consulship; but clever, quick-witted men, practised in eloquence and the law, men like Appius Claudius, should be kept to preside over the City and the Forum and be elected to the praetorship to administer justice. The day was spent on these discussions, but on the day following, by the consul's order, the elections were held for both consuls and praetors. Quintus Fabius and Publius Decius were elected consuls and Appius Claudius praetor – all in their absence; and by the decree of the Senate, ratified by the people, Lucius Volumnius had his command extended for a year.

23. There were many portents that year, to avert which the Senate decreed two days of public prayers. Wine and incense were provided at public expense, and crowds of men and women went to offer prayers. The occasion was remarkable because of a quarrel which broke out amongst the married women at the shrine of Patrician Chastity, which stands in the Cattle Market by the round temple of Hercules. Verginia, daughter of Aulus, a patrician married to a plebeian, the consul Lucius Volumnius, had been prevented by the matrons from taking part in the ceremonies on the grounds that she had married outside her patrician rank. A short altercation followed, which, when feminine tempers ran high, blazed out

into a battle of wills. Verginia proudly insisted, and with reason, that she had entered the temple of Patrician Chastity as a patrician and a chaste woman, who was the wife of the one man to whom she had been given as an unmarried girl, and was ashamed neither of her husband nor of his honours and achievements. Then she confirmed her noble words by a remarkable deed. In the Vicus Longus, where she lived, she shut off part of her great house, large enough for a shrine of moderate size, set up an altar in it, and then summoned the married plebeian women. After complaining about the insulting behaviour of the patrician ladies, 'I dedicate this altar,' she said, 'to Plebeian Chastity, and urge you to ensure that it will be said that it is tended more reverently than that other one, if that is possible, and by women of purer life. Thus, just as the men in our State are rivals in valour, our matrons may compete with each other in chastity.' This altar was then tended with almost the same ritual as the older one, so that no one but a matron of proven chaste conduct, married to one man alone, had the right to offer sacrifices. Subsequently the cult was debased by the presence of worshippers who were no longer chaste, not only matrons but women from every walk of life, and was finally forgotten.[33]

In the same year the curule aediles Gnaeus and Quintus Ogulnius put several moneylenders on trial and, when their property was confiscated, used the share which came to the public treasury to provide bronze thresholds for the Capitol and silver vessels for the three tables in the shrine of Jupiter. They also set up a statue of Jupiter in a four-horse chariot on the roof, and at the fig-tree of Romulus and Remus[34] a statue group showing the infant founders of the City being suckled by the wolf; and they made a path of squared paving-stones

33. This sounds like a typical legend devised to explain the existence of a second statue to Pudicitia, though tradition may have confused this goddess with Fortuna, who had a statue there. cf. Festus (ed. Müller), p. 242.

34. The *ficus Ruminalis* which stood at the south-west corner of the Palatine, the name of which the Romans derived from *ruma* ('breast') and Rumina, a primitive goddess of suckling (cf. Michael Grant, *Roman Myths*, pp. 115 ff., and cover picture).

from the Porta Capena to the temple of Mars. As well as this, the plebeian aediles, Lucius Aelius Paetus and Gaius Fulvius Curvus, also used the money from fines which they had exacted from the graziers they had convicted, to hold games and provide golden libation bowls for the temple of Ceres.

24. After this Quintus Fabius and Publius Decius started on their consulships, for the fifth and fourth times respectively. They had been colleagues three times as consuls and once as censors, and were renowned for the harmony between them as much as for the glory of their achievements, great though that was. This harmony was not to last for ever, though I think it was interrupted more by rivalry between the orders than by dissension between themselves. The patricians contended that Fabius should hold the command in Etruria without submitting to the normal procedure, while the plebeians put pressure on Decius to have it settled by drawing lots. At any rate there was a heated argument in the Senate, and when Fabius proved more powerful there, the matter was referred to the people.

In the public assembly, speeches were short, as was to be expected amongst military men who relied on deeds rather than words. Fabius argued that when a man had planted a tree it was intolerable that someone else should pick up the fruit from the ground beneath it; it was he who had opened up the Ciminian Forest[35] and made a way for the Romans to carry arms through its remote defiles. Why had they bothered him, at his age, if they had intended to carry on the war under another general? It was quite obvious, he said, gradually warming to his accusations, that he had chosen a rival, not a partner in command, and that Decius had been jealous during the three offices they had held together. He ended by saying that all he wanted was to be sent out to take up his command if he was thought worthy of it; he had bowed to the will of the Senate and would submit to the authority of the people.

Publius Decius complained of the Senate's injustice. As long as they could, he said, the Fathers had worked to deny the plebeians access to high office, but now that natural ability had

35. cf. IX.36.

won recognition in any class of men, they were seeking ways to disregard not only the people's decisions but also the wishes of Fortune, and to put everything into the hands of a few. All previous consuls had drawn their commands by lot, but now the Senate was giving Fabius a command without his having drawn it. If this was to do him honour, he could only say that Fabius deserved so well both of himself and of the State that he was personally prepared to promote the man's glory, provided that it did not gain lustre from insult to himself. But who could doubt, when there was one hazardous and difficult war, and the command was entrusted without drawing lots to one of the consuls, that the other was held to be superfluous and useless? Fabius was proud of his successes in Etruria; Publius Decius wanted something to be proud of too, and perhaps he would put out the fire which Fabius had left damped down, but only so that it repeatedly burst into flame without warning. In short, he was prepared to concede his colleague honours and rewards out of respect for his great age and dignity, but when danger and fighting were proposed, he conceded nothing of his own free will, nor would he ever do so. If he got nothing else from that dispute, one thing at least he would get – the people should give the orders where the people had the right to do so, and the bestowal of favours by the Senate should end. To Jupiter Best and Highest and to the immortal gods he offered this prayer: let them give him an equal chance with his colleague when lots were drawn only if they intended to grant him the same courage and good fortune in his conduct of the war. Surely it was naturally just and salutary as an example, as well as relevant to the reputation of the Roman people, if their consuls were such that the Etruscan war could be properly conducted with either of them as leader.

Fabius did no more than beg the Roman people to listen to a dispatch from the praetor Appius Claudius, which had been brought from Etruria, before the tribes were called on to vote. He then left the assembly. The people showed the same unanimity as the Senate had done in deciding that Fabius should hold the command in Etruria without lots being drawn.

25. Nearly all the younger men then gathered round the

consul, and each one gave his name, so eager were they to serve under such a commander. From the thick of the crowd surrounding him, Fabius called: 'I intend to enrol no more than four thousand infantry and six hundred cavalry; I shall take with me those of you who give your names today and tomorrow. I care more about bringing you all back enriched with spoils than about conducting a campaign with large numbers of men.' He set out with an army ready for battle, all the more confident and optimistic because he had not wanted large numbers, and made for the town of Aharna, not far from the enemy, and the camp of the praetor Appius. A few miles before he reached it he met some men who had gone out to gather wood under protection of an armed guard. When these saw the lictors riding ahead and realized that Fabius was consul, they eagerly expressed their delight and thanks to the gods and Roman people for having sent him to be their general. Then as they crowded round to hail him as consul, Fabius asked where they were going, and they answered that they were out to gather firewood. 'What, have you no rampart round your camp?' he asked. They shouted that it had a double rampart and a ditch, but they were still in mortal fear. 'Then you have quite enough wood,' he said; 'go back and pull up your stockades.' They returned to camp and there started pulling up the stakes, to the alarm of their fellows who had remained behind and of Appius himself, until they passed the word from one to another that they were acting on the orders of the consul Quintus Fabius. On the following day the camp was removed and the praetor Appius sent off to Rome. From then on the Romans had no permanent camp. Fabius maintained that it was useless for an army to settle down in one place; by marching and changing its locality it increased its mobility and physical fitness. The marches, however, were no longer than the season allowed, for the winter was not yet over.

In the early spring Fabius left the second legion near Clusium, which in former days used to be called Camars, with Lucius Scipio as propraetor in charge of the camp, and returned to Rome himself for consultation about the war. Either the decision was his own, because on consideration the war

seemed to him more serious than he had believed the reports
to indicate, or else he acted on a summons from the Senate:
the authorities are divided. Some want it to appear that he was
fetched back by the praetor Appius Claudius who exaggerated
the peril of the Etruscan war both in the Senate and before the
people, just as he had done incessantly in his dispatches. He
argued that neither a single commander nor a single army
would be enough to confront four peoples; the danger was that
whether these acted together to overpower him or carried on
separate campaigns, one man could not possibly deal with
everything at once. Appius himself had left behind two
Roman legions, and fewer than five thousand infantry and
cavalry had come with Fabius. His opinion was that the consul
Publius Decius should set out for Etruria at the earliest opportunity, to join his colleague, and Lucius Volumnius be given
the command in Samnium, but if Decius preferred to go out
to his own province, then Volumnius should set off for Etruria
to join the consul, with a regular consular army. Though the
majority were swayed by this speech, Publius Decius (it is said)
recommended that everything should be left open and free for
the decision of Quintus Fabius until Fabius should come to
Rome himself, if that were in the public interest, or send one
of his legates to give the Senate information about the extent
of the war in Etruria and to say with what forces and by how
many commanders it ought to be conducted.[36]

26. When Fabius returned to Rome, both in the Senate and
when he appeared before the people, he made a non-committal
speech, so as to give the impression that he was neither
exaggerating nor minimizing the reports about the war, and,
in accepting a second commander, was pandering to other
people's fears rather than facing any danger to himself or his
country. Besides, he asked, if they wanted to give him an
assistant in the war and a partner to share his command, how
could he possibly forget the consul Publius Decius, so often his
tried and tested colleague? There was no one else he would
prefer to work with; he would have armed forces enough if

36. A confused account, apparently of a debate before Fabius had
actually returned.

they came with Decius, and the enemy would never be too
many for them. But if his fellow-consul preferred a different
arrangement, then they should give him Lucius Volumnius to
help him. Both people and Senate as well as Publius Decius
himself left the decision entirely to Fabius, and when Decius
had shown himself ready to set out either for Samnium or for
Etruria, the public congratulations and rejoicing were such
that it looked like an anticipation of victory, and a vote of
triumph, not a war, for the consuls.

In some authorities, I find that Fabius and Decius left for
Etruria right at the start of their consulship, with no mention
of lots drawn for commands or of the rivalry between the two
which I have described. There are also some who are not
satisfied with this description but have added accusations made
by Appius before the people against Fabius in his absence, and
his stubborn opposition to Fabius when present, as well as
another quarrel between the two colleagues when Decius
insisted that each should attend to the duties he had drawn by
lot. General agreement in the records starts from the time both
consuls departed for the war.

However, before they could reach Etruria, the Senonian
Gauls in great hordes arrived in the neighbourhood of Clusium
with the intention of besieging the Roman legion encamped
there. Scipio, the camp commander, thought he should choose
a position to compensate for the insufficient numbers of his
men, and therefore led them up a hill which lay between the
town and his camp. But as he was in a hurry he had not
properly investigated the route, and reached a ridge which was
already taken by the enemy, who had approached it from the
other side. Thus the legion was heavily attacked in the rear and
completely surrounded, with the enemy bearing down on it
from all sides. Some authorities say that the legion there was
even totally destroyed, so that none survived to report it, and
no news of the disaster reached the consuls, who were not far
from Clusium, until some Gallic horsemen came in sight,
carrying heads hanging from their horses' breasts and fixed on
their spears, singing their customary song of triumph. Some
too relate that they were not Gauls but Umbrians, and the

defeat the Romans suffered was not so great. They say that some soldiers who were out foraging, under the legate Lucius Manlius Torquatus,[37] were surrounded, and that Scipio, the propraetor, came out of the camp to relieve them, renewed the battle, defeated the victorious Umbrians, and took their prisoners and spoils from them. It is more probable that defeat was suffered at the hands of the Gauls than the Umbrians, because, as so often at other times, and especially that year, what was most dreaded at Rome was a Gallic rising. And so not only did both the consuls set out for war with four legions and a strong contingent of Roman cavalry plus a thousand picked horsemen from Campania, dispatched for this campaign, and an army of allies and Latins who outnumbered the Romans, but another two armies were stationed to bar the way from Etruria, one in the Faliscan and the other in the Vatican district, not far from the City. Gnaeus Fulvius and Lucius Postumius Megellus, both propraetors, were ordered to keep a standing camp there.

27. The consuls reached the enemy in the region of Sentinum, and set up camp there about four miles away. The enemy then held consultations amongst themselves and agreed not to combine all their forces in one camp nor to open battle all together; the Gauls joined the Samnites and the Umbrians the Etruscans. A day was fixed for the battle, the Samnites and Gauls were chosen to engage in it, and during the actual fighting the Etruscans and Umbrians were to attack the Roman camp. These plans were upset by three deserters from Clusium, who came over secretly by night to Fabius and told him of the enemy's intentions. They were rewarded and sent back, so that, from time to time, as new decisions were taken, they could report on their findings. The consuls wrote to Fulvius and Postumius telling them to move their armies from their respective positions in the Faliscan and Vatican districts up to Clusium, and to destroy the enemy's lands with the utmost rigour. The devastation they carried out was reported to the Etruscans, who then withdrew from the region of

37. Possibly the son of the T. Manlius killed by a fall from his horse in 299 (ch. 11.1).

Sentinum in order to defend their own territories. At this the consuls made every effort to fight a battle in their absence. For two days they tried to draw the enemy into action; for two days nothing happened worth recounting. There were a few casualties on both sides, and appetites were whetted for a proper battle, but nothing decisive happened on the main issue. On the third day both sides came on to the battlefield in full strength.

As they stood in battle formation, a hind in flight from a wolf which had chased it down from the mountains ran across the plain between the two armies. Then the two animals turned in opposite directions, the hind towards the Gauls and the wolf towards the Romans. The wolf was given a way through the ranks, but the hind was struck down by the Gauls. At this one of the soldiers from the Roman front ranks cried out 'That is how flight and bloodshed will go – you see the beast sacred to Diana lying dead, while here the wolf of Mars is the winner, unhurt and untouched, to remind us of the race of Mars and of our Founder!'

On the right wing stood the Gauls, on the left the Samnites. Against the Samnites Quintus Fabius placed his first and third legion on the Roman right wing, while Decius drew up the fifth and sixth on the left against the Gauls. (The second and fourth were carrying on the war in Samnium under the proconsul Lucius Volumnius.)

The first clash of arms showed both sides so equally matched that, had the Etruscans and Umbrians been there, either in the battle or in the camp, wherever they had thrown their weight, the Romans would not have escaped disaster.

28. But although victory was still open to both sides and Fortune had not yet decided which way to tip the balance, the fighting was completely different on the right and left wings. The Romans with Fabius stayed on the defensive instead of pressing the attack, and were trying to prolong the battle until as late in the day as possible. Fabius was satisfied that both Samnites and Gauls were fierce fighters at the start of an attack but only needed to be withstood, for if the struggle dragged on the spirits of the Samnites would gradually flag, while the

physique of the Gauls was quite incapable of standing up to heat and strenuous effort and would soon weaken, so that though they were more than men in the early stages of a battle, they ended up by being less than women. He was therefore keeping his men fresh, with vigour unimpaired as far as he could, until the time came when the enemy usually began to fail. But Decius was more impatient, being young and high-spirited, and let loose all the resources he had at the first encounter. And since the infantry battle seemed to be going rather slowly, he called on the cavalry to attack, and, riding himself amongst the bravest of his youthful squadrons, summoned the young nobles to join him in a charge: they would win double glory, he said, if victory came first to the left wing and the cavalry. Twice they forced back the Gallic cavalry, but the second time they were carried on too far and then found themselves fighting in the midst of the companies of infantry, where they were alarmed by a new style of fighting; for the enemy, standing up and holding their weapons in chariots and wagons, bore down on them with a fearful noise of horses' hooves and wheels, and terrified the Romans' horses with the unusual din. Thus the victorious cavalry were scattered by a sort of panic frenzy, their blind flight overthrowing them, both horses and riders. Their confusion spread to the standards of the legions, and many of the first line were trampled underfoot by the horses and vehicles sweeping through the army. As soon as the Gallic infantry saw their enemies in disorder they came at them, not leaving them a moment to regain breath and recover themselves. Decius shouted to know where his men were fleeing or what hope they had in flight; he tried to stop them as they broke away and call them back when they ran. Then when he found himself powerless to stem the rout, he called on the name of his father, Publius Decius: 'Why do I longer delay,' he cried, 'the destiny of our house? Our family was granted the privilege of being sacrificed to avert dangers to our country. Now it is my turn to offer the legions of the enemy with myself as victims to Earth and the gods of the Underworld.'

With these words he told the pontiff Marcus Livius, whom

he had already ordered not to leave his side when he entered
the battle, to repeat the words whereby he could devote
himself and the enemy's legions to save the army of the
Roman nation of Quirites. He was then devoted with the same
form of prayer and dress as when his father Publius Decius had
ordered himself to be devoted at Veseris in the Latin war.[38]
After the ritual prayers he added that he was driving before
him dread and defeat, slaughter and bloodshed, the wrath of
the gods above and below, and would pollute with a deadly
curse the standards, missiles and arms of the enemy; that the
place of his own destruction would mark that of the Gauls and
Samnites. With these imprecations upon himself and the
enemy he galloped his horse into the Gallic lines, where he saw
they were thickest, and threw himself on the enemy's weapons
to meet his death.

29. From then on the battle hardly seemed to depend on
human effort. The Romans, after losing their general (which
on other occasions is generally a cause for alarm), checked their
flight and wanted to renew the fighting; the Gauls, especially
those crowding round the body of the consul, kept throwing
their javelins without aim or purpose, as if they had lost their
wits, while some of them were stupefied and could think
neither of fighting nor flight. But on the Roman side, the
pontiff Livius, to whom Decius had handed over his lictors,
telling him to act as praetor, cried out that the Romans had
won the day, now that they were freed by the consul's fate.
The Gauls and Samnites now belonged to Mother Earth and
the gods of the Underworld; Decius was carrying off the army
he had devoted, calling on it to follow him, and on the enemy's
side all was madness and terror. Then as the Romans were
restoring the battle, up came Lucius Cornelius Scipio and
Gaius Marcius, sent by order of the consul Quintus Fabius to
support his colleague, with reserves taken from the rearmost
line. There they heard of the fate of Publius Decius, a great
incentive to dare everything for the republic. And so, though
the Gauls stood close-packed with their shields overlapping in

38. cf. VIII.9.4 ff.

front of them and it did not look like an easy battle at close quarters, at the legates' command the javelins lying scattered on the ground between the two armies were gathered up and hurled against the enemy's *testudo*.[39] Most of them stuck in the shields and few pierced the bodies behind, so that the formation was broken when many fell under the shock, though unwounded. Such were the variations of Fortune on the Roman left wing.

On the right, Fabius had started, as described before, by spending the day holding back; later on, when neither the enemy's shouts nor their attacks and the missiles they threw seemed to have the same force, he told his cavalry commanders to take their squadrons round to the Samnite flank, so that at a given signal they could make a side attack with all the force they could. He ordered his own men to advance gradually and dislodge the enemy. As soon as he saw there was no resistance, and was quite certain of the enemy's fatigue, he collected all the reserve troops which he had been keeping for that moment, speeded up his legions, and signalled to the cavalry to charge. The Samnites could not sustain the onrush, and were swept headlong past the Gallic line, abandoning their allies in the thick of the battle, to seek refuge in their camp. The Gauls stayed close-packed behind the *testudo* they had formed. At this, Fabius, who had learned of his colleague's death, ordered the Campanian squadron, about five hundred strong, to leave the line, circle round, and attack the Gallic lines in the rear; then the *principes* of the third legion were to follow up closely, and, where they saw the enemy's formation broken by the cavalry charge, to press in to the kill while panic reigned. He himself vowed a temple and the enemy's spoils to Jupiter the Victor, and then rode on to the Samnite camp, where the whole terrified throng was being driven. The gates could not admit such large numbers, and some resistance was attempted right at the base of the rampart by those kept out by the jostling of their fellows. There Gellius Egnatius, the Samnite commander, fell. The Samnites were then forced inside the

39. The 'tortoise' of overlapping shields, to form a protective covering.

rampart, and after a short struggle the camp was taken and the Gauls in the rear were surrounded. 25,000 of the enemy were killed on that day and 8000 taken prisoner. Nor was it a bloodless victory; for the casualties in the army of Publius Decius amounted to 7000, while Fabius lost 1700. Fabius dispatched men to look for the body of his colleague, and then piled up the spoils taken from the enemy and burned them as a sacrifice to Jupiter the Victor. The consul's body could not be found that day, for it was buried under heaps of Gauls who had fallen dead on top of him, but next day it was found and brought back, greatly mourned by the army. Fabius then put aside all his other concerns, and celebrated the funeral of his colleague with every honour and tributes well deserved.

30. During this time in Etruria too the propraetor Gnaeus Fulvius was carrying out his campaign according to plan. Besides the great damage he did to the enemy's lands by his plundering raids, he fought a successful battle in which more than three thousand of the peoples of Perusia and Clusium were killed, and about twenty military standards were captured. The Samnite army was cut off by the Paeligni as it was making its escape through their territory, and lost about a thousand of its five thousand men.

Great is the fame of that day on which the battle was fought in the region of Sentinum, even if one sticks to the truth; but some have exaggerated it beyond belief, writing that in the enemy's army there were 600,000 infantry, 46,000 cavalry, and 1000 wheeled vehicles; and similarly, to increase the size of the Roman forces, they add the name of the proconsul Lucius Volumnius as commander with the two consuls, and join his army to their legions. The majority of the records assign the victory to the consuls, and say that Volumnius meanwhile was campaigning in Samnium, where he forced the Samnite army up Mount Tifernus, and, undeterred by the difficulty of his position, routed and put them to flight.

Quintus Fabius left the army which had been Decius's on guard in Etruria, and led his own legions back to the City, where he celebrated his triumph over the Gauls, Etruscans and Samnites. His soldiers marched behind his triumphal chariot, and their rough soldiers' songs celebrated the glorious death of Publius Decius as much as the victory of Quintus Fabius; praise of the son revived the memory of the father, a memory now matched for public service and personal fate. The soldiers received from the spoils eighty-two bronze *asses* each and a cloak and tunic, a reward for military service at that time by no means to be despised.

31. In spite of these victories there was still no peace either in Samnium or in Etruria; for war had broken out again at the prompting of the Perusini, after the consul had withdrawn his army. The Samnites came down to raid the lands of the Vescini and of Formiae, and elsewhere those of Aesernia and the area bordered by the River Volturnus. The praetor Appius Claudius was sent to confront them with the army lately commanded by Decius. Fabius dealt with the fresh outbreak in Etruria, killing 4500 of the Perusini and taking 1740 prisoners; these were ransomed for 310 *asses* each. All the other spoils were handed over to the army. The Samnite legions, some pursued by the praetor Appius Claudius, some by the proconsul Lucius Volumnius, joined each other in the Stellate region,[40] where they all took up their position near Caiatia. Appius and Volumnius also joined forces in camp. A battle was fought with the utmost fury, one side roused by exasperation with a people forever rebellious, the other resting their last hopes on the struggle. In the result, 16,300 Samnites were killed, and 2700 captured: the Roman army lost 2700 men.

This year, so fortunate in warfare, was saddened by an outbreak of plague and harassed by portents. Reports came that in several places it had rained earth, and that in the army of Appius Claudius many had been struck by lightning. The Sibylline Books were consulted on these events. In this year Quintus Fabius Gurges,[41] son of the consul, exacted fines from several married women convicted before the people of adultery; the money from the fines he used for building the temple of Venus which is near the Circus.

There are still more Samnite wars to come, though we have

40. cf. IX.44.5.   41. cf. ch. 14.10 and note 26.

now been describing them continuously for four volumes, over a period of forty-six years, from the consulship of Marcus Valerius and Aulus Cornelius, who were the first to carry arms into Samnium; and (without recapitulating now the reverses suffered by both sides in all those years, and the hardships endured, none of which could daunt those stout hearts) in the past year the Samnites had fought in the territory of Sentinum, amongst the Paeligni, near Tifernum in the Stellate plains, now with their own army, now with the addition of troops from other peoples, and had been cut to pieces by four armies under four Roman commanders. They had lost the Samnites' most distinguished general; they saw their military allies, the Etruscans, Umbrians and Gauls, in the same plight as they were themselves; they could carry on no longer, either with their own resources or with outside support, yet they would not abstain from war – so far were they from tiring of freedom even though they had not succeeded in defending it, preferring to be defeated rather than not to try for victory. Who would begrudge the length of time spent on writing or reading of wars which did not wear down the men who fought them?

32. Quintus Fabius and Publius Decius were succeeded as consuls by Lucius Postumius Megellus and Marcus Atilius Regulus. Both were assigned Samnium for their field of action, after it was reported that the Samnites had levied three armies and intended to return to Etruria with one and resume their raids on Campania with another, while making the third ready to guard their frontiers. Ill health kept Postumius in Rome, but Atilius set out at once, with the intention of crushing the enemy before they could leave Samnium, as the Senate had planned. They encountered the Samnites, as if by agreement, at a spot where they were themselves prevented from raiding Samnite territory, and they could prevent the Samnites from moving out into areas at peace with Rome and lands belonging to allies of the Roman people. When the camps were set up confronting each other, the Samnites ventured something which the Romans would hardly have dared to do, despite their many victories: they tried to storm the Roman camp. Such extreme foolhardiness is prompted by the depths of

despair. Although their rash attempt was not carried through
to the finish, it was not entirely useless. For much of the day
there was a fog so thick as to blot out the light and not only
to cut off any view beyond the rampart but also to make it
impossible for the two sides to see each other at close quarters
as they approached. The Samnites relied on this as cover, and
came right up to the Roman outpost which was on guard at
the gate, and not on the alert, when it was scarcely daylight,
and dark in any case because of the fog. The guards were
caught unawares, having neither spirit nor strength enough to
resist. The Samnites burst in at the rear of the camp through
the decuman gate, capturing the quaestor's tent and killing
Lucius Opimius Pansa, the quaestor on duty there. At this
there was a general call to arms.

33. The consul, roused by the uproar, ordered the two allied
cohorts which happened to be nearest, those from Lucania and
Suessa, to guard the general's tent, while he took command
of the legionary maniples in the main road of the camp. The
men fell in before they were properly armed, and, knowing
of the enemy's presence more from their noise than from what
they could see, found it impossible to estimate their numbers.
At first they fell back, being doubtful of their chances, and let
the enemy right into the middle of the camp; then when the
consul shouted at them to know whether they intended to be
pushed outside the rampart and afterwards make an attack on
their own camp, they raised a cheer and, making a great effort,
first stood firm and then pressed forward to force the
Samnites back. Having once set them moving, they left them
no time to recover from their initial alarm and pushed them
outside the gate and rampart. The Romans did not dare to go
on and pursue them, fearing an ambush in the murky light,
but withdrew inside their fortifications, satisfied with having
cleared their camp. About 300 of the enemy were killed; the
Roman casualties amongst the guards at the outpost and the
men surprised around the quaestor's tent came to about 730.

The Samnites' daring attempt had not been unsuccessful and
their spirits rose. Not only did they prevent the Romans from
moving on but would not even let them forage in their fields,

and the foraging parties went back to the peaceful country round Sora. Reports of these events (more disturbing than the facts warranted) reached Rome and compelled the consul Lucius Postumius to leave the City, though he had scarcely recovered his health. But before he left he issued an order to the soldiers to assemble at Sora, and he himself dedicated a temple to Victory, which as curule aedile he had built with money received from fines. He then went to join his army and led it from the region of Sora to his colleague's camp in Samnium. The Samnites then drew back, lacking confidence in their ability to withstand two armies, and the consuls went off in different directions to destroy their lands and attack their cities.

34. Postumius attempted to capture Milionia[42] first by storming it, but then, when he made little progress, he resorted to siege tactics, moved his protective sheds close up to the walls and took the town. Yet although the city was already in Roman hands, fighting continued in every quarter from the fourth till about the eighth hour. For a long time the issue was uncertain, until eventually the Romans took possession of the town. 3200 Samnites were killed and 4700 captured, besides other booty.

From there the legions were taken to Feritrum,[43] which the inhabitants had noiselessly abandoned in the night by the opposite gate, taking with them everything which they could carry or drive away. So though the consul first approached the walls as soon as he arrived with his army in regular formation, expecting the same kind of opposition as he had had at Milionia, when he found dead silence in the city and saw neither arms nor men on the walls and battlements, he held back his soldiers, who were eager to scale the deserted fortifications, in case they might rush heedlessly into some hidden trap. He ordered two squadrons of Latin allies to ride round the fortifications and make a thorough investigation. The cavalrymen found an open gate, and near it another one in the same area, and, on the roads leading from them, traces of the

42. Site unknown.   43. Also unknown.

enemy's nocturnal flight. They then rode slowly up to the gates, saw that the city could safely be crossed by roads leading straight through it, and reported to the consul that it had been evacuated: that was quite clear from its obviously deserted appearance, the fresh traces of flight, and the litter scattered around of things abandoned in the darkness and confusion. On hearing this the consul led his troops round to the side of the city which the cavalrymen had approached. He called a halt not far from the gate, and told five cavalrymen to ride into the city for a fair distance, then, if all seemed safe, three of them were to stay there together, and two to report their findings to him. When these two returned and reported that they had advanced to a point where there was a view in all directions and had found widespread silence and desertion, the consul led some light armed cohorts into the city without further delay, and ordered the rest of his army to fortify a camp meanwhile. The soldiers went in, broke down house-doors, and found a few people who were old or sick and certain objects left behind as too difficult to remove. These were seized as plunder; and from the prisoners it was learned that several of the neighbouring cities had joined together in their plans for flight; that their own people had left at the first night watch; and that they believed the Romans would find the other places deserted in the same way. What they said proved true, and the consul took possession of the abandoned towns.

35. The other consul, Marcus Atilius, had by no means so easy a campaign. He was leading his legions to Luceria, which he had heard was being attacked by the Samnites, when he was met by the enemy near the Lucerian frontier. This time anger made their strength match that of the Romans, so that the issue of the battle shifted indecisively from one side to the other. But the result was more disheartening to the Romans, who were unaccustomed to reverses, and as they left the battle they could see better than during the actual fighting how much greater their own losses were in dead and wounded. The consequent alarm which spread through the camp would have spelt severe defeat if it had seized the soldiers while fighting. Even so they spent an anxious night in the belief that the Samnites would

attack the camp any minute, or that they would have to engage their victorious enemy at daybreak. The Samnites had suffered less seriously but were no less dispirited, and as soon as it was daylight, all they wanted was to get away without a battle. But there was only one road, and that led past their enemies; once they had taken it, they appeared to be coming straight on for an attack on the Roman camp. The consul ordered the men to arm and follow him outside the rampart, while he assigned essential duties to the legates, tribunes and captains of the allies for their various commands. They all declared their own readiness for anything, but pointed out that the soldiers under them had lost heart – they had been kept awake all night by their wounds and the groans of dying men, and if the camp had been attacked before dawn, they would have panicked completely and abandoned the standards. As it was, shame kept them from actually running away, but otherwise they were beaten men.

On hearing this Atilius thought he should move amongst the men himself and talk to them. Wherever he found them slow to arm, he rebuked them. Why were they holding back and wavering? The enemy would be in the camp unless they got out of it, and they would have to fight in front of their tents if they refused to do so in front of the rampart. For men who were armed and fighting, victory was open to either side, but anyone who awaited the enemy, defenceless and unarmed, could only expect to suffer death or slavery. To his rebukes and reproaches, the men replied that they were worn out by yesterday's battle, and had no more strength left nor blood to spill, while the enemy appeared to have larger numbers than the previous day. Meanwhile the Samnites were approaching, and when the Romans had a closer look at them they cried out that they were carrying palisade stakes and doubtless intended to put a fence round the camp. Thereupon, to be sure, the consul really shouted at them that it was a shameful thing to accept such an affront and disgrace at the hands of the most cowardly of enemies. 'Are we to be blockaded in our camp,' he cried, 'to die a coward's death of hunger rather than, if need be, to die like heroes by the sword?' They must act as each thought proper for himself, and heaven grant it be for the best! But the consul, Marcus Atilius, would meet the enemy, alone if no one else would follow him, and fall amongst the Samnite standards rather than see a Roman camp so beset. The consul's words were approved by the legates and tribunes, and by all the cavalry squadrons, and top-ranking centurions.

Then at last the soldiers were moved by shame to arm, but slowly, and slowly they came out of the camp in a long, straggling column. Dejected and almost defeated they advanced towards the enemy, whose hopes and spirits stood no higher. Consequently, as soon as the Roman standards were seen, a murmur ran at once through the Samnite army from the front to the rear that, as they had feared, the Romans had come out to bar their path. There was no way open for flight; they must fall where they stood, or cut down their enemies and escape over their dead bodies.

36. They piled up their baggage in the middle, took their arms and formed a line of battle, with every man in his proper position. There was now only a small space between the two armies, and they stood still, each waiting for the other to attack first and raise the first battle-cry. Neither had any spirit for a fight, and they would have gone off in opposite directions unscathed and unhurt had both not feared that their enemy would advance on them if they gave way. The battle started slowly, without direction, whilst they were all still reluctant and uncertain; the cheer raised was half-hearted and uneven, and no one would move from where he stood.

The Roman consul, to get things moving faster, now detached a few squadrons of cavalry and sent them into the battle. Most of these were unhorsed and the rest were thrown in confusion, so that there was a rush forward by the Samnites to kill those who had fallen and by the Romans to rescue their own people. This put a little more activity into the battle; but the Samnites had run forward with rather more energy and in larger numbers, while the cavalry in their disorder trampled their own relieving troops under their terrified horses. At this the rout started which turned the entire Roman army; and now the Samnites were on the backs of the fleeing men, when the consul rode on ahead to the gate of the camp, put a guard of cavalry there, and ordered them to treat as an enemy anyone, whether Roman or Samnite, who made for the rampart. He threatened the men himself, blocking their path as they made headlong for the camp. 'Where are you going, men?' he cried. 'Here too you will find arms and fighting men, and so long as your consul lives you shall not enter the camp unless you win the day. Choose, then, whether you want to fight your fellow-citizens or the enemy!'

At the consul's words the cavalry rode round the infantry, with spears levelled to attack, and ordered them back into the battle. Not only the consul's courage but Fortune also helped, for the Samnites did not press home their attack, and there was time to wheel round the standards and turn the front lines from the camp to the enemy. At this point the Romans began to urge each other out to renew the battle; the centurions snatched the standards from the bearers and carried them forward, telling their men that the enemy were few in number and were coming on in a rabble of unformed ranks. Meanwhile the consul, with hands upraised to heaven, called out in a loud voice, so that he could be heard, that he vowed a temple to Jupiter the Stayer if the Roman army would stay their flight, resume fighting and cut down and defeat the Samnite legions. Everyone from all quarters, officers, soldiers, infantry and cavalry, threw their efforts into restoring the battle. Even the divine power of the gods appeared to be concerned for the Roman name, so easily did the tide of battle turn; the enemy were driven from the camp and soon forced back to the place where the fighting had started. There they were impeded and held up by the heap of baggage they had piled up; they then put a circle of armed men round the pile to prevent their possessions being stolen. At that point the Roman infantry bore down on them in front, while the cavalry rode round and attacked in the rear, so that between the two they were killed or captured. The number of prisoners amounted to 7800, all of whom were sent naked under the yoke; the dead were reported to be 4800. But even the Romans had no joy of their victory, for when the consul counted up his losses over the two days, they came to 7800 men.

During these events in Apulia, the Samnites made an attempt with a second army on Interamna, a Roman colony on the Latin Way, but failed to take it. They laid waste the countryside and were carrying off a mixed haul of plunder, including men and cattle and the settlers they had captured, when they encountered the victorious consul returning from Luceria, and not only lost their booty but were cut down themselves as they straggled along in a long and overburdened column. The consul issued a proclamation recalling the owners of the plunder to Interamna to identify and recover their property, then left his army there and departed for Rome to hold the elections. He applied for a triumph, but was refused the honour, on the grounds that he had lost so many thousands from his army and had sent the Samnite prisoners under the yoke, without any agreement on terms.[44]

37. The other consul, Postumius, had taken his army into Etruria when there was no further reason for campaigning in Samnium, and began by destroying the countryside round Volsinii. Then, when the people came out to defend their territory, he defeated them in a battle not far from their town walls. 2800 Etruscans were killed, while the rest were saved by being so near their city. The army moved on to the territory of Rusellae, where not only were the fields laid waste but the town captured as well. More than 2000 were taken prisoner, but rather fewer than that number killed fighting around the walls. However, the peace which was made that year in Etruria was more celebrated and important than the campaign had been. Three highly powerful cities, the principal ones in Etruria – Volsinii, Perusia and Arretium – applied for a peace settlement, and agreed with the consul that in return for clothing and grain for the troops they should be permitted to send representatives on their behalf to Rome; they were granted a truce for forty years. An immediate fine of 5000 *asses* was imposed on each city.

44. i.e. he was blamed for letting the Samnites off with no more than a humiliation.

In view of his achievements the consul asked the Senate for a triumph, more because it was customary than with any hope of being granted one. When he saw that some were for refusing because he had been rather slow leaving the City, and others because he had moved out of Samnium into Etruria without an order from the Senate, and that his critics were divided between his personal enemies and his colleague's friends, who wished to console Atilius for his own rebuff by denying a triumph to Postumius as well, he addressed the senators as follows. 'My respect for your dignity, Conscript Fathers, still cannot make me forget that I am consul. By the same right of command with which I conducted my campaigns, now that these are successfully completed with the subjection of Samnium and Etruria, with victory won and peace settled, I intend to celebrate my triumph.' With this he left the Senate. An argument then broke out amongst the people's tribunes, some saying that they would veto this unprecedented triumph, others that they would support the consul's rights against the opposition of their colleagues. The question was raised at an assembly and Postumius summoned to appear. He quoted the case of the consuls Marcus Horatius and Lucius Valerius, and the recent one of Gaius Marcius Rutulus,[45] father of the current censor, whose triumphs had not been authorized by the Senate but commanded by the people, and added that he too would have referred the matter to the people had he not known that there were tribunes who were the property of the nobles and would obstruct the law; but the wishes and good-will of the people when united carried the same weight with him as any commands, and always would. On the following day, with the support of three tribunes, against the intervention of seven, and the unanimous opposition of the Senate, Postumius held his triumph, while the people gathered in crowds to see it.

This was another year for which the records are conflicting. According to Claudius,[46] Postumius captured several cities in Samnium but was defeated and put to flight in Apulia, and,

45. Four times consul and the first plebeian dictator (VII.17.6).
46. Q. Claudius Quadrigarius; cf. VI.42, note 52.

being wounded himself, was forced to take refuge with a few of his men in Luceria, while it was Atilius who campaigned in Etruria and the triumph celebrated was his. Fabius[47] writes that both consuls campaigned in Samnium and near Luceria, that the army was taken across to Etruria (by which consul he does not say), that both sides suffered heavy losses near Luceria, and that during the battle the temple was vowed to Jupiter the Stayer, as Romulus had vowed before. He says, though, that only the sanctuary, that is, the site consecrated for the temple, had been marked out, but that this year the Senate at last took action under pressure of its religious duty, seeing that the State had been put under obligation twice by the same vow, and gave orders for the temple to be built.

38. The following year was marked both by a consul distinguished for his father's glory and equally for his own, namely Lucius Papirius Cursor, and by a large-scale war ending in a victory such as no one up to that day had won over the Samnites, except the consul's father, Lucius Papirius.[48] The Samnites, as it happened, had put the same sort of effort into their preparations, and had furnished their campaign with all the riches they could lavish on splendid arms; they had even invoked the support of the gods by a kind of initiation ceremony for their army through an ancient form of oath. But first they had held a levy throughout Samnium under a new ruling that anyone of military age who did not report for service under the generals' proclamation or left the army without their permission should forfeit his life to Jupiter. Then the whole army was told to report at Aquilonia, where the entire strength of Samnium assembled – around 40,000 men.

There a site practically in the centre of the camp, extending up to 200 feet in all directions, was fenced round with hurdles of wickerwork and hide and roofed with linen. In it sacrifice was offered, following the words read from an old linen roll; the priest was an aged man named Ovius Paccius, who claimed to derive the ritual from an ancient religious practice of the Samnites which their ancestors had observed when laying

47. Q. Fabius Pictor, the historian; see VIII.30, note 31.
48. cf. IX.40.2 ff.

secret plans for taking Capua from the Etruscans.[49] When the
sacrifice had been duly performed, the general, through his
attendant, ordered all those who ranked highest in birth and
feats of arms to be summoned, and they were brought in one
by one. As well as other ritual objects to fill the mind with awe,
there were altars in the middle of a completely enclosed area,
slaughtered victims lying about, and centurions standing
round with drawn swords.[50] The man was brought up to the
altars more like a victim for sacrifice than a participant in the
ceremony, and obliged to swear not to divulge anything seen
or heard there. Then he was forced to take a fearful form of
oath bringing down a curse on his own head and on his
household and family if he did not go into battle where his
generals led, and if he either fled from battle himself, or did
not immediately kill anyone he saw doing likewise. At first
some refused to take this oath; they were beheaded round the
altars and left lying there amongst the piles of victims to be
a warning to the rest not to refuse. When the leading Samnites
had bound themselves by this curse, ten of them were singled
out by the general by name and told that they were each to
choose another man and continue until their numbers reached
16,000.[51] They were called the 'Linen Legion' after the covering of the enclosure in which the nobles had been bound by
oath, and were given splendid arms and crested helmets to
make them stand out amongst the rest. Rather more than
20,000 men[52] made up another army, which neither in
physique, military renown nor equipment was inferior to the
Linen Legion. This was the size and strength of the Samnite
army which encamped near Aquilonia.

39. The consuls left the City, Spurius Carvilius, who had
been allocated the veteran legions which Marcus Atilius, consul
of the year before, had left in the territory of Interamna, being
the first to leave. He set out with his army, entered Samnium

49. cf. IV.37.1. The Etruscan city of Volturnum had been renamed
Capua.
50. These must be the 'armed priests' of ch. 41.3.
51. cf. IX.39.5, where the Etruscans follow a similar practice.
52. The figure of 24,000 would be consistent with that given in §4.

and captured the Samnite town of Amiternum while the enemy were occupied with their superstitious practices and holding secret councils. About 2800 were killed there and 4270 prisoners taken. Papirius enrolled a new army, as the Senate had decreed he should, with which he stormed and captured the city of Duronia; he took fewer prisoners than his colleague, but killed many more. Both places yielded a rich haul of plunder. Then the consuls ranged widely over Samnium, destroying mainly the area round Atina, after which Carvilius arrived outside Cominium, and Papirius outside Aquilonia, where the main strength of the Samnites was established. For some time Papirius allowed no respite from skirmishing, while avoiding a set battle; the days were spent in harassing the enemy when they were quiet and retreating when they offered resistance, in threats rather than real attacks. Anything started or stopped at Cominium; the result of every activity, however slight, was made known from day to day. The other Roman camp was twenty miles away, and Papirius was influenced by his absent colleague's plans in all his operations, while as the crucial moment approached, Carvilius paid more attention to what went on in Aquilonia than to his siege of Cominium.

Lucius Papirius was now sufficiently prepared for battle in every way, and sent a message to his colleague that if the auspices permitted, he intended to engage the enemy on the following day. It was necessary, he said, that Carvilius should also make as vigorous an attack on Cominium as he could, so that no lifting of pressure there should allow the Samnites to send relief to Aquilonia. The messenger had a day for the journey, and returned in the night to report that Carvilius approved of the decision. Once he had sent off the messenger, Papirius addressed his troops. He spoke at length about war in general, and had much to say about the enemy's present equipment, which he thought more for useless show than for efficiency in action. Crested helmets dealt no wounds, and Roman javelins could pierce shields which were painted and gilded; gleaming white tunics worn for battle would be stained with blood when swords came into action. Some time earlier a gilt and silvered Samnite army had been completely wiped

out by his own father,[53] and the spoils of victory had brought
their captors more glory than they had given their owners
when carried as arms. Perhaps his name and family had been
granted the privilege of being sent out as leaders to confront
the greatest efforts on the part of the Samnites, and of bringing
back such spoils to be the prized adornment even of public
places. The immortal gods, he added, were on their side, as a
result of treaties so often sought and so often broken; and now
if it were possible to guess what the attitude of the gods might
be – they had never been more hostile to any army than to this
one. It was spattered with the mingled blood of man and beast
from its unspeakable rite, marked out for the twofold wrath
of the gods, dreading on the one hand the gods called to
witness the treaties struck with the Romans, and on the other
the curses called down on oaths sworn to break those treaties.
It had taken its oath unwillingly, and hated it when sworn; at
one and the same time it feared its gods, its fellows and its foe.

40. All this Papirius had learned from information brought
by deserters, and now described to his soldiers. They were
already enraged of their own accord, and now with high hopes
of both gods and men they clamoured for battle with a single
voice. They resented the struggle's being postponed until the
following day, and were exasperated by the delay of a day and
a night. Papirius had now received his colleague's answer, and
at the third watch of the night, he rose silently and sent the
keeper of the sacred chickens to take the auspices. In the camp
there was no class of men untouched by lust for battle; high
and low all were equally keyed up; general and army could
witness each other's eagerness. The general impatience spread
even to those taking the auspices, for when the chickens
refused to eat, the keeper ventured to conceal the truth and told
the consul that the omens could not be more favourable.[54]
Papirius was delighted, announced that the auspices were excellent, and that the army would go into action with the gods'

53. In 308; cf. IX.40.
54. He reported a *tripudium solistimum,* the 'dancing' of corn as it
fell from the beaks of pecking chickens. cf. Cicero, *de Divinatione*
II.34.72; I.15.28.

support. He then displayed the signal for battle. As the army took the field, it so happened that a deserter reported that twenty Samnite cohorts, each about four hundred strong, had set out for Cominium. Papirius immediately sent a messenger to his colleague, to inform him of this, and gave orders himself for the troops to quicken their pace. He had stationed the reserves in their proper places and put officers in command of them, Lucius Volumnius on the right wing and Lucius Scipio on the left, with the other legates, Gaius Caedicius and Titus Trebonius, in charge of the cavalry. He then ordered Spurius Nautius to have the pack-saddles taken off the mules and with three cohorts of allied troops to make a rapid detour on to a hill which was in full view, and then to show himself at the height of the battle raising as much dust as he could.[55]

While the general was occupied with these plans, an argument broke out amongst the chicken-keepers about the auspices for the day. This was overheard by some of the Roman cavalry, who thought it should not be ignored, and reported to Spurius Papirius, the consul's nephew, that there was doubt about the auspices. This young man had been born before scepticism was taught about the gods; he made inquiries about the matter so as not to repeat unconfirmed rumours, and reported it to the consul. 'For what you have done,' replied Papirius, 'congratulations on your honour and diligence; but anyone taking the auspices who makes a false report brings retribution for his offence on his own head. As far as I am concerned, I was told that the corn had danced, and that is a splendid omen for the Roman people and the army.' He then ordered the centurions to place the keepers of chickens in the front line. The Samnites also advanced their standards, and the army followed in its ornate armour, a splendid spectacle even for Roman eyes. Before the first shout and encounter the chicken-keeper fell in front of the standards, struck by a random javelin, and, when this was reported to Papirius, 'The gods are here in the battle,' he cried, 'and the guilty have met their deserts!' As he spoke a raven in front of him croaked loud

55. cf. the similar device in VII.14.7–10.

and clear. Delighted with the omen, he declared that never had the gods been more actively present to intervene in human affairs; then he gave the command for the battle-cry and trumpets to sound.

41. The battle was savagely fought, but in widely differing spirit. The Romans were swept into the fray by fury, hope, zest for the encounter, thirst for their enemies' blood; the Samnites for the most part were reluctantly impelled by necessity and their superstitious fears to resist rather than to attack. Nor would they have withstood the first shout and onset of the Romans, accustomed to defeat as they had now been for several years, had not another powerful and deep-seated terror prevented them from flight. In their minds' eye they had all the set-up of that secret ritual and the armed priests, the mingled heaps of butchered men and beasts, the altars bespattered with the blood of such abomination amongst that of ordinary victims, the fearful imprecation and dreadfully worded oath, designed to invoke a curse on household and family: these were the bonds that kept them from their flight, as they held out in dread more of their fellows than of their foes. The Romans pressed on from both wings and from the centre, and cut them down as they stood transfixed with terror of gods and men. Their resistance was tardy, coming as it did from men who were kept from running away only by their fears.

The carnage had now nearly reached the standards when a cloud of dust was seen coming on obliquely, apparently raised by the approach of a great army. It was Spurius Nautius (some say it was Octavius Maecius) leading the allied cavalry. They were stirring up more dust than their numbers warranted, for the servants riding the mules were trailing leafy branches along the ground. Their arms and standards in the van were seen through the dust-storm, while a higher and denser cloud of dust following behind suggested that a body of cavalry was bringing up the rear. This deceived the Romans as well as the Samnites, and the consul confirmed the error by calling out along the front ranks, loudly enough for his voice to reach the enemy, that Cominium was taken and here was his victorious colleague: they must try for victory too before the other army should gain all the glory. This he said while mounted on his horse, and then ordered the tribunes and centurions to clear a path to let the cavalry through. He had previously told Trebonïus and Caedicius that when they saw him shaking his raised spear they should lead a cavalry charge against the enemy with all the force they could. Everything went as he wanted, in accordance with his previous plans: ways were opened through the files, the cavalry dashed forward, rode at the enemy's centre with levelled spears, and broke the Samnite ranks wherever they attacked. Close behind came Volumnius and Scipio to strike down the disorganized men.

Then at last, when the power of gods and men was broken, the Linen Cohorts were routed; sworn and unsworn fled alike, fearing no one but their enemies. The infantry who survived the battle were driven into the camp or to Aquilonia; the nobles and cavalry took refuge in Bovianum. The cavalry was pursued by cavalry, infantry by infantry: the Roman wings pressed on in different directions, the right to the Samnite camp, the left to the city. The camp was the first to fall to Volumnius, while Scipio was still dealing with more stubborn resistance near the town, not so much because defeated men show more courage but because walls are a better protection against armed assailants than a rampart, and stones can be thrown from them to hold off an attack. Scipio realized that the reduction of a fortified city would be a slow business unless it could be completed before the enemy rallied from their initial panic and recovered their spirits, and he asked his troops whether they were prepared to put up with the fact that the other wing had captured the camp while they, though victors in battle, were driven back from the city gates. When the men all shouted their refusal, he himself led the way to the gate, his shield held over his head, and the rest followed, formed a *testudo*, and burst their way into the town. Pushing the Samnites off, they seized the parts of the walls round the gate, but did not venture further into the city because their numbers were so small.

42. The consul was unaware of the situation at first, and

thought only of withdrawing his army, for the sun was now
rapidly sinking, and the approach of night made everything
dangerous and suspect even to the victors. He rode further on,
to see on the right that the camp was taken, while on the left
the shouts from the fighting in the city were mingled with
shrieks of terror, for that happened to be the time of the
struggle at the gate. He rode nearer and saw his own men
on the walls; knowing then that the decision had already been
taken for him, since the audacity of a few had given him a great
opportunity, he ordered the troops he had withdrawn to be
recalled and advance into the city. They went in on the side
nearest them, and rested for the night, as it was growing dark;
during the night the town was abandoned by the enemy.

At Aquilonia that day 20,340 Samnites were killed and 3870
taken prisoner, with the capture of ninety-seven military standards. Tradition also records that practically no other general
appeared so cheerful in action, whether because of Scipio's
natural temperament or his confidence of success. The same
resilience of mind made it possible for him not to be held back
from giving battle even by the argument about the auspices,
and at the height of the struggle, when it was customary to
vow temples to the immortal gods, he had already vowed to
Jupiter the Victor that if he routed the enemy's legions he
would pour him out a small cupful of wine and honey before
he took a drink of strong wine himself. That vow pleased the
gods, who changed the auspices for the best.[56]

43. The other consul was equally fortunate in action at
Cominium. At dawn he brought his forces up to the walls and
encircled the town, placing a strong body of supporting troops
to prevent any break-out through the gates. He was already
giving the signal when the alarming message reached him
about the pending arrival of the twenty cohorts[57]; this halted
his attack and forced him to recall part of his forces, who were
all prepared and eager to storm the town. He ordered the
legate Decimus Brutus Scaeva to take the first legion, ten

56. Papirius was showing his high spirits; but Pliny (NH XIV.91)
saw it as an instance of sparing use of wine.
57. Those mentioned in ch. 40.

cohorts of allied troops and the cavalry, and advance to confront the enemy's reinforcements. Wherever he encountered them he was to block their route and hold them up, and give battle if the situation required it – at all costs this force must not be allowed to approach Cominium. He himself gave orders for scaling ladders to be brought up to the walls from all sides, and came right up to the gates under cover of a *testudo*. As the gates were broken open there was a simultaneous attack from all round the walls. Though the Samnites had had sufficient courage to keep the Romans from approaching the city until they saw armed men on the walls, once the fighting was no longer carried on by missiles at long range but became hand-to-hand, and their opponents had managed with an effort to climb from the plain (thereby overcoming the difficulties of their position, which had given them some anxiety) and were now having an easy battle on the level with an enemy who was no match for them, they abandoned the towers and battlements and all collected in the forum. There for a while they made a last desperate effort to turn the tide of battle. Then they threw down their weapons and about 11,400 men surrendered to the consul. The dead numbered some 4880.

Such were the events at Cominium and Aquilonia. A third battle had been expected in the area between the two cities, but there was no sign of the enemy. They had been recalled by their leaders when seven miles from Cominium without taking part in either battle. Darkness was beginning to fall when they were already in sight of both the camp and Aquilonia and were halted by the noise, which was equally loud from both directions. Then from the site of the camp, which had been fired by the Romans, the widespread flames gave clear indication of definite disaster and checked them from going on further. They threw themselves on the ground here and there, just where they were, without removing their arms or taking any precautions, and spent the whole night restlessly awaiting and dreading the dawn. They were still wondering which way to march at the first signs of daylight, when the Roman cavalry, who had pursued the Samnites after they left Aquilonia in the night, caught sight of them, saw there were large numbers of men unprotected by earthworks or outposts, and quickly put them to flight. They had also been seen from the walls of Aquilonia, and were soon followed by some legionary cohorts. But the infantry could not catch them up as they fled, though about 280 of the rearguard were killed by the cavalry, abandoning in their panic a large quantity of arms and eighteen military standards. The remainder made their way to Bovianum, relatively unscathed in spite of so much haste and confusion.

44. The rejoicing in each Roman army was increased by the good fortune enjoyed by the other. Each consul, with the other's agreement, handed over the town he had taken to the troops to plunder, and, when the houses were emptied, set it on fire. On the same day as Aquilonia and Cominium were burnt to the ground, the consuls combined their camps to the mutual delight of their legions and themselves. In full sight of the two armies Carvilius commended his men as each merited and gave awards; and Papirius, who had fought his battle on many fronts – in line of battle, round the enemy's camp and round the city – presented armlets and golden crowns to Spurius Nautius, his nephew Spurius Papirius, four centurions and a maniple of front-line troops: Nautius for the operation whereby he had terrorized the enemy as if he had had a large force behind him, young Papirius for his distinguished service with the cavalry both in battle and on the night when he had harassed the fleeing Samnites[58] after their secret departure from Aquilonia, the centurions and soldiers for being the first to take the gate and walls of Aquilonia. He also presented all members of the cavalry with helmet ornaments and armlets of silver for their outstanding service in many fields.

A council was then called to decide whether the time had now come to withdraw from Samnium either both or at least one of the armies; it was agreed that in view of the Samnite collapse, the best course would be to persevere with anything that remained, and redouble hostilities so that Samnium could be completely subjected before it was handed over to the

58. There is no reference to this in ch. 42.

succeeding consuls. Now that there was no Samnite army left
which was able to meet them in pitched battle, the only form
of warfare left to the Romans was to attack Samnite cities: by
destroying these they could enrich the army with plunder
and wipe out their enemies as they fought for their altars and
hearths. And so, after sending letters to the Senate and Roman
people reporting their achievements, the consuls parted;
Papirius marched his legions on to attack Saepinum, while
Carvilius took his army to Velia.

45. The consuls' letters were heard both in the Senate and
in the assembly with immense delight, and the general rejoicing was expressed in the personal enthusiasm shown during a
four-day thanksgiving. It was a great victory for the Roman
people, and also one which was most opportune, as news
reached them about the same time that fighting had broken
out again amongst the Etruscans. People began to wonder how
they could have withstood Etruria if anything had gone
against them in Samnium, for it was the alliance with the
Samnites that had encouraged the Etruscans, and when both
consuls and the entire strength of Rome had been diverted to
Samnium they had seized their chance to revolt while the
Roman people were fully occupied. Envoys from the allies
were brought into the Senate by the praetor Marcus Atilius,
and complained that their lands were being burnt and destroyed by the Etruscans on their borders, because they refused
to break with the Roman people; they besought the Conscript
Fathers to defend them against the violence and injustice of
their common enemy. They were given the answer that the
Senate would ensure that their allies would not regret their
loyalty: the Etruscans would shortly meet with the same fate
as the Samnites. All the same, there would have been no great
hurry to deal with the Etruscans if news had not come that the
Falisci as well, who had been friendly to Rome for many
years, had taken up arms with the Etruscans. They were too
near to Rome for the Senate not to feel increasingly anxious,
and it was decided to send fetial priests to demand redress.
When this was refused, war was declared on the Falisci by
the people's command at the Senate's behest, and the consuls

were ordered to draw lots to decide which of them should take his army across to Etruria.

Carvilius had already taken the Samnite towns of Velia, Palumbinium and Herculaneum[59] – Velia within a few days and Palumbinium the same day as he had come up to the walls. However, at Herculaneum he had to fight a regular battle, where the result was at first uncertain and his losses greater than the enemy's; then he set up camp, shut in the enemy behind their walls, stormed the town and took it. Up to 10,000 men were killed in these three towns, and rather more were taken prisoner. When the consuls cast lots for their commands, Carvilius drew Etruria, an answer to prayer for his men, who could not endure the bitter cold in Samnium.

Papirius at Saepinum found a larger Samnite force confronting him. His men were often attacked in a regular battle, often while on the march, and often around the city itself when they had to check the enemy's attempts to break out. This was no siege, but war on equal terms, for the Samnites protected the walls with arms and men just as much as their walls protected them. At last Papirius by sheer fighting forced the enemy into a real position of siege, and, by a mixture of attack and use of siege-works in the blockade, he took the town. In their exasperation, the Romans showed more savagery than when the town fell: 7400 men were killed and fewer than 3000 taken prisoner. The plunder, which was extensive, as the Samnites had gathered their possessions together in a few cities, was handed over to the army.

46. Everything was now deep in snow and it was impossible to remain out of doors. Papirius accordingly withdrew his army from Samnium. On his arrival at Rome he was unanimously voted a triumph, and this he celebrated while still in office in splendid style, as was the custom of those times. Infantry and cavalry marched or rode past, a striking spectacle in their decorations; many civic crowns were to be seen, and many which had been won for being first over a rampart or a town wall. The spoils won from the Samnites were inspected

59. Three unknown sites.

and compared for splendour and fine craftsmanship with those Papirius's father had won, which were well known from their frequent display in public places. Several Samnite nobles, famous for their own and their fathers' deeds, were led along as prisoners. The weight of heavy bronze carried came to 2,533,000 pounds, and was said to have come from the sale of prisoners; the silver, which had been taken from the cities, weighed 1830 pounds. All the bronze and silver was deposited in the treasury, and the soldiers were given nothing from the booty. The resentment this caused amongst the people was increased when a tax was collected to provide pay for the troops; for had Papirius forgone the glory of paying the money captured into the treasury, the army could then have been given a gratuity out of the booty as well as their regular pay. Papirius dedicated the temple of Quirinus. In no ancient authority can I find that it was vowed during the actual fighting, nor indeed would it have been possible to complete it in so short a time. His father had made the vow when he was dictator, and the son as consul carried out the dedication and embellished the temple with the enemy's spoils. These were captured in such quantities that they provided ornaments for the Forum as well as the temple, and were also shared out among the allies and neighbouring colonies for the decoration of their temples and public places. After his triumph Papirius took his army to winter in Vescinian territory, as that was an area liable to be molested by the Samnites.

Meanwhile in Etruria the consul Carvilius prepared to start with an assault on Troilum.[60] 470 of the wealthiest inhabitants bargained with him to be allowed to leave in return for a large sum of money, and these he allowed to go. The remaining population and the town itself he took by direct attack. After this he stormed five fortresses in well-secured positions. 2400 of the enemy were killed there and fewer than 2000 taken prisoner. He also granted a year's truce to the Falisci, who were seeking peace, after settling for 100,000 *asses* of heavy bronze and a year's pay for his army. After these operations

60. Site unknown.

he returned to Rome for his triumph, which was not as
glorious as his colleague's for his victory over the Samnites, but
matched it when the Etruscan war was taken into account. He
deposited in the treasury 380,000 pounds of heavy bronze, and
with the remaining money from the spoils he contracted for
a temple to Fors Fortuna to be built next to the temple which
had been dedicated to that goddess by King Servius Tullius.
The soldiers were given 102 *asses* each from the booty, and the
centurions and cavalry twice the sum, a gift all the more
gratefully received because of their niggardly treatment by
Papirius. Carvilius's popularity protected his legate Lucius
Postumius from the people: he had been indicted by Marcus
Scantius, a people's tribune, and it was said he had escaped
judgement by the people when he had been appointed legate.
After that it was easier to threaten him with prosecution than
to carry this through.

47. Now that the year had run its course, new people's
tribunes took up office, but as there was a flaw in their election
they were replaced after five days. The lustral rite was performed that year by the censors Publius Cornelius Arvina and
Gaius Marcius Rutulus, and the population figures registered
came to 262,321. The censors were the twenty-sixth pair since
the first two, and the *lustrum* was the nineteenth. This year for
the first time those awarded crowns for gallantry in action
wore them when watching the Roman Games, and, also for
the first time, palm branches were presented to the winners,
a custom taken over from the Greeks. In the same year the
curule aediles who gave these games successfully prosecuted
several graziers,[61] and with money from their fines paved the
road from the temple of Mars as far as Bovillae.[62]

Lucius Papirius held the consular elections, and announced
the appointment of the new consuls, Quintus Fabius Gurges,
son of Maximus, and Decimus Junius Brutus Scaeva. Papirius
himself was elected praetor.

61. Neither here nor when fines were exacted before (ch. 23.12)
is it clear what was the graziers' offence: probably that of pasturing
cattle on public lands.
62. i.e. the Via Appia.

The year had been a happy one in many ways, but this was hardly adequate consolation for one major disaster: the plague which raged through town and countryside alike. The devastation it caused was thought to be an evil omen, and the Sibylline Books were consulted to find what limit or remedy the gods proposed for its ravages. The Books revealed that Aesculapius must be summoned from Epidaurus to Rome; however, because the consuls were busy with the war, nothing was done about it that year except that one day was set apart for supplication to the god.[63]

63. The summary of the lost Book XI tells how envoys went to Epidaurus and brought back the snake which embodied Aesculapius (Greek Asclepius, god of healing), and how it chose the Insula Tiberina for the god's sanctuary. The story is told at length by Ovid in *Metamorphoses* XV.622 ff.

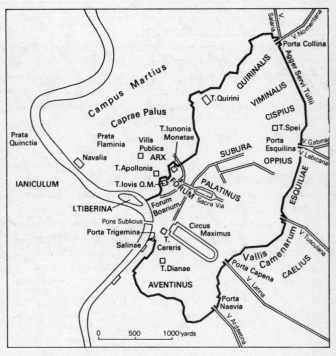

MAP I. ROME

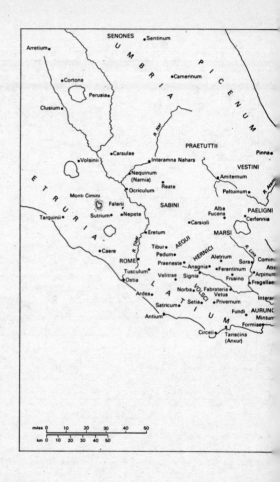

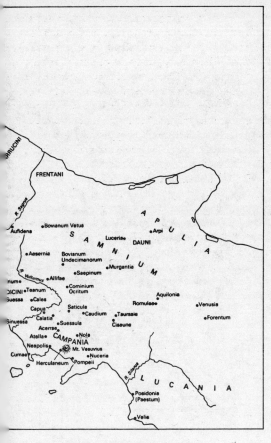

MAP 2. CENTRAL ITALY

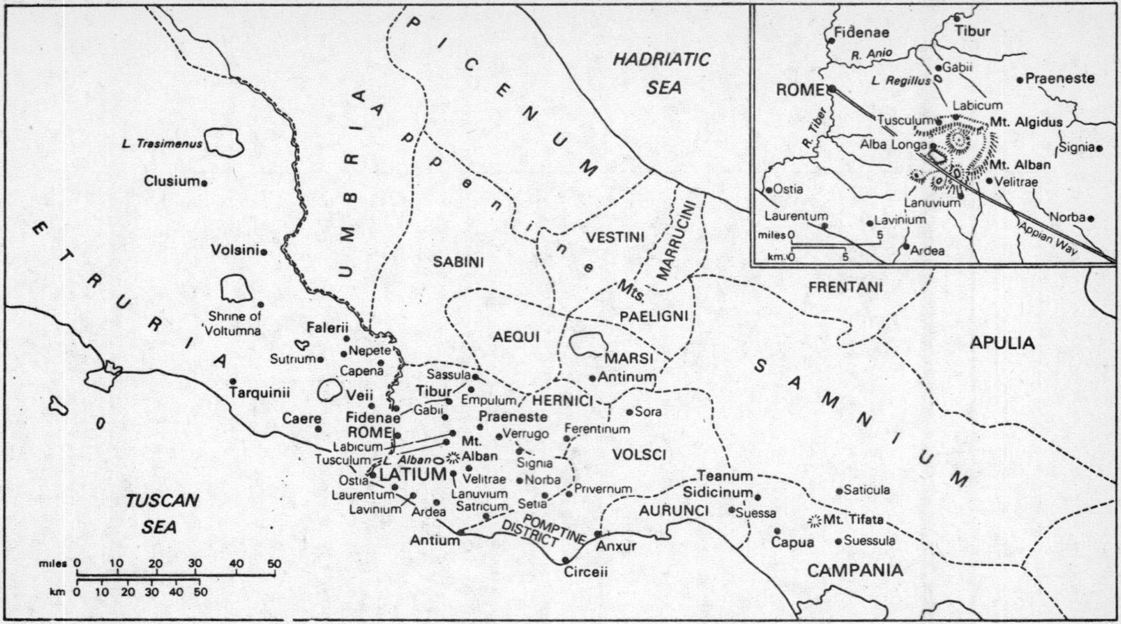

MAP 3. WESTERN CENTRAL ITALY

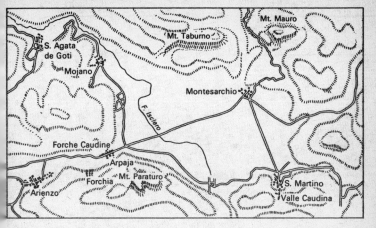

MAP 4. THE VALLEY OF THE CAUDINE FORKS

INDEX

INDEX

Acerrae, 27, 182

Acheron, river, 191, 192n.; Acheros, 192

Adriatic Sea, 29, 192n.

Aelius Paetus, L. (plebeian aedile 295), 321

Aelius Paetus, P., 179, 224, 299

Aelius Tubero, Q. (annalist), 21–22, 300 and n.

Aemilian law, 263–6

Aemilius, L. (*trib. mil.* 389), 38–39, 44, 65–6, 79, 87

Aemilius, T. (*quinquevir*), 124, 158

Aemilius, Mamercus (dictator 434), 263–4

Aemilius Mamercus (Mamercinus), L. (consul 366), 97, 152, 157, 181, 185, 191, 246

Aemilius Mamercinus, Ti. (consul 339), 174–5

Aemilius Barbula, Q. (consul 316), 246–7, 258, 260–61

Aemilius Cerretanus, Q. (consul 325), 209–10

Aemilius Papus, M. (dictator 320), 224

Aemilius Paulus, M. (consul 302), 289, 292

Aenaria, island, 188

Aequi, 31, 40–42, 46, 52, 136, 140, 284–6, 289, 300

Aequicoli, 304

Aesculapius, god, 356 and n.

Aesernia, 332

Aharna, 323

Alba, Albans, 95, 110, 128–9, 134, 151, 163, 289; Alban citadel, 128; Alban mount, 134

Albinius, M. (*trib. mil.* 379), 76

Aletrium, 280, 282

Alexander (king of Epirus), 18, 27, 160 and n., 182, 191–3, 240

Alexander the Great, 16–17, 19, 160, 193, 239–45

Alexandria, 191

Allia, river, 38, 74–5, 113, 220n.

Allifae, 193, 271 and n., 279

Amiternum, 344

Anagnia, 280

Aniensis tribe, 301

Anio, river, 95, 107

Annius of Setia, L., 14, 19, 160–63

Antiochus the Great, 244 and n.

Antistius, L. (*trib. mil.* 379), 76

Antium, Antiates, 44–8, 73, 78–80, 129, 132, 157, 174–9, 243, 246

Antonius, M., (*mag. eq.* 332) 181

Anxur, 27, 151

Apollo, god, 124, 298

Appian Way: *see* Via Appia

Apuleius Pansa, Q. (consul 300), 295, 300

Apulia, Apulians, 27, 95, 97, 131, 193, 195, 209–10, 214, 216, 232, 235–40, 243, 245, 254, 308, 340

Aqua Appia, 257 and n.

MORE ABOUT PENGUINS, PELICANS
AND PUFFINS

For further information about books available from Penguins please write to Dept EP, Penguin Books Ltd, Harmondsworth, Middlesex UB7 0DA.

In the U.S.A.: For a complete list of books available from Penguins in the United States write to Dept DG, Penguin Books, 299 Murray Hill Parkway, East Rutherford, New Jersey 07073.

In Canada: For a complete list of books available from Penguins in Canada write to Penguin Books Canada Limited, 2801 John Street, Markham, Ontario L3R 1B4.

In Australia: For a complete list of books available from Penguins in Australia write to the Marketing Department, Penguin Books Australia Ltd, P.O. Box 257, Ringwood, Victoria 3134.

In New Zealand: For a complete list of books available from Penguins in New Zealand write to the Marketing Department, Penguin Books (N.Z.) Ltd, Private Bag, Takapuna, Auckland 9.

In India: For a complete list of books available from Penguins in India write to Penguin Overseas Ltd, 706 Eros Apartments, 56 Nehru Place, New Delhi 110019.

LIVY

THE EARLY HISTORY OF ROME

Translated by Aubrey de Selincourt
With an introduction by Robert Ogilvie

'An epic poet in prose' – in these apt words Michael Grant evokes both the stylistic brilliance and the imaginative genius of Livy (59 B.C.–A.D. 17).

The Early History of Rome contains the first five books of his monumental work, and proceeds from the foundation of Rome through the history of the seven kings, the establishment of the Republic and its internal struggles, up to Rome's recovery after the fierce Gallic invasion of the fourth century B.C.

Here readers will encounter the famous story of Romulus and Remus among a number of other familiar legends and tales.

ROME AND THE MEDITERRANEAN

Translated by Henry Bettenson
with an introduction by A. H. McDonald

This volume, which contains fifteen books from Livy's masterly History of Rome from Its Foundations, traces the final stages of Roman aggrandizement up to 167 B.C.: the defeat of the Hellenistic Kings in the three 'preventive' Eastern wars, from which Rome emerged as ruler of the Mediterranean.

However Livy does not neglect affairs at Rome; the bitter feuding, the debates and oratory, Cato's celebrated Censorship and the repression in 186 B.C. of the subversive rites of Bacchus are described with a vivid and dramatic immediacy as Livy brings Rome to life in a crucial phase of her development.

and

THE WAR WITH HANNIBAL

Translated by Aubrey de Selincourt
with an introduction by Betty Radice

CLASSICS IN TRANSLATION IN PENGUINS

☐ *Remembrance of Things Past* **Marcel Proust**

☐ Volume One: *Swann's Way, Within a Budding Grove* £7.95
☐ Volume Two: *The Guermantes Way, Cities of the Plain* £7.95
☐ Volume Three: *The Captive, The Fugitive, Time Regained* £7.95

Terence Kilmartin's acclaimed revised version of C. K. Scott Moncrieff's original translation, published in paperback for the first time.

☐ *The Canterbury Tales* **Geoffrey Chaucer** £2.95

'Every age is a Canterbury Pilgrimage . . . nor can a child be born who is not one of these characters of Chaucer' – William Blake

☐ *Gargantua & Pantagruel* **Rabelais** £3.95

The fantastic adventures of two giants through which Rabelais (1495–1553) caricatured his life and times in a masterpiece of exuberance and glorious exaggeration.

☐ *The Brothers Karamazov* **Fyodor Dostoevsky** £4.95

A detective story on many levels, profoundly involving the question of the existence of God, Dostoevsky's great drama of parricide and fraternal jealousy triumphantly fulfilled his aim: 'to find the man in man . . . [to] depict all the depths of the human soul.'

☐ *Fables of Aesop* £1.95

This translation recovers all the old magic of fables in which, too often, the fox steps forward as the cynical hero and a lamb is an ass to lie down with a lion.

☐ *The Three Theban Plays* **Sophocles** £2.95

A new translation, by Robert Fagles, of *Antigone, Oedipus the King* and *Oedipus at Colonus*, plays all based on the legend of the royal house of Thebes.

CLASSICS IN TRANSLATION
IN PENGUINS

☐ **The Treasure of the City of Ladies**
Christine de Pisan £2.95

This practical survival handbook for women (whether royal courtiers or prostitutes) paints a vivid picture of their lives and preoccupations in France, *c.* 1405. First English translation.

☐ **La Regenta** Leopoldo Alas £10.95

This first English translation of this Spanish masterpiece has been acclaimed as 'a major literary event' – *Observer*. 'Among the select band of "world novels" . . . outstandingly well translated' – John Bayley in the *Listener*

☐ **Metamorphoses** Ovid £2.95

The whole of Western literature has found inspiration in Ovid's poem, a golden treasury of myths and legends that are linked by the theme of transformation.

☐ **Darkness at Noon** Arthur Koestler £2.50

'Koestler approaches the problem of ends and means, of love and truth and social organization, through the thoughts of an Old Bolshevik, Rubashov, as he awaits death in a G.P.U. prison' – *New Statesman*

☐ **War and Peace** Leo Tolstoy £4.95

'A complete picture of human life;' wrote one critic, 'a complete picture of the Russia of that day; a complete picture of everything in which people place their happiness and greatness, their grief and humiliation.'

☐ **The Divine Comedy: 1 Hell** Dante £2.25

A new translation by Mark Musa, in which the poet is conducted by the spirit of Virgil down through the twenty-four closely described circles of hell.

CLASSICS IN TRANSLATION IN PENGUINS

☐ *The Magic Mountain* **Thomas Mann**   £4.95

Set in a sanatorium high in the Swiss Alps, this is modern German literature's most spectacular exploration of love and death, and the relationships between them.

☐ *The Good Soldier Švejk* **Jaroslav Hašek**   £4.95

The first complete English translation, with illustrations by Josef Lada. 'Hašek was a humorist of the highest calibre . . . A later age will perhaps put him on a level with Cervantes and Rabelais' – Max Brod

These books should be available at all good bookshops or news-agents, but if you live in the UK or the Republic of Ireland and have difficulty in getting to a bookshop, they can be ordered by post. Please indicate the titles required and fill in the form below.

NAME _____ BLOCK CAPITALS

ADDRESS _____

_____

_____

Enclose a cheque or postal order payable to The Penguin Bookshop to cover the total price of books ordered, plus 50p for postage. Readers in the Republic of Ireland should send £IR equivalent to the sterling prices, plus 67p for postage. Send to: The Penguin Bookshop, 54/56 Bridlesmith Gate, Nottingham, NG1 2GP.

You can also order by phoning (0602) 599295, and quoting your Barclaycard or Access number.

Every effort is made to ensure the accuracy of the price and availability of books at the time of going to press, but it is sometimes necessary to increase prices and in these circumstances retail prices may be shown on the covers of books which may differ from the prices shown in this list or elsewhere. This list is not an offer to supply any book.

This order service is only available to residents in the UK and the Republic of Ireland.

● ● ●